Visual QuickStart Guide

QuickBooks Pro 2006 for Macintosh

Maria Langer

 Peachpit Press

Visual QuickStart Guide

QuickBooks Pro 2006 for Macintosh

Maria Langer

Peachpit Press
1249 Eighth Street
Berkeley, CA 94710
510-524-2178 • 800-283-9444
510-524-2221 (fax)

Find us on the World Wide Web at: www.peachpit.com

Peachpit Press is a division of Pearson Education

Editor: Nancy Davis, Tracy O'Connell
Indexer: Julie Bess
Cover Design: Peachpit Press
Production: Maria Langer, David Van Ness

Colophon

This book was produced with Adobe InDesign CS and Adobe Photoshop 7 on a Power Macintosh Dual G5 running Mac OS X 10.4. The fonts used were Utopia, Meta Plus, PIXymbols Command, and ITC Zapf Dingbats. Screenshots were created using Snapz Pro on an eMac.

ISBN 0-321-34894-X

9 8 7 6 5 4 3 2 1

Printed and bound in the United States of America

Dedication

To Mike

Thanks!

To Nancy Davis and Tracy O'Connell, for having patience with my wait, wait, *hurry!* completion of this book. (Hmmm…didn't we go through the same thing last time around?)

To David Van Ness, for—as usual—making production such a pleasure.

To Julie Bess, for preparing another great index.

To Peggy Chang at Intuit Inc., for getting me the information I needed to write this book. And to Intuit Inc., for keeping real accounting alive on Mac OS.

And to Mike, for the usual reasons.

www.marialanger.com

Table of Contents

Introduction .... **xv**
Introduction to QuickBooks Pro 2006 .... *xv*
Accounting with QuickBooks .... *xvi*
Accounts .... *xvii*
Double-Entry Accounting .... *xix*
Forms & Lists .... *xix*

Chapter 1: **Getting Started with QuickBooks** **1**
Getting Started *1*
Installing QuickBooks *2*
To install QuickBooks Pro *2*
To launch QuickBooks for the first time *3*
Opening an Existing Company File *4*
To open & update an existing company file when you first open QuickBooks *5*
To open a company file with the Open Company command *6*
To open a company file from the Finder *6*
To convert a Quicken file for use with QuickBooks *6*
Using the New Company Setup Assistant *8*
To open the New Company Setup Assistant *9*
To complete the General section of the New Company Setup Assistant *9*
To complete the Income & Expenses section of the New Company Setup Assistant *17*
To complete the Income Details section of the New Company Setup Assistant *19*
To complete the Opening Balances section of the New Company Setup Assistant *22*
To complete the Documents section of the New Company Setup Assistant *26*

Chapter 2: **Working with Lists 29**

Working with Lists *29*
To view a list *31*
To print a list *31*
To close a list *31*
To sort a list *32*
To return a list to the default sort order *32*
To toggle between hierarchical & flat views *32*
To make an item inactive *33*
To make an item active *33*
Chart of Accounts *34*
To add an account *36*
To modify an account *37*
To delete an account *38*
Item List *39*
To add a new service item, non-inventory part item, or other charge item *41*
To add a new inventory part item *44*
To add a subtotal item *46*
To add a group item *47*
To add a discount item *49*
To add a payment item *51*
To add a sales tax item *53*
To add a sales tax group item *54*
To modify an item *55*
To add custom fields for an item *56*
To delete an item *57*
Class List *58*
To add a class *59*
To modify a class *60*
To delete a class *60*
Customer:Job List *61*
To add a customer *61*
To add a job to a customer *65*
To modify a customer or job *66*
To delete a customer or job *66*
Vendor List *67*
To add a vendor *67*
To modify a vendor *70*
To delete a vendor *70*

Employee List 71
To add an employee 71
To modify an employee 73
To delete an employee 73
Other Names List 74
To add a name 74
To modify a name 75
To delete a name 76
To Do List 77
To add a to do note 77
To modify a to do note 78
To mark a to do note as done 79
To delete a to do note 79
Customer Type, Vendor Type, & Job Type Lists 80
To add a customer, vendor, or job type 80
To modify a customer, vendor, or job type 81
To delete a customer, vendor, or job type 82
Terms List 83
To add a terms definition 84
To modify a terms 85
To delete a terms definition 85
Customer Message, Payment Method, & Ship Via Lists 86
To add a customer message, payment method, or shipping method 87
To modify a customer message, payment method, or shipping method 88
To delete a customer message, payment method, or shipping method 88
Reminders List 89
To show or hide details in the Reminders list 89
To view a reminder item 89

Chapter 3: **Entering Sales** **91**
Sales & Accounts Receivable 91
Entering Sales 92
To create an invoice or enter a sales receipt 93
To include billable items, expenses, and time in an invoice or sales receipt 98
Using Estimates 101
To create an estimate 101
To create an invoice based on an estimate 104

Working with Invoices, Sales Receipts, & Estimates 105
To view an invoice, sales receipt, or estimate 105
To modify or delete an invoice, sales receipt, or estimate 106
Receiving Payments 107
To apply a payment to open invoices 107
To modify or delete a payment 109
To view an invoice's payment history 110
Making Deposits 111
To deposit checks & cash 112
To record credit card deposits 113
To modify or delete a deposit 114
Assessing Finance Charges 115
To set up finance charges 115
To assess finance charges 117
Adjusting Customer Accounts 118
To create a credit memo or refund 118
To enter statement charges 121

Chapter 4: **Making Payments 123**
Making Payments 123
Writing Checks 125
To write a check 126
Entering Bills & Credits 130
To enter a bill 131
To enter a credit 134
Entering Credit Card Charges & Credits 135
To enter a credit card charge or credit 135
Paying Bills 139
To pay a bill 140
Paying Sales Tax 142
To pay sales tax 143

Chapter 5: **Downloading Transactions 145**
Downloading Transactions 145
Signing Up for Transaction Download 146
To determine whether your financial institution supports QuickBooks Web Connect 146
To sign up for transaction download 147
To log into your bank or credit card company's Web site 147
Downloading QuickBooks Transactions 148
To complete the first transaction download for an account 148
To complete subsequent transaction downloads for an account 151

Reviewing Downloaded Transactions 152
To review downloaded transactions 153

Chapter 6: **Working with Transactions** **155**
Working with Transactions 155
Viewing Account Registers 156
To view an account register 156
Entering Special Transactions 158
To enter a transaction in the General Journal Entry window 159
To modify a General Journal entry 161
To enter a transaction in an account register window 162
Searching for Transactions 165
To search for a transaction 165
To perform another search 167
To work with a found transaction 167
Working with Transactions 168
To open a transaction 168
To modify a transaction 169
To delete or void a transaction 169
Memorizing & Scheduling Transactions 170
To memorize a transaction 171
To open the Memorized Transaction List window 172
To use a memorized transaction 172
To delete a memorized transaction 173
To modify the settings for a memorized transaction 173
To set reminder & scheduling options for a memorized transaction 174
Tracking Time 175
To enter a single activity 176
To enter multiple activities on a weekly timesheet 177
Reconciling Accounts 179
To reconcile an account 180

Chapter 7: **Tracking Inventory** **183**
Tracking Inventory 183
Creating Purchase Orders 185
To view the Purchase Order list 185
To view a specific purchase order 185
To create a purchase order 186
To modify a purchase order 189
To delete a purchase order 189

Receiving Items & Entering Bills 190
To receive items & enter a corresponding bill 191
To receive items without entering a corresponding bill 193
To enter a bill for received items 195
Adjusting Inventory Balances 196
To conduct a physical inventory 197
To adjust inventory quantities 198
To adjust inventory values 199

Chapter 8: **Processing Payroll** **201**
Processing Payroll with QuickBooks 201
Getting Started with PayCycle 203
To open PayCycle for the first time 203
To open PayCycle after the first time 204
To open your To Do list 204
To set up your pay schedule & policies 205
To add employees 208
To accept the Customer Service Agreement 211
To complete state tax setup 212
To complete other setup tasks 212
Preparing QuickBooks for Payroll Processing 213
To add payroll accounts to QuickBooks 214
To identify which QuickBooks accounts you use for Payroll 214
Creating Paychecks 215
To create paychecks 215

Chapter 9: **Reporting Results** **219**
Reporting Results 219
Creating QuickReports & Using QuickZoom 221
To create a QuickReport for an account 221
To create a QuickReport from a list 222
To use QuickZoom 222
Creating Reports with the Reports Menu 223
To create a report with the Reports menu 224
Creating Reports with the Report Finder 225
To create a report with the Report Finder 227
Customizing Reports 228
To set report customization options 231
To set report filters 233
To set report formatting options 234
To format a report header & footer 235

Creating Graphs 236
To create a graph with the Reports menu 237
To create a graph with the Report Finder 237
To customize a graph 238
Memorizing Reports 239
To memorize a report 239
To recreate a memorized report 240
To delete a memorized report 240
Setting Up Budgets 241
To set up budgets 241

Chapter 10: **Printing** **243**
Printing 243
Setting Up to Print 244
To set up for printing invoices, statements, estimates, or purchase orders 244
To set up for printing reports, graphs, & lists 246
To set up for printing checks 247
To set up for printing labels 249
To set up for printing 1099s 250
Printing Forms 251
To print invoices, sales receipts, credit memos, or purchase orders 251
To print statements 253
To print checks 255
To print mailing labels 256
To print 1099s 258
Printing Lists & Reports 260
To print a list 260
To print a report 260
Using the Print Dialog 261
To set options in the Print dialog & print 261

Chapter 11: **Customizing QuickBooks** **263**
Customizing QuickBooks 263
QuickBooks Preferences 264
To open & set QuickBooks preferences 264
Views preferences 265
Data Entry preferences 266
Reminders preferences 267
Graphs preferences 267
Company File Backups preferences 268
Contact Sync preferences 270

Company Settings ... 271
To open & set Company Settings ... 271
Company Information settings ... 272
Transactions settings ... 273
Inventory/Purchase Orders/Estimates settings ... 274
Purchase Order Format & Estimate Format settings ... 275
Sales/Invoicing settings ... 278
Sales Receipt Format, Credit Memo Format, Invoice Format, & Statement Format settings ... 279
Checks settings ... 280
Check Format settings ... 280
Reporting settings ... 281
Report Format settings ... 282
Report Header/Footer settings ... 283
Statement of Cash Flows Report ... 284
Sales Tax settings ... 284
Time Tracking settings ... 285
Payroll settings ... 285
Jobs settings ... 285
Passwords settings ... 286
1099s settings ... 287
Configuring the Toolbar ... 288
To configure the toolbar ... 288

Appendix A: **Menus & Shortcut Keys ... 291**
Menus & Shortcut Keys ... 291
QuickBooks Menu ... 291
File Menu ... 292
Back Up submenu ... 292
Restore submenu ... 292
Import submenu ... 292
Export submenu ... 292
Utilities submenu ... 292
Print Setup submenu ... 292
Print Forms submenu ... 292
Edit Menu ... 293
Lists Menu ... 294
Customer & Vendor Profile submenu ... 294
Company Menu ... 294
Customers Menu ... 294
Time Tracking submenu ... 294

Vendors Menu 295
  Inventory Activities submenu 295
Employees Menu 295
  Time Tracking submenu 295
Banking Menu 295
Reports Menu 296
  Company & Financial submenu 296
  Customers & Receivables submenu 296
  Sales submenu 296
  Jobs & Time submenu 296
  Vendors & Payables submenu 297
  Purchases submenu 297
  Inventory submenu 297
  Banking submenu 297
  Accountant & Taxes submenu 297
  Budgets submenu 297
  List submenu 297
Window Menu 298
Help Menu 298

Index 299

Introduction

Introduction to QuickBooks Pro 2006

QuickBooks Pro 2006 is the latest version of Intuit Inc.'s powerful double-entry accounting software for Macintosh users. Designed primarily for small and medium sized businesses, QuickBooks Pro can handle sales, cash receipts, invoicing and accounts receivable, purchase orders and accounts payable, and inventory management. Its intuitive, forms-based interface is customizable and easy to use. It's no wonder that QuickBooks is the top-selling Mac OS accounting software.

This Visual QuickStart Guide will help you learn QuickBooks by providing step-by-step instructions, plenty of illustrations, and a generous helping of tips. On these pages, you'll find everything you need to know to get up and running quickly with QuickBooks—and a lot more!

This book was designed for page flipping. Use the thumb tabs, index, or table of contents to find the topics for which you need help. If you're brand new to QuickBooks, however, I recommend that you begin by reading at least the first two chapters. In them, you'll find the information you need to install and configure QuickBooks and to manage the lists of information you'll use in all QuickBooks transactions.

This introduction provides a review of basic accounting principles with an emphasis on how they apply in QuickBooks Pro.

Accounting with QuickBooks

To use QuickBooks, it's extremely helpful to have a good understanding of basic bookkeeping or accounting principles. Unlike Intuit's personal accounting software, Quicken, QuickBooks has a more robust feature set that requires accounting knowledge to use it effectively.

This part of the introduction provides a brief overview of accounting principles as they apply to QuickBooks.

✔ Tips

- Quicken is a personal finance software package published by Intuit, Inc. Although it may offer enough features to meet the bookkeeping needs of some small businesses, it lacks many of the business accounting features found in QuickBooks.
- A complete discussion of accounting principles is far beyond the scope of this book. If you are unfamiliar with the basics covered in this overview, I highly recommend that you obtain additional training before using QuickBooks for your company's accounting needs.

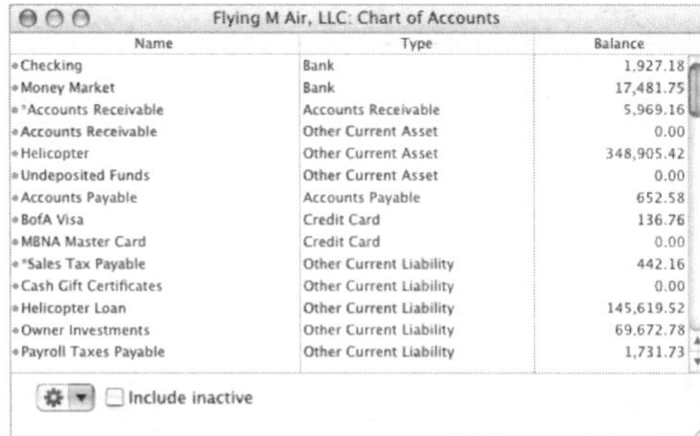

Flying M Air, LLC: Chart of Accounts

Name	Type	Balance
Checking	Bank	1,927.18
Money Market	Bank	17,481.75
*Accounts Receivable	Accounts Receivable	5,969.16
Accounts Receivable	Other Current Asset	0.00
Helicopter	Other Current Asset	348,905.42
Undeposited Funds	Other Current Asset	0.00
Accounts Payable	Accounts Payable	652.58
BofA Visa	Credit Card	136.76
MBNA Master Card	Credit Card	0.00
*Sales Tax Payable	Other Current Liability	442.16
Cash Gift Certificates	Other Current Liability	0.00
Helicopter Loan	Other Current Liability	145,619.52
Owner Investments	Other Current Liability	69,672.78
Payroll Taxes Payable	Other Current Liability	1,731.73

Include inactive

Figure 1 The first few accounts in a custom Chart of Accounts.

Accounts

All transactions are recorded in *accounts*. An account is a record of amounts for a specific thing or category. QuickBooks enables you to maintain a custom Chart of Accounts to meet your needs (**Figure 1**).

In standard accounting, there are five types of accounts (**Table 1**):

- **Asset** accounts track the value of what you own or what is owed to you. QuickBooks supports five types of asset accounts: Bank, Accounts Receivable, Other Current Asset, Fixed Asset, and Other Asset.
- **Liability** accounts track what you owe. QuickBooks supports four types of liabilities: Accounts Payable, Credit Card, Other Current Liability, and Long Term Liability.
- **Equity** accounts track owner investments and draws, as well as the net value of the business (assets – liabilities).

Continued on next page...

Table 1

Account Types Supported by QuickBooks

QuickBooks Account Type	Standard Account Type	Purpose
Bank	Asset	Funds on deposit in a financial institution.
Accounts Receivable	Asset	Amounts owed to you by customers.
Other Current Asset	Asset	Other current assets.
Fixed Asset	Asset	Fixed assets.
Other Asset	Asset	Other non-current assets.
Accounts Payable	Liability	Amounts you owe vendors.
Credit Card	Liability	Credit card accounts.
Other Current Liability	Liability	Other current liability.
Long Term Liability	Liability	Long-term debt, including loans.
Equity	Equity	Owners' equity.
Income	Income	Amounts received for the sale of goods or services.
Other Income	Income	Other non-sales income.
Cost of Goods Sold	Expense	Expense directly related to the manufacture of goods sold.
Expense	Expense	Expense not directly related to the manufacture of goods sold.
Other Expense	Expense	Other expense.

Continued from previous page.

- **Income** accounts track incoming funds. QuickBooks supports two types of income accounts: Income and Other Income.
- **Expense** accounts track outgoing funds. QuickBooks supports three types of expense accounts: Cost of Goods Sold, Expense, and Other Expense.

Accounts can be categorized into two main groups:

- **Balance sheet accounts** are those that appear on a standard balance sheet: Asset, Liability, and Equity accounts. These account balances show values as of a specific date.
- **Income statement accounts** are those that appear on a standard income or profit and loss statement: Income and Expense accounts. The amounts in these accounts are totaled over a predefined period to quantify performance in terms of net profit or loss.

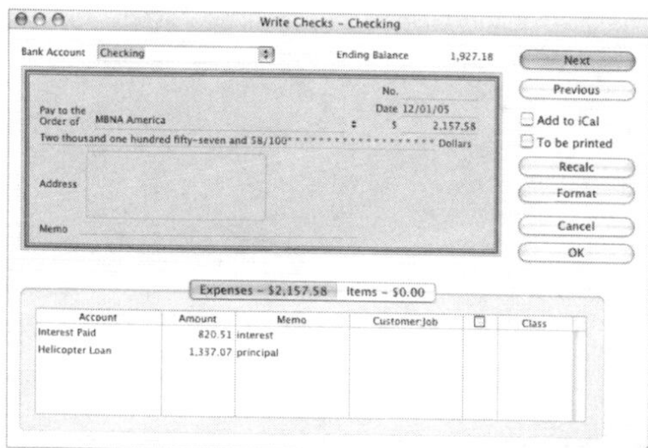

Figure 2 QuickBooks uses intuitive forms—like this Write Checks form—to gather information about transactions.

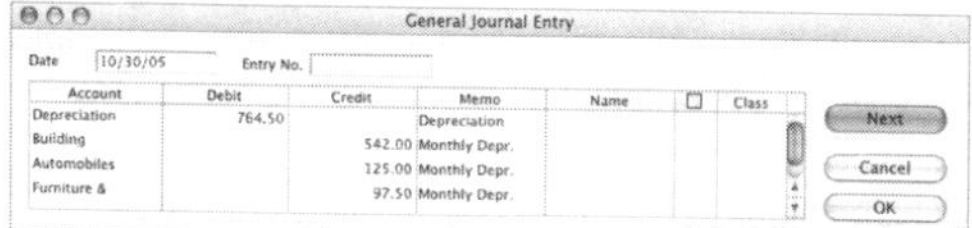

Figure 3 If you want to use the General Journal Entry form, you'd better know the difference between a debit and a credit.

Table 2

How Debits and Credits Affect an Account's Balance or Total

Account Type	Debit to...	Credit to...
Asset	Increase balance	Decrease balance
Liability	Decrease balance	Increase balance
Equity	Decrease balance	Increase balance
Income	Decrease total	Increase total
Expense	Increase total	Decrease total

Double-Entry Accounting

QuickBooks Pro enables you to maintain a standard *double-entry* accounting system. In a double-entry accounting system, every accounting entry has two parts that must balance: a debit and a credit.

For example, suppose you write a check to pay for your company's electric bill. The check reduces the balance in your checking account and increases the amount spent on electricity. To record this transaction, you would debit the Electricity expense account and credit the Checking asset account for the same amount.

Do you need to know debits and credits to enter basic transactions—such as a check—in QuickBooks? Not really. QuickBooks will handle the debits and credits for you, based on how you fill in forms (**Figure 2**). But if you want to take advantage of its General Journal Entry form (**Figure 3**), you should fully understand how each type of transaction works and the effect of debits and credits on account balances.

✔ Tip

- **Table 2** provides some guidelines for how debits and credits affect an account's balance or total.

Forms & Lists

QuickBooks makes extensive use of forms (**Figures 2 and 3**) to gather information for transactions. You fill in a form using information already set up in QuickBooks lists. When you complete the entry, QuickBooks automatically debits or credits account balances based on the information you provided.

Getting Started with QuickBooks 1

Getting Started

Before you can use QuickBooks Pro to manage your company's finances, you need to install it and configure it for your use.

Installation is as easy as drag-and-drop, as you'll learn in the first part of this chapter. Copying QuickBooks to your computer's hard disk takes just minutes.

Configuring QuickBooks is a bit more time-consuming. Fortunately, QuickBooks comes with a New Company Setup Assistant, which makes the job easy. You'll use it to enter general information about your company, as well as specific information for accounts and opening balances.

This chapter explains how to install QuickBooks and use the New Company Setup Assistant to set basic company options.

✔ Tip

- This chapter assumes you are installing QuickBooks on a computer running Mac OS X 10.4 or later. QuickBooks 2006 is also compatible with Mac OS X 10.3.9, although some features require Mac OS X 10.4 to work.

Installing QuickBooks

Installing QuickBooks Pro is as easy as dragging the QuickBooks application file from a CD window to the Applications folder on your hard disk.

Figure 1 The QuickBooks Pro 2006 CD icon appears on the desktop.

To install QuickBooks Pro

1. Insert the QuickBooks CD into your disc drive.

   The QuickBooks Pro 2006 CD icon appears on the desktop (**Figure 1**).

2. If necessary, double-click the icon to open the disc window (**Figure 2**).

3. Drag the QuickBooks Pro 2006 application icon onto the Applications folder on your hard disk (**Figure 3**).

4. Wait while QuickBooks is copied to your hard disk. A standard Copy window appears while it works (**Figure 4**). When the Copy window disappears, you're ready to use QuickBooks.

5. Eject the QuickBooks Pro 2006 CD and store it in a safe place in case you ever need to reinstall.

✔ Tip

- In step 3, if you prefer, you can drag the QuickBooks Pro 2006 application icon to the Applications folder in any Finder window's Sidebar.

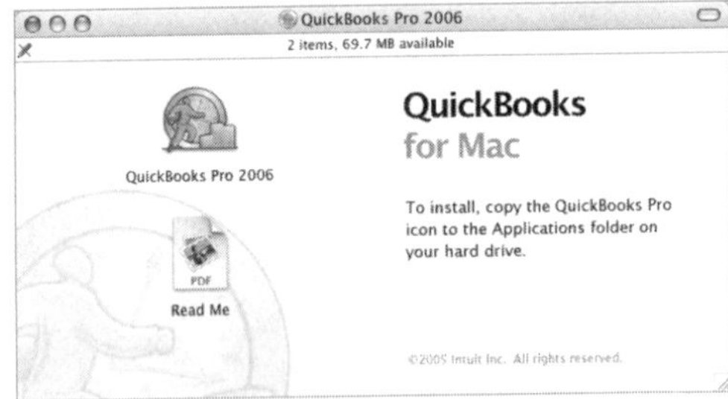

Figure 2 Double-clicking the CD icon displays the contents of the disc in a Finder window.

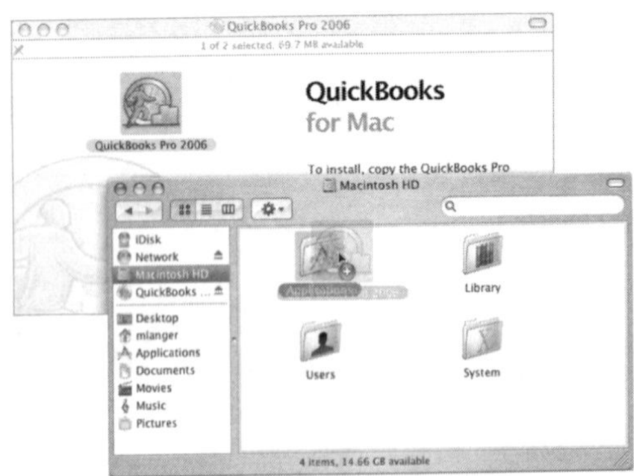

Figure 3 Drag the QuickBooks Pro 2006 application icon to your Applications folder.

Figure 4 The Copy window appears while QuickBooks is copied to your hard disk.

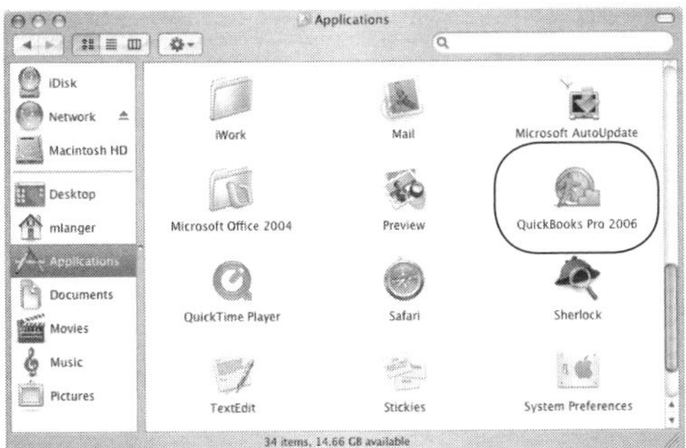

Figure 5 The QuickBooks Pro 2006 application icon should appear in your Applications folder.

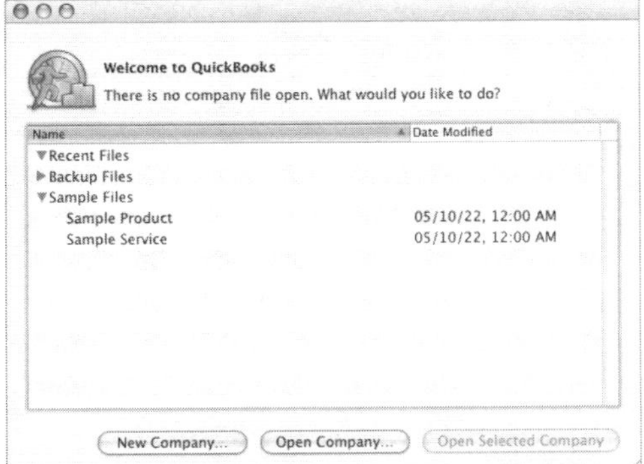

Figure 6 When you open QuickBooks Pro for the first time, a window like this one appears.

To launch QuickBooks for the first time

1. Open the Applications folder on your hard disk (**Figure 5**).
2. Locate and double-click the QuickBooks Pro 2006 application icon (**Figure 5**).
3. The Welcome to QuickBooks window appears (**Figure 6**). You have several options:
   - ▲ If you're a new QuickBooks user and want to create a new company file, click the New Company button. Then follow the instructions in the section titled "Using the new Company Setup Assistant" later in this chapter.
   - ▲ If you're upgrading to QuickBooks 2006 from a previous version of QuickBooks, click the Open Company button. Then follow the instructions in the section titled "To open & update an existing company file when you first open QuickBooks" later in this chapter.
   - ▲ If you'd like to explore the features of QuickBooks using sample company files, select the Sample Product or Sample Service item in the Sample Files list and click Open Selected Company.
   - ▲ If this isn't the first time you've launched QuickBooks and a company file appears in the Recent Files list, you can open that file by selecting it and clicking Open Selected Company.

✔ Tip

- ■ The first time you launch QuickBooks, a dialog may appear asking you to register. Follow the instructions in that dialog to complete the registration process.

Opening an Existing Company File

There are several ways to open an existing company file for use with QuickBooks:

- Click Open Company in the Welcome to QuickBooks window that appears when you launch QuickBooks for the first time (**Figure 6**).
- Use the File menu's Open Company command (**Figure 11**).
- Double-click the company file's icon in a Finder window.

You can also use the Import From Quicken Files command to convert a Quicken data file for use with QuickBooks.

This part of the chapter explores each of these options.

✔ Tips

- When you open a company file created with a previous version of QuickBooks, QuickBooks makes an archival copy of that file with a different name before converting it to the current version of QuickBooks and opening it for use.
- Quicken is a personal finance software package by Intuit Inc. You can learn more about Quicken at `www.quicken.com`.

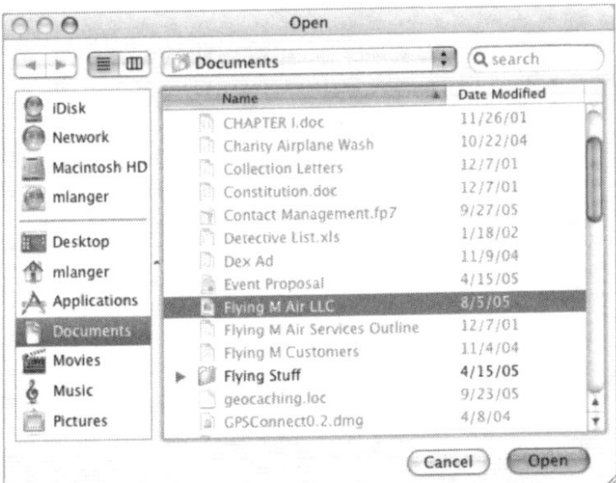

Figure 7 Use a standard Open dialog to locate, select, and open an existing QuickBooks company file.

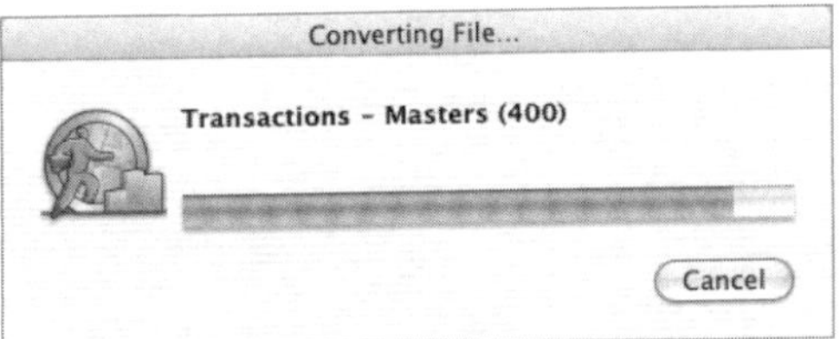

Figure 8 When you open a company file created with a previous version of QuickBooks, the file is converted to the new QuickBooks format.

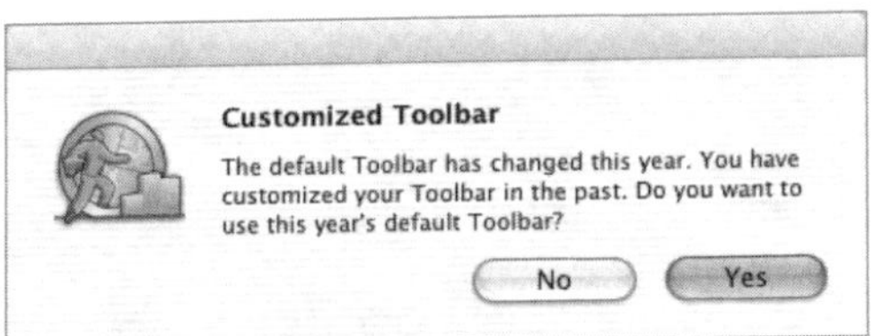

Figure 9 If your old QuickBooks company file had a customized toolbar,a dialog like this appears.

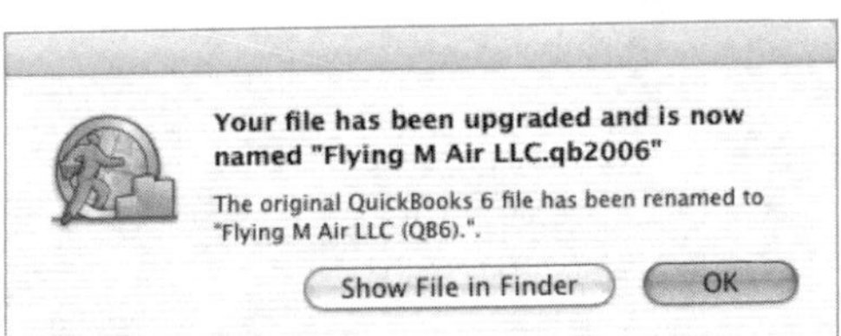

Figure 10 QuickBooks tells you when it upgrades a file and lets you know what the original file's name is.

To open & update an existing company file when you first open QuickBooks

1. In the Welcome to QuickBooks window that appears when you first launch QuickBooks (**Figure 6**), click the Open Company button.
2. In the Open dialog (**Figure 7**), locate and select the company file you want to open.
3. Click Open.

   If you have opened a company file created with a previous version of QuickBooks, a few things may happen:

   ▲ A Converting File dialog appears, showing conversion progress (**Figure 8**).

   ▲ A Customized Toolbar dialog may appear (**Figure 9**). Click Yes if you want your toolbar to match the one illustrated throughout this book.

   ▲ A dialog like the one in **Figure 10** appears, explaining that QuickBooks has made a copy of the original file. Click OK.

The company file opens in QuickBooks, displaying the same windows that were open when you last closed the file.

To open a company file with the Open Company command

1. Choose File > Open Company (**Figure 11**).
2. Follow steps 2 and 3 in the previous section to finish opening the file.

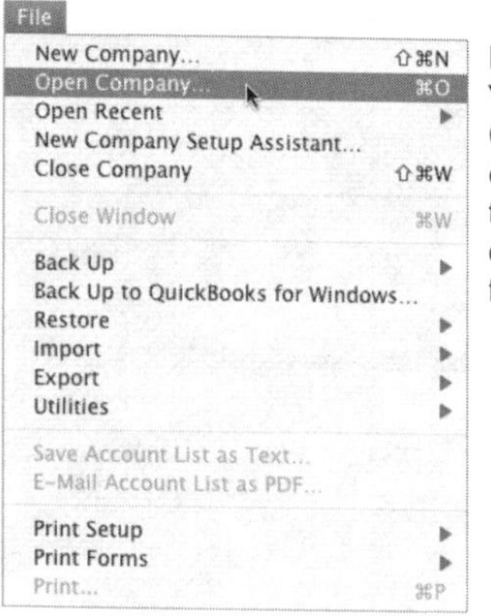

Figure 11 You can use the Open Company command under the File menu to open a company file.

To open a company file from the Finder

1. In the Finder, locate the icon for the company file you want to open (**Figure 12**).
2. Double-click the company file icon. If necessary, QuickBooks launches. The company file opens, displaying the same windows that were open when you last closed the file.

Flying M Air LLC.qb2006

Figure 12 A QuickBooks company file icon.

✔ Tip

- This is probably the fastest way to open a specific QuickBooks company file. You may want to make an alias of this file and keep it in the Mac OS X Dock so it's easy to find and open.

To convert a Quicken file for use with QuickBooks

1. Choose File > Import > From Quicken File (**Figure 13**).
2. A Convert from Quicken dialog like the one in **Figure 14** appears. Click No.
3. In the Select dialog that appears (**Figure 15**), locate and select the Quicken data file you want to convert.
4. Click Open.
5. Use the Create a new QuickBooks file dialog that appears (**Figure 16**) to name and save the converted file.
6. If a dialog like the one in **Figure 17** appears, click Yes or No to indicate whether the Quicken file includes an

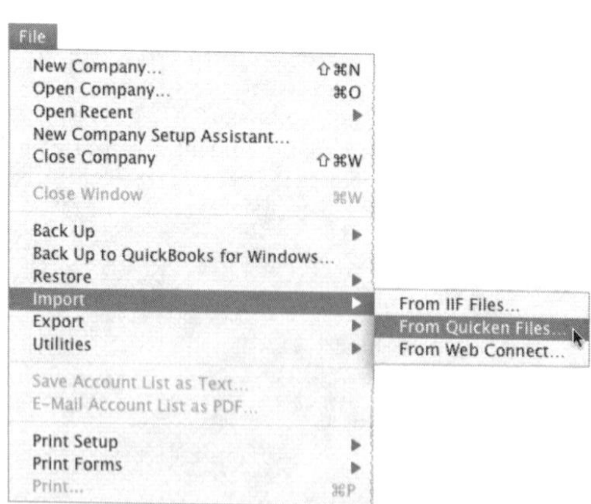

Figure 13 The Import submenu includes a command for converting a Quicken data file.

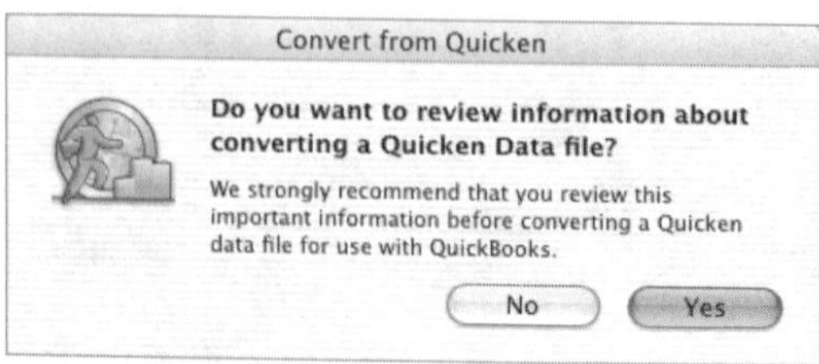

Figure 14 A dialog like this asks if you want to review conversion information.

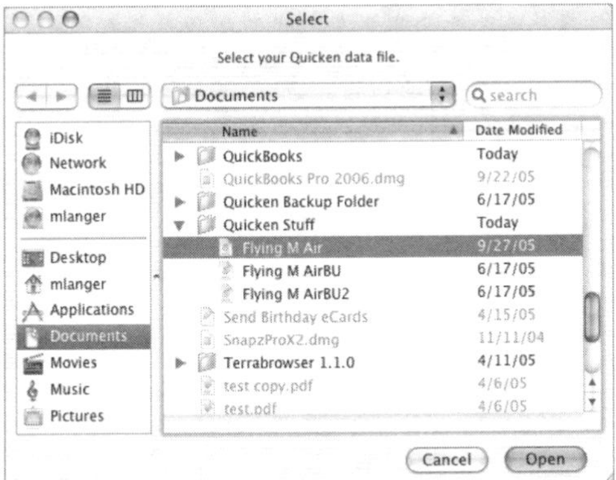

Figure 15 Use this dialog to locate, select, and open the Quicken file you want to convert.

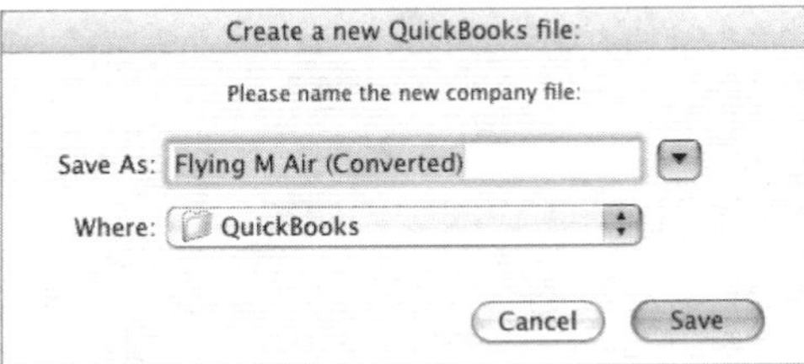

Figure 16 Enter a name and choose a disk location to save the converted file.

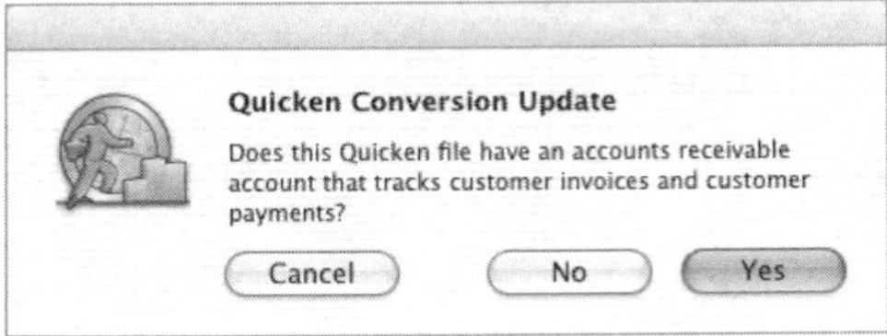

Figure 17 Indicate whether your Quicken data file includes an accounts receivable account...

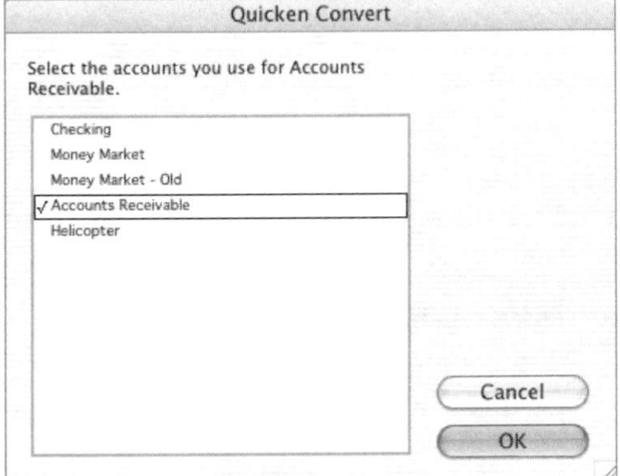

Figure 18 ...and if so, which account it is.

accounts receivable account to track customer invoices and payments. If you click Yes, you can use a dialog like the one in **Figure 18** to select the accounts receivable account and click OK.

7. Wait while QuickBooks converts the file. It displays a status dialog as it works (**Figure 19**).

8. When the conversion is complete, QuickBooks displays a Quicken Conversion Results window (**Figure 20**). Read it to learn about any problems with the conversion and click OK to dismiss it.

   The new QuickBooks data file opens and is ready for use.

✔ Tip

- If you click Yes in step 2, a QuickBooks Help window opens with some additional information about converting from Quicken. Click the window's close button to dismiss it when you're done.

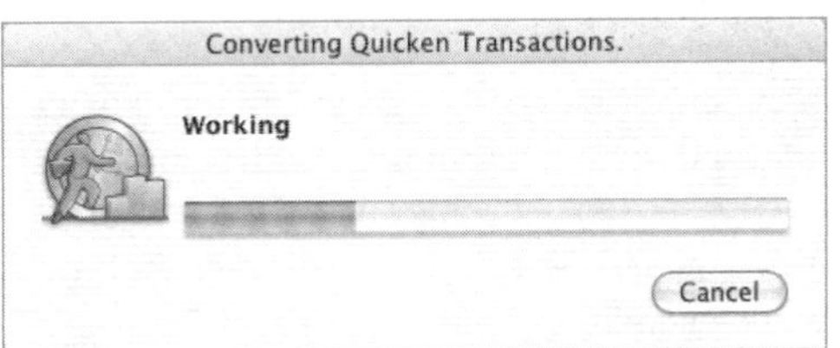

Figure 19 This dialog appears while QuickBooks makes the conversion.

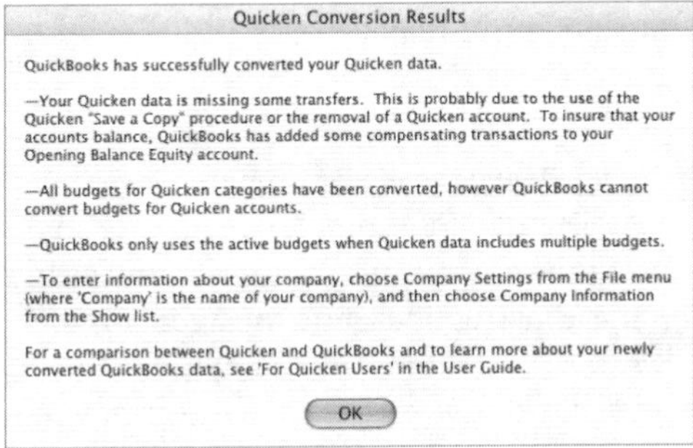

Figure 20 Read about the results of the conversion in a dialog like this one.

Using the New Company Setup Assistant

If you have not used QuickBooks before or you want to set up QuickBooks for a new company, you must create a new QuickBooks company file. The company file you create will be customized to include all of the accounts and other information you need to record transactions and track the finances for your company.

QuickBooks's New Company Setup Assistant makes creating a new company file easy. It walks you, step-by-step, through the setup process, prompting you for information along the way.

The New Company Setup Assistant is organized into five main sections, each of which has two or more topics of information. You read the information in one screen and enter data as requested, then click the Next button to move on. At any point in the process, you can go back to a previous screen or skip ahead or back to another topic.

This part of the chapter provides step-by-step instructions for completing each section and topic of the New Company Setup Assistant. Although it does not provide details on how you can create accounts or items with the Assistant, it shows you how you can enter basic information, set preferences, and learn more about how QuickBooks helps you track your company's finances.

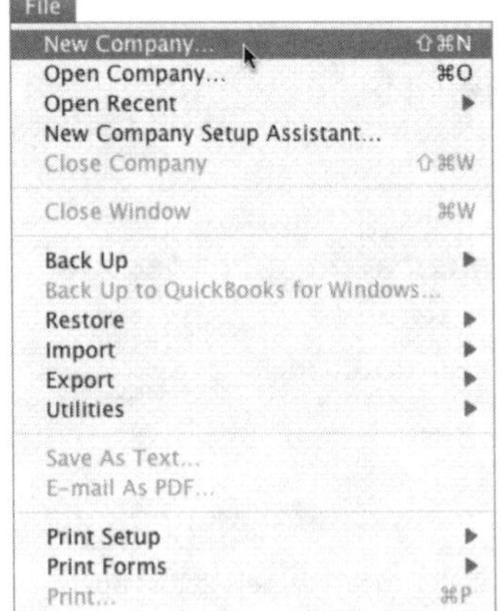

Figure 21 To create a new company file, choose New Company from the File menu.

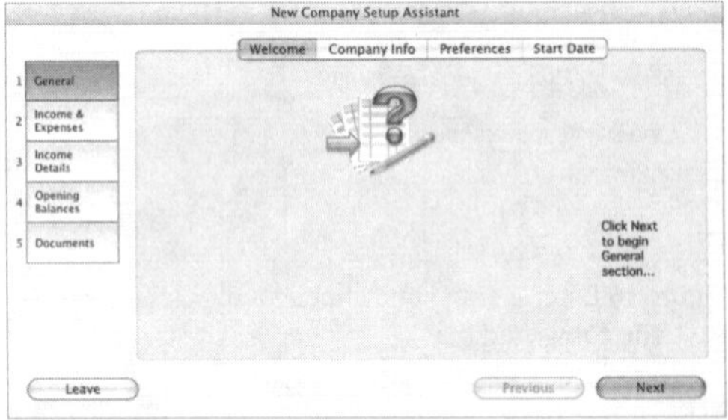

Figure 22 The first screen of the New Company Setup Assistant dialog.

✔ Tips

- If you leave the New Company Setup Assistant before completing it, you can resume at any time. To find your place in these instructions, find the figure for the screen you see on your computer, then use the cross-references in the numbered steps to find the step that goes with it.
- Click the More button in any screen to learn more about the available options.
- The setup hints illustrated in screenshots throughout this chapter are for a retail business, because that's the business I selected in step 14. The hints that appear for your business type may vary.

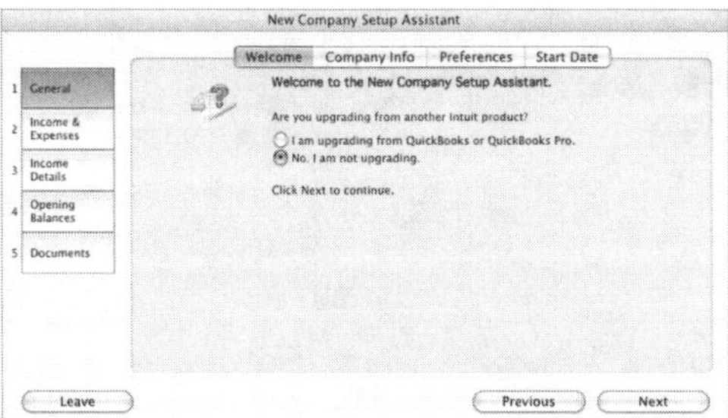

Figure 23 The Welcome to the New Company Setup Assistant screen.

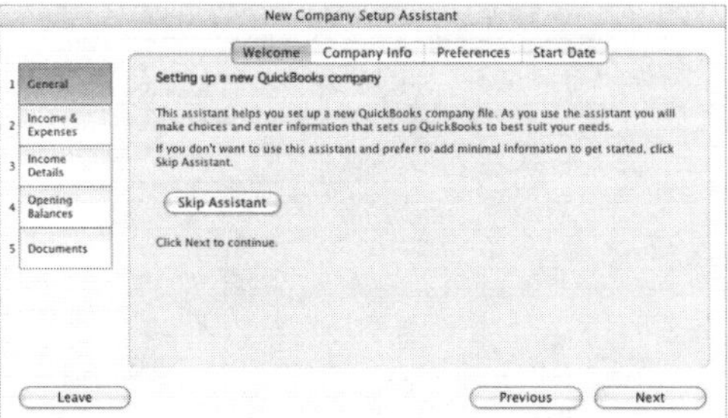

Figure 24 The Setting up a new QuickBooks company screen.

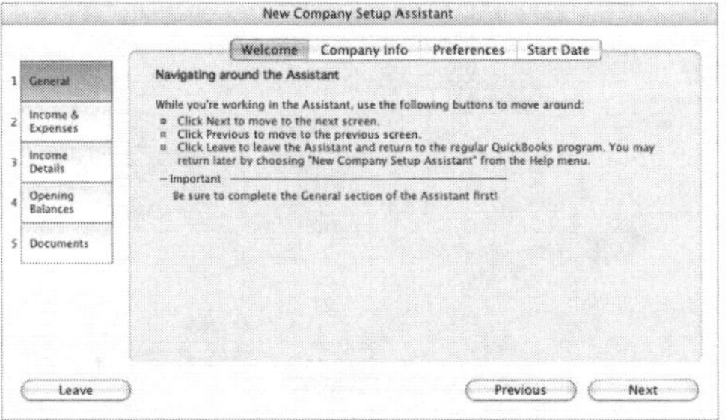

Figure 25 The Navigating around the Assistant screen.

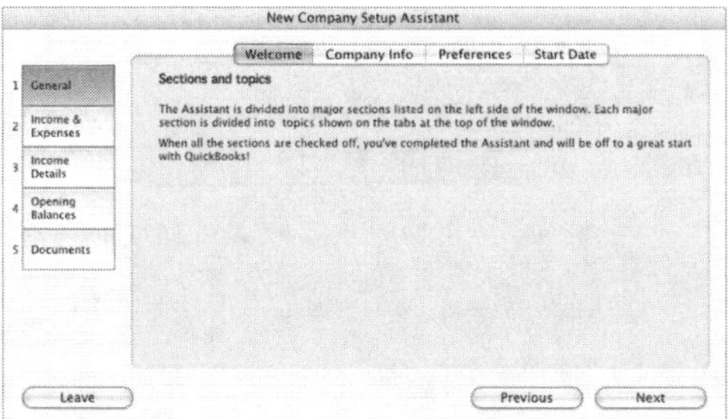

Figure 26 The Sections and topics screen.

To open the New Company Setup Assistant

In the Welcome to QuickBooks window (**Figure 6**), click the New Company button.

Or

Choose File > New Company (**Figure 21**).

The first screen of the New Company Setup Assistant appears (**Figure 22**).

✔ Tips

- You can leave the New Company Setup Assistant at any time by clicking the Leave button in any screen. QuickBooks will save all information you have entered up to that point.
- You can open the New Company Setup Assistant for an existing company company file by choosing File > New Company Setup Assistant.

To complete the General section of the New Company Setup Assistant

1. If necessary, open the New Company Setup Assistant (**Figure 22**).
2. Click the Next button.
3. In the Welcome to the New Company Setup Assistant screen (**Figure 23**), select the radio button labeled No, I'm not upgrading and click Next.
4. Read the information in the Setting up a new QuickBooks company screen (**Figure 24**) and click Next.
5. Read the information in the Navigating around the Assistant screen (**Figure 25**) and click Next.

Continued on next page...

Continued from previous page.

6. Read the information in the Sections and topics screen **(Figure 26)** and click Next.
7. Read the information in the Feel free to change your answers screen **(Figure 27)** and click Next.
8. Read the information in the Welcome completed screen **(Figure 28)** and click Next.
9. Read the information in the General: Company Information screen **(Figure 29)** and click Next.
10. In the Your company name screen **(Figure 30)**, enter the public and legal names of your business in the appropriate boxes. If your business uses the same name on invoices and checks as it does on legal documents, enter the same name in each box. Then click Next.
11. In the Your company address screen **(Figure 31)**, enter the complete address for your company in the box and choose your country from the pop-up menu. Then click Next.

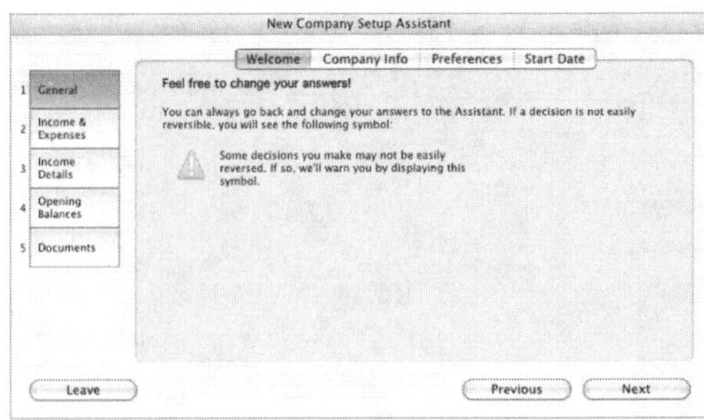

Figure 27 The Feel free to change your answers screen.

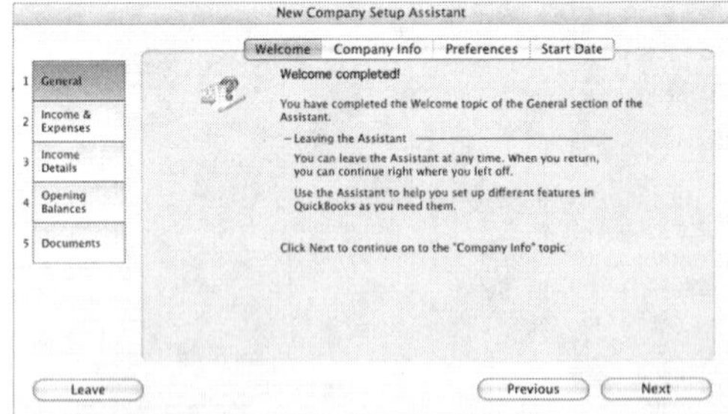

Figure 28 The Welcome completed screen.

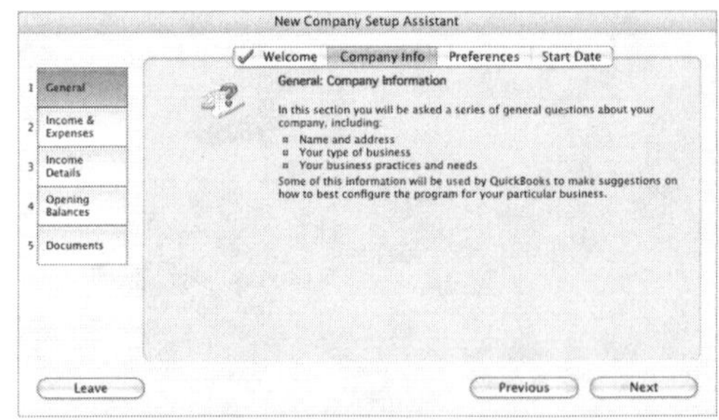

Figure 29 The General: Company Information screen.

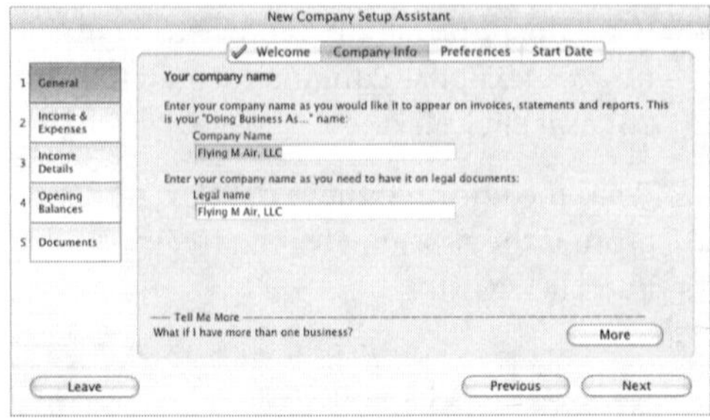

Figure 30 The Your company name screen.

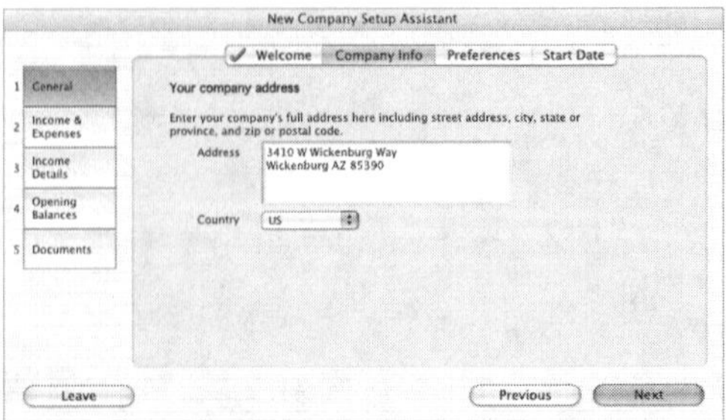

Figure 31 The Your company address screen.

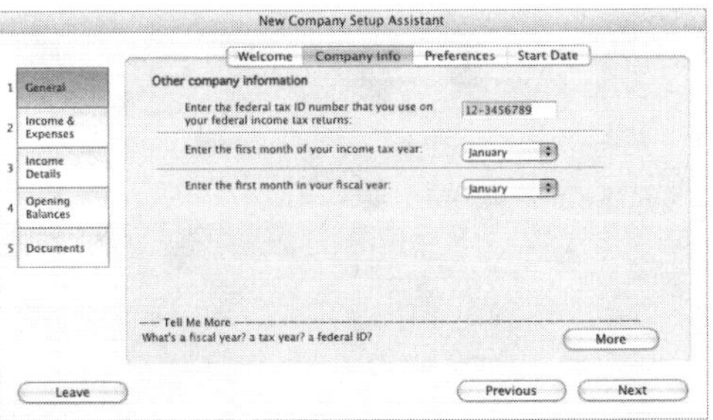

Figure 32 The Other company information screen.

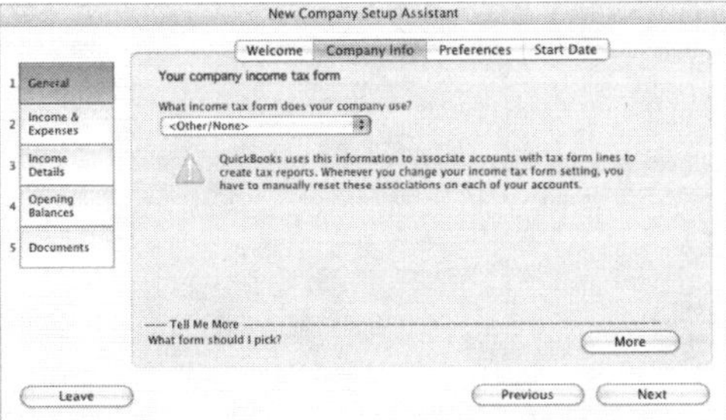

Figure 33 The Your company income tax form screen.

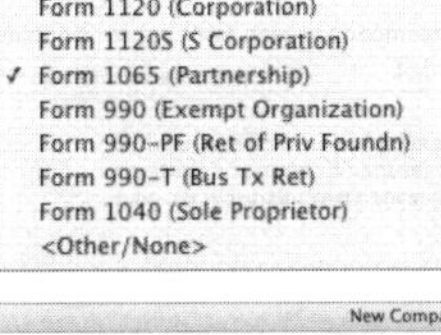

Figure 34 Use this pop-up menu to select the tax form you use for reporting business income.

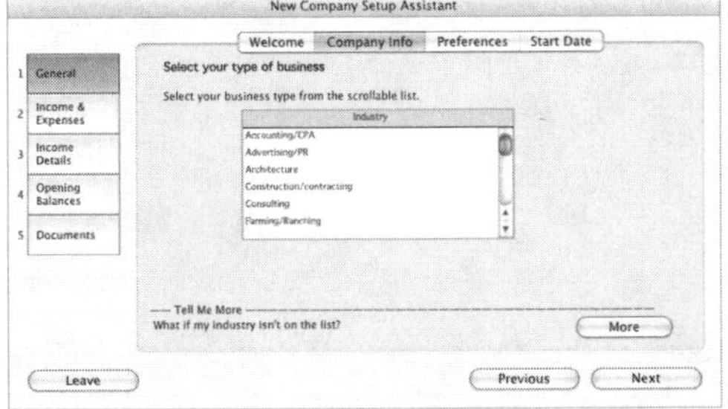

Figure 35 The Select your type of business screen.

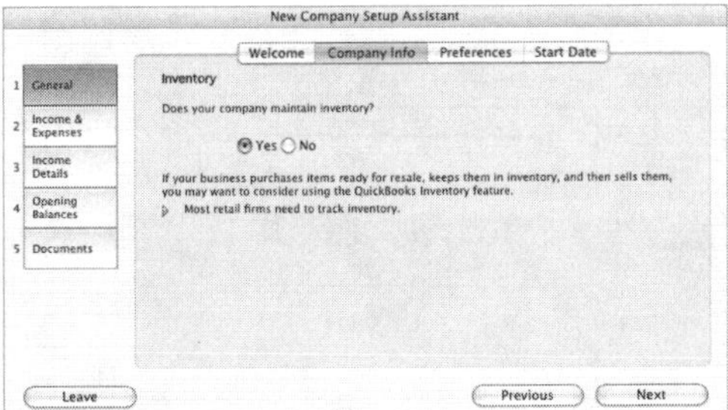

Figure 36 The Inventory screen.

12. In the Other company information screen (**Figure 32**), enter the following information and click Next.
    - ▲ **Federal Tax ID number** is the number you use on your federal income tax returns for the business. Enter the number as you want it to appear on reports and tax forms.
    - ▲ **First month of income tax year** is the month your tax year begins. For most businesses, this is January, but if you're using a different tax year, choose an option from the pop-up menu.
    - ▲ **First month of fiscal year** is the month your fiscal year begins. If your fiscal year starts in a month other than January, choose the month from the pop-up menu.
13. In the Your company income tax form screen (**Figure 33**), choose the form you use for filing your business's tax returns from the pop-up menu (**Figure 34**) and click Next.
14. In the Select your type of business screen (**Figure 35**), select a business type from the Industry scrolling list. The type you select will determine which accounts QuickBooks creates automatically for you, so it's a good idea to select a business type that's close to yours. Then click Next. If you select an industry that doesn't normally have inventory, skip ahead to step 19.
15. In the Inventory screen (**Figure 36**), select an option to indicate whether your company tracks inventory. The answer you select determines whether the Assistant will prompt you for inventory information. Then click Next. If you selected No, skip ahead to step 19.

Continued on next page...

Continued from previous page.

16. The Assistant displays the Should I use QuickBooks for inventory screen (**Figure 37**). You have two main options:
    - ▲ **Show Help** displays a QuickBooks Help window with information about the inventory tracking features. When you are finished reading this information, click the window's close button to dismiss it and continue.
    - ▲ **Next** moves to the next screen without displaying help information.
17. In the Enabling Inventory screen (**Figure 38**), select an option to indicate whether you want to use QuickBooks to track your inventory. Then click Next.
18. The Product sales with QuickBooks inventory screen appears next (**Figure 39**). You have two options:
    - ▲ **Show Help** displays a PDF document with information about how you can use QuickBooks for your industry. You can print this document or save it for later reference. When you're finished working with it, quit the application in which it is displayed to return to QuickBooks.
    - ▲ **Next** moves to the next screen without displaying more information.
19. Read the information in the Setup hints for your business screen (**Figure 40**) and click Next.

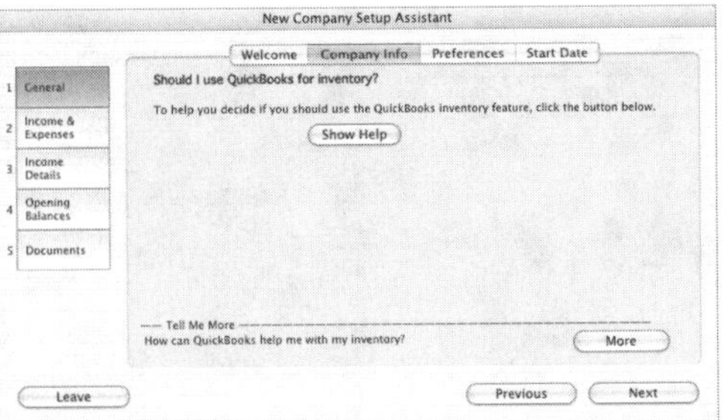

Figure 37 The Should I use QuickBooks for inventory screen.

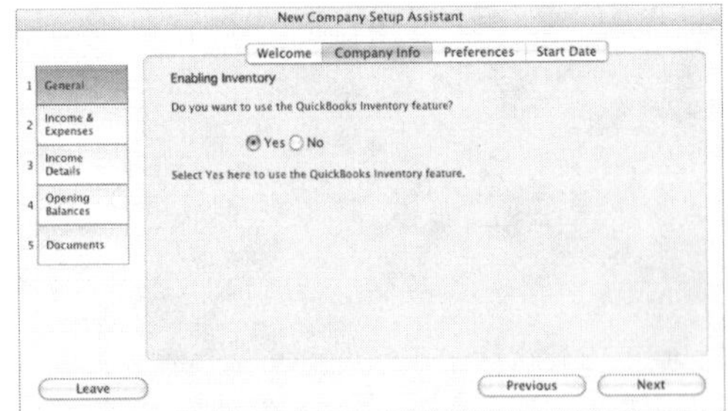

Figure 38 The Enabling Inventory screen.

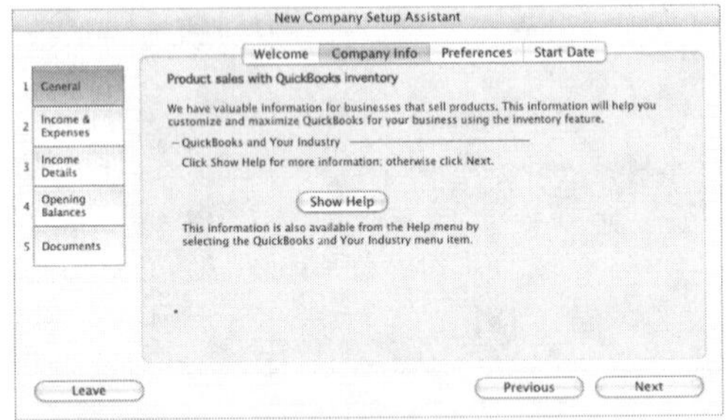

Figure 39 The Product sales with QuickBooks Inventory screen.

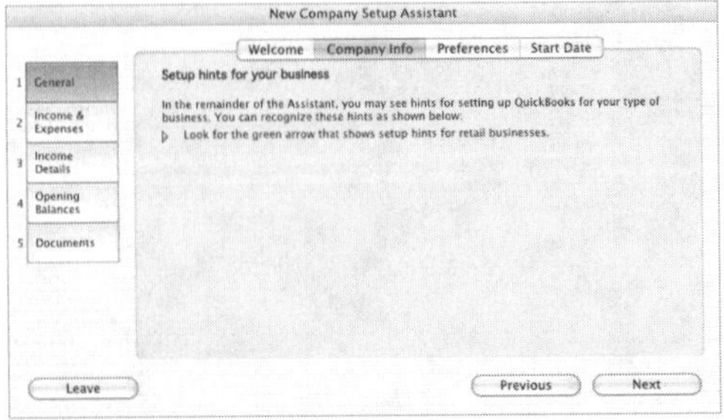

Figure 40 The Setup hints for your business screen.

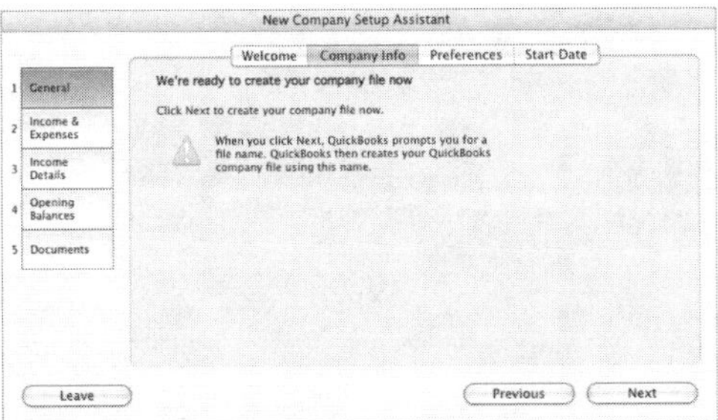

Figure 41 The We're ready to create your company file now screen.

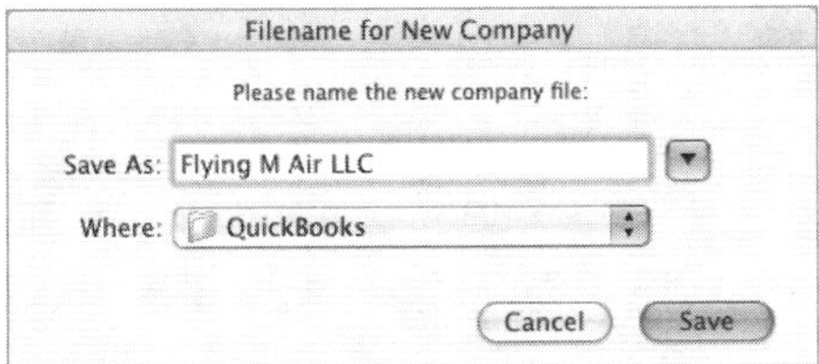

Figure 42 The Filename for New Company dialog.

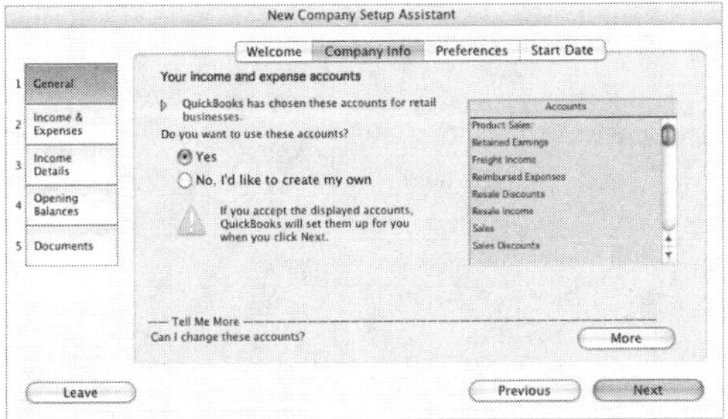

Figure 43 The Your income and expense accounts screen.

20. Read the information in the We're ready to create your company file now screen **(Figure 41)** and click Next.

21. Use the Filename for New Company dialog that appears **(Figure 42)** to enter a name and select a location for the company file. By default, QuickBooks suggests the QuickBook folder inside your Documents folder. Click Save.

22. In the Your income and expense accounts screen **(Figure 43)**, select an option to determine whether you want to accept the income and expense accounts QuickBooks can automatically create for your business. These steps assume you select Yes; I provide instructions for creating accounts in **Chapter 2**. Click Next.

23. Read the information in the Company Info completed screen **(Figure 44)** and click Next.

24. Read the information in the What are preferences screen **(Figure 45)** and click Next.

Continued on next page...

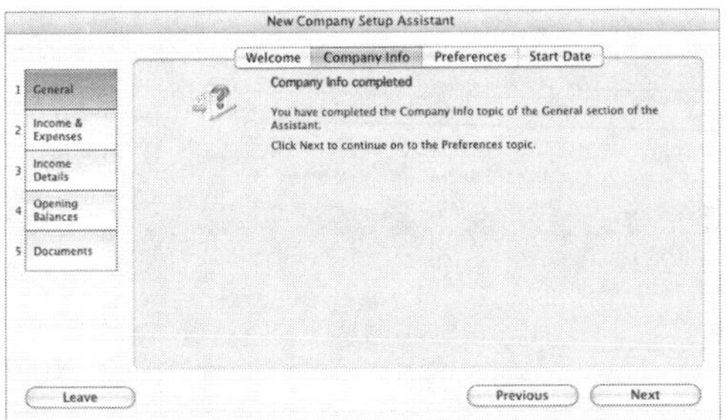

Figure 44 The Company Info completed screen.

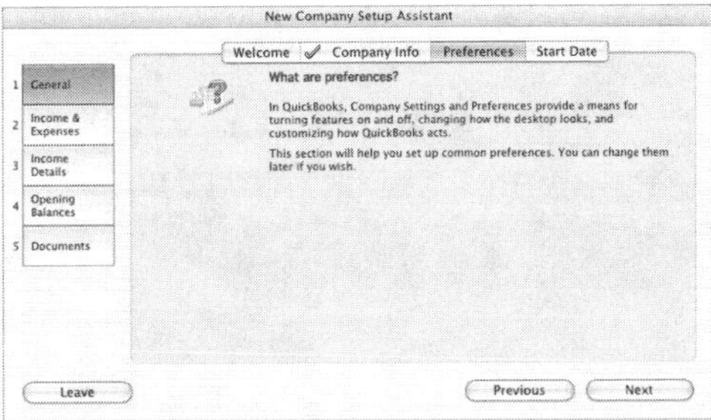

Figure 45 The What are preferences screen.

Continued from previous page.

25. In the Sales tax screen **(Figure 46)**, select an option to indicate whether you collect sales tax from your customers. Then click Next. If you selected No, skip ahead to step 28.

26. In the Single or multiple sales tax rates screen **(Figure 47)**, select an option to indicate whether you collect sales tax for a single or for multiple tax agencies. Then click Next. If you selected Multiple, click Next in the next screen that appears and skip ahead to step 28.

27. In the Sales tax information screen **(Figure 48)**, enter information about the sales tax and click Next:

- **Short name** is an internally used name for the tax.
- **Description** is the text to appear on invoices and similar documents for the sales tax line.
- **Sales tax rate** is the sales tax rate, entered as a percentage.
- **Government agency** is the name of the government agency to which you pay the sales tax.

28. In the Your invoice format screen **(Figure 49)**, select the invoice format you prefer. When you select a different option, the preview changes to show you what it might look like. Then click Next.

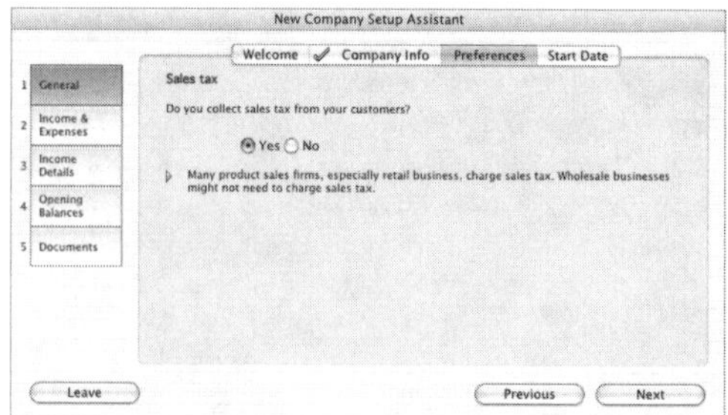

Figure 46 The Sales tax screen.

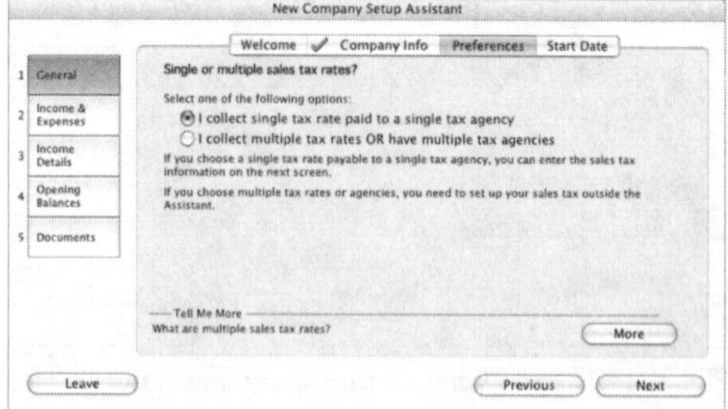

Figure 47 The Single or multiple sales tax rates screen.

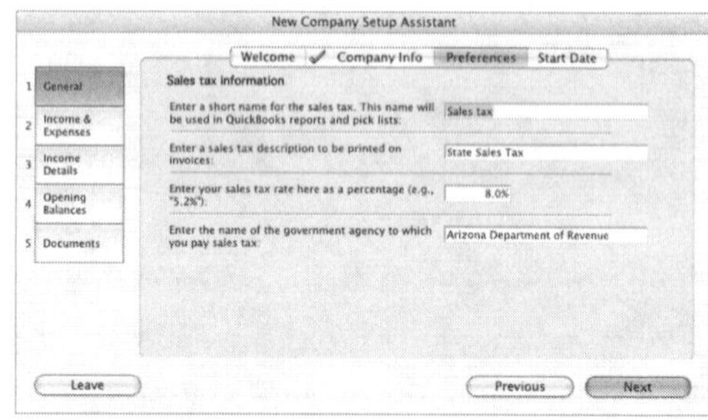

Figure 48 The Sales tax information screen.

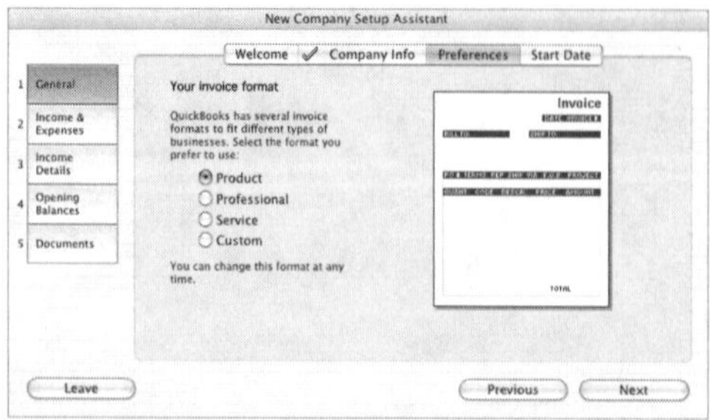

Figure 49 The Your invoice format screen.

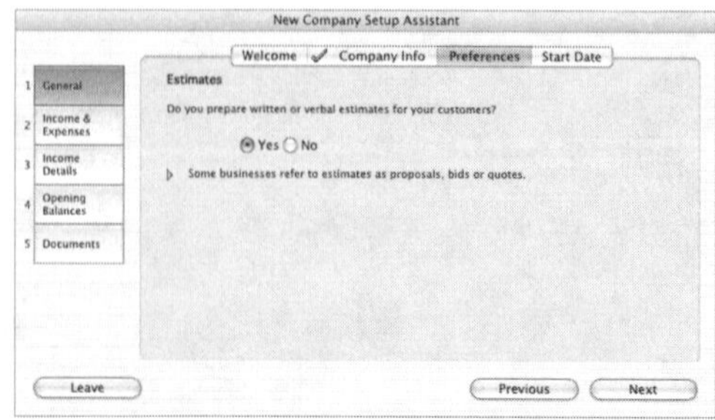

Figure 50 The Estimates screen.

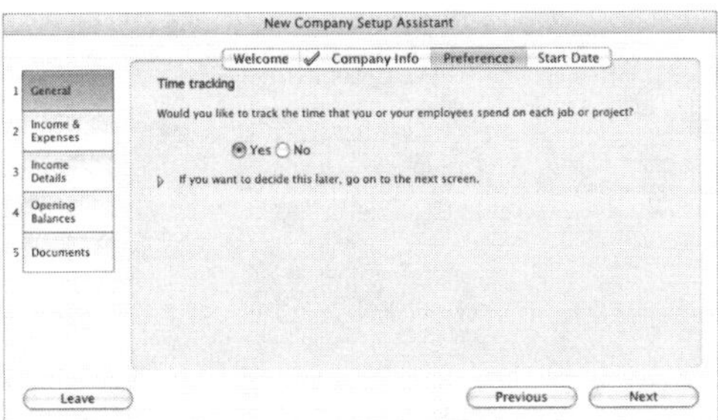

Figure 51 The Time tracking screen.

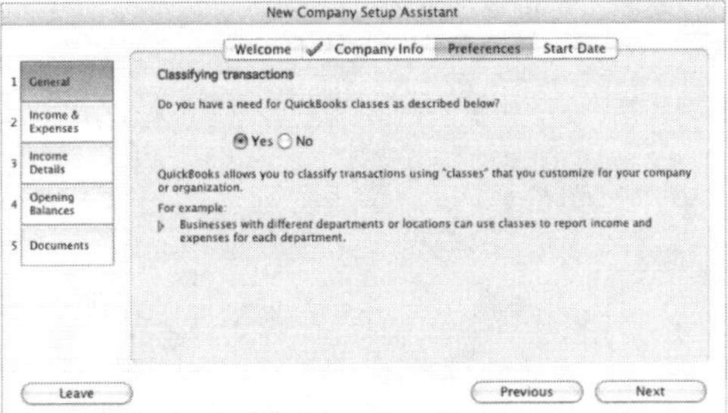

Figure 52 The Classifying transactions screen.

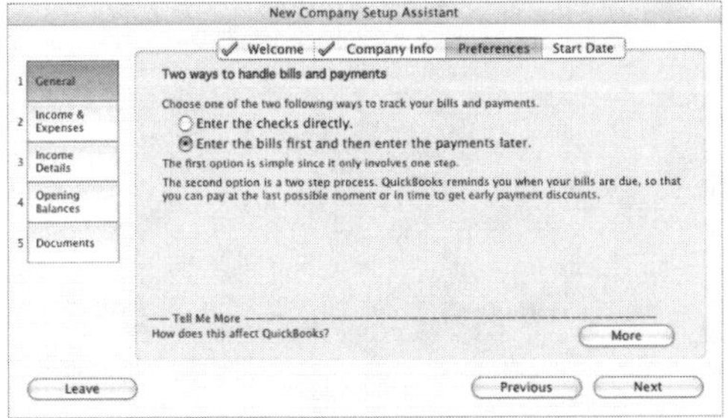

Figure 53 The Two ways to handle bills and payments screen.

29. In the Estimates screen (**Figure 50**), select an option to indicate whether you prepare estimates for customers. Then click Next.
30. In the Time tracking screen (**Figure 51**), select an option to indicate whether you want to track time spent on jobs or projects. Then click Next.
31. In the Classifying transactions screen (**Figure 52**), select an option to indicate whether you want to use QuickBooks' class feature to classify transactions. Then click Next.
32. In the Two ways to handle bills and payments screen (**Figure 53**), select an option to indicate whether you want to pay bills by simply entering checks or by entering the bills and then entering payments later. Then click Next.
33. In the Reminders list screen (**Figure 54**), select an option to indicate when you want to see a Reminders List. Then click Next.
34. Read the information in the Preferences completed screen (**Figure 55**) and click Next.

Continued on next page...

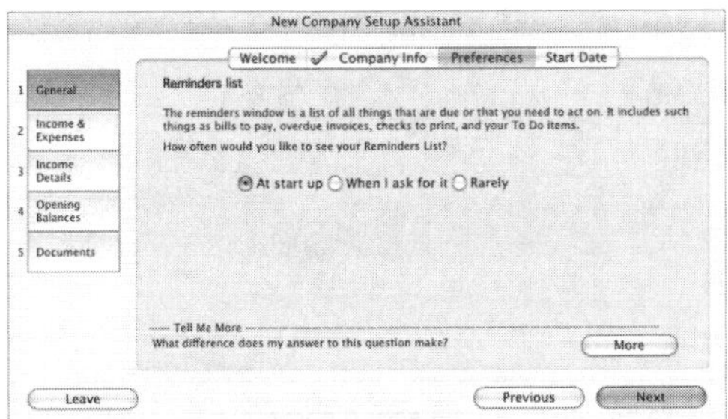

Figure 54 The Reminders list screen.

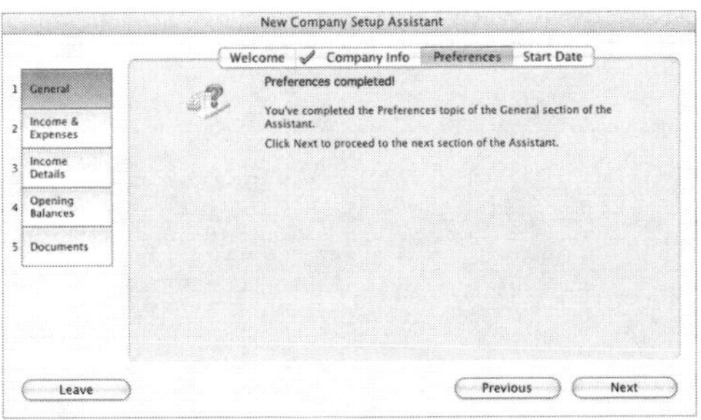

Figure 55 The Preferences completed screen.

Continued from previous page.

35. Read the information in the Understanding your QuickBooks start date screen **(Figure 56)** and click Next.

36. Read the information in the Information for your start date screen **(Figure 57)**. At this point, you may want to make a decision and get the documents listed in this screen ready. Then click Next.

37. In the Choose your QuickBooks start date screen **(Figure 58)**, enter your desired start date in the box using *MM/DD/YYYY* format. Then click Next.

38. Read the information in the General section completed screen **(Figure 59)** and click Next.

39. Continue following instructions in the next section.

✔ Tips

- The appearance of the Filename for New Company dialog **(Figure 42)** will vary if the dialog has been expanded to show location details. You can click the button beside the filename to expand or collapse the dialog.

- Although you can use any date as a start date for QuickBooks, I highly recommend that you start with the beginning of a fiscal or tax year. This makes it possible to have complete financial records in QuickBooks for that entire year and the future.

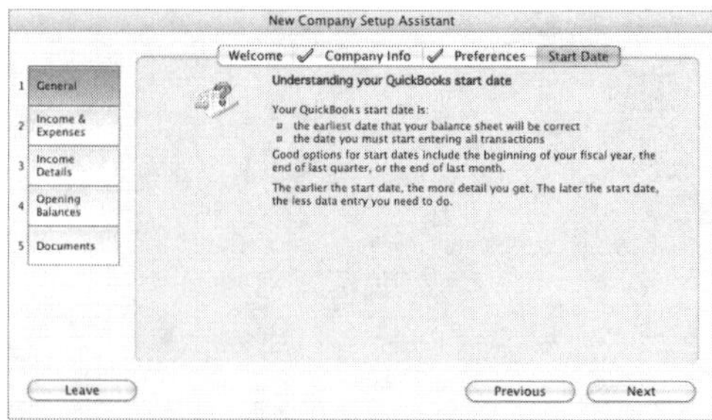

Figure 56 The Understanding your QuickBooks start date screen.

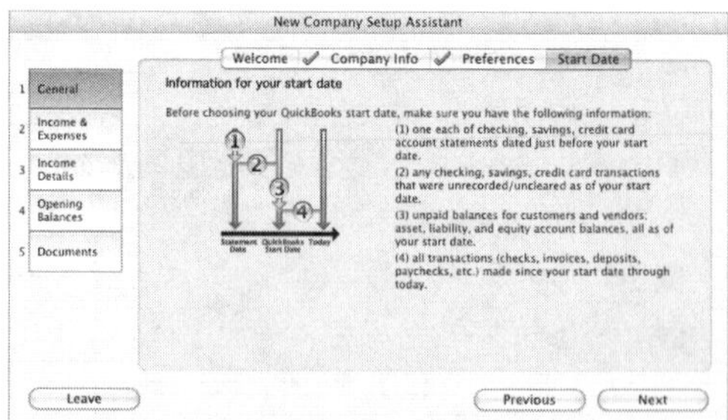

Figure 57 The Information for your start date screen.

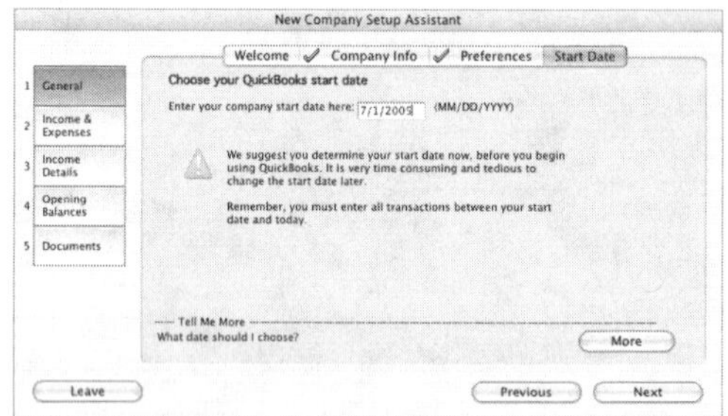

Figure 58 The Choose your QuickBooks start date screen.

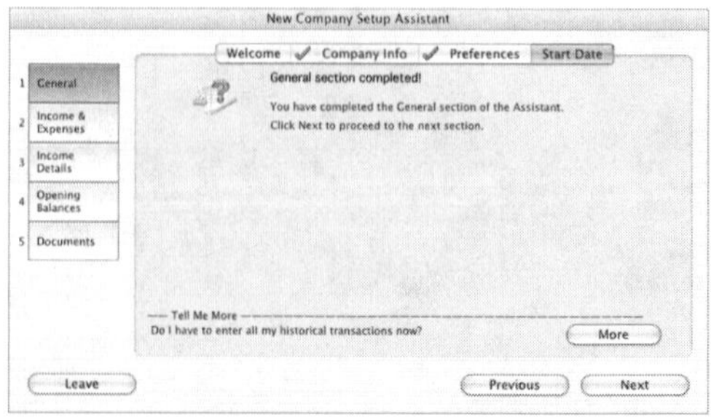

Figure 59 The General section completed screen.

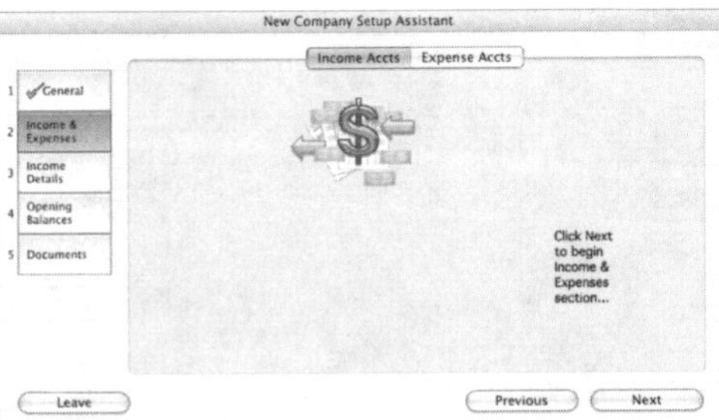

Figure 60 The first screen of the Income & Expenses section.

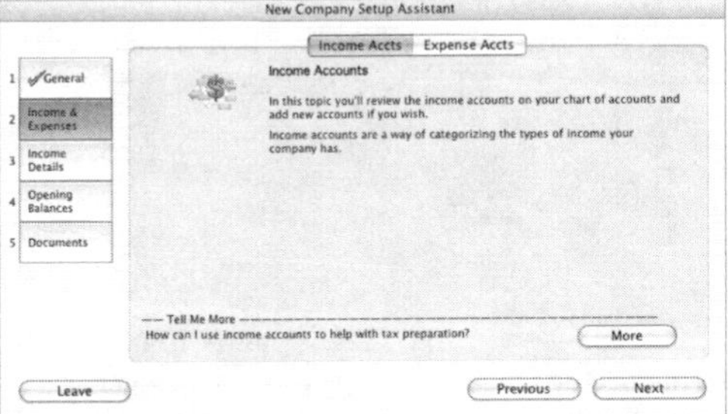

Figure 61 The Income Accounts screen.

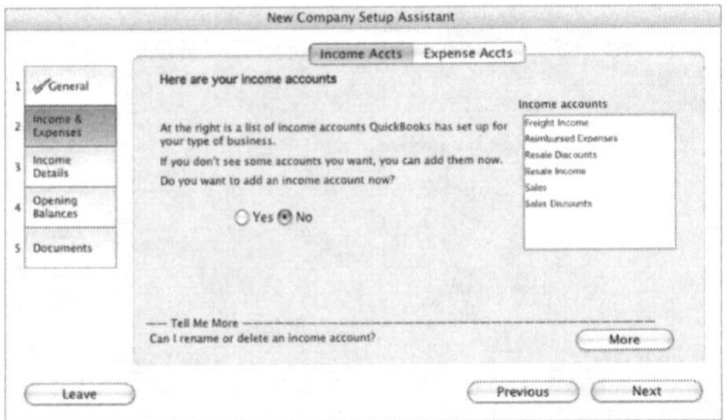

Figure 62 The Here are your income accounts screen.

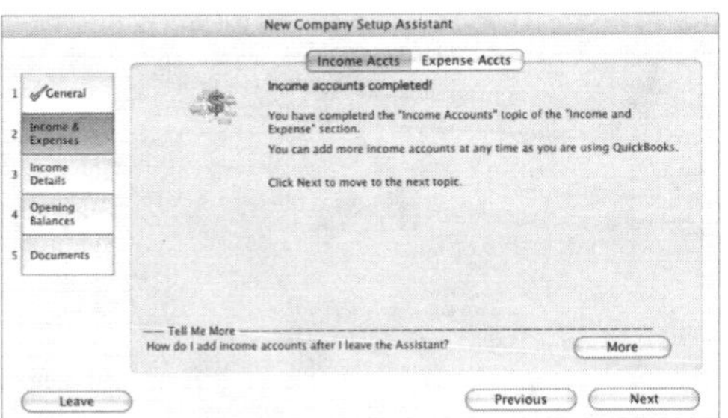

Figure 63 The Income accounts completed screen.

To complete the Income & Expenses section of the New Company Setup Assistant

1. If necessary, open the New Company Setup Assistant and click the Income & Expenses button on the left side of the window.
2. If necessary, click the Income Accts button to display the first screen of the Income & Expenses section (**Figure 60**).
3. Click Next.
4. Read the information in the Income Accounts screen (**Figure 61**) and click Next.
5. Look over the list of accounts in the Here are your income accounts screen (**Figure 62**). QuickBooks creates this list based on the type of business you indicated earlier in the setup process.
   - ▲ To add another account now, select Yes, click Next, and follow the instructions that appear to add one or more accounts.
   - ▲ To continue without adding accounts, select No and click Next.
6. Read the information in the Income accounts completed screen (**Figure 63**) and click Next.

Continued on next page...

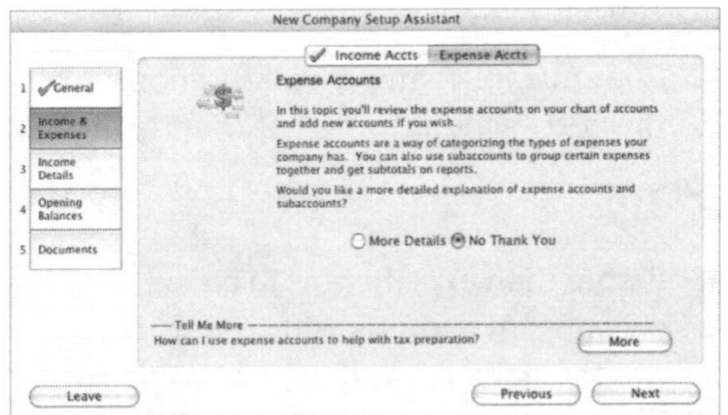

Figure 64 The Expense Accounts screen.

Continued from previous page.

7. In the Expense Accounts screen **(Figure 64)**, you have two options:
   - ▲ **More Details** displays a series of screens that provides more information about expense accounts. If you select this option, click Next until you have viewed all information.
   - ▲ **No Thank You** does not display any additional information when you click Next.
8. In the Set up all of your accounts screen **(Figure 65)**, select Minimum accounts and click Next.
9. Read the information in the Minimum expense accounts for QuickBooks Pro screen **(Figure 66)** and click Next.
10. Look over the list of accounts in the Here are your expense accounts screen **(Figure 67)**. QuickBooks creates this list based on the type of business you indicated earlier in the setup process.
    - ▲ To add another account now, select Yes, click Next, and follow the instructions that appear to add one or more accounts.
    - ▲ To continue without adding accounts, select No and click Next.
11. Read the information in the Expense accounts completed screen **(Figure 68)** and click Next.
12. Continue following the instructions in the next section.

✔ Tip

- Rather than explain how to create accounts two ways—with and without the Assistant—I explain how to create them without the Assistant in **Chapter 2**. You'll probably use that method most.

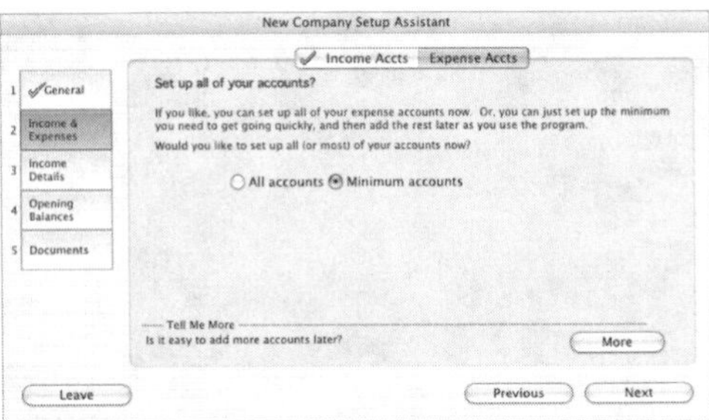

Figure 65 The Set up all of your accounts screen.

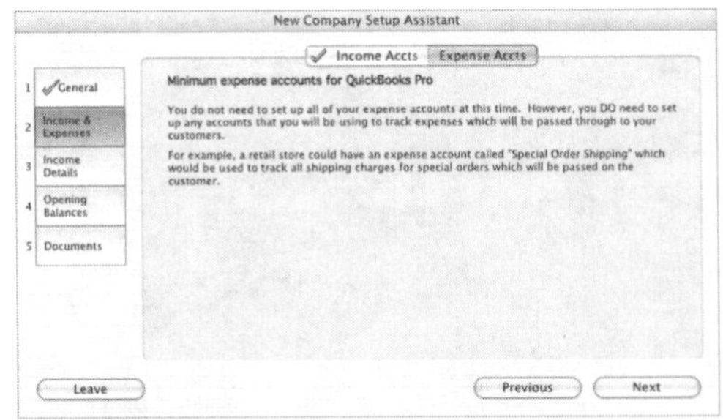

Figure 66 The Minimum expense accounts for QuickBooks Pro screen.

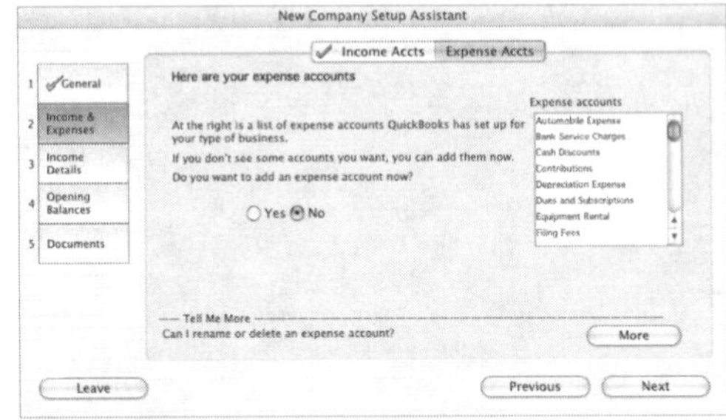

Figure 67 The Here are your expense accounts screen.

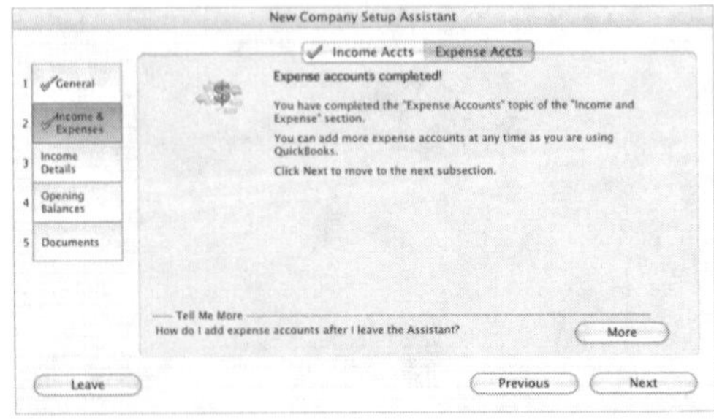

Figure 68 The Expense accounts completed screen.

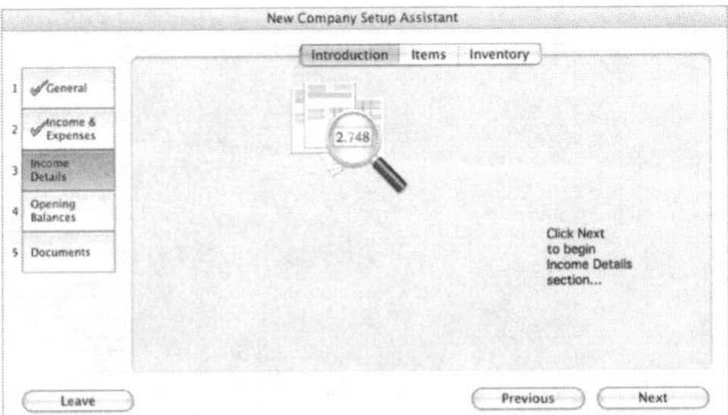

Figure 69 The first screen of the Income Details section.

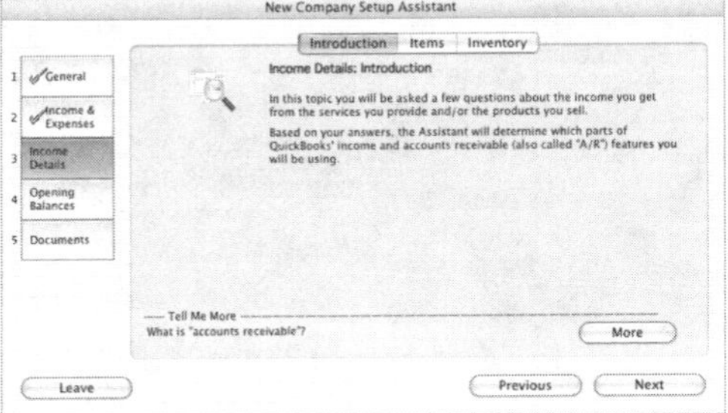

Figure 70 The Income Details: Introduction screen.

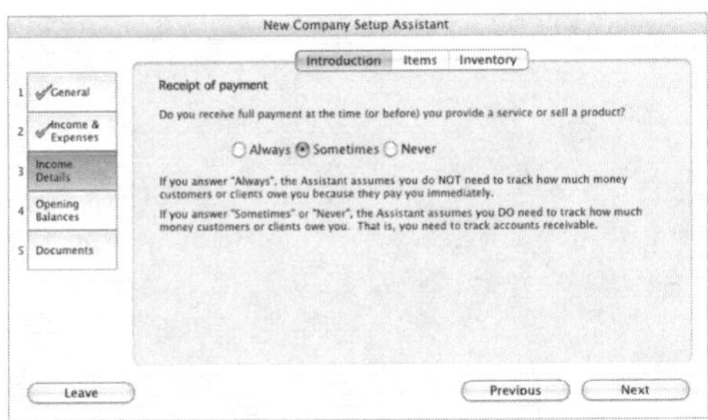

Figure 71 The Receipt of payment screen.

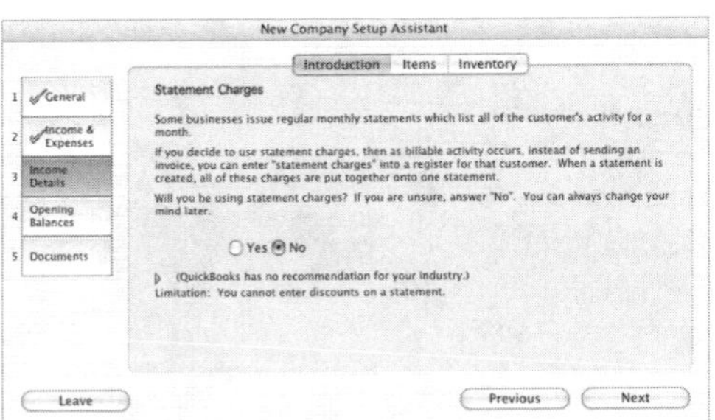

Figure 72 The Statement Charges screen.

To complete the Income Details section of the New Company Setup Assistant

1. If necessary, open the New Company Setup Assistant and click the Income Details button on the left side of the window.
2. If necessary, click the Introduction button to display the first screen of the Income Details section **(Figure 69)**.
3. Click Next.
4. Read the information in the Income Details: Introduction screen **(Figure 70)** and click Next.
5. In the Receipt of payment screen **(Figure 71)**, select one of the three options and click Next:
   - ▲ **Always** tells QuickBooks that you don't need to track accounts receivable. If you select this option, skip ahead to step 7.
   - ▲ **Sometimes** tells QuickBooks that you do need to track accounts receivable, but you also need to account for immediate cash receipts.
   - ▲ **Never** tells QuickBooks that you do need to track accounts receivable but you don't need to account for immediate cash receipts.
6. In the Statement Charges screen **(Figure 72)**, select an option to indicate whether you want to bill your customer on a monthly statement rather than invoicing when billable activity occurs. Then click Next.
7. Read the information in the Introduction completed screen **(Figure 73)** and click Next.

Continued on next page...

Continued from previous page.

8. Read the information in the Income Details: Items screen (**Figure 74**) and click Next.
9. In the Service Items screen (**Figure 75**), select an option:
   - ▲ To add a service item now, select Yes, click Next, and follow the instructions that appear to add one or more items.
   - ▲ To continue without adding service items, select No and click Next.
10. In the Non-inventory Parts screen (**Figure 76**), select an option:
    - ▲ To add a non-inventory part item now, select Yes, click Next, and follow the instructions that appear to add one or more items.
    - ▲ To continue without adding non-inventory part items, select No and click Next.
11. In the Other Charges screen (**Figure 77**), select an option:
    - ▲ To add items for other charges now, select Yes, click Next, and follow the instructions that appear to add one or more items.
    - ▲ To continue without adding items for other charges, select No and click Next.

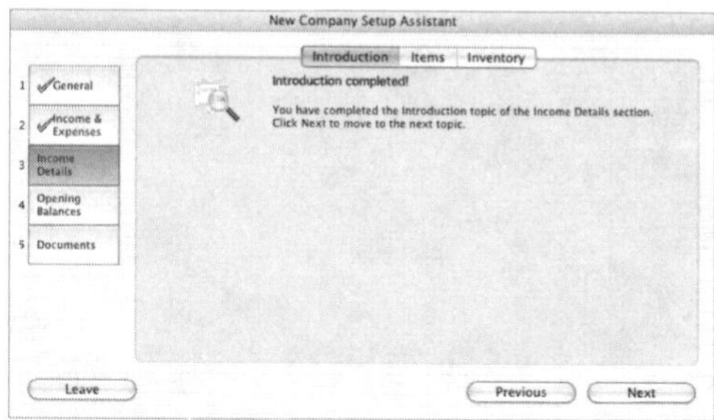

Figure 73 The Introduction completed screen.

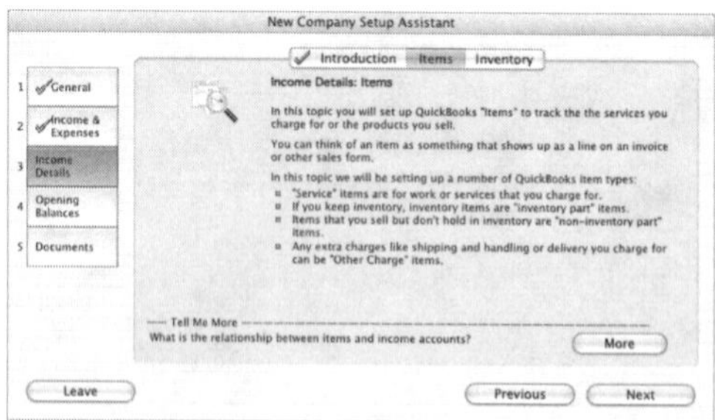

Figure 74 The Income Details: Items screen.

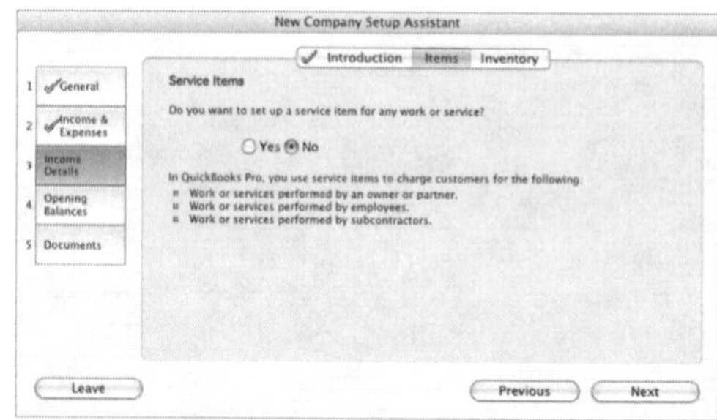

Figure 75 The Service Items screen.

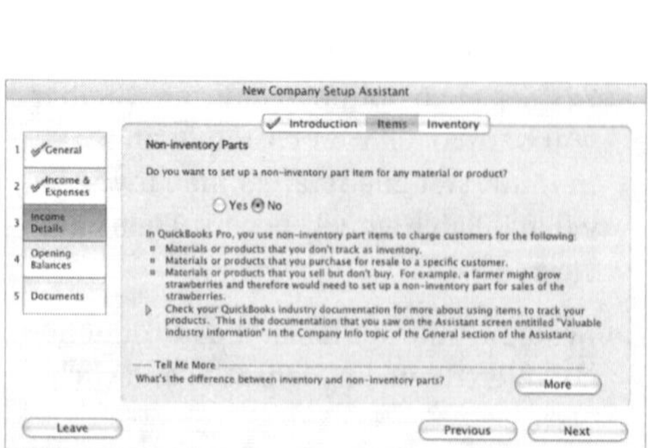

Figure 76 The Non-inventory Parts screen.

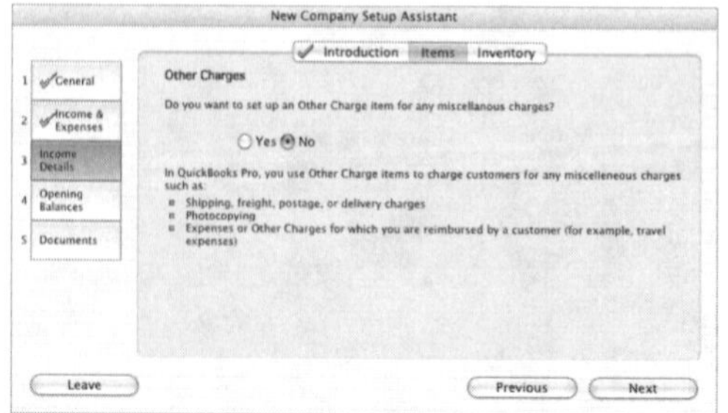

Figure 77 The Other Charges screen.

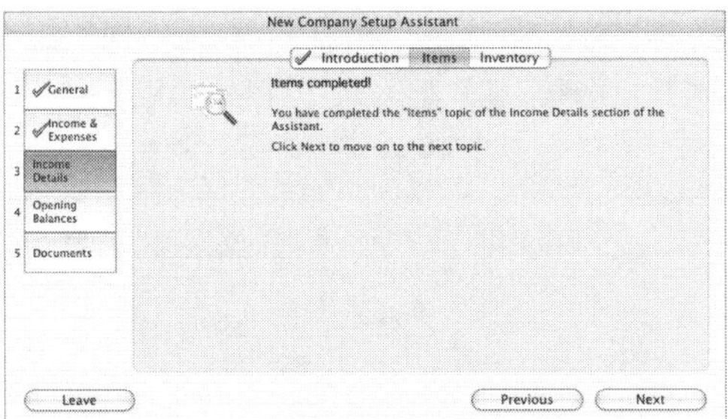

Figure 78 The Items completed screen.

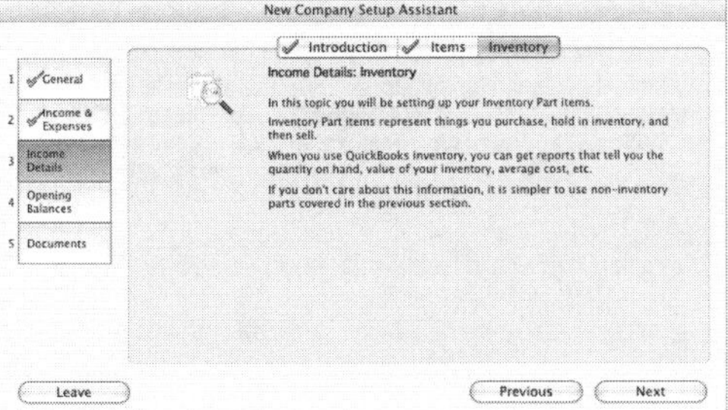

Figure 79 The Income Details: Inventory screen.

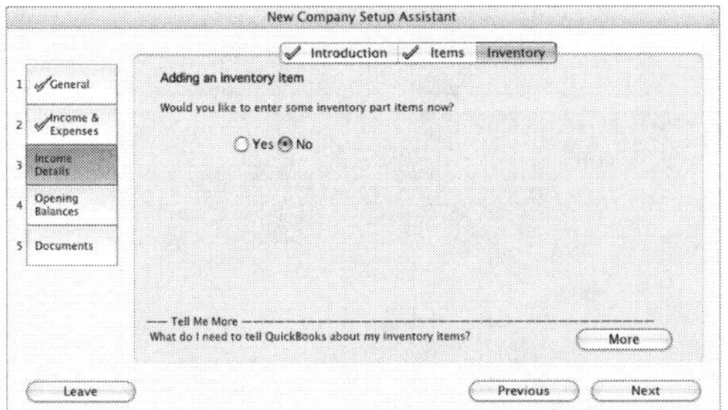

Figure 80 The Adding an inventory item screen.

12. Read the information in the Items completed! screen (**Figure 78**) and click Next.

13. Read the information in the Income Details: Inventory screen (**Figure 79**) and click Next.

14. In the Adding an inventory item screen (**Figure 80**), select an option:
    - ▲ To add an inventory item now, select Yes, click Next, and follow the instructions that appear to add one or more items.
    - ▲ To continue without adding inventory items, select No and click Next.

15. Continue following the instructions in the next section.

✔ Tips

- If you're not sure what to select in step 6, select No. QuickBooks enables you to prepare both invoices and monthly statements.
- Rather than explain how to create service items, non-inventory part items, other charges, and inventory part items two ways—with and without the Assistant—I explain how to create them without the Assistant in **Chapter 2**. I believe that's the method you'll use most as you work with QuickBooks.

To complete the Opening Balances section of the New Company Setup Assistant

1. If necessary, open the New Company Setup Assistant and click the Opening Balances button on the left side of the window.
2. If necessary, click the Introduction button to display the first screen of the Opening Balances section (**Figure 81**).
3. Click Next.
4. Read the information in the Opening Balances: Introduction screen (**Figure 82**) and click Next.
5. Read the information in the Information to have on hand screen (**Figure 83**) and click Next.
6. Read the information in the Opening Balances: Customers screen (**Figure 84**) and click Next.
7. In the Enter customers screen (**Figure 85**), select an option:
   - ▲ To add a customer now, select Yes, click Next, and follow the instructions that appear to add one or more customers.
   - ▲ To continue without adding customers, select No and click Next.

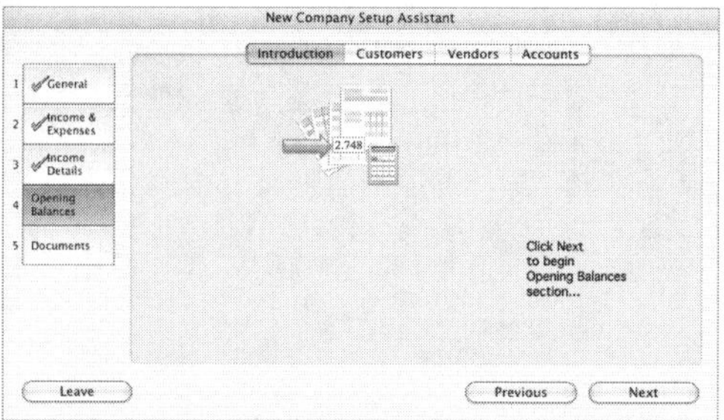

Figure 81 The first screen of the Opening Balances section.

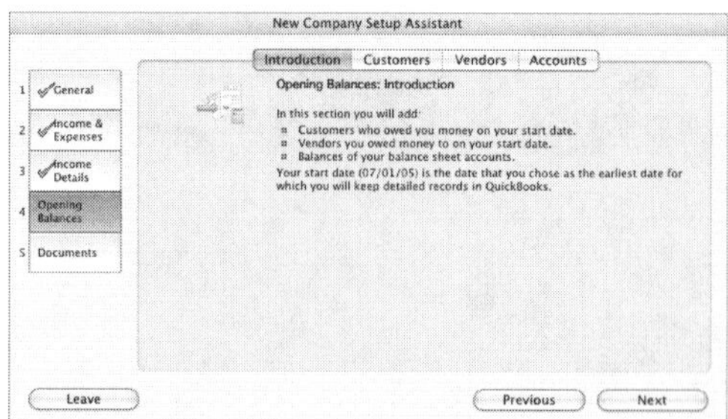

Figure 82 The Opening Balances: Introduction screen.

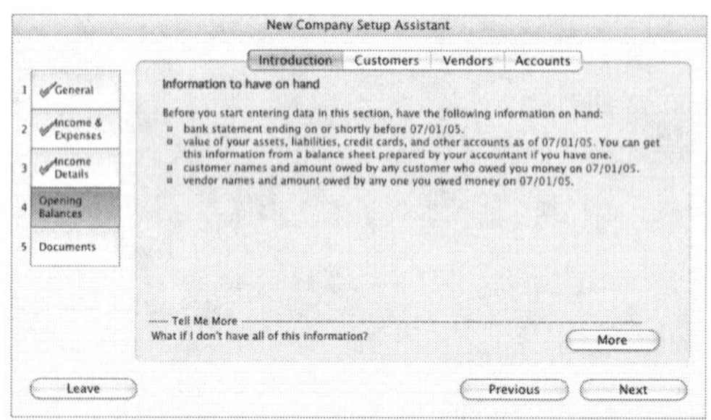

Figure 83 The Information to have on hand screen.

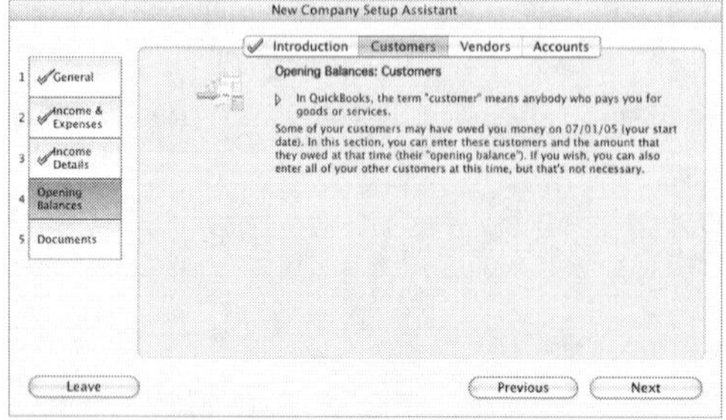

Figure 84 The Opening Balances: Customers screen.

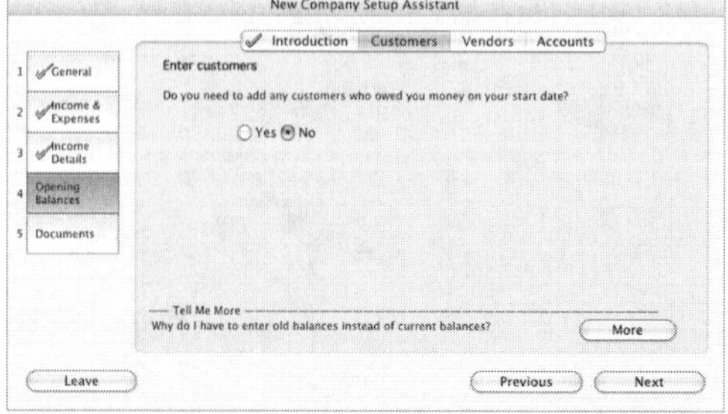

Figure 85 The Enter customers screen.

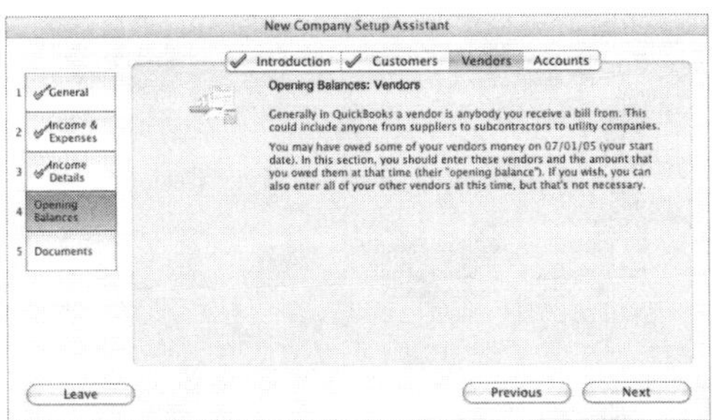

Figure 86 The Opening Balances: Vendors screen.

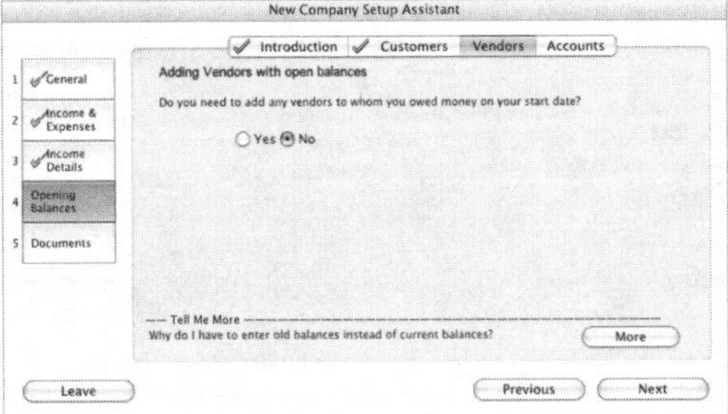

Figure 87 The Adding Vendors with open balances screen.

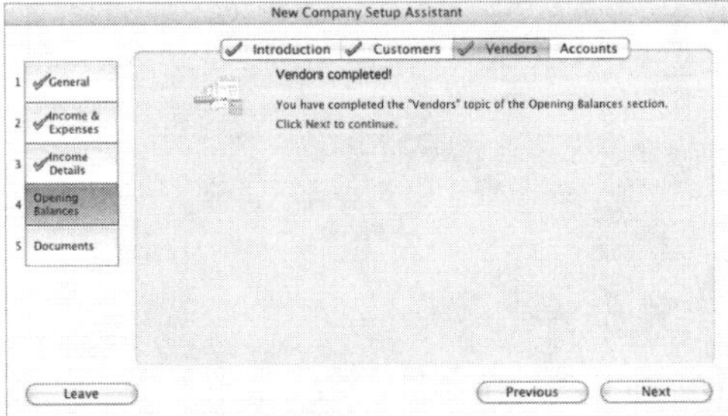

Figure 88 The Vendors completed screen.

8. Read the information in the Opening Balances: Vendors screen (**Figure 86**) and click Next.

9. In the Adding Vendors with open balances screen (**Figure 87**), select an option:

   ▲ To add a vendor now, select Yes, click Next, and follow the instructions that appear to add one or more vendors.

   ▲ To continue without adding vendors, select No and click Next.

10. Read the information in the Vendors completed screen (**Figure 88**) and click Next.

11. Read the information in the Opening Balances: Accounts screen (**Figure 89**) and click Next.

12. In the Credit card accounts screen (**Figure 90**), select an option:

    ▲ To add a credit card account now, select Yes, click Next, and follow the instructions that appear to add one or more credit card accounts.

    ▲ To continue without adding credit card accounts, select No and click Next.

Continued on next page...

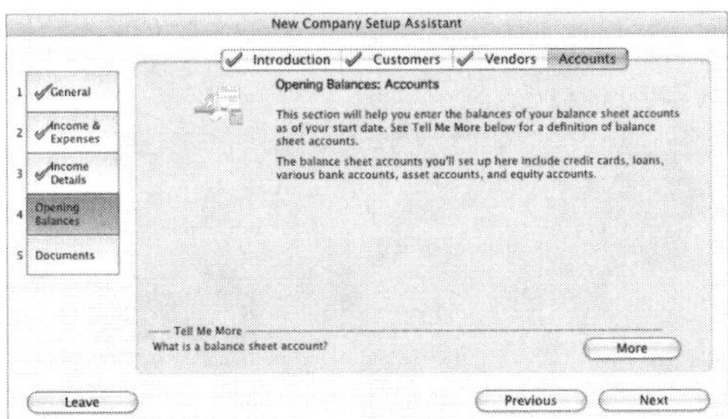

Figure 89 The Opening Balances: Accounts screen.

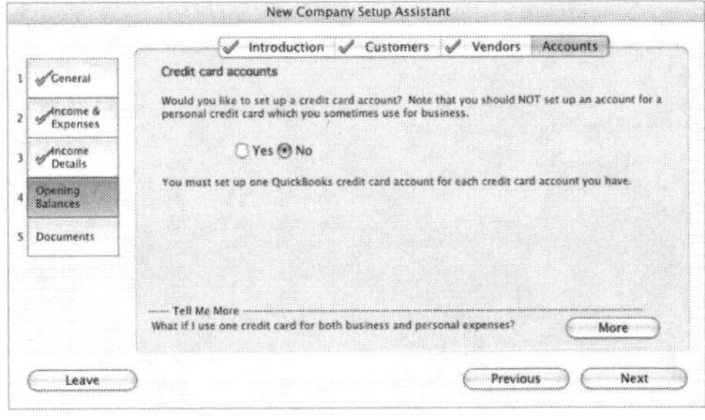

Figure 90 The Credit card accounts screen.

Continued from previous page.

13. In the Adding lines of credit screen **(Figure 91)**, select an option:
    - ▲ To add a line of credit now, select Yes, click Next, and follow the instructions that appear to add one or more lines of credit.
    - ▲ To continue without adding lines of credit, select No and click Next.

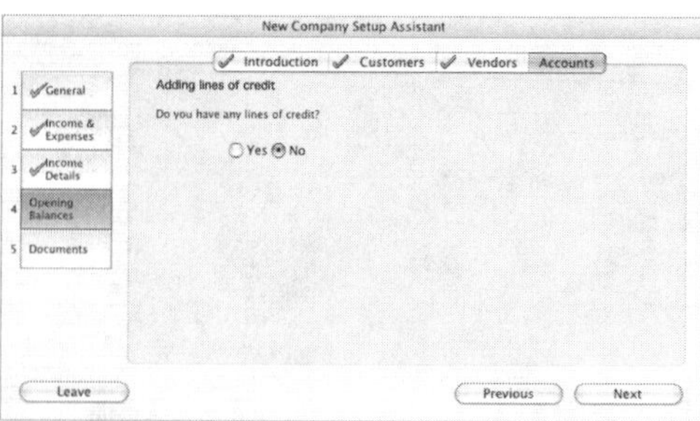

Figure 91 The Adding lines of credit screen.

14. In the Loans and Notes Payable screen **(Figure 92)**, select an option:
    - ▲ To add a loan now, select Yes, click Next, and follow the instructions that appear to add one or more loans.
    - ▲ To continue without adding loans, select No and click Next.

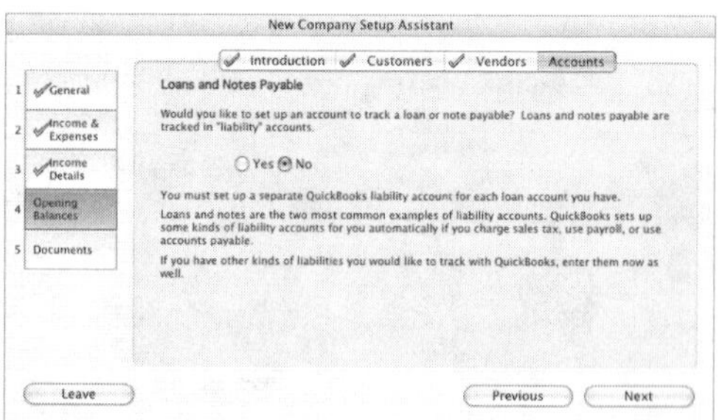

Figure 92 The Loans and Notes Payable screen.

15. In the Bank accounts screen **(Figure 93)**, select an option:
    - ▲ To add a bank account now, select Yes, click Next, and follow the instructions that appear to add one or more bank accounts.
    - ▲ To continue without adding bank accounts, select No and click Next.

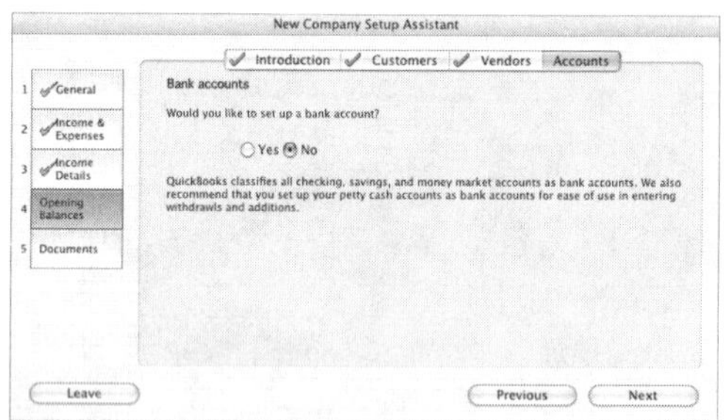

Figure 93 The Bank accounts screen.

16. Read the information in the Introduction to assets screen **(Figure 94)** and click Next.

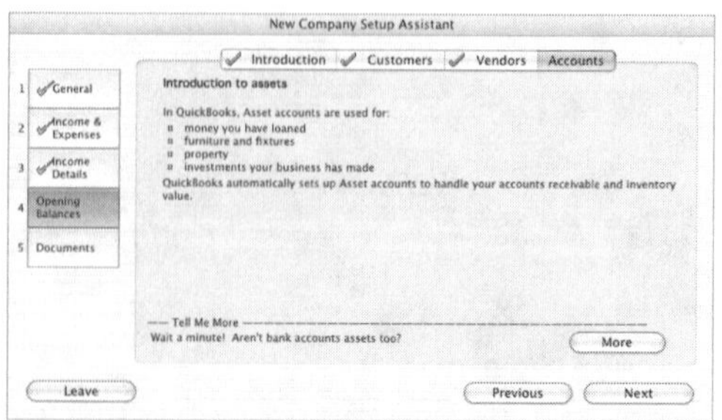

Figure 94 The Introduction to assets screen.

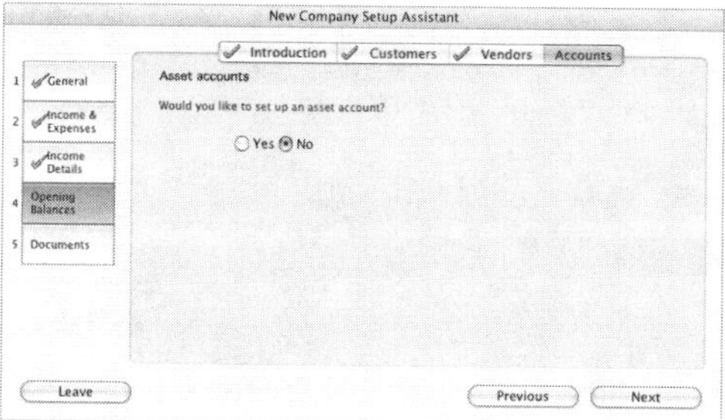

Figure 95 The Asset accounts screen.

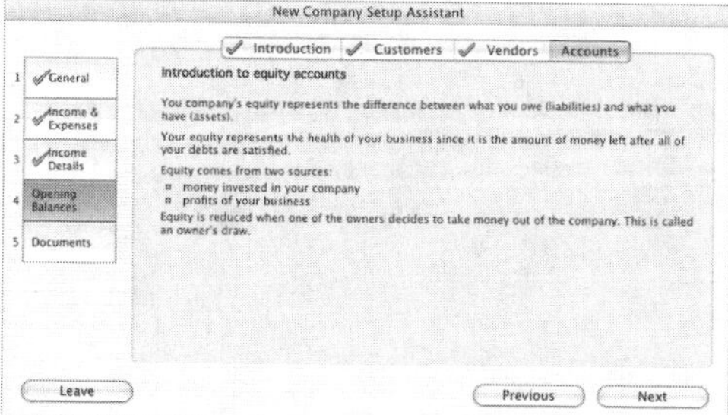

Figure 96 The Introduction to equity accounts screen.

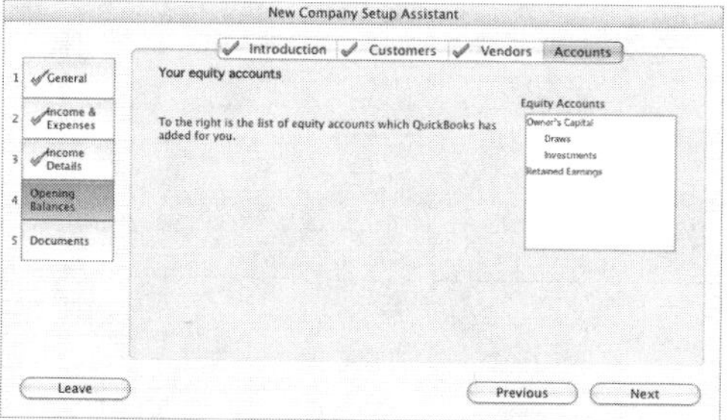

Figure 97 The Your equity accounts screen.

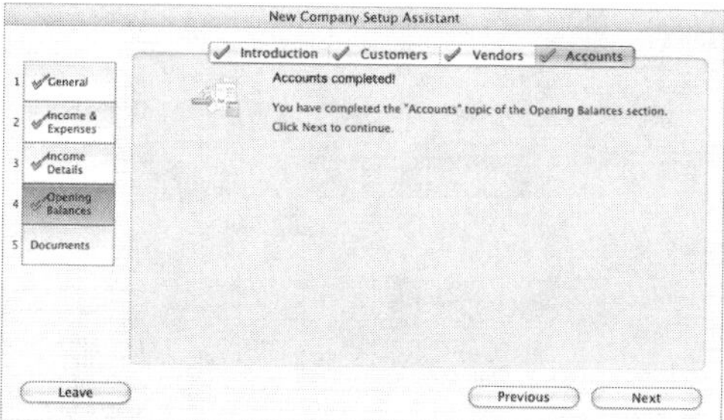

Figure 98 The Accounts completed screen.

17. In the Asset accounts screen (**Figure 95**), select an option:
    - ▲ To add an asset account now, select Yes, click Next, and follow the instructions that appear to add one or more asset accounts.
    - ▲ To continue without adding asset accounts, select No and click Next.
18. Read the information in the Introduction to equity accounts screen (**Figure 96**) and click Next.
19. In the Your equity accounts screen (**Figure 97**), review the list of equity accounts. QuickBooks creates equity accounts based on the type of business you selected earlier in the setup process. Click Next.
20. Read the information in the Accounts completed screen (**Figure 98**) and click Next.
21. Continue following the instructions in the next section.

✔ Tip

- Rather than explain how to create accounts two ways—with and without the Assistant—I explain how to create them without the Assistant in **Chapter 2**. I believe that's the method you'll use most as you work with QuickBooks.

To complete the Documents section of the New Company Setup Assistant

1. If necessary, open the New Company Setup Assistant and click the Documents button on the left side of the window.
2. If necessary, click the Documents button to display the first screen of the Documents section **(Figure 99)**.
3. Click Next.
4. Read the information in the Documents screen **(Figure 100)** and click Next.
5. QuickBooks displays a series of screens that include buttons you can click to access topics in QuickBooks help **(Figures 101 through 106)**. In each screen, you have two options:

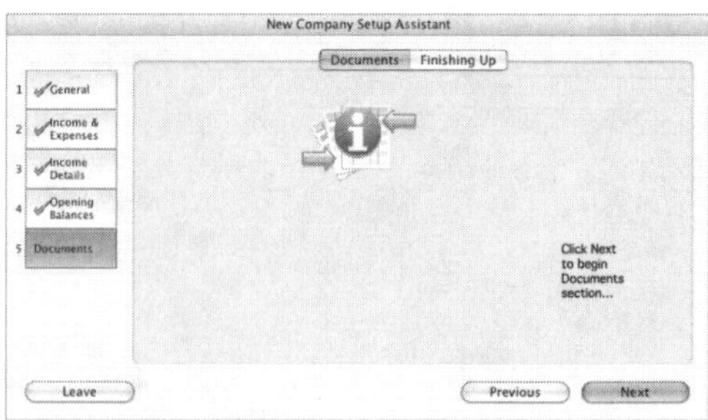

Figure 99 The first screen of the Documents section.

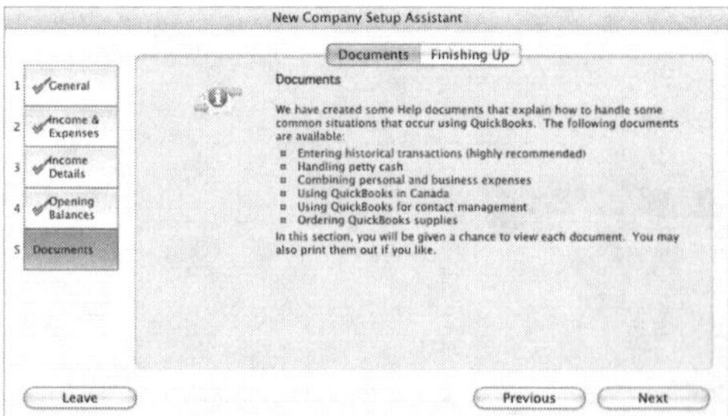

Figure 100 The Documents screen.

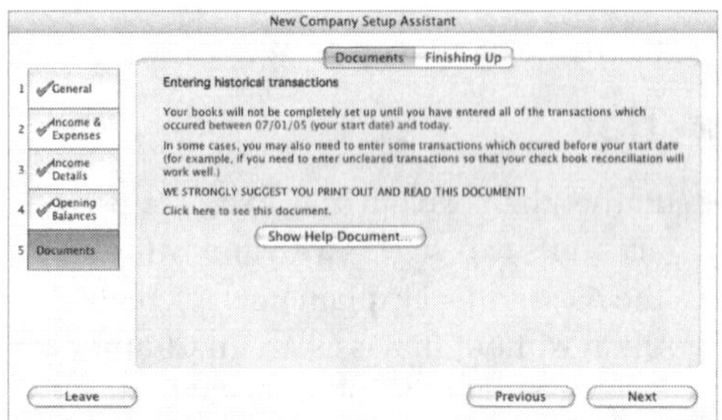

Figure 101 The Entering historical transactions screen.

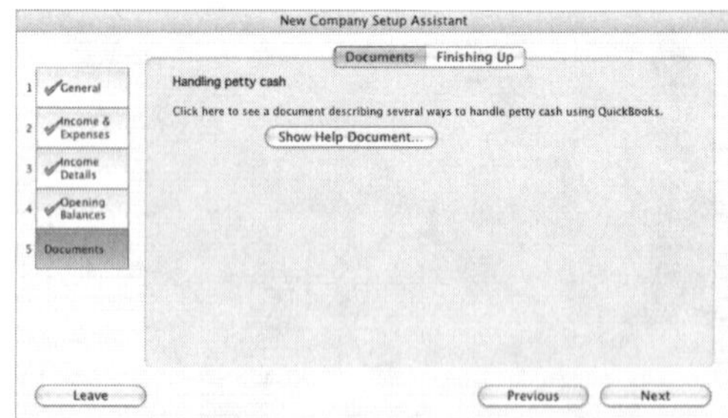

Figure 102 The Handling petty cash screen.

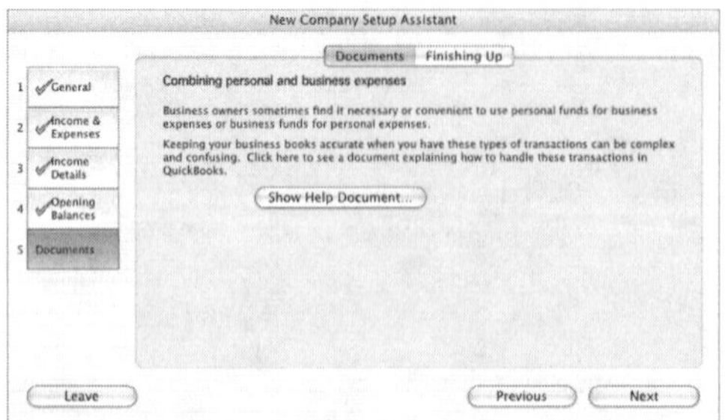

Figure 103 The Combining personal and business expenses screen.

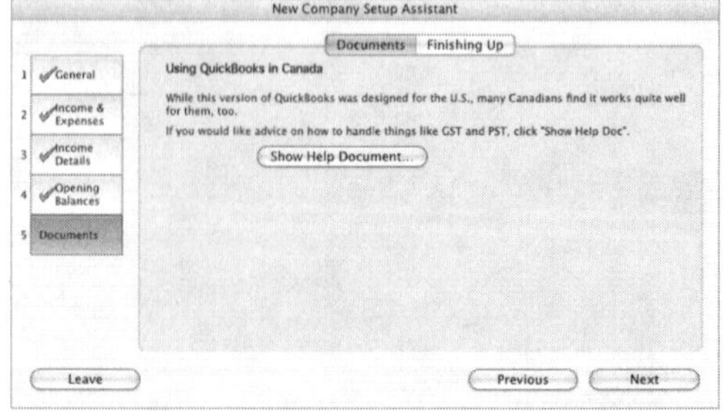

Figure 104 The Using QuickBooks in Canada screen.

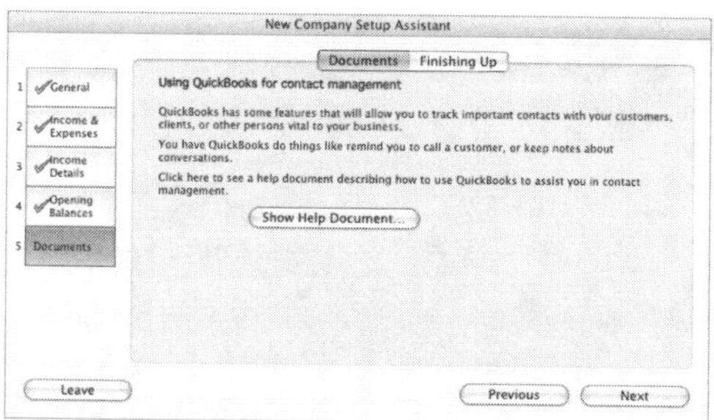

Figure 105 The Using QuickBooks for contact management screen.

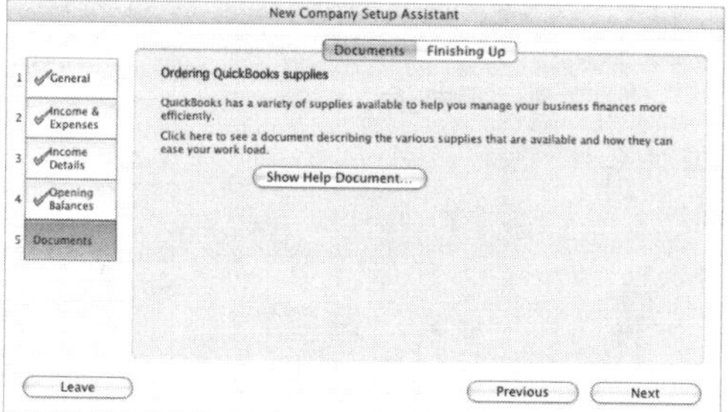

Figure 106 The Ordering QuickBooks supplies screen.

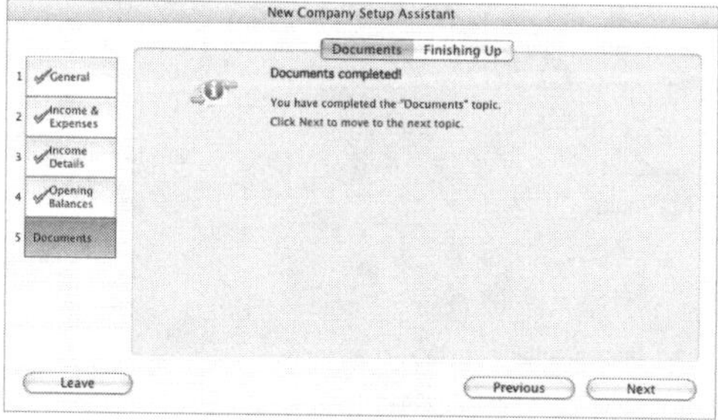

Figure 107 The Documents completed! screen.

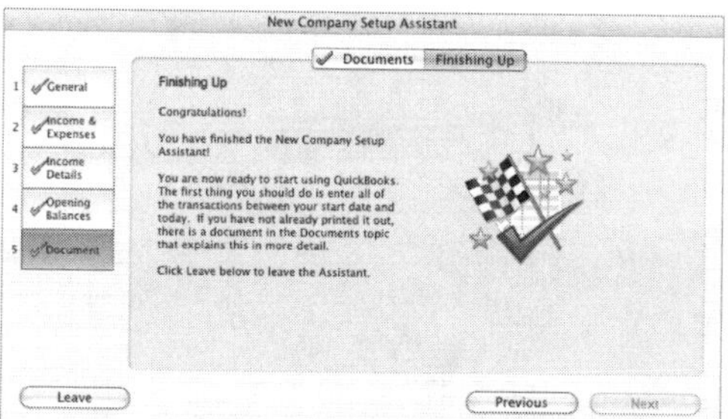

Figure 108 The Finishing Up screen.

- ▲ **Show Help Document** displays a QuickBooks Help window with information about the topic. When you finish working with this window, click its close button to dismiss it and click Next in the New Company Setup Assistant window to continue.
- ▲ **Next** continues without displaying a help document.

6. Read the information in the Documents completed screen (**Figure 107**) and click Next.
7. Read the information in the Finishing Up screen (**Figure 108**) and click Leave.

✔ Tips

- If you are brand new to QuickBooks, I highly recommend that you review each of these documents. They provide valuable insights about using QuickBooks that can help save you time and prevent errors.
- If you are a Canadian user, be sure to read the document about using QuickBooks in Canada (**Figure 104**). This book assumes QuickBooks is being used in the United States and does not provide specific information for Canadian users.

Working with Lists

Lists
Chart of Accounts ⇧⌘A
Items ⇧⌘I
Classes
Customer:Jobs ⇧⌘J
Vendors ⇧⌘V
Employees ⇧⌘E
Other Names
Customer & Vendor Profile ▶
Memorized Transactions ⇧⌘M

Customer Types
Vendor Types
Job Types
Terms
Customer Messages
Payment Methods
Ship Via

Figure 1 The Lists menu and its Customer & Vendor Profile submenu.

Working with Lists

QuickBooks keeps track of the information you enter, including most configuration information, in lists. QuickBooks has many different lists, most of which are accessible through its Lists menu and Customer & Vendor Profile submenu (**Figure 1**):

- **Chart of Accounts** is a list of the accounts created for your business.
- **Items** is a list of the products, services, and other items you sell.
- **Classes** is a list of the classifications you may use to further categorize transactions.
- **Customer: Jobs** is a list of the customers you sell to and the jobs you work on.
- **Vendors** is a list of the vendors you buy inventory, supplies, and services from.
- **Employees** is a list of your employees.
- **Other Names** is a list of other individuals or organizations you deal with.
- **Memorized Transactions** is a list of transactions you use over and over.
- **Customer Types** is a list of types of customers.
- **Vendor Types** is a list of types of vendors.
- **Job Types** is a list of types of jobs.
- **Terms** is a list of payment terms.

Continued on next page...

Continued from previous page.

- **Customer Messages** is a list of messages that can appear on invoices and other documents.
- **Payment Methods** is a list of payment methods you accept.
- **Ship Via** is a list of shipping methods you use.

Other lists within QuickBooks include:

- **Purchase Order List**, accessible under the Vendors menu (**Figure 2**), lists all purchase orders.
- **To Do List**, accessible under the Company menu (**Figure 3**), is a list of reminders you create for things you need to do.
- **Reminders**, which is also accessible under the Company menu (**Figure 3**), is the QuickBooks Reminders list.

This chapter provides details about most of these lists. It explains how to view and print each list and how you can modify lists to add, remove, or change the names of items on them. It also provides a good overview of many of QuickBooks's features.

✔ Tips

- If you didn't customize the QuickBooks setup with the New Company Setup Assistant, use the information in this chapter to create custom list items and enter balances for your company.
- This chapter does not include coverage of the Purchase Orders or Memorized Transactions lists. I discuss these lists in **Chapters** 7 and **6** respectively.

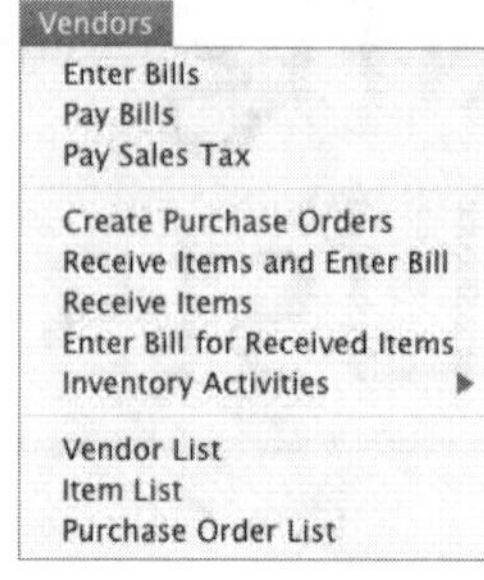

Figure 2 The Purchase Order List is only accessible under the Vendors menu.

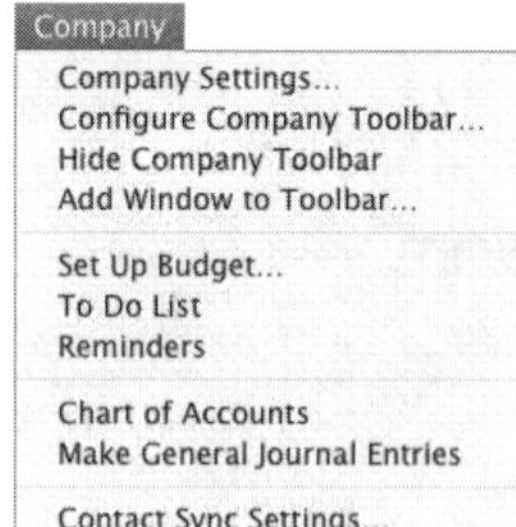

Figure 3 The Company menu includes the To Do List and Reminders commands.

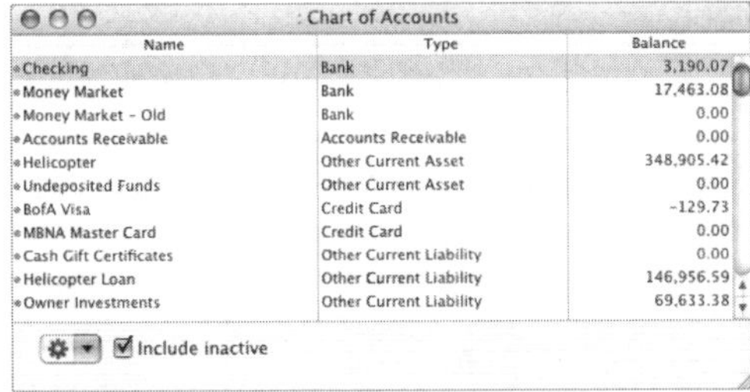

Figure 4 The Chart of Accounts window with the Chart of Accounts QuickBooks created automatically.

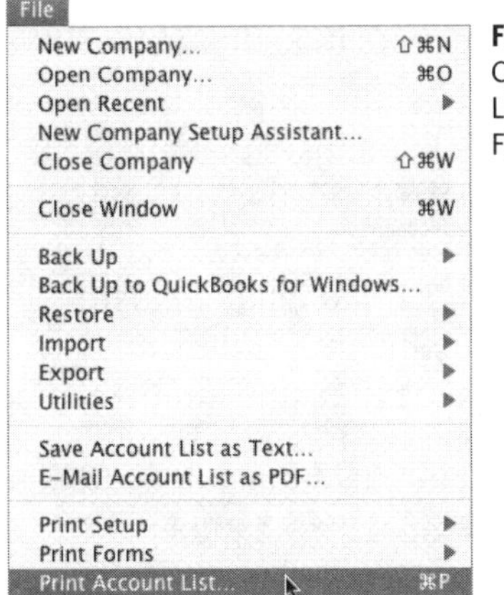

Figure 5 Choose Print List from the File menu.

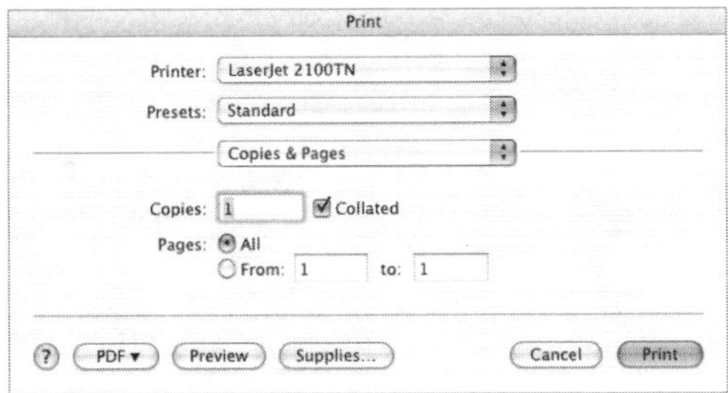

Figure 6 The Print dialog.

To view a list

Choose the name of the list from the menu or submenu on which it appears.

Or

Click the toolbar button for the list you want to view.

The list appears in a window. **Figure 4** shows an example of a list window for the Chart of Accounts list; other list windows are illustrated throughout this chapter.

To print a list

1. Make sure the window for the list you want to print is active (**Figure 4**).
2. Choose File > Print *List Type* List (**Figure 5**), or press [⌘ P]. The exact wording of this command varies depending on the list that is active.
3. In the Print dialog (**Figure 6**), click Print.

   The list prints.

✔ Tips

- You can identify an active window by its title bar. In Mac OS X, the title bar will include colored buttons. In Mac OS 9, the title bar will have horizontal stripes.
- I explain how to print other items from within QuickBooks, such as checks and reports, in **Chapter 10**. That chapter also explains how to set printing options for lists to change margins or print in landscape view.

To close a list

Click the window's close button. The list window closes.

To sort a list

Click the column you want to sort by:

- Click once to sort in ascending order.
- Click twice to sort in descending order.

To return a list to the default sort order

Choose Show Sorted List from the Action pop-up menu (**Figure 7**).

To toggle between hierarchical & flat views

- To view subitems indented beneath their parent items (**Figure 8**), choose Hierarchical View from the Action pop-up menu (**Figure 7**).
- To view all items at the same indentation level (**Figure 9**), choose Flat View from the Action pop-up menu (**Figure 7**).

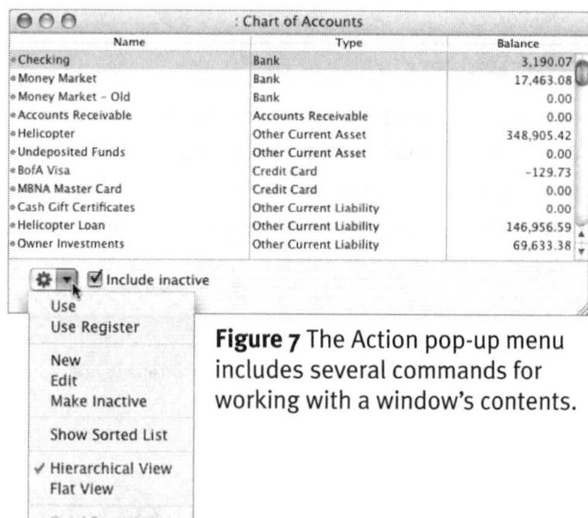

Figure 7 The Action pop-up menu includes several commands for working with a window's contents.

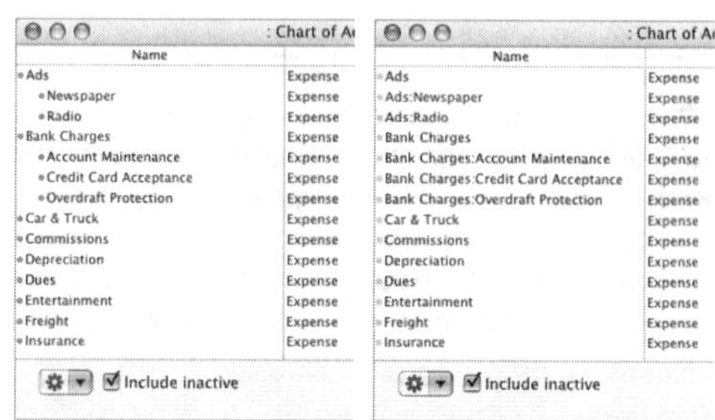

Figures 8 & 9 The same portion of a chart of accounts, in hierarchical view (left) and flat view (right).

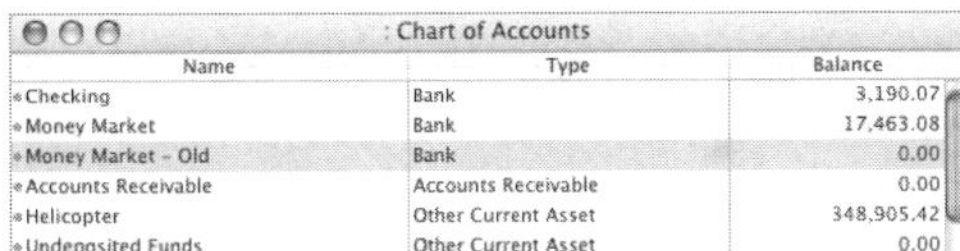

Chart of Accounts

Name	Type	Balance
Checking	Bank	3,190.07
Money Market	Bank	17,463.08
Money Market - Old	Bank	0.00
Accounts Receivable	Accounts Receivable	0.00
Helicopter	Other Current Asset	348,905.42
Undeposited Funds	Other Current Asset	0.00

Figure 10 Select the item you want to hide.

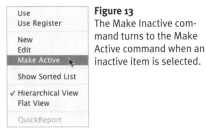

Chart of Accounts

Name	Type	Balance
Checking	Bank	3,190.07
Money Market	Bank	17,463.08
Money Market - Old	Bank	0.00
Accounts Receivable	Accounts Receivable	0.00
Helicopter	Other Current Asset	348,905.42
Undeposited Funds	Other Current Asset	0.00

Figure 11 When you make an item inactive, its name turns gray...

Chart of Accounts

Name	Type	Balance
Checking	Bank	3,190.07
Money Market	Bank	17,463.08
Accounts Receivable	Accounts Receivable	0.00
Helicopter	Other Current Asset	348,905.42
Undeposited Funds	Other Current Asset	0.00

Figure 12 ...or it simply disappears from the list.

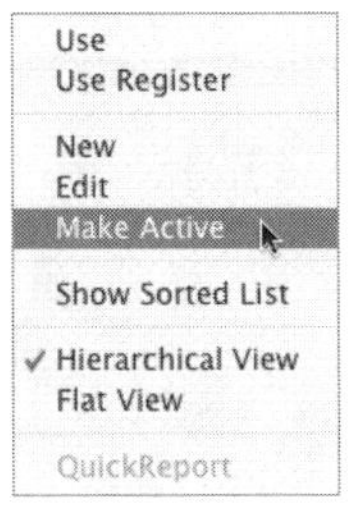

Figure 13
The Make Inactive command turns to the Make Active command when an inactive item is selected.

To make an item inactive

1. Select the item you want to hide (**Figure 10**).
2. Choose Make Inactive from the Action pop-up menu (**Figure 7**). The selected item turns gray (**Figure 11**) if the Include inactive checkbox is turned on or disappears (**Figure 12**) if the inactive check box is turned off.

✓ Tips

- Making an item inactive does not remove any data from your company file. This feature is a good way to remove unused items without actually deleting them.
- You cannot use an inactive item in a transaction.

To make an item active

1. If necessary, turn on the Include inactive check box so you can see all inactive items (**Figure 7**).
2. Select the item you want to make active (**Figure 11**).
3. Choose Make Active from the Action pop-up menu (**Figure 13**). The item's name turns black and you can use it again.

Chart of Accounts

The Chart of Accounts is perhaps the most important list within QuickBooks. It lists all of the accounts your company uses to track its finances.

QuickBooks supports 15 types of accounts, which can be broken down into the two categories discussed in the **Introduction**:

- **Balance Sheet accounts** include asset, liability, and owner's equity accounts:
  - **Bank** is for bank accounts, such as checking, savings, and money market accounts.
  - **Accounts Receivable** is for money owed to your company by others, such as your customers. Accounts Receivable is often abbreviated *A/R*.
  - **Other Current Asset** is for assets likely to be converted into cash or used up within a year. This might include prepaid expenses, petty cash, short-term notes receivable, and security deposits.
  - **Fixed Asset** is for long-term notes receivable and depreciable assets your company owns, such as buildings, furniture, and equipment.
  - **Other Asset** is for other assets that cannot be categorized elsewhere.
  - **Accounts Payable** is for money your company owes to others, such as vendors. Accounts Payable is often abbreviated *A/P*.
  - **Credit Card** is for your company's credit card accounts.
  - **Other Current Liability** is for amounts your company will pay within a year, such as sales tax and short-term loans.

  - ▲ **Long Term Liability** is for amounts your company will pay over a period longer than a year, such as mortgages and long-term notes payable.
  - ▲ **Equity** is for owner's equity, including investments, draws, and retained earnings.

- ◆ **Income Statement accounts** include income and expense accounts:
  - ▲ **Income** is for income from the sale of goods and services.
  - ▲ **Cost of Goods Sold** is for the costs related to items sold.
  - ▲ **Expense** is for the expenses incurred in doing business.
  - ▲ **Other Income** is for other receipts not directly related to doing business, such as a gain on the sale of some used equipment.
  - ▲ **Other Expense** is for other expenses not directly related to doing business, such as a loss on the sale of some used equipment.

The Chart of Accounts list includes accounts and subaccounts. *Subaccounts*, which appear indented beneath their parent accounts, are like subcategories for an account—they make it possible to group related accounts so they are summarized together in reports. **Figure 8**, for example, shows several layers of subaccounts.

When you use the New Company Setup Assistant to create a QuickBooks data file, you are offered an opportunity to add accounts to the default Chart of Accounts QuickBooks creates for you based on your business type. But you can also add and modify accounts at any time while you use QuickBooks. This part of the chapter explains how. If you have not set up accounts for your company, this is a good time to do so.

To add an account

1. In the Chart of Accounts, choose New from the Action pop-up menu (**Figure 7**).

   Or

   With the Chart of Accounts list window active, choose Edit > New Account or press [⌘ N].

   The New Account dialog appears (**Figure 14**).

2. Choose a type of account from the Type pop-up menu (**Figure 15**).
3. Set options for the account as follows:
   - **Name** is the name of the account.
   - **Description** is a brief description for the account. This field is optional.
   - **Bank No./Card No./Note** is for additional information about the account. The label on this box varies depending on the type of account you choose in step 2. For example, if you chose Bank, the box is labeled *Bank No.* (**Figure 14**) for your bank account number and if you chose Expense, the box is labeled *Note* (**Figure 16**).
   - **Subaccount of** tells QuickBooks that the account is a subaccount of another account. If you turn on this check box, choose the parent account from the account drop-down list that appears beside it. **Figure 16** shows an example for setting up a subaccount called Radio under a parent account called Ads.
   - **Tax Line** is a specific line on one of Quicken's tax reports. Choose an option from the Tax Line pop-up menu (**Figure 17**). Normally, this option is only used for income or expense accounts.

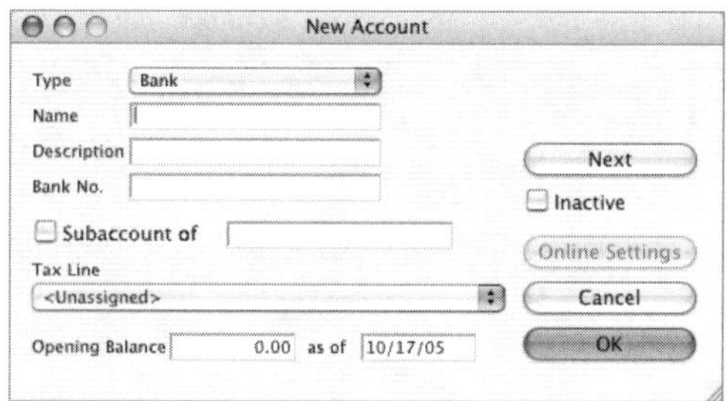

Figure 14 The New Account dialog.

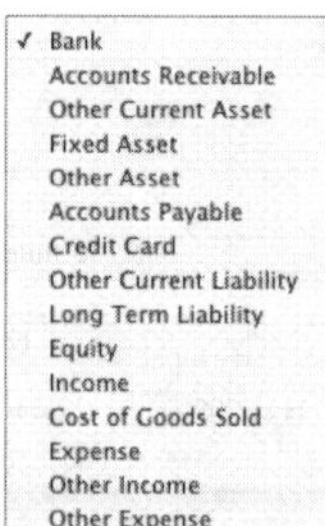

Figure 15 The Type pop-up menu.

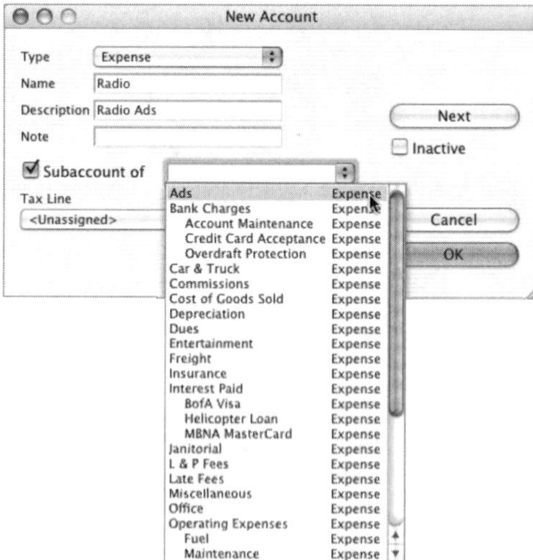

Figure 16 An example of a subaccount being created. Choose the parent account from the drop-down list of accounts.

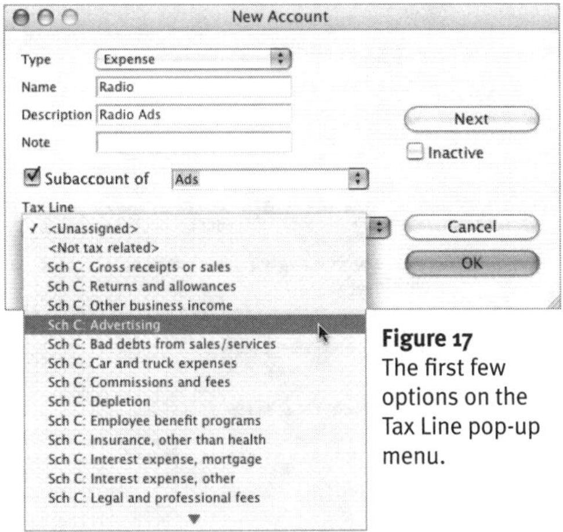

Figure 17 The first few options on the Tax Line pop-up menu.

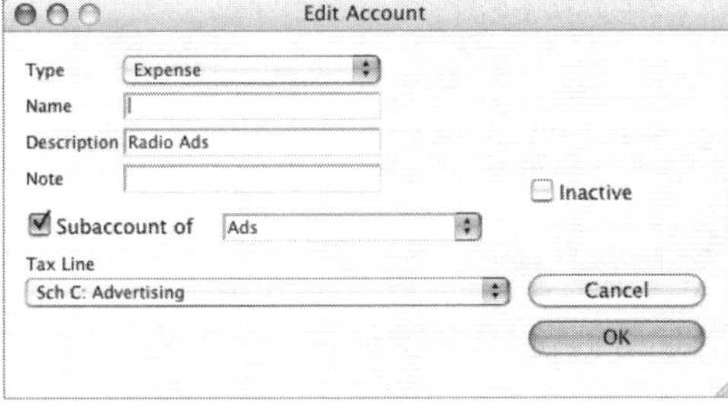

Figure 18 The Edit Account dialog.

- ▲ **Opening Balance** and **as of** enable you to enter the opening balance amount and date for certain Balance Sheet accounts.
- ▲ **Inactive** makes the account inactive.

4. To save the account and create another new one, click Next. The New Account dialog appears again (**Figure 14**). Repeat steps 2 through 4.

   Or

   To save the account without creating another new one, click OK.

   The account is added to the Chart of Accounts list.

✔ Tips

- Only accounts that are the same type you chose in step 2 appear in the Subaccount of pop-up menu. A subaccount cannot be a different type than its parent account.
- I explain how to set up online options for the account types that support them in **Chapter 5**.

To modify an account

1. In the Chart of Accounts list window (**Figure 4**), select the name of the account you want to modify.
2. Choose Edit from the Action pop-up menu, choose Edit > Edit Account, or press ⌘E.

   The Edit Account dialog appears (**Figure 18**).
3. Make changes as desired in the dialog.
4. Click OK.

To delete an account

1. In the Chart of Accounts list window **(Figure 4)**, select the name of the account you want to delete.
2. Choose Edit > Delete Account or press [⌘ D].
3. One of three dialogs appears, depending on the account you selected:
   - ▲ If you selected an account that has subaccounts, a dialog like the one in **Figure 19a** appears. Click OK, then remove all the account's subaccounts and try to delete the account again.
   - ▲ If you selected an account that was created by QuickBooks for a special purpose, a dialog like the one in **Figure 19b** appears. Click OK.
   - ▲ If you selected an account that has a balance or was used in a transaction, a dialog like the one in **Figure 19c** appears. Click OK. The account cannot be deleted unless all transactions have been removed and the balance is zero.
   - ▲ If you selected an account you created that does not have subaccounts or transactions, the account is deleted without a confirmation dialog.

✔ Tip

- If you delete an account that QuickBooks created, it will automatically recreate the account if it needs to. Generally, I don't recommend deleting any account that QuickBooks created.

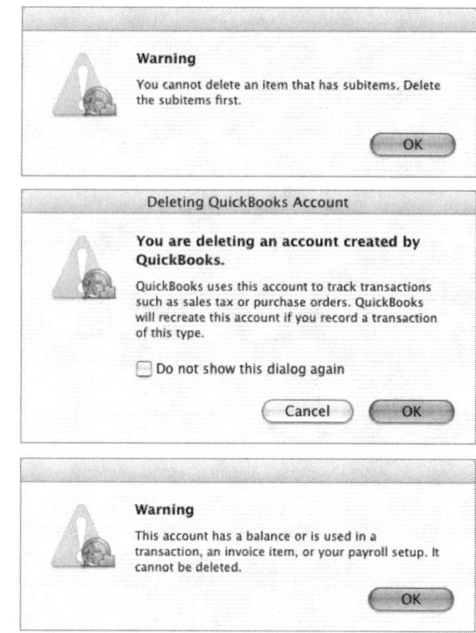

Figures 19a, 19b, & 19c One of these dialogs appears when you attempt to delete an account.

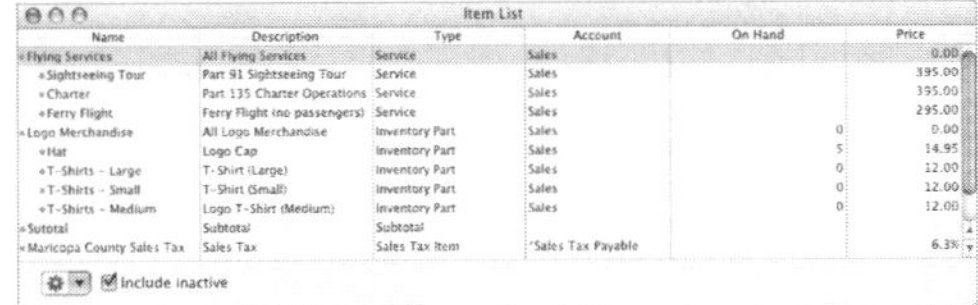

Name	Description	Type	Account	On Hand	Price
Flying Services	All Flying Services	Service	Sales		0.00
Sightseeing Tour	Part 91 Sightseeing Tour	Service	Sales		395.00
Charter	Part 135 Charter Operations	Service	Sales		395.00
Ferry Flight	Ferry Flight (no passengers)	Service	Sales		295.00
Logo Merchandise	All Logo Merchandise	Inventory Part	Sales	0	0.00
Hat	Logo Cap	Inventory Part	Sales	5	14.95
T-Shirts - Large	T-Shirt (Large)	Inventory Part	Sales	0	12.00
T-Shirts - Small	T-Shirt (Small)	Inventory Part	Sales	0	12.00
T-Shirts - Medium	Logo T-Shirt (Medium)	Inventory Part	Sales	0	12.00
Sutotal	Subtotal	Subtotal			
Maricopa County Sales Tax	Sales Tax	Sales Tax Item	Sales Tax Payable		6.3%

Figure 20 An example of an Item List window with several items already created.

Item List

The Item List (**Figure 20**) includes all products and services your company buys or sells, as well as other calculations. By maintaining a complete and accurate list of items, you can quickly and easily create invoices, estimates, and purchase orders.

QuickBooks supports 10 types of items:

- **Service** is for services you charge for or purchase. Examples include consulting services or specialized labor.
- **Inventory Part** is for merchandise or parts you buy, keep track of in inventory, and resell.
- **Non-inventory Part** is for materials or parts you buy but don't track as inventory. Some items, such as component materials, may be resold while others, such as office supplies, may be part of your company's overhead.
- **Other Charge** is for other charges that are not services, labor, materials, or parts. Examples could include delivery charges, service charges, or rent.
- **Subtotal** is for calculating a total prior to applying a discount or charge that covers several items.
- **Group** is for quickly entering several individual items already on the Item List. For example, a specific group item might include two inventory parts, a service, and an other charge item.
- **Discount** is for subtracting an amount from a subtotal. To apply a discount to more than one item, use a subtotal item and then apply the discount to that.

Continued on next page...

Continued from previous page.

- **Payment** is for a payment received at the time you prepare an invoice. It reduces the total due on the invoice.
- **Sales Tax Item** is for applying a single sales tax to a sale.
- **Sales Tax Group** is for applying two or more sales taxes to the same sale.

When you use the New Company Setup Assistant to create a QuickBooks data file, you are offered an opportunity to add items to the default Item List that QuickBooks creates for you based on sales tax questions. But you can also add and modify items at any time while you use QuickBooks. This part of the chapter explains how. If you have not set up items for your company, this is a good time to do so.

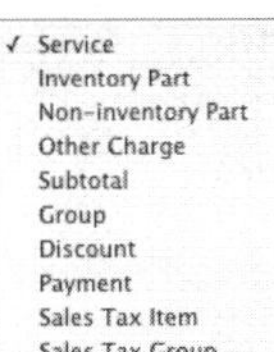

Figure 21 The Type pop-up menu.

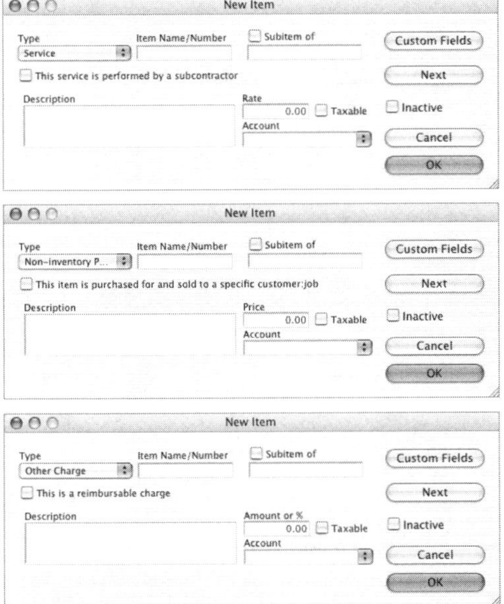

Figures 22a, 22b, & 22c The New Item dialogs for a service item (top), non-inventory part item (middle), and other charge item (bottom).

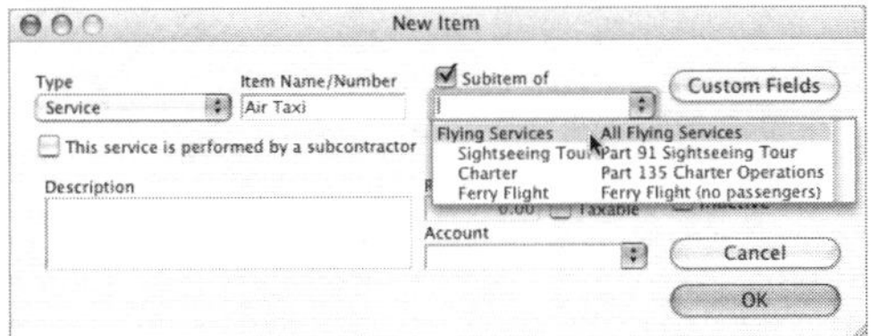

Figure 23 Creating an item that is a subitem of another item.

To add a new service item, non-inventory part item, or other charge item

1. In the Item List window (**Figure 20**), choose New from the Action pop-up menu.

   Or

   With the Item List window open and active, choose Edit > New Item or press ⌘ N.

   The New Item dialog appears.

2. If necessary, choose Service, Non-inventory Part, or Other Charge from the Type pop-up menu (**Figure 21**). The dialog changes to offer options for the appropriate type of item (**Figures 22a, 22b, and 22c**).

3. Set options for the item as follows:

   ▲ **Item Name/Number** is the name or number of the item. This is an internally-used identifier that your customers or suppliers won't see.

   ▲ **Subitem of** check box tells QuickBooks that the item is a subitem of another item. If you turn on this check box, choose an option from the drop-down list beneath it (**Figure 23**).

   ▲ **Description** is the description of the item as it should appear on invoices and estimates.

   ▲ **Rate**, **Price**, or **Amount or %** is the per unit or percent charge for the item.

   ▲ **Taxable** identifies the item as taxable so sales tax can be applied to it.

   ▲ **Account** is the account that income from the sale of this item will be recorded in. Normally, this will be an income account.

Continued on next page...

Continued from previous page.

4. If a service is performed by someone who is not on your payroll, turn on the This service is performed by a subcontractor check box (**Figure 22a**).

   Or

   If a non-inventory part is purchased for a specific customer, turn on the This item is purchased for and sold to a specific customer:job check box (**Figure 22b**).

   Or

   If an other charge is reimbursable, turn on the This is a reimbursable charge check box (**Figure 22c**).

   The dialog expands to include additional fields (**Figures 24a, 24b, and 24c**). Fill in fields as follows:

   ▲ **Description on Purchase Transactions** is the description that would appear on a purchase order to buy this service from the vendor.

   ▲ **Cost** is the cost the vendor charges for the item.

   ▲ **Expense Account** is the account you record the expense in. Normally, this will be an expense account.

   ▲ **Preferred Vendor** is the vendor you most often purchase this item from.

5. To make the item inactive, turn on the Inactive check box.

6. To save the item and create another item, click the Next button.

   Or

   To save the item without creating another item, click OK.

   The item is added to the Item List.

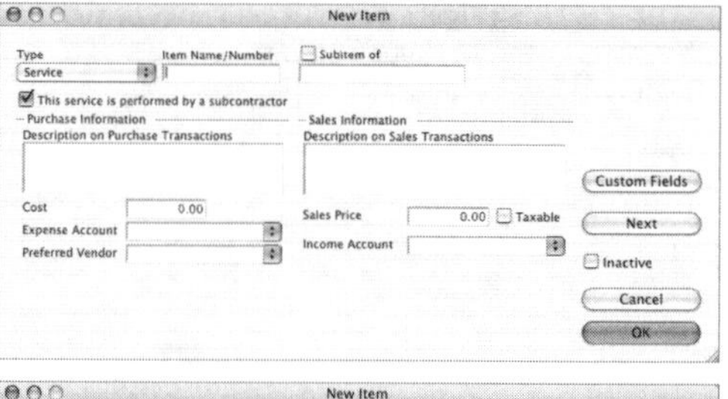

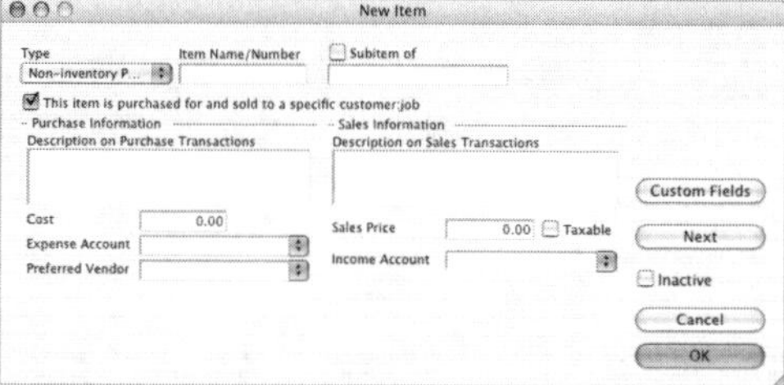

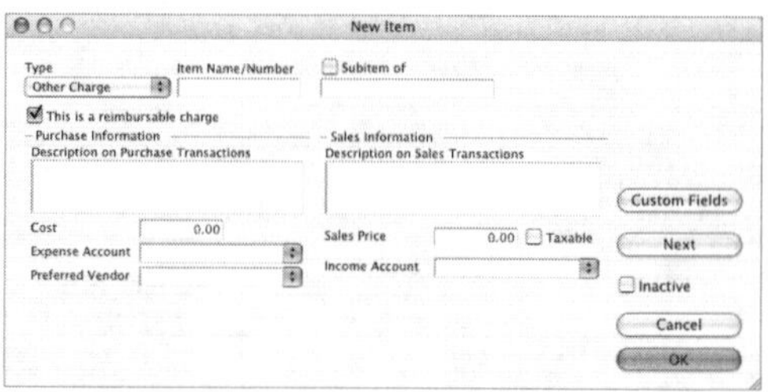

Figures 24a, 24b, & 24c When you indicate that the service, part, or other charge is purchased for resale, the New Item dialog expands so you can enter more information.

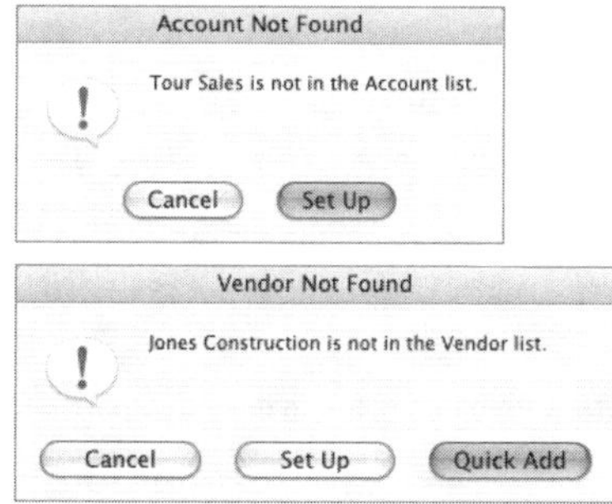

Figures 25a & 25b These dialogs appear when you attempt to enter a non-existent account (top) or vendor (bottom).

✔ Tips

- Text in the Description box or Description on Sales Transactions box may be seen by customers, so it's a good idea to be clear and to check spelling and punctuation before moving on to the next field.
- If the item's cost, price, or rate varies, leave it set to 0.00. You can then enter the correct value when you use the item.
- If an account or vendor does not exist when you need to enter it, enter its name in the box, then click the Set Up button in the dialog that appears (**Figure 25a or 25b**) when you advance to the next field. Then follow the instructions in the appropriate section of this chapter to create the account or vendor.
- I explain how to add custom fields for an item later in this chapter.

To add a new inventory part item

1. In the Item List window **(Figure 20)**, choose New from the Action pop-up menu.

   Or

   With the Item List window open and active, choose Edit > New Item or press ⌘N.

   The New Item dialog appears.

2. Choose Inventory Part from the Type pop-up menu **(Figure 21)**. The dialog changes to offer options for inventory part items **(Figure 26)**.

3. Set options for the inventory part item as follows:

   - **Item Name/Number** is the name or number of the item. This is an internally-used identifier that your customers or suppliers won't see.
   - **Subitem of** check box tells QuickBooks that the item is a subitem of another item. If you turn on this check box, choose an option from the drop-down list beneath it **(Figure 23)**.
   - **Description on Purchase Transactions** is the description that would appear on a purchase order to buy this item from a vendor.
   - **Cost** is the price the vendor charges for the item.
   - **COGS Account** is the account the cost of the item is charged to when purchased.
   - **Preferred Vendor** is the vendor you most often purchase this item from.
   - **Description on Sales Transactions** is the description of the item as it should appear on invoices and estimates.

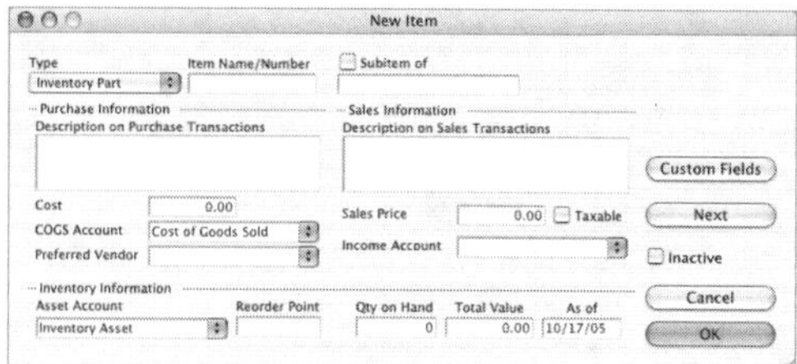

Figure 26 The New Item dialog for an inventory part item.

- **Sales Price** is the per unit price you charge for the item.
- **Taxable** identifies the item as taxable so sales tax can be applied to it.
- **Income Account** is the account that income from the sale of this item will be recorded in.
- **Asset Account** is the account that the value of the inventory item is recorded in. This should be an asset account.
- **Reorder Point** is the number of units remaining on hand that should trigger a reorder reminder.
- **Qty on Hand** is the number of units currently in inventory.
- **Total Value** is the value of the current inventory. QuickBooks calculates this amount based on the item cost and quantity on hand, but you can override it with a different value if necessary.
- **As of** is the date of the inventory information.

4. To make the item inactive, turn on the Inactive check box.
5. To save the inventory part item and create another item, click the Next button.

   Or

   To save the inventory part item without creating another item, click OK.

   The item is added to the Item List.

✔ Tips

- Text in the Description on Sales Transactions box (**Figure 26**) will be seen by customers, so it's a good idea to be clear and to check spelling and punctuation before moving on to the next field.
- If the item's cost or sales price varies, leave it set to 0.00. You can then enter the correct cost or sales price when you use the item.
- If an account or vendor does not exist when you need to enter it, enter its name in the box, then click the Set Up button in the dialog that appears (**Figure 25a or 25b**) when you advance to the next field. Then follow the instructions in the appropriate section of this chapter to create the account or vendor.
- I explain how to add custom fields for an item later in this chapter.

To add a subtotal item

1. In the Item List window (**Figure 20**), choose New from the Action pop-up menu.

   Or

   With the Item List window open and active, choose Edit > New Item or press ⌘N.

   The New Item dialog appears.

2. Choose Subtotal from the Type pop-up menu (**Figure 21**). The dialog changes to offer options for a subtotal item (**Figure 27**).

3. Set options for the item as follows:
   - ▲ **Item Name/Number** is the name or number of the item. This is an internally-used identifier that your customers or suppliers won't see.
   - ▲ **Description** is the description of the item as it should appear on invoices and estimates.

4. To make the item inactive, turn on the Inactive check box.

5. To save the subtotal item and create another item, click the Next button.

   Or

   To save the subtotal item without creating another item, click OK.

   The item is added to the Item List.

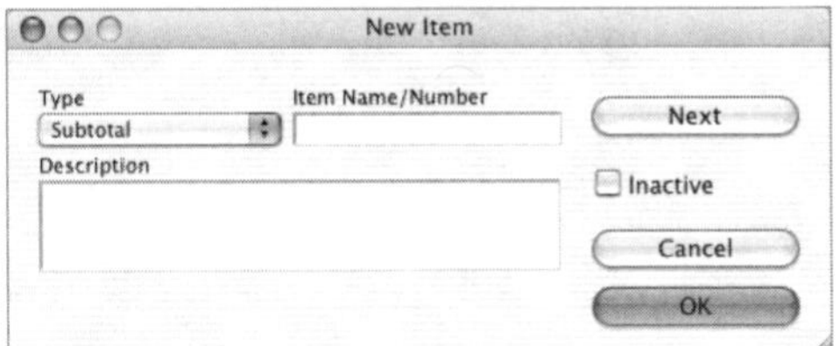

Figure 27 The New Item dialog for a subtotal item.

✔ Tip

- Text in the Description box (**Figure 27**) will be seen by customers, so it's a good idea to be clear and to check spelling and punctuation before moving on to the next field.

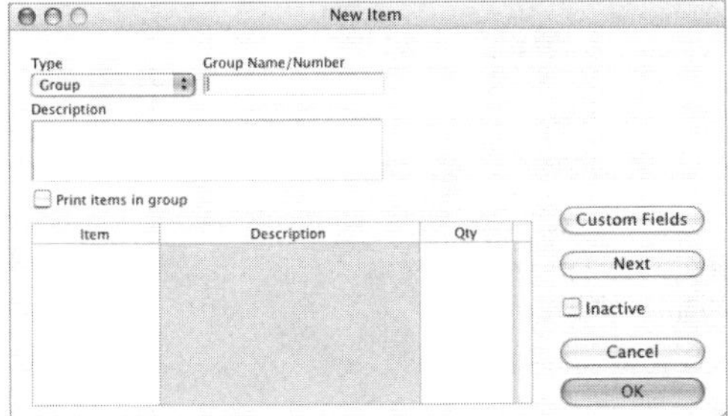

Figure 28 The New Item dialog for a group item.

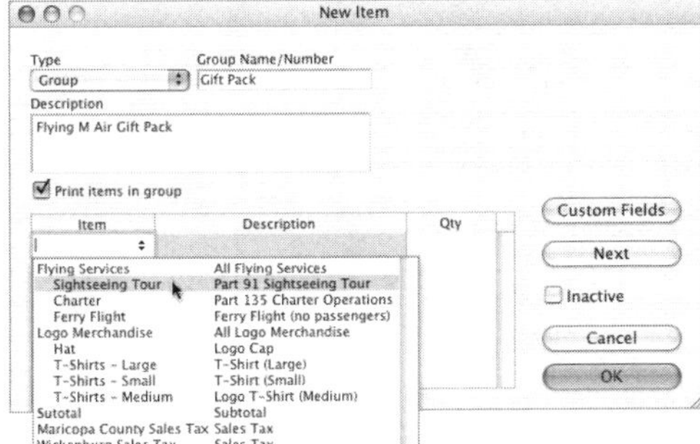

Figure 29 Use a drop-down list to select an item to include in the group.

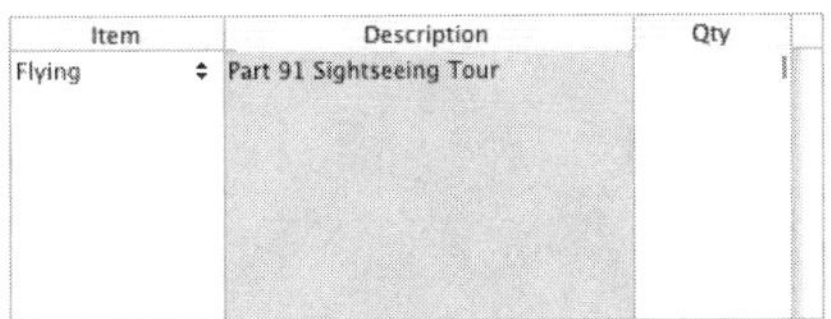

Figure 30 The item's description appears beside it in the list.

To add a group item

1. Make sure you have already added all items that will be part of the group to the Item List.
2. In the Item List window (**Figure 20**), choose New from the Action pop-up menu.

   Or

   With the Item List window open and active, choose Edit > New Item or press ⌘N.

   The New Item dialog appears.
3. Choose Group from the Type pop-up menu (**Figure 21**). The dialog changes to offer options for a group item (**Figure 28**).
4. Set options for the item as follows:
   - ▲ **Group Name/Number** is the name or number of the item. This is an internally-used identifier that your customers or suppliers won't see.
   - ▲ **Description** is the description of the item as it should appear on invoices and estimates.
   - ▲ **Print items in group** tells QuickBooks to print the description of each item in the group when the group is used. Leaving this check box turned off prints only the name of the group.
5. To add an item to the group, click in the first row under Item in the scrolling list to display a drop-down list of items (**Figure 29**) and select the item you want to add. Its description appears in the list beside it (**Figure 30**). Then enter a quantity in the Qty column beside the item.

Continued on next page...

Continued from previous page.

6. Repeat step 5 to add additional items to the group. **Figure 31** shows an example of what the list of items in the group might look like when you're finished.
7. To make the item inactive, turn on the Inactive check box.
8. To save the group item and create another item, click the Next button.

   Or

   To save the group item without creating another item, click OK.

   The item is added to the Item List.

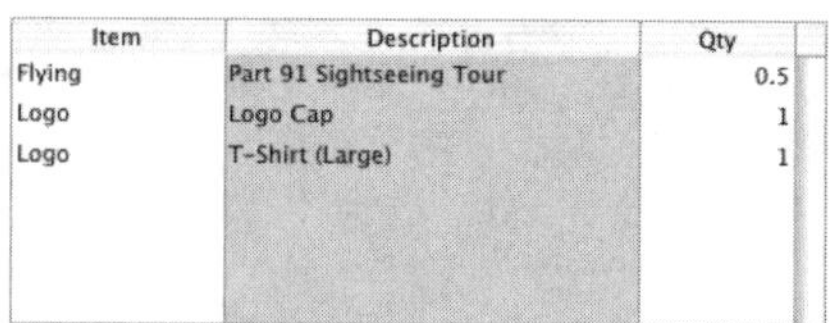

Item	Description	Qty
Flying	Part 91 Sightseeing Tour	0.5
Logo	Logo Cap	1
Logo	T-Shirt (Large)	1

Figure 31 Here's what a group's contents list might look like.

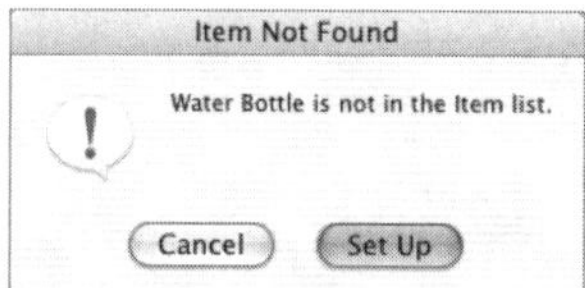

Figure 32 This dialog appears if you attempt to enter the name of an item that doesn't exist.

✔ Tips

- Text in the Description box (**Figure 22**) will be seen by customers, so it's a good idea to be clear and to check spelling and punctuation before moving on to the next field.
- A group can contain almost any combination of item types.
- QuickBooks automatically calculates the price or rate of a group based on the prices or rates of individual items in the group.
- If an item does not exist when you need to enter it, enter its name in the box, then click the Set Up button in the dialog that appears (**Figure 32**) when you advance to the next field. Then follow the instructions in the appropriate section of this chapter to create the item.
- I explain how to add custom fields for an item later in this chapter.

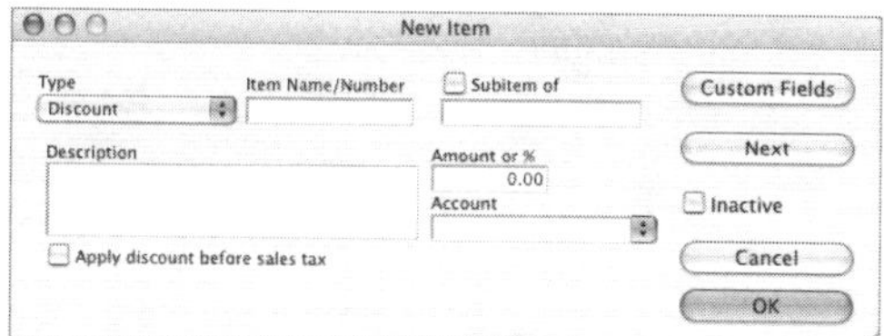

Figure 33 The New Item dialog for a discount item.

To add a discount item

1. In the Item List window (**Figure 20**), choose New from the Action pop-up menu.

   Or

   With the Item List window open and active, choose Edit > New Item or press ⌘N.

   The New Item dialog appears.

2. Choose Discount from the Type pop-up menu (**Figure 21**). The dialog changes to offer options for a discount item (**Figure 33**).

3. Set options for the item as follows:
   - ▲ **Item Name/Number** is the name or number of the item. This is an internally-used identifier that your customers or suppliers won't see.
   - ▲ **Subitem of** check box tells QuickBooks that the item is a subitem of another item. If you turn on this check box, choose an option from the drop-down list beneath it (**Figure 23**).
   - ▲ **Description** is the description of the item as it should appear on invoices and estimates.
   - ▲ **Amount or %** is the per unit or percent discount for the item.
   - ▲ **Account** is the account that the discount will be recorded in.
   - ▲ **Apply discount before sales tax** tells QuickBooks to apply the discount to the item, group, or subtotal before it calculates sales tax.

4. To make the item inactive, turn on the Inactive check box.

Continued on next page...

Continued from previous page.

5. To save the discount item and create another item, click the Next button.

   Or

   To save the discount item without creating another item, click OK.

   The item is added to the Item List.

✔ Tips

- Text in the Description box may be seen by customers, so it's a good idea to be clear and to check spelling and punctuation before moving on to the next field.
- If the item's amount or percent varies, leave it set to 0.00. You can then enter the correct value when you use the item.
- If an account does not exist when you need to enter it, enter its name in the Account box and click the Set Up button in the dialog that appears (**Figure 25a**) when you advance to the next field. Then follow the instructions in the appropriate section of this chapter to create the account.
- I explain how to add custom fields for an item later in this chapter.

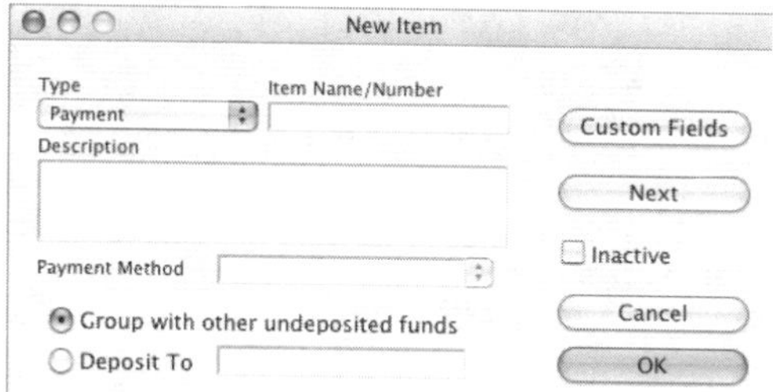

Figure 34 The New Item dialog for a payment item.

To add a payment item

1. In the Item List window (**Figure 20**), choose New from the Action pop-up menu.

   Or

   With the Item List window open and active, choose Edit > New Item or press [⌘ N].

   The New Item dialog appears.

2. Choose Payment from the Type pop-up menu (**Figure 21**). The dialog changes to offer options for a payment item (**Figure 34**).

3. Set options for the item as follows:

   ▲ **Item Name/Number** is the name or number of the item. This is an internally-used identifier that your customers or suppliers won't see.

   ▲ **Description** is the description of the item as it should appear on invoices and estimates.

   ▲ **Payment Method** is the method by which the payment was received.

4. Select one of the two radio buttons to determine what was done with the payment that was received:

   ▲ **Group with other undeposited funds** records the payment with other undeposited funds. You can later create a deposit, as discussed in **Chapter 3**.

   ▲ **Deposit To** is the account that the payment was deposited to.

5. To make the item inactive, turn on the Inactive check box.

Continued on next page...

Continued from previous page.

6. To save the payment item and create another item, click the Next button.

   Or

   To save the payment item without creating another item, click OK.

   The item is added to the Item List.

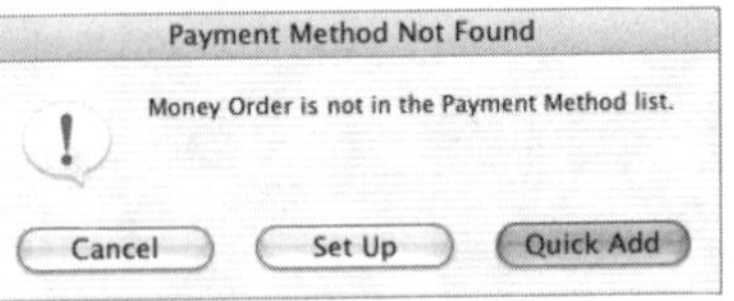

Figure 35 This dialog appears if you try to enter a payment method that doesn't exist.

✔ Tips

- Text in the Description box may be seen by customers, so it's a good idea to be clear and to check spelling and punctuation before moving on to the next field.
- If an account or payment method does not exist when you need to enter it, enter its name in the box and click the Set Up button in the dialog that appears (**Figure 25a or 35**) when you advance to the next field. Then follow the instructions in the appropriate section of this chapter to create the account or payment method.
- I explain how to add custom fields for an item later in this chapter.

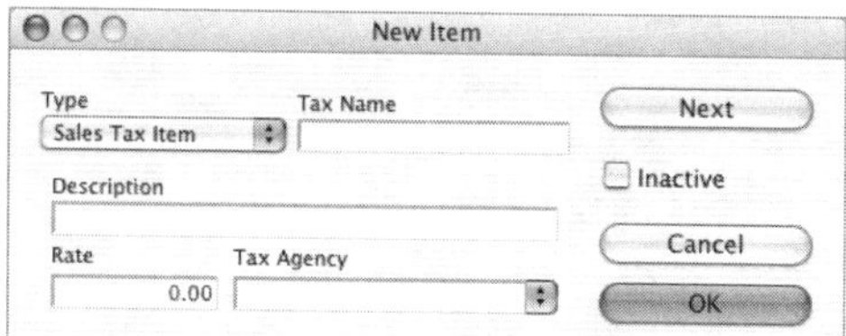

Figure 36 The New Item dialog for a sales tax item.

✔ Tip

- If a sales tax agency name does not exist in the Vendor List when you need to enter it, enter its name in the Tax Agency box and click the Set Up button in the dialog that appears (**Figure 25b**) when you advance to the next field. Then follow the instructions in the appropriate section of this chapter to create the vendor.

To add a sales tax item

1. In the Item List window (**Figure 20**), choose New from the Action pop-up menu.

   Or

   With the Item List window open and active, choose Edit > New Item or press ⌘N.

   The New Item dialog appears.

2. Choose Sales Tax Item from the Type pop-up menu (**Figure 21**). The dialog changes to offer options for a sales tax item (**Figure 36**).

3. Set options for the item as follows:
   - **Tax Name** is the name of the tax. This is an internally-used identifier that your customers or suppliers won't see.
   - **Description** is the description of the item as it should appear on invoices and estimates.
   - **Rate** is the percentage rate of the tax.
   - **Tax Agency** is the name of the agency you pay the tax to. This could be a vendor or other name.

4. To make the item inactive, turn on the Inactive check box.

5. To save the sales tax item and create another item, click the Next button.

   Or

   To save the sales tax item without creating another item, click OK.

   The item is added to the Item List.

To add a sales tax group item

1. Make sure you have already added all items that will be part of the group to the Item List.
2. In the Item List window (**Figure 20**), choose New from the Action pop-up menu.

   Or

   With the Item List window open and active, choose Edit > New Item or press ⌘ N.

   The New Item dialog appears.
3. Choose Sales Tax Group from the Type pop-up menu (**Figure 21**). The dialog changes to offer options for a sales tax group item (**Figure 37**).
4. Set options for the item as follows:
   - ▲ **Group Name/Number** is the name or number of the item. This is an internally-used identifier that your customers or suppliers won't see.
   - ▲ **Description** is the description of the item as it should appear on invoices and estimates.
5. To add an item to the group, click in the first row under Tax Item in the scrolling list to display a drop-down list of sales tax items (**Figure 38**) and select the item you want to add. Its description appears in the list beside it (**Figure 39**).
6. Repeat step 5 to add additional items to the group. **Figure 40** shows an example of what the dialog might look like when you're finished.
7. To make the item inactive, turn on the Inactive check box.

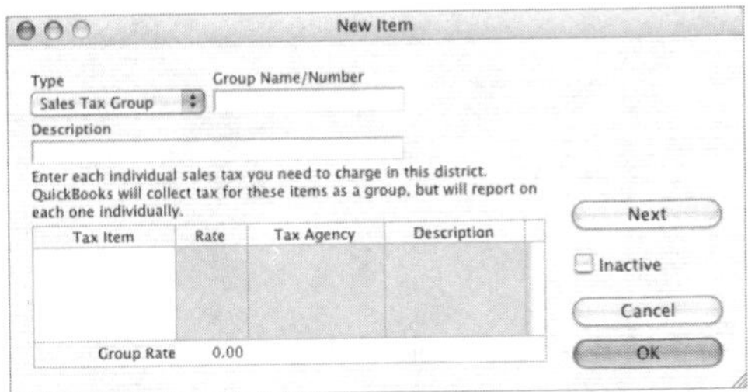

Figure 37 The New Item dialog for a sales tax group item.

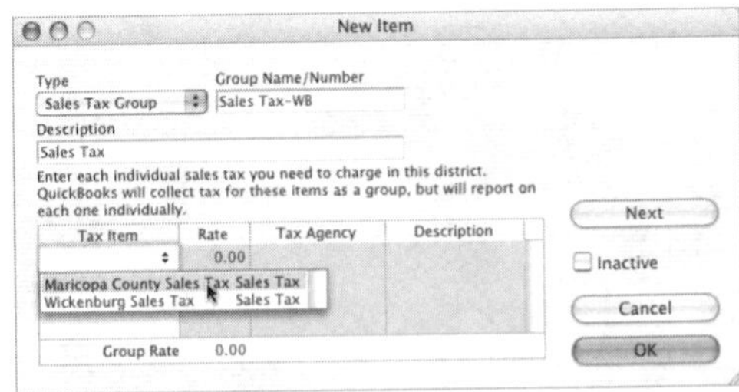

Figure 38 Select a sales tax item from the drop-down list.

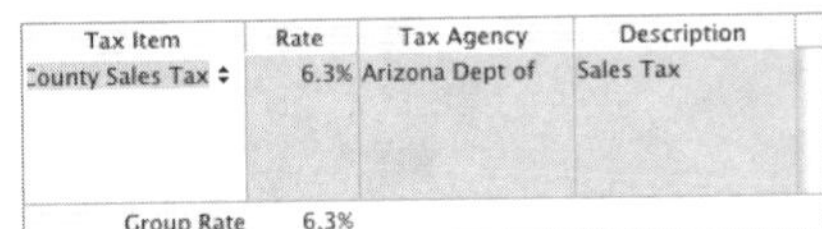

Tax Item
Rate
Tax Agency
Description
County Sales Tax
6.3%
Arizona Dept of
Sales Tax
Group Rate
6.3%

Figure 39 The item and its information appear in the tax items list.

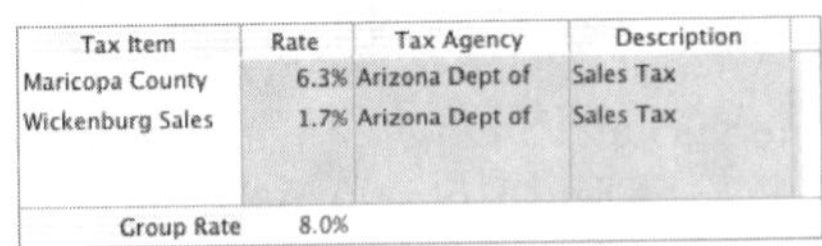

Figure 40 This example shows sales tax for two overlapping jurisdictions (county and town) added together as a group.

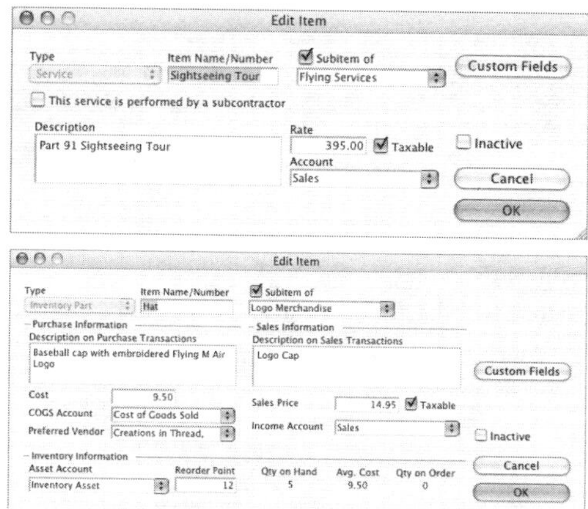

Figures 41a & 41b The Edit Item dialog for a service item (top) and an inventory part item (bottom).

✔ Tip

- Changes you make to an item's setting are effective on a go-forward basis only. For example, if you change an item's price, the new price will only appear on new invoices and estimates—not existing ones.

8. To save the sales tax group item and create another item, click the Next button.

   Or

   To save the sales tax group item without creating another item, click OK.

   The item is added to the Item List.

✔ Tips

- Text in the Description box (**Figure 38**) will be seen by customers, so it's a good idea to be clear and to check spelling and punctuation before moving on to the next field.
- QuickBooks automatically calculates the rate of a sales tax group based on the rates of individual items in the group.
- If a sales tax item does not exist when you need to enter it, enter its name in the box, then click the Set Up button in the dialog that appears (**Figure 32**) when you advance to the next field. Then follow the instructions in the appropriate section of this chapter to create the item.

To modify an item

1. In the Item List window (**Figure 20**), select the name of the item you want to modify.
2. Choose Edit from the Action pop-up menu.

   Or

   Choose Edit > Edit Item or press ⌘ E.

   The Edit Item dialog appears. It looks a lot like the New Item dialog you used to create the item, but certain fields cannot be modified. **Figures 41a and 41b** show examples.
3. Make changes as desired in the dialog.
4. Click OK.

To add custom fields for an item

1. In the New Item or Edit Item dialog, click the Custom Fields button.
2. If no custom fields have been defined for items, an Information dialog like the one in **Figure 42** appears. Click OK.
3. The Custom Fields dialog appears (**Figure 43** or **46**). If this dialog includes a field you want to use (**Figure 46**), skip ahead to step 8.
4. Click the Define Fields button.
5. In the Define Custom Fields for Items dialog (**Figure 44**), enter labels for the fields you want to add in the Label boxes. Then turn on the check box beside each label you want to use for the item.
6. Click OK.
7. Another information dialog appears (**Figure 45**). Click OK.

   The fields you created and enabled appear in the Custom Fields dialog (**Figure 46**).
8. Enter the value you want for the field in the box beside the field name.
9. Click OK. The information you entered is added to the item, but does not appear in the New Item or Edit Item dialog.

✔ Tips

- Not all item types support custom fields. The Custom Fields button only appears in the New Item or Edit item dialog for items that support custom fields.
- In steps 2 and 7, you can turn on the Do not show this dialog again check box to prevent the Information dialogs in **Figure 42** and **45** from appearing again.

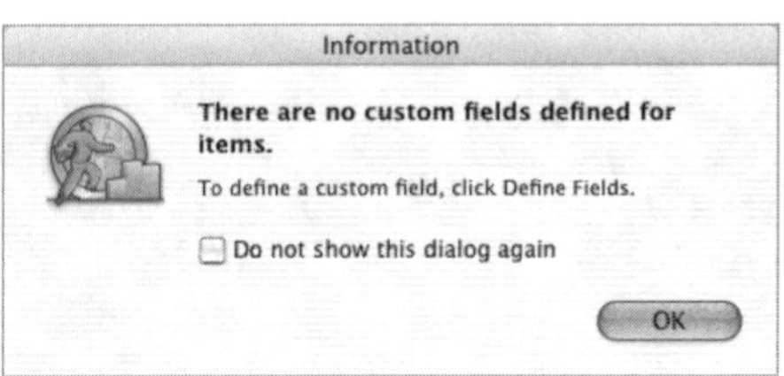

Figure 42 This Information dialog appears if no custom fields have been defined for items.

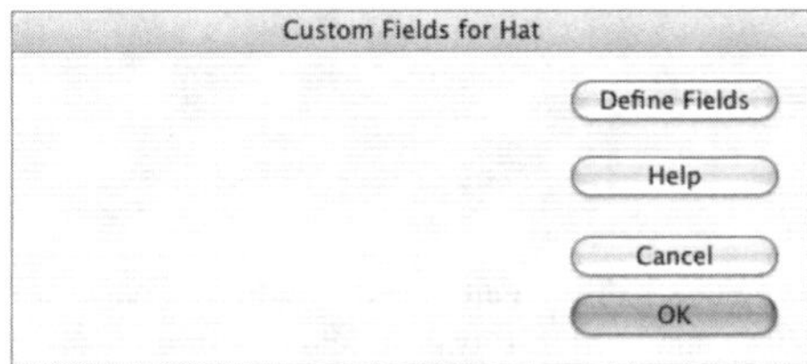

Figure 43 The Custom Fields dialog before any custom fields have been defined for an item.

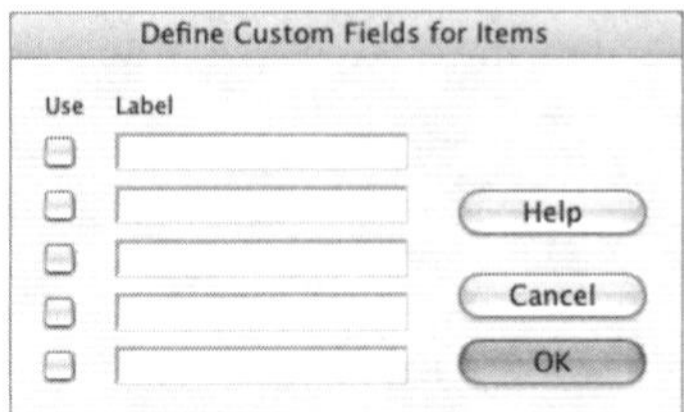

Figure 44 The Define Custom Fields for Items dialog.

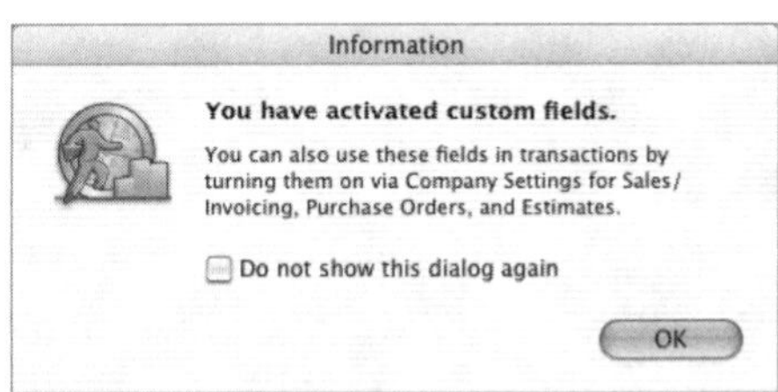

Figure 45 This dialog appears when you activate custom fields for an item.

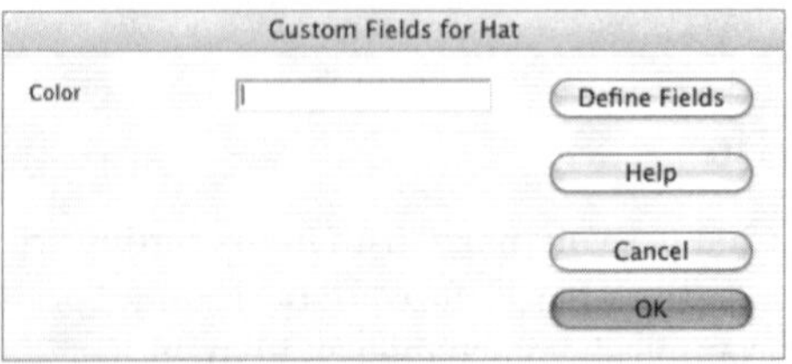

Figure 46 The Custom Fields dialog with one custom field activated for use.

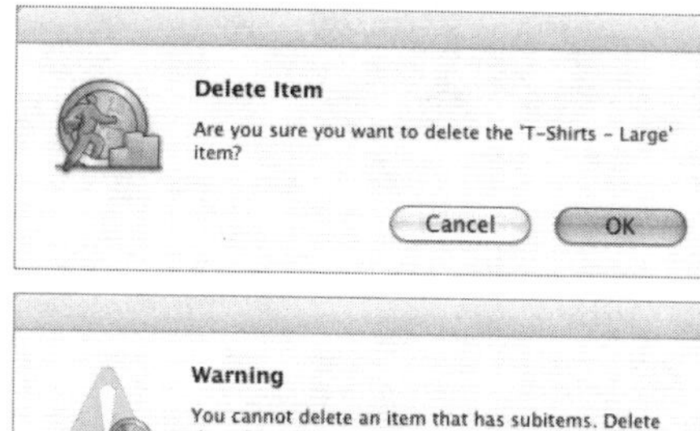

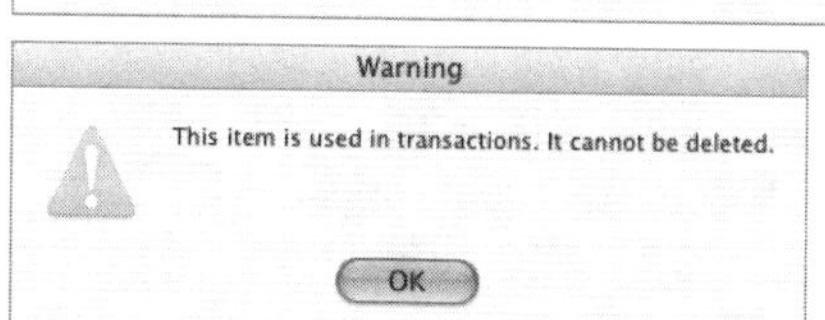

Figures 47a, 47b, & 47c One of these dialogs will appear when you try to delete an item.

To delete an item

1. In the Item List window (**Figure 20**), select the name of the item you want to delete.
2. Choose Edit > Delete Item or press ⌘D.
3. One of three dialogs appears, depending on the item you selected:
   - ▲ If you selected an item you created that does not have subitems, a dialog like the one in **Figure 47a** appears. Click OK.
   - ▲ If you selected an item that has subitems, a dialog like the one in **Figure 47b** appears. Click OK, then remove all of the item's subitems and try to delete the item again.
   - ▲ If you selected an item that has been used in a transaction, a dialog like the one in **Figure 47c** appears, explaining that you cannot delete the item. Click OK.

Class List

Classes, which appear in the Class List window (**Figure 48**), offer a way to categorize transactions for reporting purposes.

Suppose, for example, that your company has three different departments, each with its own revenue and expenses. You can set up three classes—one for each department—and, when you enter a transaction for a department, you can include its class information in the transaction. This makes it easy to create reports for any of the departments or for the entire company, with separate columns of information for each department.

This part of the chapter explains how to set up and work with the Class List.

✔ Tips

- The use of classes is completely optional within QuickBooks.
- Like accounts and items, classes can be subdivided into *subclasses* to group related classes together.

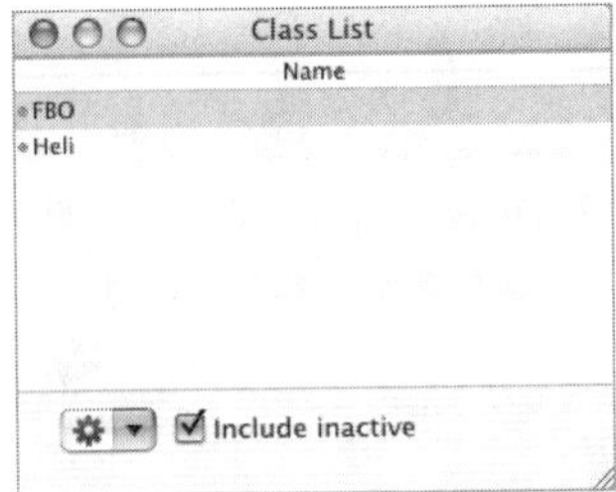

Figure 48 The Class List window with two classes defined.

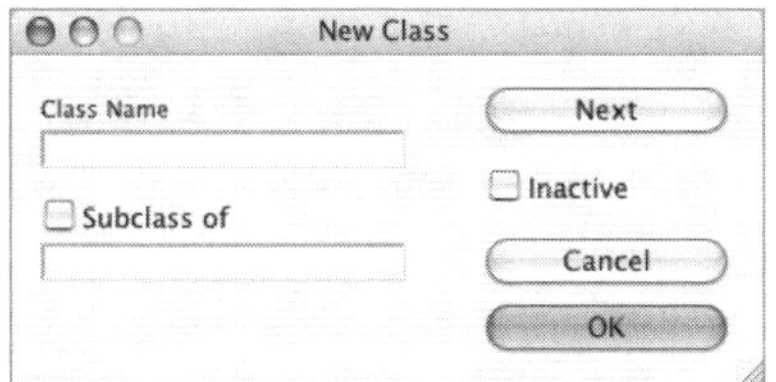

Figure 49 The New Class dialog.

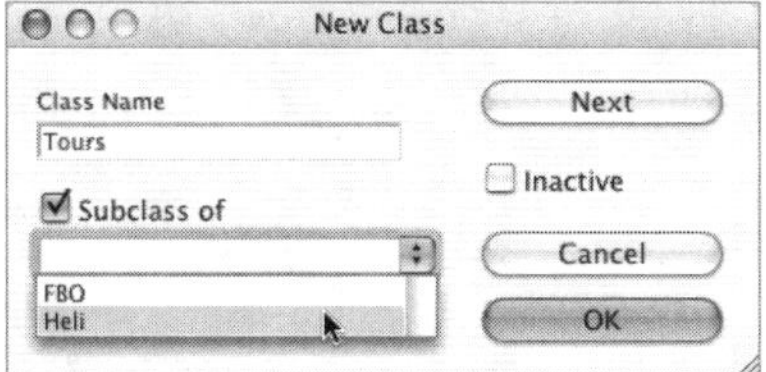

Figure 50 Selecting a parent class for a subclass.

To add a class

1. In the Class List window (**Figure 48**), choose New from the Action pop-up menu.

   Or

   With the Class List window active, choose Edit > New Class or press [⌘ N].

   The New Class dialog appears (**Figure 49**).

2. Enter a name for the class in the Class Name box.

3. If the class is a subclass of another class, turn on the Subclass of check box and choose a class from the drop-down list (**Figure 50**).

4. To make the class inactive, turn on the Inactive check box.

5. To save the class and create another new one, click Next.

   Or

   To save the class without creating another new one, click OK.

   The class is added to the Class List.

✔ Tip

- I recommend keeping class names short. This will make it easier to enter them in transactions.

To modify a class

1. In the Class List window **(Figure 48)**, select the name of the class you want to modify.
2. Choose Edit from the Action pop-up menu.

   Or

   Choose Edit > Edit Class or press [⌘ E].

   The Edit Class dialog appears **(Figure 51)**.
3. Make changes as desired in the dialog.
4. Click OK.

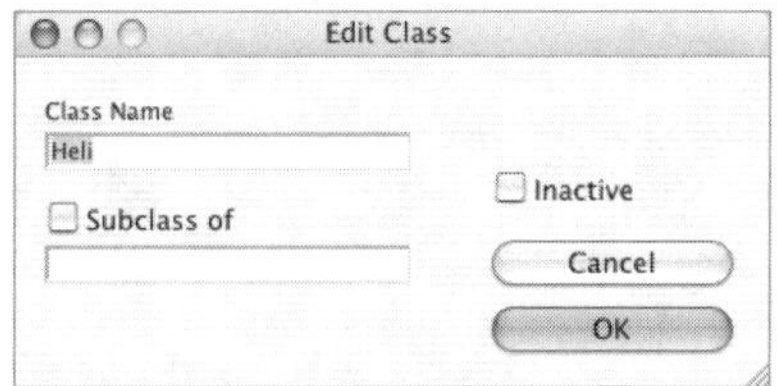

Figure 51 The Edit Class dialog.

To delete a class

1. In the Class List window **(Figure 48)**, select the name of the class you want to delete.
2. Choose Edit > Delete Class or press [⌘ D].
3. One of three dialogs appears, depending on the class you selected:
   - ▲ If you selected a class that does not have subclasses, a dialog like the one in **Figure 52a** appears. Click OK.
   - ▲ If you selected a class that has subclasses, a dialog like the one in **Figure 52b** appears. Click OK, then remove all of the class's subclasses and try to delete the class again.
   - ▲ If you selected a class that has been used in a transaction, a dialog like the one in **Figure 52c** appears. Click OK.

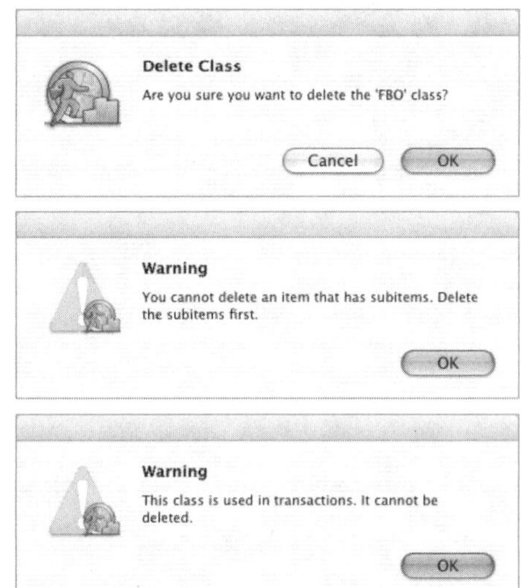

Figures 52a, 52b, & 52c A dialog like one of these appears when you try to delete a class.

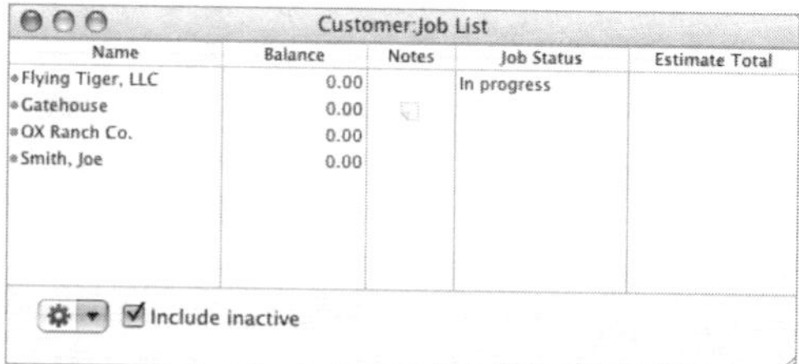

Figure 53 The Customer:Job List window with a few customers created.

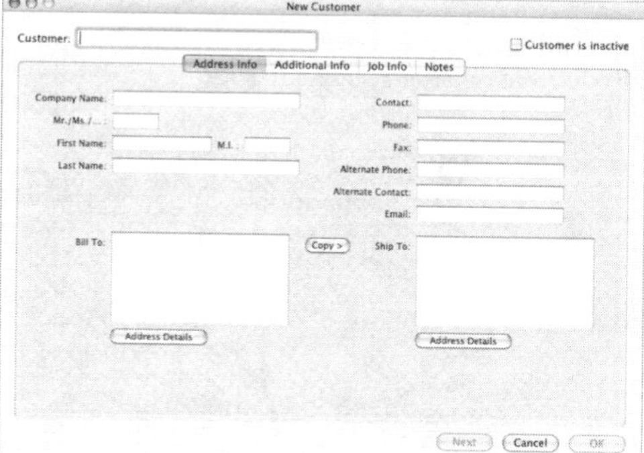

Figure 54 The Address Info pane of the New Customer dialog.

Customer:Job List

QuickBooks keeps track of customer and related job information in the Customer:Job List (**Figure 53**). You use this list when you create invoices, estimates, and other documents for specific customers.

QuickBooks enables you to store a wealth of information about each customer and a related job, including contact, categorization, tax, and job status data. Although this information is used internally by QuickBooks, you can also use it as the basis for a detailed contact database of your customers.

This part of the chapter explains how you can enter and maintain customer and job information in the Customer:Job List.

To add a customer

1. In the Customer:Job List window (**Figure 53**), choose New from the Action pop-up menu.

   Or

   With the Customer:Job List window active, choose Edit > New Customer:Job or press [⌘][N].

   TheNew Customer dialog appears (**Figure 54**).

2. Enter a name for the customer in the Customer box. This is the name that will appear in menus and lists throughout QuickBooks.

3. If necessary, click the Address Info button (**Figure 54**). Enter information in fields as desired:

   ▲ **Company Name** is the name of the customer's company. This can be the same as what you entered in the Customer box.

Continued on next page...

Continued from previous page.

- **Mr./Ms./...** is a title for the customer.
- **First Name** is the customer's first name.
- **M.I.** is the customer's middle initial.
- **Last Name** is the customer's last name.
- **Contact** is the name of a contact person for the customer.
- **Phone** is the customer's voice phone number.
- **Fax** is the customer's fax number.
- **Alternate Phone** is an alternative phone number for the customer.
- **Alternate Contact** is an alternative contact person for the customer.
- **Email** is the customer's e-mail address.
- **Bill To** is the customer's billing address. To enter each part of the address in a different address field, click the Address Details button, use the form that appears **(Figure 55)** and click OK.
- **Ship To** is the customer's shipping address. You can click the Address Details button to enter each part of the address in a different field **(Figure 55)** or click the Copy button to copy the Bill To address to the Ship to box.

4. Click the Additional Info button **(Figure 56)**. Enter information in fields as desired:
   - **Customer Type** is the type of customer. This drop-down list displays the contents of the Customer Type List, which I cover later in this chapter.
   - **Terms** is the customer's payment terms. This drop-down list displays the contents of the Terms List, which I cover later in this chapter.

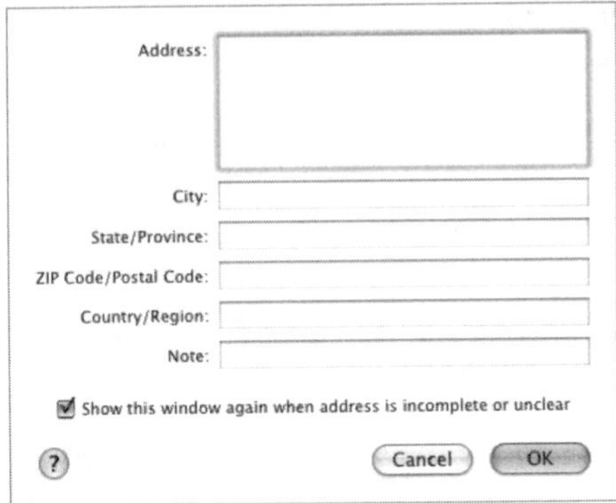

Figure 55 You can use this dialog to enter each part of the address in a separate field.

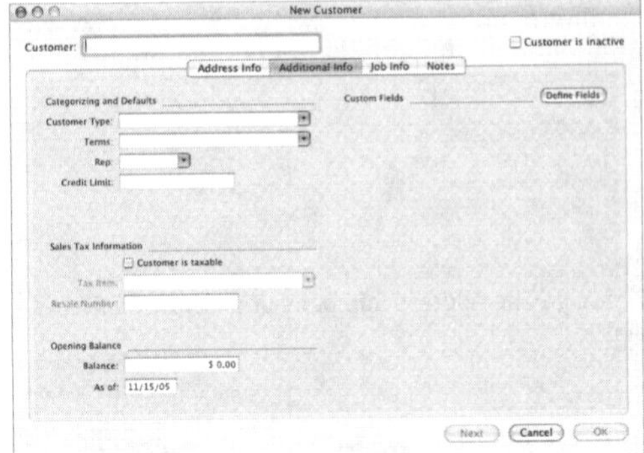

Figure 56 The Additional Info pane of the New Customer dialog.

ADDING CUSTOMERS

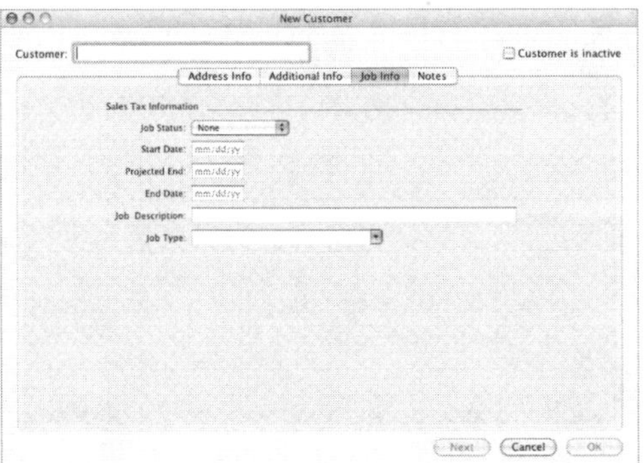

Figure 57 The Job Info pane of the New Customer dialog.

- **Rep** is the employee assigned to the customer. This drop-down list displays the initials of all employees in the Employee List, which I cover later in this chapter.
- **Credit Limit** is the customer's credit limit. QuickBooks uses this information to notify you when a customer exceeds its credit limit.
- **Customer is taxable** tells QuickBooks that the customer pays sales tax on taxable items.
- **Tax Item** is the sales tax that should be billed to the customer. This list displays all of the sales tax items and groups in the Item List. I discuss the Item List earlier in this chapter.
- **Resale Number** is the customer's resale number, which you should have on file if the customer is not taxable.
- **Opening Balance** is the opening balance for the customer's account. Enter the amount and the balance date in the appropriate fields.

5. Click the Job Info button (**Figure 57**). Enter information in fields as desired:
   - **Job Status** is the current status for the job. The pop-up menu's options include None, Pending, Awarded, In Progress, Closed, and Not Awarded.
   - **Start Date** is the job's start date.
   - **Projected End** is the job's estimated end date.
   - **End Date** is the job's actual end date.
   - **Job Description** is a brief description of the job.
   - **Job Type** is the type of job. This drop-down list displays the contents of the Job Type List, which I cover later in this chapter.

Continued on next page...

Continued from previous page.

6. To add Notes or To Do items for a customer, click the Notes button **(Figure 58)**. Then:
   - ▲ To add a date-stamped note for the customer, click the Date Stamp button and enter the note after the date stamp in the window **(Figure 59)**.
   - ▲ To add a To Do item for the customer, click the New To Do button. Then follow the instructions in the section titled "To add a To Do List note" later in this chapter.
7. To make the customer inactive, turn on the Customer is inactive check box.
8. To save the customer and create another new one, click Next. The Edit new customer dialog appears again **(Figure 54)**. Repeat steps 2 through 7.

   Or

   To save the customer without creating another new one, click OK.

   The customer is added to the Customer: Job List.

✔ Tips

- It is not necessary to add every single customer you do business with. Instead, just enter information for customers you work with on a regular basis, those you bill, or those you want to track activity for.
- In step 2, if the customer is a person and you want to sort customers by last name, enter the customer's last name first, like this: *Langer, Maria.*
- In steps 3, 4, and 5, it is not necessary to enter information into all of the fields. Just use the fields you need.

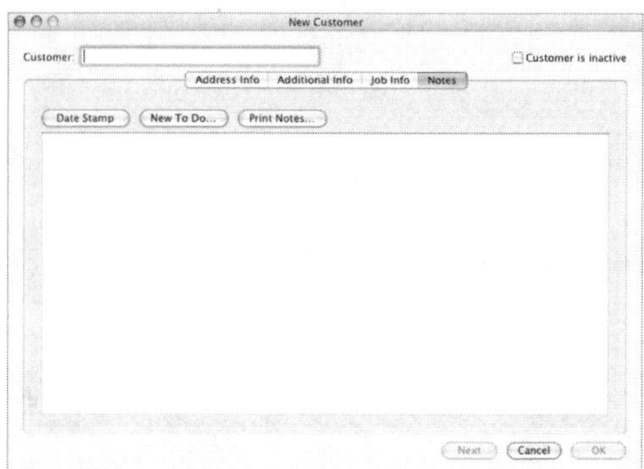

Figure 58 The Notes pane of the New Customer dialog.

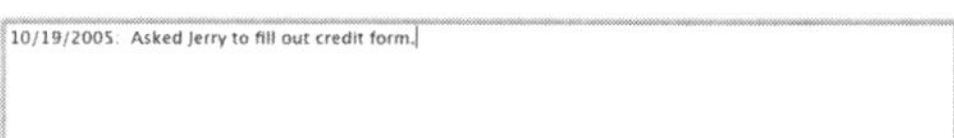

Figure 59 You can easily created date-stamped notes for a customer.

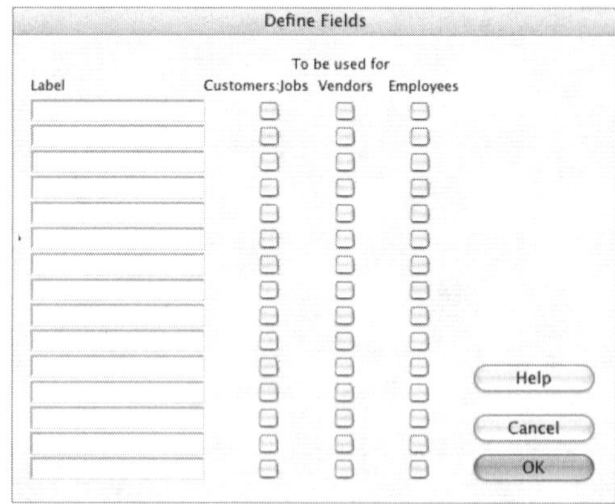

Figure 60 The Define Fields dialog enables you to add fields for customers, vendors, and employees.

- Clicking the Define Fields button in the Additional Info pane of the New Customer dialog **(Figure 56)** displays a dialog like the one in **Figure 60**, which you can use to create custom fields for customers, vendors, and employees.

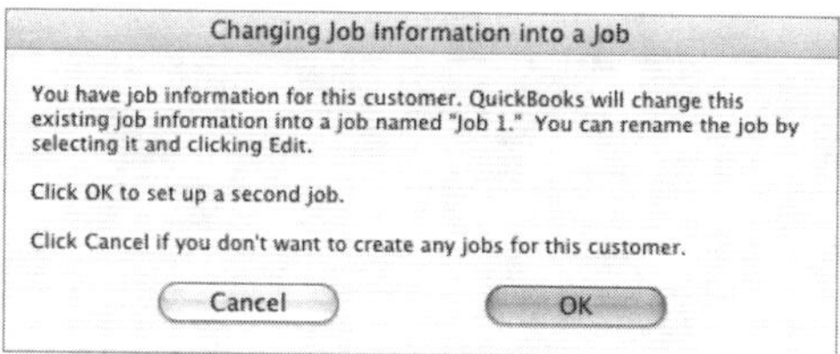

Figure 61 This dialog appears when you add a job to a customer that already has one job entered.

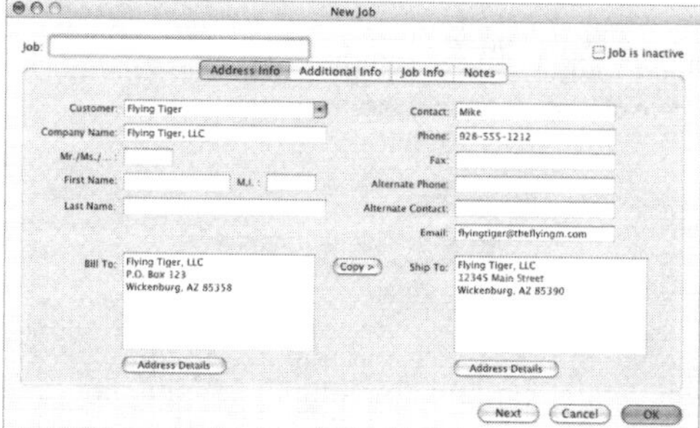

Figure 62 The New job dialog looks a lot like theNew Customer dialog.

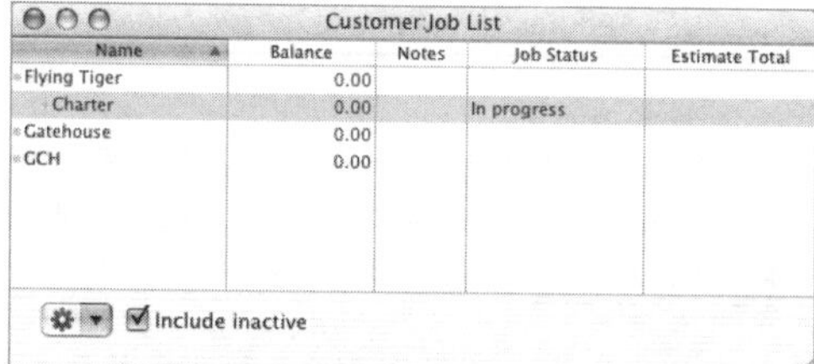

Figure 63 A customer's jobs appear indented beneath the customer name in the Customer:Job List window.

To add a job to a customer

1. In the Customer:Job List window (**Figure 53**), select the name of the customer you want to add a job to.
2. Choose Add Job from the Action pop-up menu.
3. If the customer already has information for one job entered for it, a dialog like the one in **Figure 61** appears. Click OK.
4. The New Job dialog appears (**Figure 62**). This dialog looks and works very much the same as the New Customer dialog (**Figure 54**), but it is already filled in with information about the customer.

   Enter a name for the job in the Job Name box.
5. Make changes as necessary in fields in the four panes of the dialog: Address Info, Additional Info, Job Info, and Notes. These changes apply to the job.
6. Click OK. The new job appears indented beneath the customer name in the Customer:Job List window (**Figure 63**).

✔ Tip

- If you need help with step 5, consult steps 3 through 5 in the section titled "To add a customer" earlier in this chapter.

To modify a customer or job

1. In the Customer:Job List window (**Figure 53**), select the name of the customer or job you want to modify.
2. Choose Edit from the Action pop-up menu.

   Or

   Choose Edit > Edit Customer:Job or press [⌘][E].

   The *Customer Name* (**Figure 64**) or *Job Name* (**Figure 65**) dialog appears.
3. Make changes as desired in each pane of the dialog.
4. Click OK.

To delete a customer or job

1. In the Customer:Job List window (**Figure 53**), select the name of the customer or job you want to delete.
2. Choose Edit > Delete Customer:Job or press [⌘][D].
3. One of three dialogs appears, depending on the customer or job you selected:
   - ▲ If you selected a customer or job that has not been used in any transactions, a dialog like the one in **Figure 66a** appears. Click OK.
   - ▲ If you selected a customer or job that has been used in a transaction, a dialog like the one in **Figure 66b** appears. Click OK.
   - ▲ If you selected a customer with multiple individual jobs, a dialog like the one in **Figure 66c** appears. Click OK. You'll have to delete the jobs before you can delete the customer.

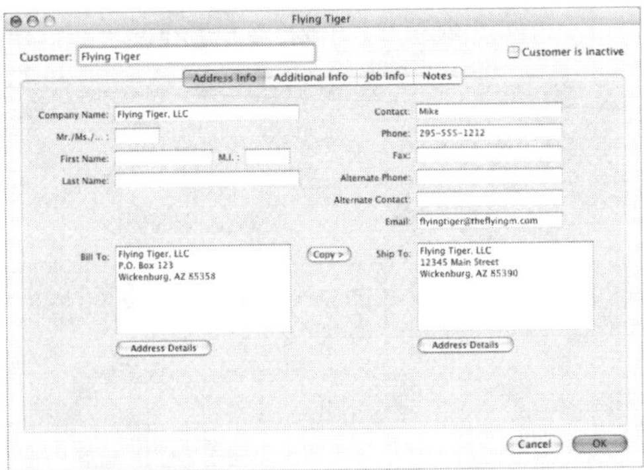

Figure 64 The Address Info pane of the *Customer Name* dialog.

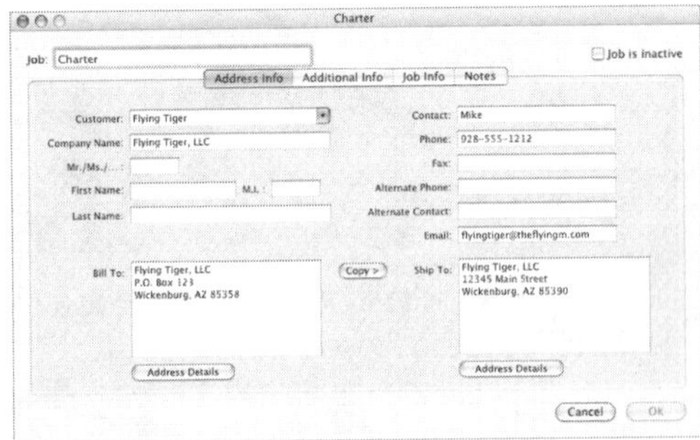

Figure 65 The Address Info pane of the *Job Name* dialog.

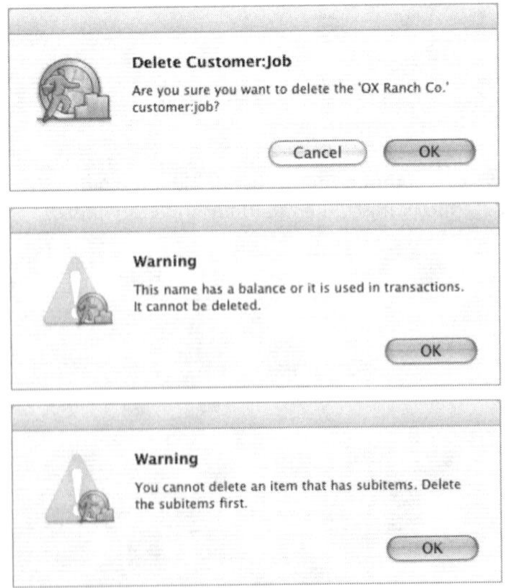

Figures 66a, 66b, & 66c One of these dialogs appears when you try to delete a customer or job.

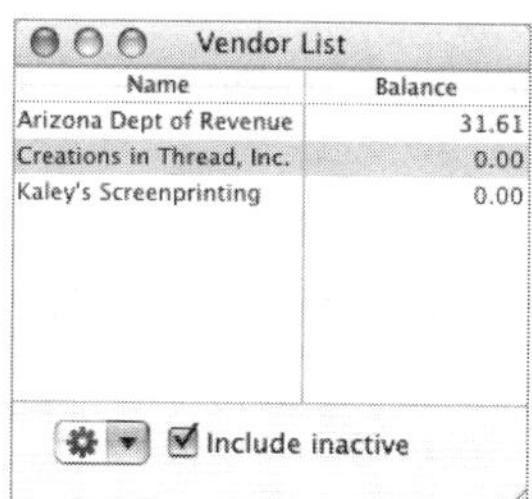

Figure 67 The Vendor List window with a few vendors already created.

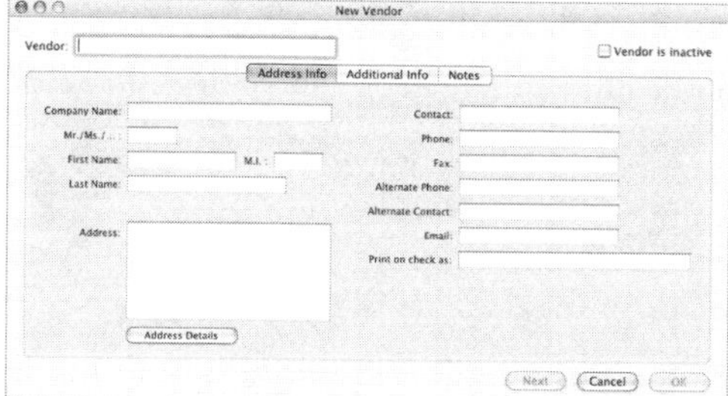

Figure 68 The Address Info pane of the New Vendor dialog.

Vendor List

QuickBooks keeps track of vendor information in the Vendor List (**Figure 67**). You use this list when you create purchase orders, checks, and other documents for specific vendors.

Like the Customer:Job List discussed in the previous section, the Vendor List can contain a great deal of information about each vendor. This information is used internally by QuickBooks, and can also be used as the basis for a detailed contact database of your suppliers.

This part of the chapter explains how you can enter and maintain vendor information in the Vendor List.

To add a vendor

1. In the Vendor List window (**Figure 67**), choose New from the Action pop-up menu.

   Or

   With the Vendor List window active, choose Edit > New Vendor or press [⌘ N].

   The New Vendor dialog appears (**Figure 68**).

2. Enter a name for the vendor in the Vendor box. This is the name that will appear in menus and lists throughout QuickBooks.

3. If necessary, click the Address Info button (**Figure 68**). Enter information in fields as desired:

   ▲ **Company Name** is the name of the vendor's company. This can be the same as what you entered in the Vendor box.

Continued on next page...

Adding Vendors

Continued from previous page.

- **Mr./Ms./...** is a title for the vendor.
- **First Name** is the vendor's first name.
- **M.I.** is the vendor's middle initial.
- **Last Name** is the vendor's last name.
- **Address** is the vendor's address. To enter each part of the address in a different address field, click the Address Details button, use the form that appears (**Figure 55**) and click OK.
- **Contact** is the name of a contact person for the vendor.
- **Phone** is the vendor's voice phone number.
- **Fax** is the vendor's fax number.
- **Alternate Phone** is an alternative phone number for the vendor.
- **Alternate Contact** is an alternative contact person for the vendor.
- **Email** is the vendor's e-mail address.
- **Print on Check as** is the name of the vendor as it should be printed on checks.

4. Click the Additional Info button (**Figure 69**). Enter information in fields as desired:
    - **Account No.** is the account number you want to appear in the Memo field on checks you send to the vendor. In most instances, this will be your company's account number with the vendor.
    - **Type** is the type of vendor. This drop-down list displays the contents of the Vendor Type List, which I cover later in this chapter.
    - **Terms** are the payment terms. This drop-down list displays the contents of the Terms List, which I cover later in this chapter.

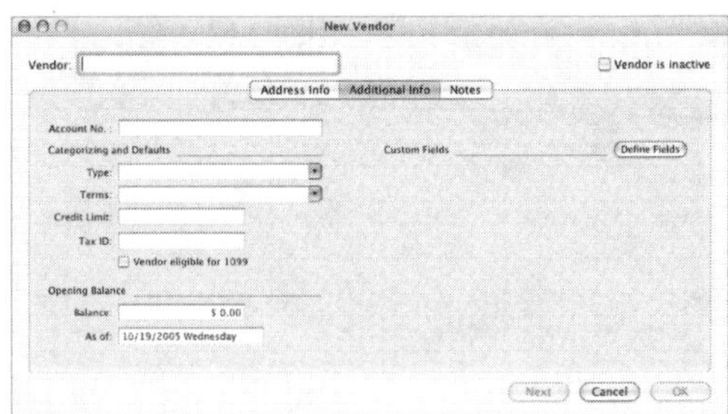

Figure 69 The Additional Info pane of the New Vendor dialog.

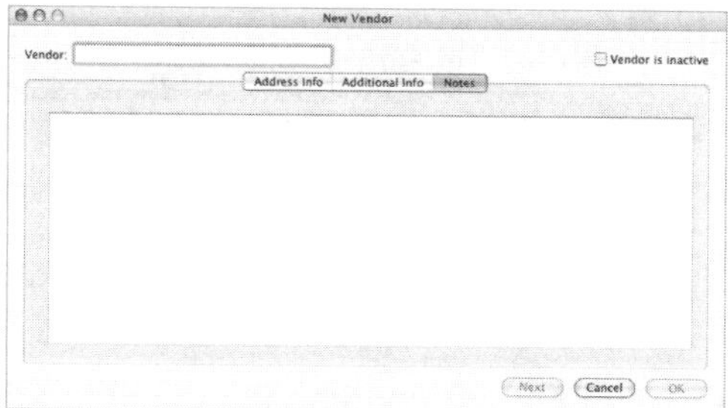

Figure 70 The Notes pane of the New Vendor dialog.

- ▲ **Credit Limit** is your credit limit with the vendor. QuickBooks uses this information to notify you when you exceed your credit limit.
- ▲ **Tax ID** is the tax identification number provided by the vendor.
- ▲ **Vendor eligible for 1099** indicates that a 1099 form should be prepared for the vendor at year-end as required by the IRS.
- ▲ **Opening Balance** is the opening balance for the vendor's account. Enter the amount and the balance date in the appropriate fields.

5. To add Notes for a vendor, click the Notes button (**Figure 70**). Then enter your note in the big box.
6. To make the vendor inactive, turn on the Vendor is inactive check box.
7. To save the vendor and create another new one, click Next. The New Vendor dialog appears again (**Figure 68**). Repeat steps 2 through 6.

   Or

   To save the vendor without creating another new one, click OK.

   The vendor is added to the Vendor List.

✔ Tips

- It is not necessary to add every single vendor you do business with. Instead, just enter information for vendors you work with on a regular basis, those who bill you, those you write checks to, or those you want to track activity for.
- In step 2, if the vendor is a person and you want to sort vendors by last name, enter the vendor's last name first, like this: *Langer, Maria.*
- In steps 3 through 5, it is not necessary to enter information into all of the fields. Just use the fields you need.
- Clicking the Define Fields button in the Additional Info pane of the New Vendor dialog (**Figure 69**) displays a dialog like the one in **Figure 60**, which you can use to create custom fields for customers, vendors, and employees.

To modify a vendor

1. In the Vendor List window (**Figure 67**), select the name of the vendor you want to modify.
2. Choose Edit from the Action pop-up menu.

   Or

   Choose Edit > Edit Vendor or press ⌘E.

   The *Vendor Name* dialog appears (**Figure 71**).
3. Make changes as desired in the three panes of the dialog.
4. Click OK.

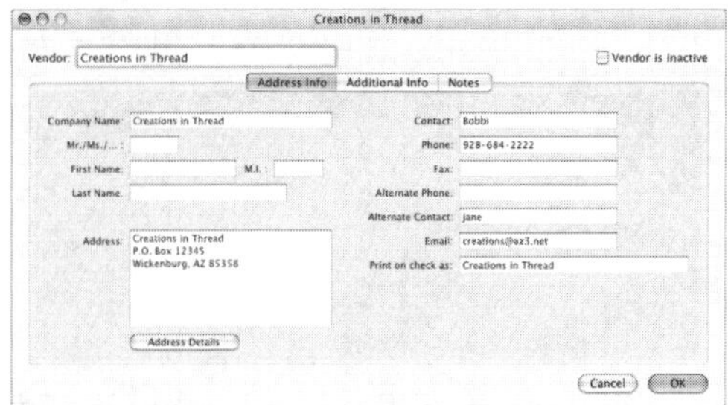

Figure 71 The Address Info tab of the *Vendor Name* dialog.

To delete a vendor

1. In the Vendor List window (**Figure 67**), select the name of the vendor you want to delete.
2. Choose Edit > Delete Vendor or press ⌘D.
3. One of three dialogs appears, depending on the vendor you selected:
   - If you selected a vendor that has not been used in any transactions, a dialog like the one in **Figure 72a** appears. Click OK.
   - If you selected a vendor that has been used in a transaction, a dialog like the one in **Figure 72b** appears. Click OK.
   - If you selected a vendor which is a taxing agency used by a sales tax item, a dialog like the one in **Figure 72c** appears. Click OK.

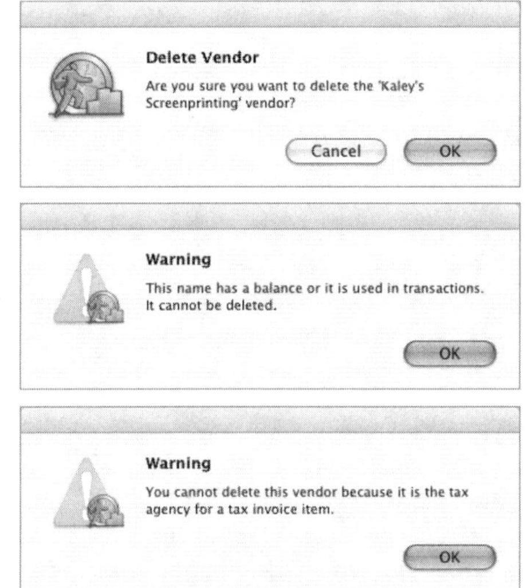

Figures 72a, 72b, & 72c One of these dialogs will appear when you attempt to delete a vendor.

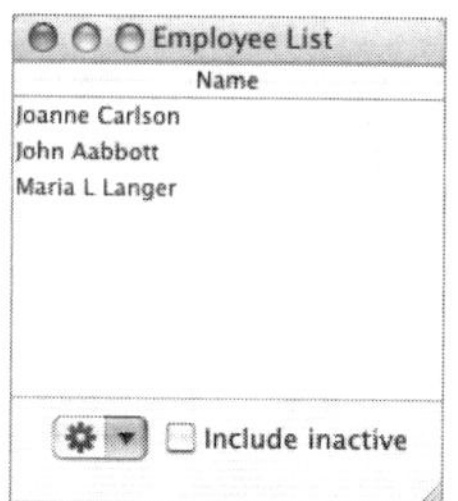

Figure 73 The Employee List window with three employees created.

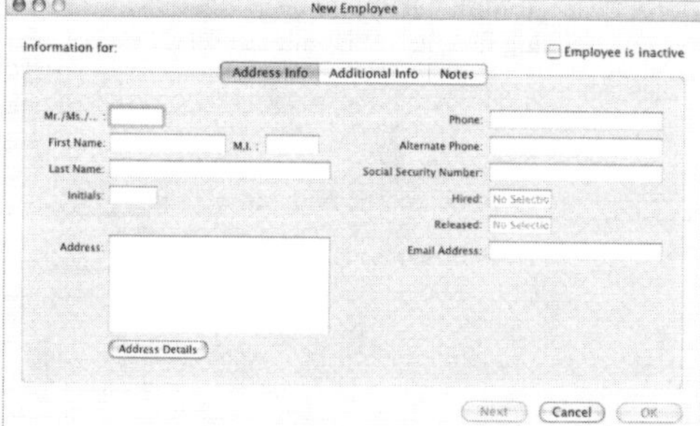

Figure 74 The Address Info pane of the New Employee dialog.

Employee List

QuickBooks keeps track of employee information in the Employee List (**Figure 73**). You use this list to identify sales reps in transactions or to track employee time—especially billable time.

This part of the chapter explains how you can enter and maintain employee information in the Employee List.

To add an employee

1. In the Employee List window (**Figure 73**), choose New from the Action pop-up menu.

   Or

   With the Employee List window active, choose Edit > New Employee or press ⌘N.

   The New Employee dialog appears (**Figure 74**).

2. If necessary, click the Address Info button (**Figure 74**). Enter information in fields as desired:
   - **Mr./Ms./...** is a title for the employee.
   - **First Name** is the employee's first name.
   - **M.I.** is the employee's middle initial.
   - **Last Name** is the employee's last name.
   - **Initials** is the employee's initials. This field is filled in automatically based on what you enter in the previous three fields.
   - **Address** is the employee's address. To enter each part of the address in a different address field, click the Address Details button, use the form that appears (**Figure 55**) and click OK.
   - **Phone** is the employee's voice phone number.

Continued on next page...

Continued from previous page.

- **Alternate Phone** is an alternative phone number for the employee.
- **Social Security Number** is the employee's social security number.
- **Hired** is the date the employee was hired.
- **Released** is the date the employee resigned, was laid off, or was fired.
- **Email Address** is the employee's e-mail address.

3. Click the Additional Info button. As shown in **Figure 75**, this pane is empty by default, but you can add fields to it and enter information into those custom fields.
4. To add Notes for an employee, click the Notes button (**Figure 76**). Then enter your note in the big box.
5. To make the employee inactive, turn on the Employee is inactive check box.
6. To save the employee and create another new one, click Next. The Edit dialog appears again (**Figure 74**). Repeat steps 2 through 5.

   Or

   To save the employee without creating another new one, click OK.

   The employee is added to the Employee List.

✔ Tip

- Clicking the Define Fields button in the Additional Info pane of the New Employee dialog (**Figure 75**) displays a dialog like the one in **Figure 60**, which you can use to create custom fields for customers, vendors, and employees.

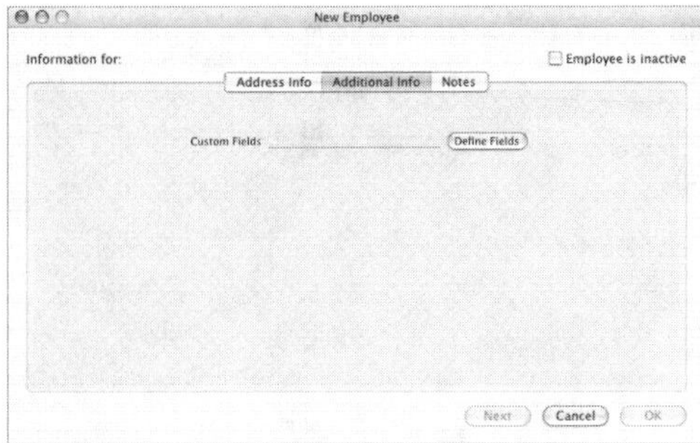

Figure 75 The Additional Info pane of the New Employee dialog has no fields unless you define some.

Figure 76 The Notes pane of the New Employee dialog.

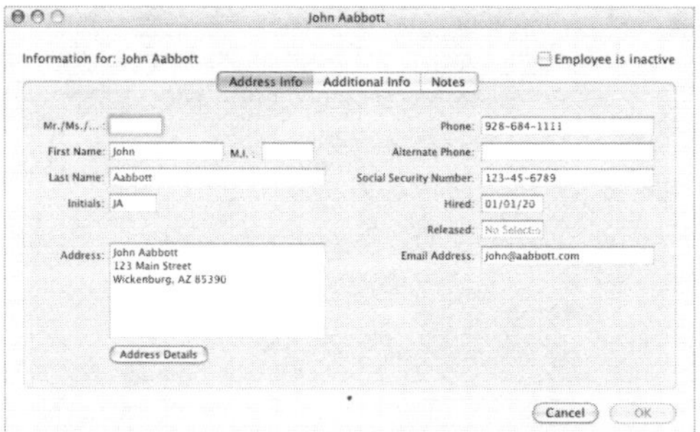

Figure 77 The Address Info pane of the *Employee Name* dialog.

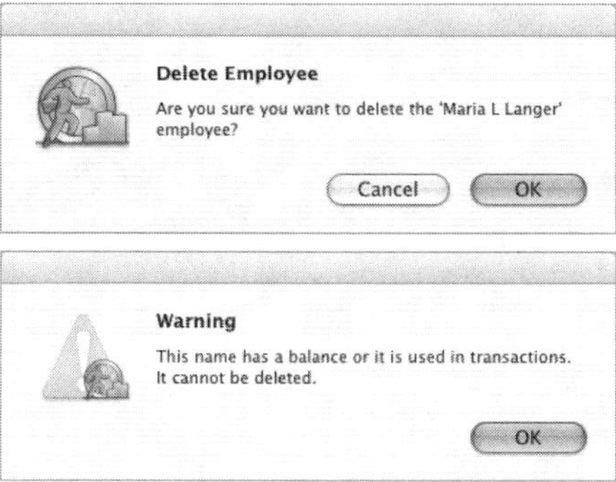

Figures 78a & 78b One of these dialogs appears when you try to delete an employee.

To modify an employee

1. In the Employee List window (**Figure 73**), select the name of the employee you want to modify.
2. Choose Edit from the Action pop-up menu.

   Or

   Choose Edit > Edit Employee or press [⌘][E].

   The *Employee Name* dialog appears (**Figure 77**).
3. Make changes as desired in the three panes of the dialog.
4. Click OK.

To delete an employee

1. In the Employee List window (**Figure 73**), select the name of the employee you want to delete.
2. Choose Edit > Delete Employee or press [⌘][D].
3. One of two dialogs appears, depending on the employee you selected:
   - ▲ If you selected an employee that has not been used in any transactions, a dialog like the one in **Figure 78a** appears. Click OK.
   - ▲ If you selected an employee that has been used in a transaction, a dialog like the one in **Figure 78b** appears. Click OK.

Other Names List

QuickBooks's Other Names List (**Figure 79**) enables you to enter contact information for individuals and companies that are not customers, vendors, or employees. You can then use this information from within QuickBooks.

This part of the chapter explains how you can maintain the Other Names List.

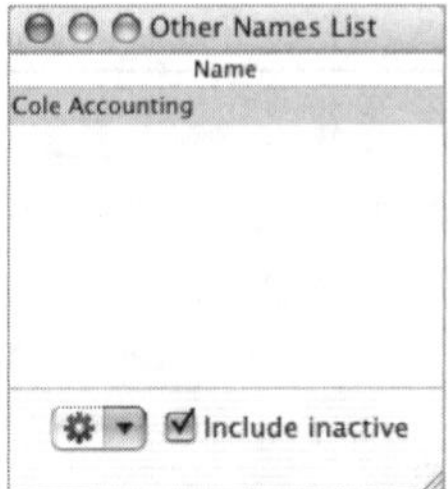

Figure 79 The Other Names List window with one other name created.

To add a name

1. In the Other Names List window (**Figure 79**), choose New from the Action pop-up menu.

   Or

   With the Other Names List window active, choose Edit > New Other Name or press ⌘N.

   The New Name dialog appears (**Figure 80**).

2. If necessary, click the Address Info button (**Figure 80**).

3. Enter information in fields as desired:

   ▲ **Name** is the name as you want it to appear in pop-up menus and drop-down lists throughout QuickBooks.

   ▲ **Company Name** is the name of the company.

   ▲ **Mr./Ms./...** is a title for the name.

   ▲ **First Name** is the first name.

   ▲ **M.I.** is the middle initial.

   ▲ **Last Name** is the last name.

   ▲ **Address** is the address. To enter each part of the address in a different address field, click the Address Details button, use the form that appears (**Figure 55**) and click OK.

   ▲ **Contact** is the name of a contact.

   ▲ **Phone** is the voice phone number.

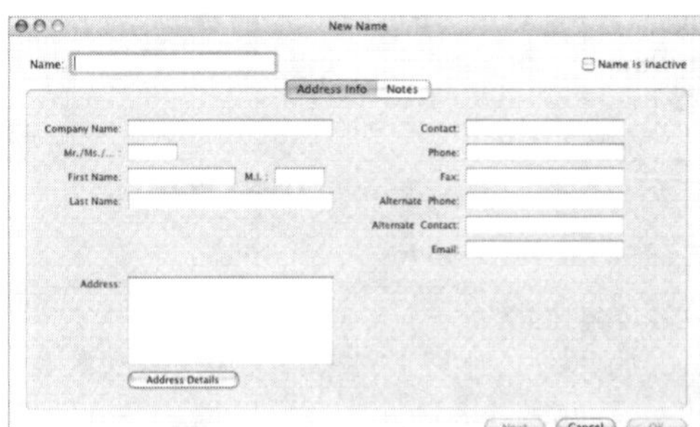

Figure 80 The New Name dialog.

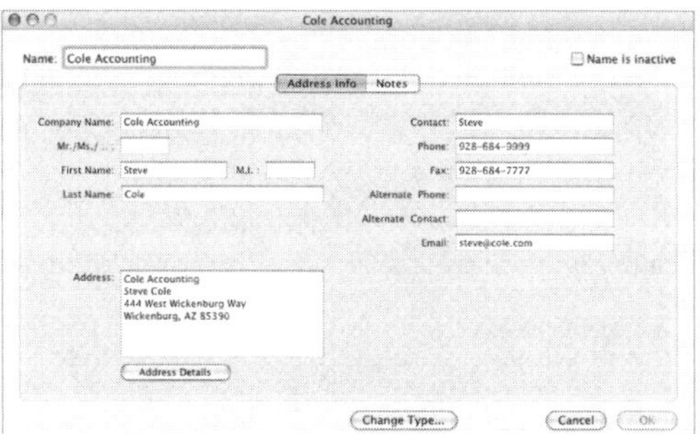

Figure 81 The *Name* dialog.

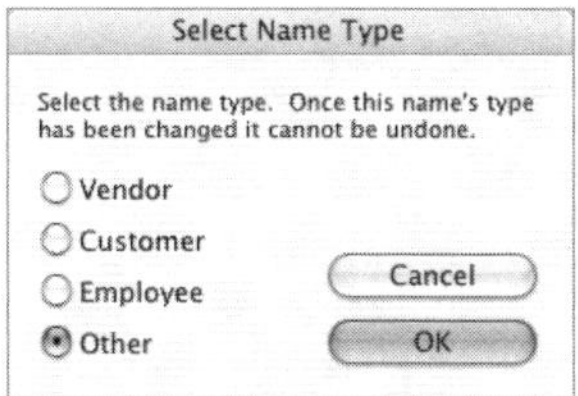

Figure 82 Use this dialog to change the type of name from Other to Vendor, Customer, or Employee.

- **Fax** is the fax number.
- **Alternate Phone** is an alternative phone number.
- **Alternate Contact** is the name of an alternative contact.
- **Email** is the associated e-mail address.

4. To make the name inactive, turn on the Name is inactive check box.
5. To save the name and create another new one, click Next. The Edit dialog appears again (**Figure 80**). Repeat steps 2 through 4.

   Or

   To save the name without creating another new one, click OK.

   The name is added to the Other Names List.

To modify a name

1. In the Other Names List window (**Figure 79**), select the name you want to modify.
2. Choose Edit from the Action pop-up menu.

   Or

   Choose Edit > Edit Other Name or press [Cmd-E].

   The *Name* dialog appears (**Figure 81**).
3. Make changes as desired in the dialog.
4. Click OK.

✔ Tip

- To change the type of name, click the Change Type button in step 3. Then select a type of name in the Select Name Type dialog (**Figure 82**) and click OK. The name is moved from the Other Names List to the list you specified.

To delete a name

1. In the Other Names List window (**Figure 79**), select the name you want to delete.
2. Choose Edit > Delete Other Name or press [⌘ ⌘][D].
3. One of two dialogs appears, depending on the name you selected:
   - ▲ If you selected a name that has not been used in any transactions, a dialog like the one in **Figure 83a** appears. Click OK.
   - ▲ If you selected a name that has been used in a transaction, a dialog like the one in **Figure 83b** appears. Click OK.

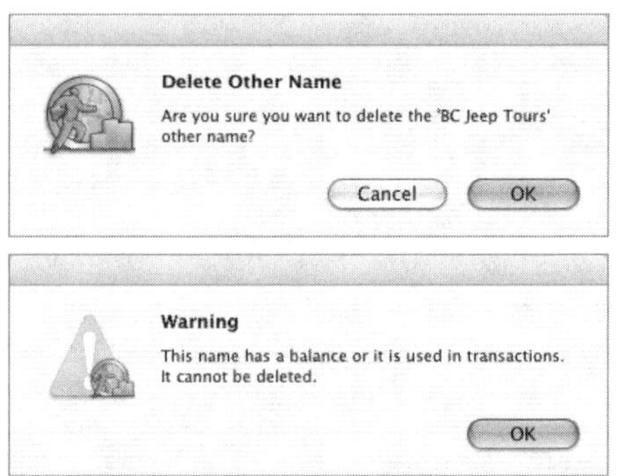

Figures 83a & 83b One of these dialogs appears when you try to delete a name from the Other Names List.

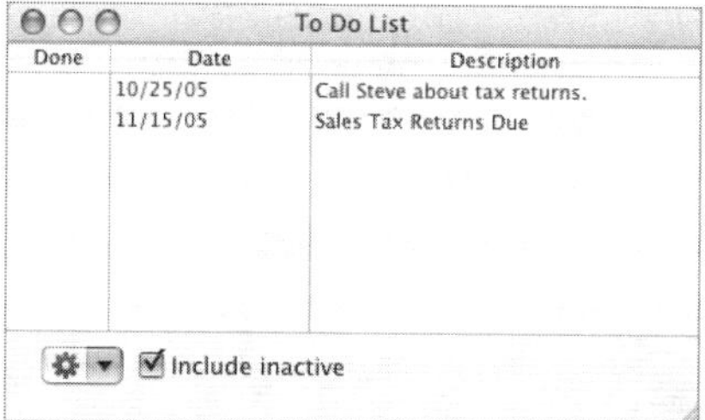

Figure 84 The To Do List window.

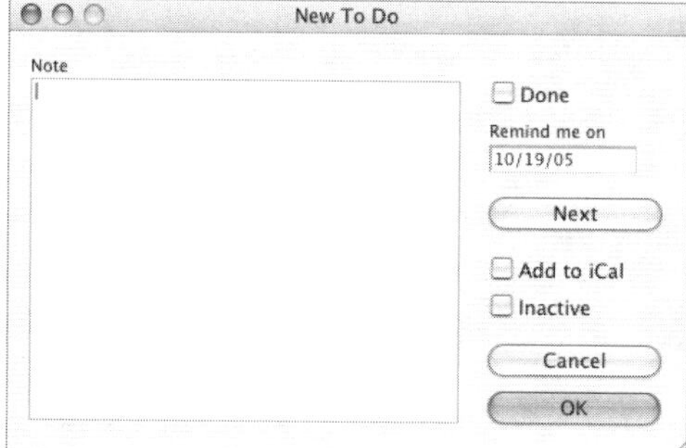

Figure 85 The New To Do dialog.

To Do List

QuickBooks includes a To Do List that you can use to remind you about things you need to do for your business. These notes, which are date-driven, appear in the To Do List window (**Figure 84**) as well as the Reminders window (**Figure 104**), which I discuss later in this chapter.

In this part of the chapter, I explain how to set up To Do List items, how to mark completed items as Done, and how to manage the To Do List's contents.

To add a to do note

1. In the To Do List window (**Figure 84**), choose New from the Action pop-up menu.

   Or

   With the To Do List window active, choose Edit > New To Do Note or press [⌘][N].

   The New To Do dialog appears (**Figure 85**).

2. Enter a description of what you need to do in the Note box.
3. Enter the date you want to be reminded in the Remind me on box.
4. If you have already completed the item, turn on the Done check box.
5. To add the To Do note to your iCal calendar, turn on the Add to iCal check box.
6. To make the To Do note inactive, turn on the Inactive check box.

Continued on next page...

Continued from previous page.

7. To save the to do note and create another new one, click Next. The New To Do dialog appears again (**Figure 85**). Repeat steps 2 through 6.

   Or

   To save the to do note without creating another new one, click OK.

   The note is added to the To Do List.

✔ Tips

- You can also display the New To Do dialog (**Figure 85**) by clicking the New To Do button in the Notes pane for a customer (**Figure 58**).
- If you turned on the Add to iCal check box in step 5, QuickBooks creates a new "all-day" event for that date in the QuickBooks 2006 for Mac calendar it creates in iCal (**Figure 86**).

To modify a to do note

1. In the To Do List window (**Figure 84**), select the to do note you want to modify.
2. Choose Edit from the Action pop-up menu.

   Or

   Choose Edit > Edit To Do Note or press ⌘E.

   The Edit To Do dialog appears (**Figure 87**).
3. Make changes as desired in the dialog.
4. Click OK.

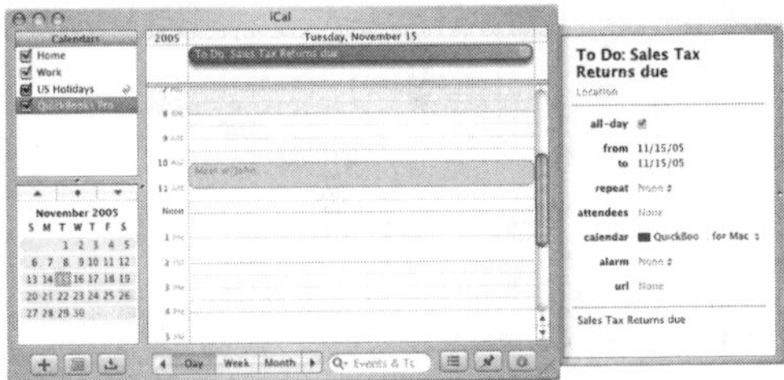

Figure 86 QuickBooks can add to do items to iCal as events.

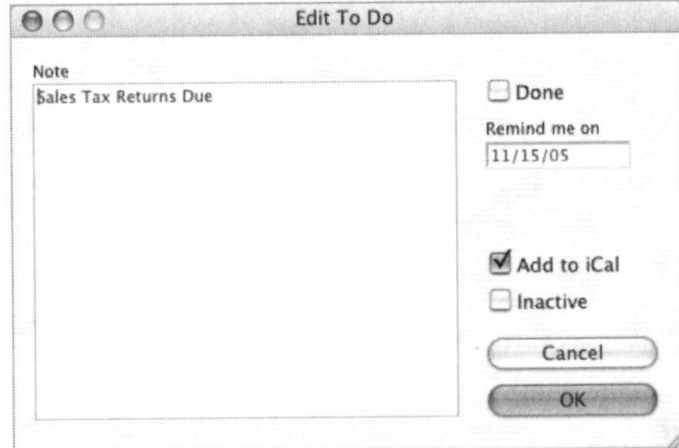

Figure 87 The Edit To Do dialog.

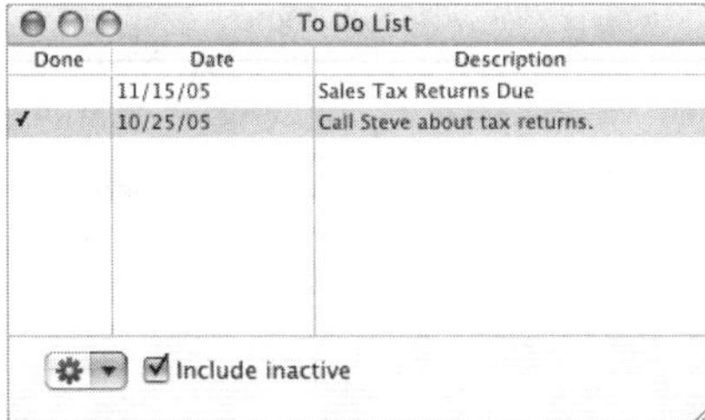

Figure 88 When you mark an item as done, a check mark appears beside it in the To Do List window.

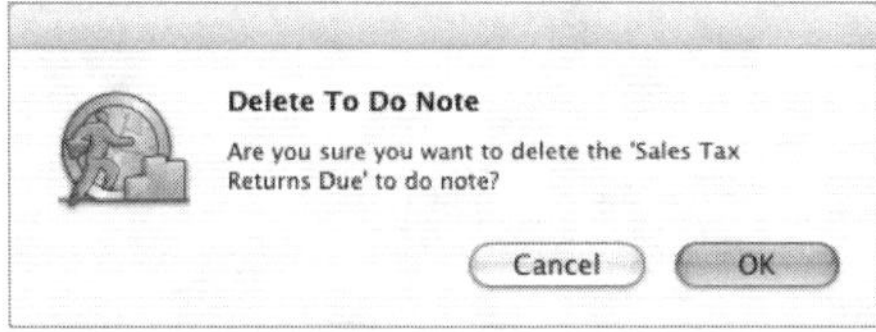

Figure 89 Click OK to confirm that you want to delete the to do note.

To mark a to do note as done

1. In the To Do List window (**Figure 84**), select the to do note you want to mark as done.
2. Choose Mark as 'Done' from the Action pop-up menu. A check mark appears in the Done column beside the note (**Figure 88**).

✔ Tip

- To do notes that are done do not appear in the Reminders window (**Figure 104**).

To delete a to do note

1. In the To Do List window (**Figure 84**), select the to do note you want to delete.
2. Choose Edit > Delete To Do Note or press [⌘][D].
3. A confirmation dialog appears (**Figure 89**). Click OK.

Customer Type, Vendor Type, & Job Type Lists

The Customer Type List (**Figure 90a**), Vendor Type List (**Figure 90b**), and Job Type List (**Figure 90c**) enable you to create categories for customers, vendors, and jobs. These categories can then be used in reports to group, sort, and filter transactions.

This part of the chapter explains how to add types and maintain these lists.

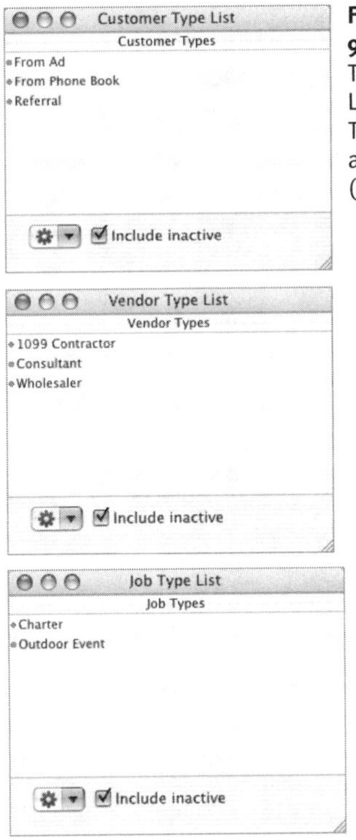

Figures 90a, 90b, & 90c The Customer Type List (top), Vendor Type List (middle), and Job Type List (bottom).

✔ Tips

- You don't have to use customer, vendor, or job types when adding customers or vendors or entering transactions that include Customer Type,Vendor Type, or Job Type fields. This QuickBooks feature is entirely optional.
- Customer, vendor, and job types can include *subtypes*. This enables you to group several types within one main type.

To add a customer, vendor, or job type

1. In the Customer Type List window (**Figure 90a**), Vendor Type List window (**Figure 90b**), or Job Type List window (**Figure 90c**) choose New from the Action pop-up menu.

   Or

   With the Customer Type List, Vendor Type List, or Job Type List window active, choose Edit > New Customer Type, Edit > New Vendor Type, or Edit > New Job Type, or press [⌘ N].

   The New Customer Type (**Figure 91a**), New Vendor Type (**Figure 91b**), or New Job Type (**Figure 91c**) dialog appears.

2. Enter the type in the Customer Type (**Figure 91a**), Vendor Type (**Figure 91b**), or Job Type Name (**Figure 91c**) box.

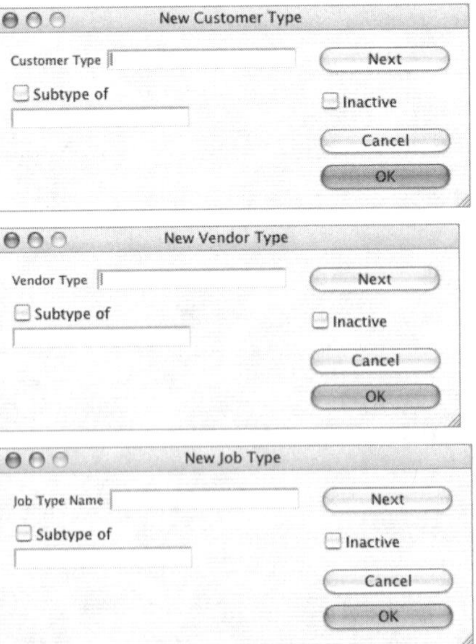

Figures 91a, 91b, & 91c The New Customer Type (top), New Vendor Type (middle), and New Job Type (bottom) dialogs.

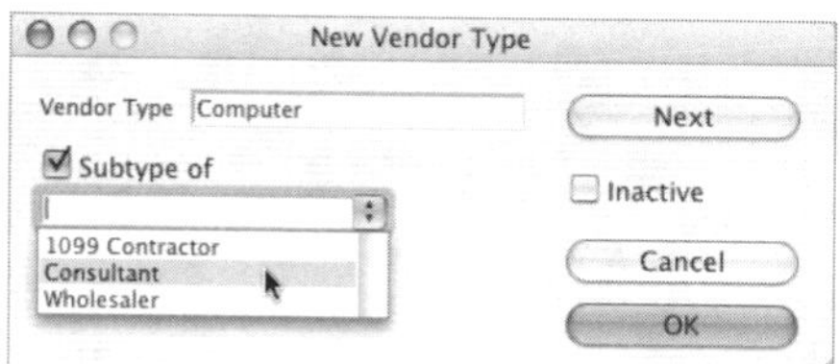

Figure 92 To make a type a subtype, choose a type from the drop-down list.

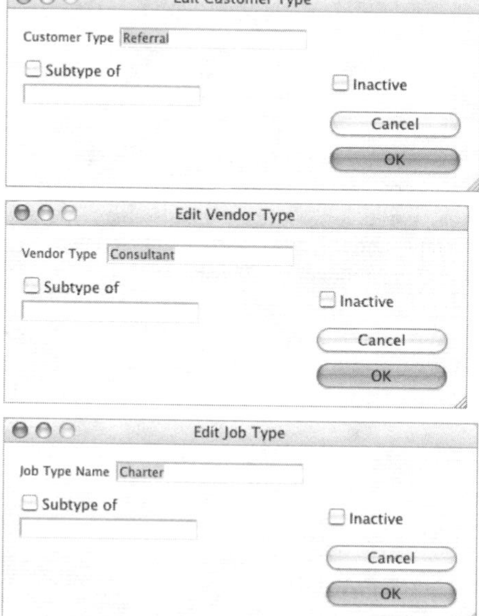

Figures 93a, 93b, & 93c The Edit Customer Type (top), Edit Vendor Type (middle), and Edit Job Type (bottom) dialogs.

3. If the type is a subtype of another type, turn on the Subtype of check box and select an option from the drop-down list that appears beneath it (**Figure 92**).
4. To mark a type as inactive, turn on the Inactive check box.
5. To save the type and create another new one, click Next. The New Customer Type (**Figure 91a**), New Vendor Type (**Figure 91b**),or New Job Type (**Figure 91c**) dialog appears again. Repeat steps 2 through 4.

   Or

   To save the type without creating another new one, click OK.

   The type is added to the list.

To modify a customer, vendor, or job type

1. In the Customer Type List window (**Figure 90a**), Vendor Type List window (**Figure 90b**), or Job Type List window (**Figure 90c**), select the type you want to modify.
2. Choose Edit from the Action pop-up menu.

   Or

   Choose Edit > Edit Customer Type, Edit > Edit Vendor Type, or Edit > Edit Job Type, or press [⌘][E].

   The Edit Customer Type (**Figure 93a**), Edit Vendor Type (**Figure 93b**), or Edit Job Type (**Figure 93c**) dialog appears.
3. Make changes as desired in the dialog.
4. Click OK.

To delete a customer, vendor, or job type

1. In the Customer Type List window (**Figure 90a**), Vendor Type List window (**Figure 90b**), or Job Type List window (**Figure 90c**), select the type you want to delete.
2. Choose Edit > Delete Customer Type, Edit > Delete Vendor Type, or Edit > Delete Job Type, or press ⌘D.
3. A confirmation dialog appears (**Figure 94a, 94b, or 94c**). Click OK.

✔ Tip

- You cannot delete a customer, vendor, or job type that has been used in a transaction.

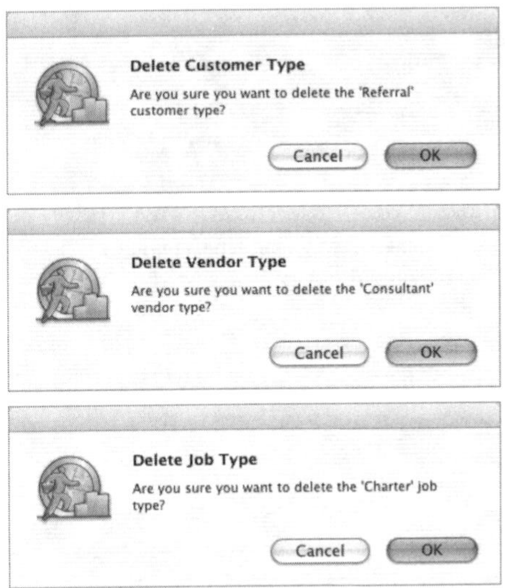

Figures 94a, 94b, & 94c The Delete Customer Type (top), Delete Vendor Type (middle), and Delete Job Type (bottom) confirmation dialogs.

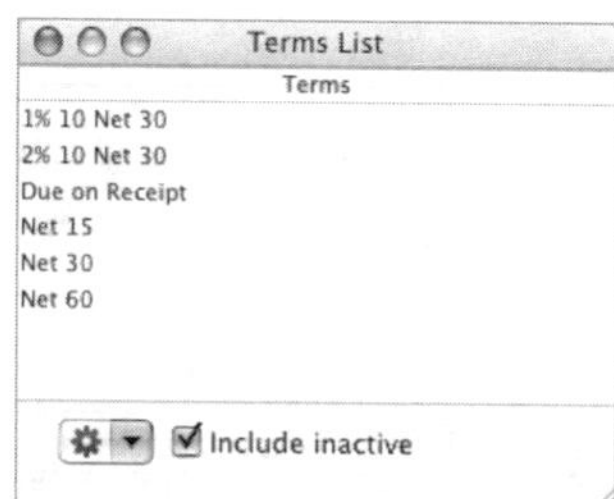

Figure 95 The Terms List window with some terms defined.

Terms List

The Terms List (**Figure 95**) enables you to maintain a list of payment terms. You use these terms when creating invoices and recording bills. When used properly, payment terms can automate reminders, finance fees, discounts, and other billing-related features.

QuickBooks supports two kinds of payment terms:

- **Standard** terms are those based on the invoice date. They can include a due date, discount percentage, and discount date. For example, *1% 10 Net 30* terms means that the net amount of the invoice is due in 30 days, but if it's paid in 10 days, there's a 1% discount.
- **Date Driven** terms are those based on the day of the month. They include due dates based on a calendar month and can include a discount percentage and discount date. For example, you can set up a date-driven terms that requires payment by the 25th of the month unless the invoice date is between the 20th and the 25th; then it's due on the 25th of the following month. These same terms can include a 1% discount if paid before the 10th of the month.

This part of the chapter explains how to set up and modify payment terms on the Terms List.

To add a terms definition

1. In the Terms List window (**Figure 95**), choose New from the Action pop-up menu.

   Or

   With the Terms List window active, choose Edit > New Terms, or press [⌘N].

   The New Terms dialog appears (**Figure 96**).

2. Enter a name for the terms in the Terms box.

3. Select the radio button for the type of terms you want.

4. Set options for Standard terms:

   ▲ **Net due in** is the number of days from the invoice date that the full amount is due.

   ▲ **Discount percentage is** is the percent discount that can be applied to the full amount.

   ▲ **Discount if paid within** is the number of days from the invoice date that the invoice must be paid by to be eligible for the discount.

   Or

   Set options for Date Driven terms:

   ▲ **Net due before the** is the day of the month the full amount is due.

   ▲ **Due the next month if issued within** is the number of days between the invoice date and the normal due date that would make the invoice due the following month.

   ▲ **Discount percentage is** is the percent discount that can be applied to the full amount.

   ▲ **Discount if paid before the** is the day of the month the invoice must be paid by to be eligible for the discount.

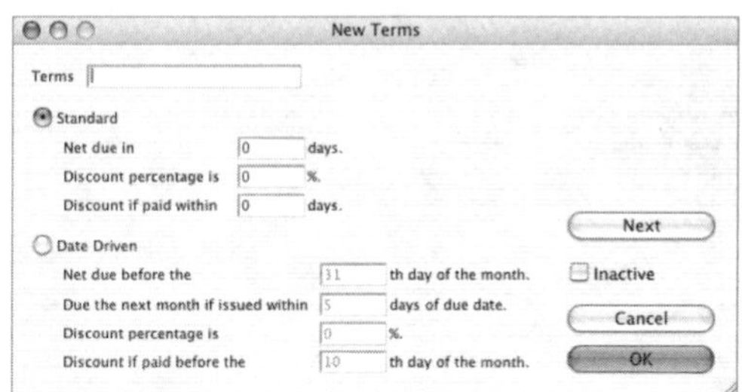

Figure 96 The New Terms dialog.

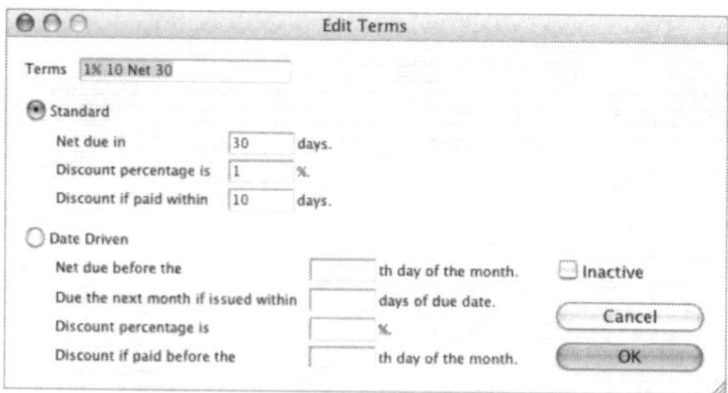

Figure 97 The Edit Terms dialog.

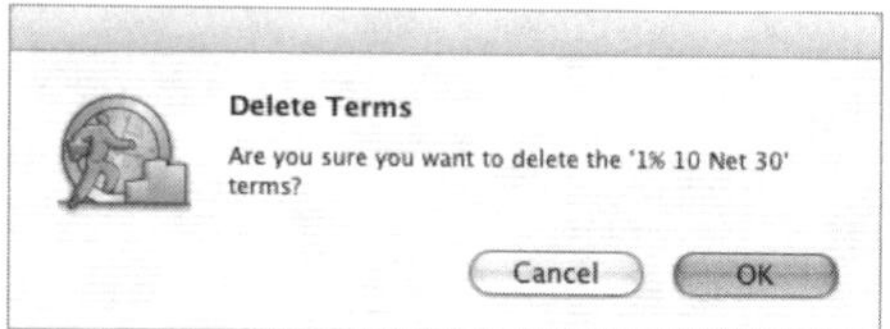

Figure 98 This confirmation dialog appears when you try to delete terms.

5. To make the terms inactive, turn on the Inactive check box.

6. To save the terms and create another new one, click Next. The New Terms dialog appears again (**Figure 96**). Repeat steps 2 through 5.

   Or

   To save the terms without creating another new one, click OK.

   The new terms definition is added to the list.

To modify a terms

1. In the Terms List window (**Figure 97**), select the terms you want to modify.

2. Choose Edit from the Action pop-up menu.

   Or

   Choose Edit > Edit Terms, or press [⌘ ⌘][E].

   The Edit Terms dialog appears (**Figure 97**).

3. Make changes as desired in the dialog.

4. Click OK.

To delete a terms definition

1. In the Terms List window (**Figure 95**), select the terms you want to delete.

2. Choose Edit > Delete Terms, or press [⌘ ⌘][D].

3. A confirmation dialog appears (**Figure 98**). Click OK.

✔ Tip

- You cannot delete a terms definition that has been used in a transaction.

Modifying & Deleting Terms

Customer Message, Payment Method, & Ship Via Lists

QuickBooks' Customer Message List (**Figure 99a**), Payment Method List (**Figure 99b**), and Ship Via List (**Figure 99c**) enable you to include additional information and comments on invoices, estimates, and other documents you create with QuickBooks. Although customer messages aren't used internally by QuickBooks, payment methods and shipping methods can be used in reports to group, sort, and filter transactions.

This part of the chapter explains how to build and maintain these lists.

✔ Tip

- You don't have to use customer messages, payment methods, or ship via list entries when entering transactions that include Customer Message, Payment Method, or Ship Via fields. This QuickBooks feature is entirely optional.

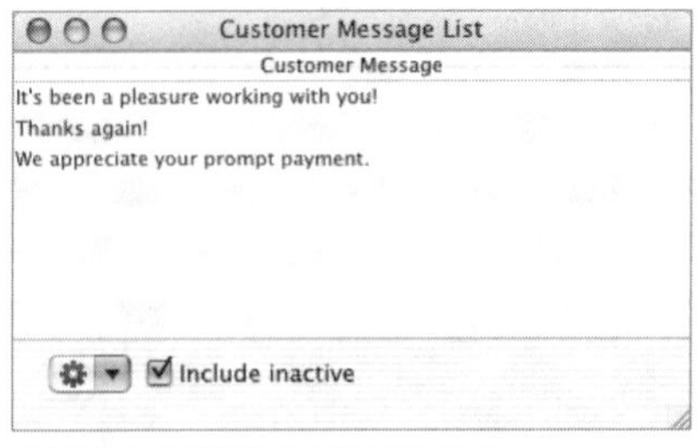

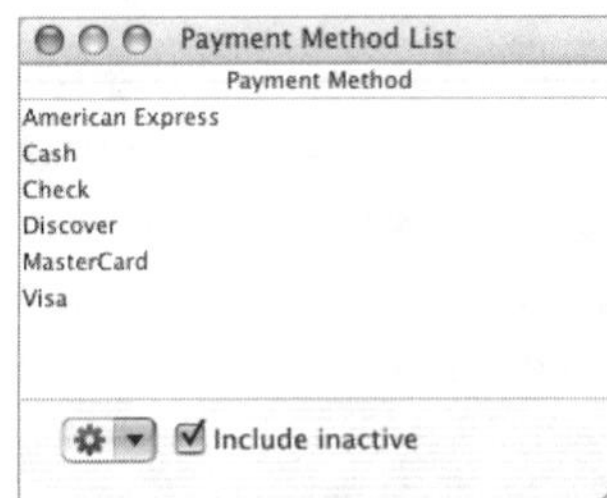

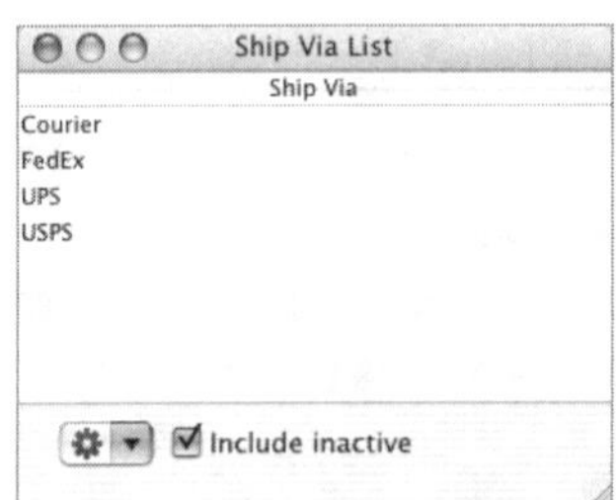

Figures 99a, 99b, & 99c The Customer Message (top), Payment Method (middle), and Ship Via (bottom) List windows.

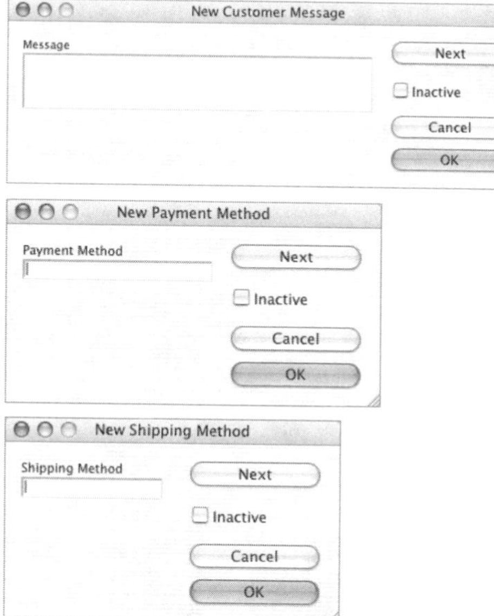

Figures 100a, 100b, & 100c The New Customer Message (top), New Payment Method (middle), and New Shipping Method (bottom) dialogs.

To add a customer message, payment method, or shipping method

1. In the Customer Message List (**Figure 99a**), Payment Method List (**Figure 99b**), or Ship Via List (**Figure 99c**) window, choose New from the Action pop-up menu.

   Or

   With the Customer Message List, Payment Method List, or Ship Via List window active, choose Edit > New Customer Message, Edit > New Payment Method, or Edit > New Shipping Method, or press [⌘][N].

   The New Customer Message (**Figure 100a**), New Payment Method (**Figure 100b**), or New Shipping Method (**Figure 100c**) dialog appears.

2. Enter a name for the item in the Message, Payment Method, or Shipping Method box.

3. To make the customer message, payment method, or shipping method inactive, turn on the Inactive check box.

4. To save the item and create another new one, click Next. The New Customer Message (**Figure 100a**), New Payment Method (**Figure 100b**), or New Shipping Method (**Figure 100c**) dialog appears again. Repeat steps 2 and 3.

   Or

   To save the item without creating another new one, click OK.

   The item is added to the list.

To modify a customer message, payment method, or shipping method

1. In the Customer Message List (**Figure 99a**), Payment Method List (**Figure 99b**), or Ship Via List (**Figure 99c**) window, select the item you want to modify.
2. Choose Edit from the Action pop-up menu.

   Or

   Choose Edit > Edit Customer Message, Edit > Edit Payment Method, or Edit > Edit Shipping Method, or press ⌘E.

   The Edit Customer Message (**Figure 101a**), Edit Payment Method (**Figure 101b**), or Edit Shipping Method (**Figure 101c**) dialog appears.
3. Make changes as desired in the dialog.
4. Click OK.

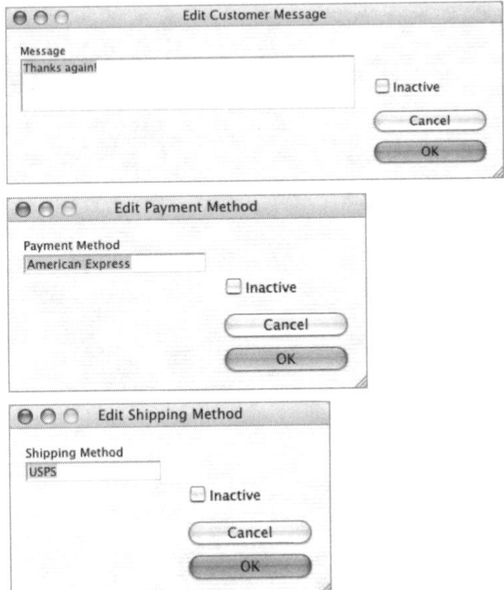

Figures 101a, 101b, & 101c The Edit Customer Message (top), Edit Payment Method (middle), and Edit Shipping Method (bottom) dialogs.

To delete a customer message, payment method, or shipping method

1. In the Customer Message List (**Figure 99a**), Payment Method List (**Figure 99b**), or Ship Via List (**Figure 99c**) window, select the item you want to delete.
2. Choose Edit > Delete Customer Message, Edit > Delete Payment Method, or Edit > Delete Shipping Method, or press ⌘D.
3. A confirmation dialog appears (**Figure 102a, 102b, or 102c**). Click OK.

✔ Tip

- You cannot delete an item that has been used in a transaction.

Figures 102a, 102b, & 102c Use a dialog like one of these to confirm that you want to delete a customer message (top), payment method (middle), or shipping method (bottom).

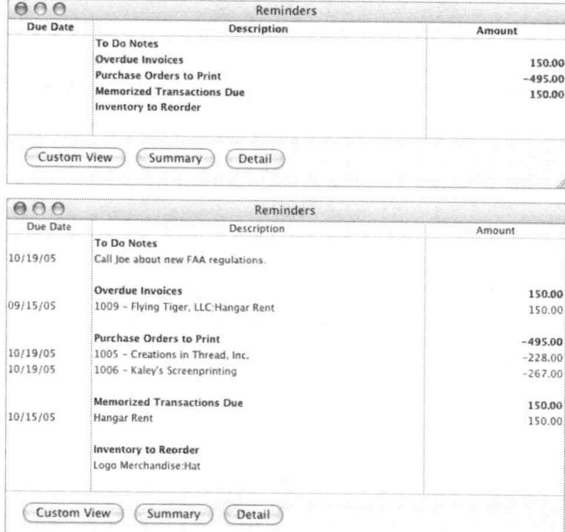

Figures 103 & 104 The Reminders window showing the summary (top) and details (bottom).

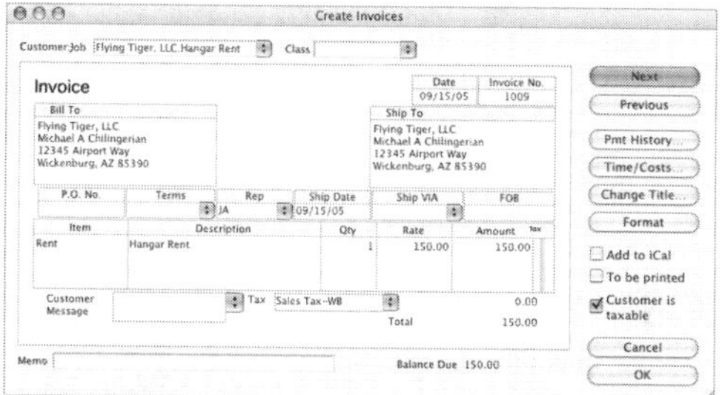

Figure 105 The Create Invoices window for a reminder transaction.

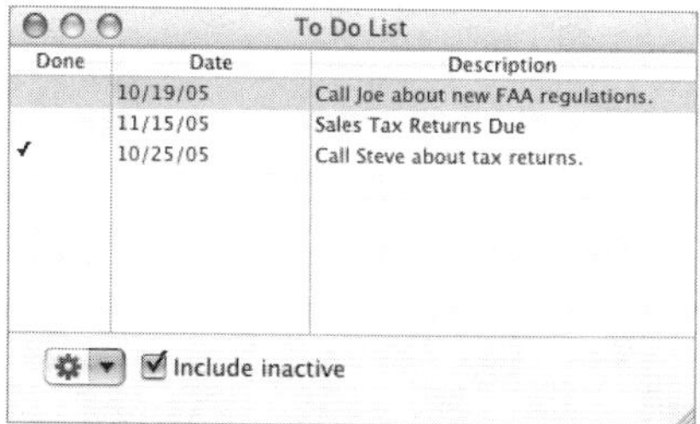

Figure 106 The To Do List window for reminder items.

Reminders List

QuickBooks maintains a Reminders list (**Figures 103 and 104**) that helps you remember to do things. This list includes to do notes you have created, overdue invoices, checks to print, memorized transactions due, and more. QuickBooks automatically keeps track of all reminders for you based on information you provided when you created related items.

This part of the chapter explains how you can work with the Reminders list.

To show or hide details in the Reminders list

Click one of the buttons at the bottom of the Reminders window:

- **Custom View** shows the amount of detail you specified in the Reminder Preferences window. I explain how to set preferences for reminders in **Chapter 11**.
- **Summary** (**Figure 103**) shows only the types and total amounts due for each type of reminder.
- **Detail** (**Figure 104**) shows the individual reminder items for each type of reminder.

To view a reminder item

1. If necessary, click the Detail button to view all individual reminders.
2. Double-click the reminder you want to view. The reminder appears in its transaction (**Figure 105**) or list (**Figure 106**) window.

Entering Sales

Sales & Accounts Receivable

Sales transactions are those that show an exchange of goods and services for payment or a promise to pay. Every successful business should record some kind of sales transaction—the more, the better!

Because QuickBooks integrates all aspects of accounting, every time you enter a sales transaction, you affect balances in other QuickBooks accounts. For example, when you enter a customer name for an invoice, the amount of the invoice increases the customer's account balance. Customer *accounts receivable* can also be affected by payments received, finance charges, and credits for returns.

This chapter explains how to use QuickBooks to enter sales and estimates. It also explains how to monitor and adjust your customers' accounts receivable balances to ensure that you receive proper payment on a timely basis.

Entering Sales

QuickBooks supports two main types of sales:

- **Invoices** are for sales on account. When you create an invoice, you identify the customer account so the amount of the invoice can be added to the customer's account balance.
- **Cash Sales** are for sales for which you receive immediate payment, either by cash, check, or credit card. When you enter a cash sale, no accounts receivable balances are affected.

You enter each type of sale with a form that includes all of the fields you'll need for that kind of sale. These forms are virtually identical, so if you know how to enter one type of sale, you can easily enter the other.

To get the most out of QuickBooks, it's a good idea to take advantage of all of the fields that appear in sales forms. Most form fields correspond to QuickBooks lists. Before you begin to enter sales, the following lists should be up to date; you can find instructions in **Chapter 2** for adding, modifying, and removing list items.

- For both invoices and cash sales:
  - Customer:Job
  - Class
  - Employee (for Rep field)
  - Ship Via
  - Item
  - Customer Message
- For invoices only:
  - Terms
- For cash sales only:
  - Payment Method

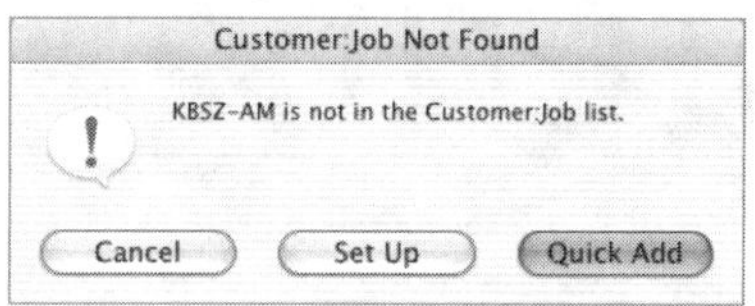

Figure 1 A dialog like this appears when you attempt to enter information that has not already been entered in its corresponding list.

✔ Tip

- If you attempt to fill in a form field with an item that does not exist in the corresponding list, a dialog like the one in **Figure 1** appears. You have three options:
  - **Cancel** returns to the sale form so you can change the entry in the field.
  - **Set Up** displays the appropriate dialog so you can enter all details for the new list entry.
  - **Quick Add** adds the entry name to the appropriate list without giving you an opportunity to enter entry details.

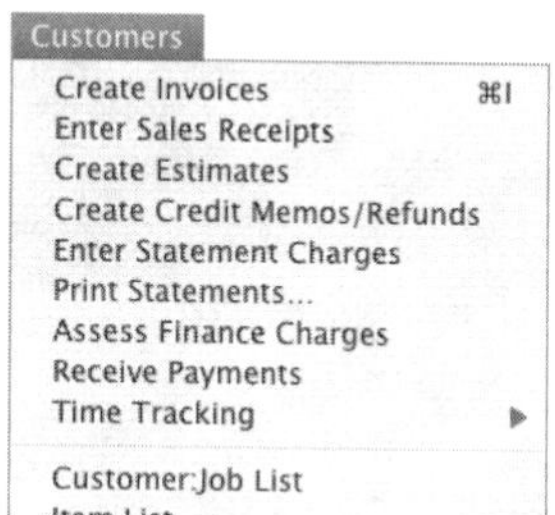

Figure 2 The Customers menu.

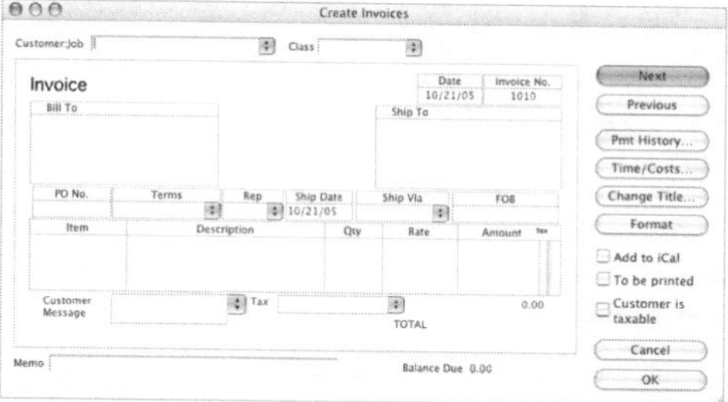

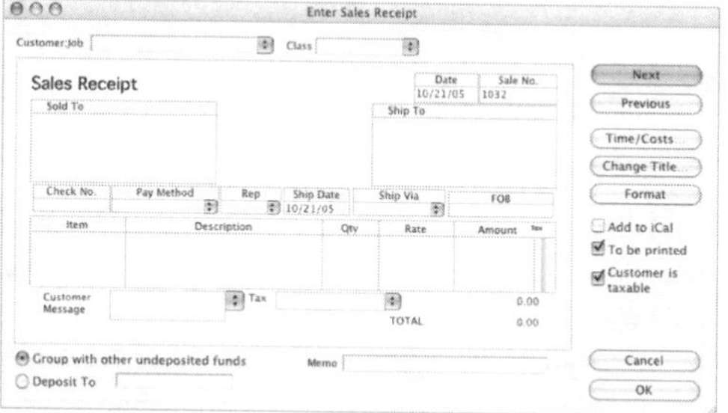

Figures 3 & 4 Blank invoice (top) and sales receipt (bottom) forms for product sales.

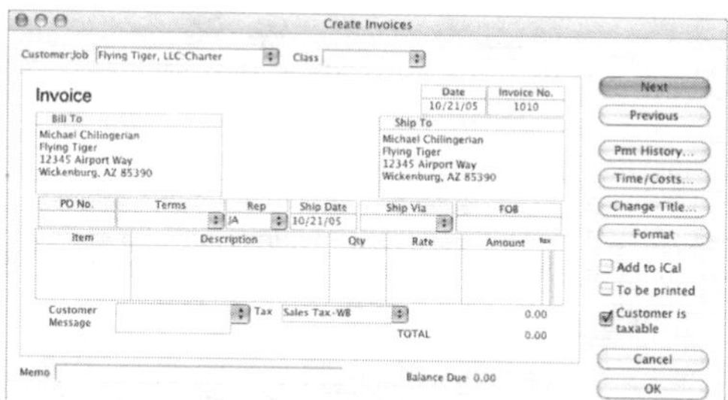

Figure 5 When you choose a customer, other fields are filled in automatically based on customer information.

To create an invoice or enter a sales receipt

1. Choose Customers > Create Invoices (**Figure 2**) or press ⌘ I. The Create Invoices window appears (**Figure 3**).

   Or

   Choose Customers > Enter Sales Receipts (**Figure 2**). The Enter Sales Receipt window appears (**Figure 4**).

2. Choose a customer from the Customer:Job drop-down list. The Bill To, Ship To, Terms, and Rep fields should fill in automatically with information for that customer (**Figure 5**).

3. If desired, choose a class from the Class drop-down list.

4. Enter information or change the entries in the following fields if necessary:

   ▲ **Date** is the invoice or sale date. By default, the current date is automatically entered, but you can change the date if you need to.

   ▲ **Invoice No.** or **Sale No.** is the invoice or sale number. This field is automatically incremented by one from the previous form, so you should not need to change the number.

   ▲ **Bill To** or **Sold To** is the customer name and address for billing or payment purposes.

   ▲ **Ship To** is the customer name and address for shipping purposes.

   ▲ **PO No.** is the customer's purchase order number, if one was provided. This field appears on invoice forms only.

Continued on next page...

Continued from previous page.

- **Terms** refers to the payment terms for the customer. This field appears on invoice forms only.
- **Check No.** is the customer's check number, if payment was made by check. This field appears on sales receipt forms only.
- **Pay Method** is the payment method. This field appears on sales receipt forms only.
- **Rep** is the sales representative. This drop-down list displays initials for your employees.
- **Ship Date** is the date the items that were purchased were or will be shipped.
- **Ship Via** is the shipping method to be used to ship the items.
- **FOB** is the FOB (free on board) location for shipping.

5. Choose the name of an item sold from the Item drop-down list (**Figure 6**). The Description, Rate, and Amount fields fill in automatically (**Figure 7**), but you can change them if desired. Enter a quantity in the Qty field for the line to update the amount (**Figure 8**).
6. Repeat step 5 for each item you want to include on the invoice or sales receipt. **Figure 9** shows an example with three line items.
7. If the customer is required to pay sales tax, turn on the Customer is taxable check box and choose the correct tax item or tax group from the Tax drop-down list. QuickBooks calculates the sales tax and total (**Figure 10**).
8. If desired, choose a message from the Customer Message drop-down list.

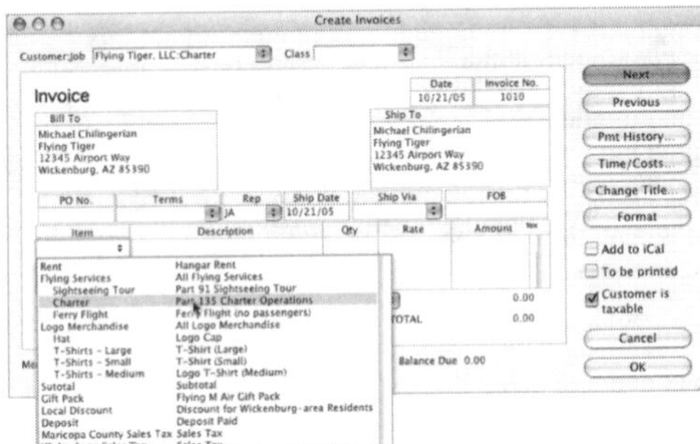

Figure 6 The Item drop-down list includes all items in the Item List.

Item	Description	Qty	Rate	Amount	Tax
Flying	Part 135 Charter Operations		395.00	395.00	T

Figure 7 When you choose an item, its information appears on its invoice line.

Item	Description	Qty	Rate	Amount	Tax
Flying	Part 135 Charter Operations	1.3	395.00	513.50	T

Figure 8 Enter a quantity to calculate the amount.

Item	Description	Qty	Rate	Amount	Tax
Flying	Part 135 Charter Operations	1.3	395.00	513.50	T
Logo	Logo Cap	2	14.95	29.90	T
Logo	Logo T-Shirt (Medium)	1	12.00	12.00	T

Figure 9 Here's an example with several line items entered.

Item	Description	Qty	Rate	Amount	Tax
Flying	Part 135 Charter Operations	1.3	395.00	513.50	T
Logo	Logo Cap	2	14.95	29.90	T
Logo	Logo T-Shirt (Medium)	1	12.00	12.00	T

Customer Message | Tax: Sales Tax-WB | 44.43
TOTAL 599.83

Figure 10 If the customer is taxable, QuickBooks calculates the tax due based on the tax item or tax group you choose from the Tax drop-down list.

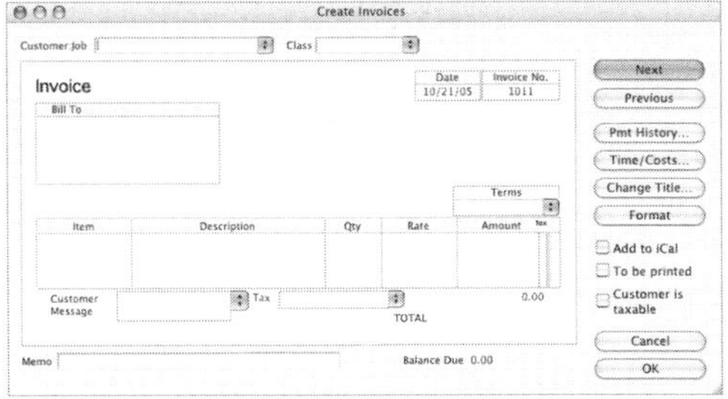

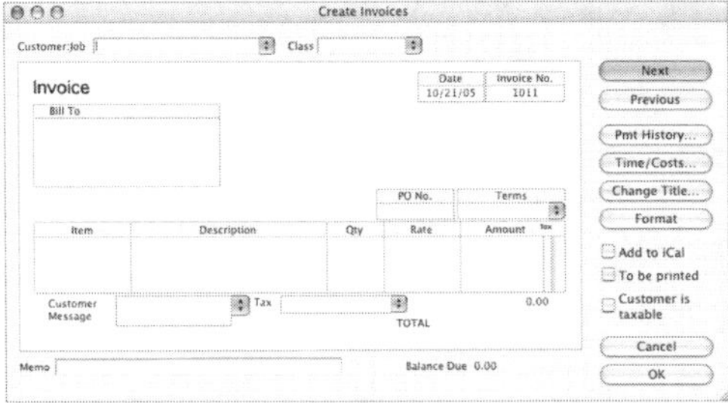

Figures 11 & 12 QuickBooks has two other built-in invoice formats: Professional (top) and Service (bottom). The only difference between these two forms is that the Service Invoice includes a field for P.O.

Figures 13 & 14 QuickBooks also has two other built-in sales receipt formats: Professional (top) and Service (bottom). The only difference between these two forms is that the Service Sales Receipt includes a field for P.O.

9. For a sales receipt, choose one of the radio buttons at the bottom of the window:
   - **Group with other undeposited funds** records the amount of the sale in the Undeposited Funds account for depositing into another account later.
   - **Deposit To** enables you to choose an appropriate account from a drop-down list.
10. To create an iCal reminder for the invoice or sales receipt, turn on the Add to iCal check box.
11. To print the invoice or sales receipt with other invoices or sales receipts, turn on the To be printed check box.
12. To save the invoice or sales receipt and create another new one, click Next.

    Or

    To save the invoice or cash sale without creating another new one, click OK.

    QuickBooks makes an entry sound and saves the transaction.

✔ Tips

- The exact appearance of the Create Invoices or Enter Sales Receipt window depends on options you set when you used the New Company Setup Assistant, as discussed in **Chapter 1**, as well as whether you have customized the invoice or cash sale format. **Figures 3 and 4** show a Product invoice form and a Product sales receipt form. The other built-in invoice formats are Professional (**Figure 11**) and Service (**Figure 12**). Similarly, the other built-in sales receipt formats are Professional (**Figure 13**) and Service (**Figure 14**). If a field mentioned in these instructions does not appear on the form

Continued on next page...

Continued from previous page.

you see, don't worry about it. I explain how to create custom invoices and sales receipts in **Chapter 11**.

- It is not necessary to create a Customer: Job List entry for every customer. Instead, consider creating a single Customer:Job List entry called "Cash Sale" or "Counter Sale" and using that for sales receipts when you do not need to store customer-specific information.
- To change the title that appears at the top of the printed invoice or sales receipt, click the Change Title button. Then enter a new title in the Set Title dialog that appears (**Figure 15**) and click OK. Your change affects only the currently displayed invoice or sales receipt.
- A *T* appears in the Tax column beside each taxable item (**Figure 10**). You can change the taxability of an item for that invoice by clicking in the Tax column beside the item to toggle the *T* on or off.
- To insert a line item above the currently selected line item, choose Edit > Insert Line (**Figure 16**) or press ⌘Y. Then enter information on the new line that appears.
- To delete a line item, position the insertion point anywhere in the line and choose Edit > Delete Line (**Figure 16**) or press ⌘B. The line is removed.
- To include a subtotal beneath line items, insert a subtotal item. QuickBooks automatically calculates a subtotal of all items above the subtotal item (**Figure 17**). To use a subtotal item, it must exist in the Item List; I explain how to work with the Item List in **Chapter 2**.

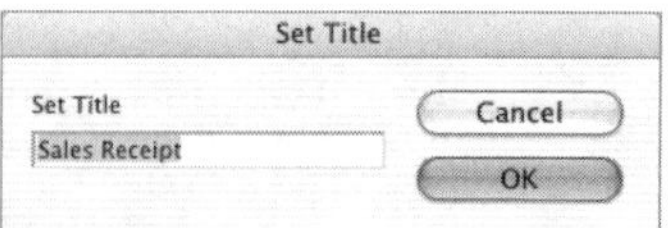

Figure 15 Use the Set Title dialog to change the title of the currently displayed invoice or sales receipt.

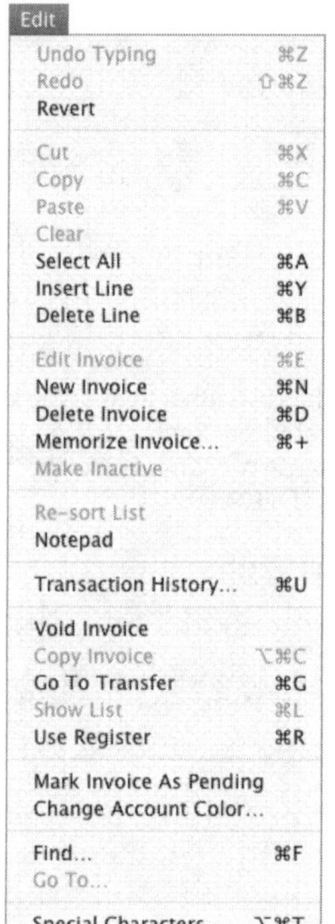

Figure 16 Use the Edit menu to insert or delete line items.

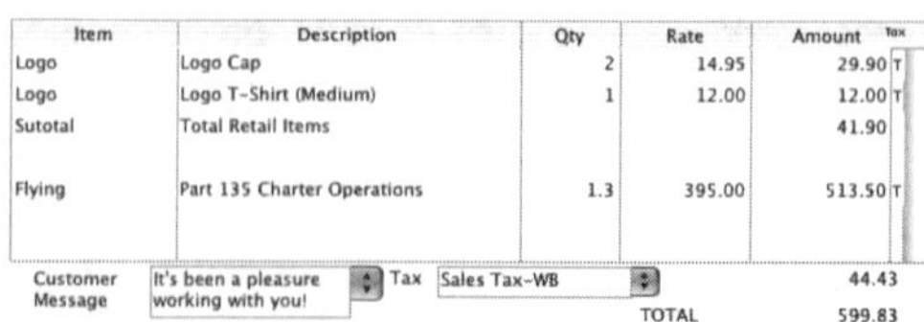

Item	Description	Qty	Rate	Amount	Tax
Logo	Logo Cap	2	14.95	29.90	T
Logo	Logo T-Shirt (Medium)	1	12.00	12.00	T
Sutotal	Total Retail Items			41.90	
Flying	Part 135 Charter Operations	1.3	395.00	513.50	T

Figure 17 A subtotal adds all the items above it.

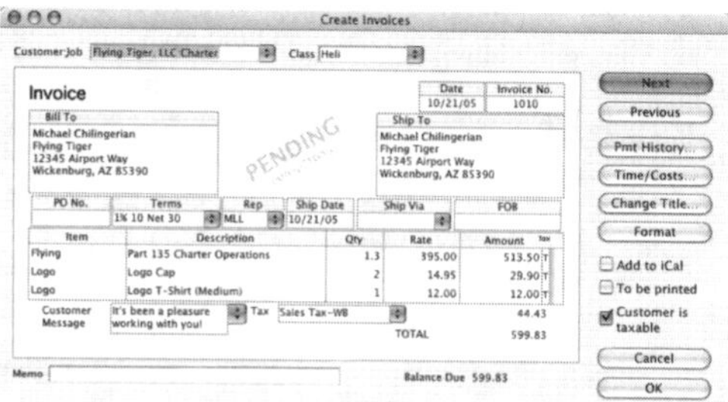

Figure 18 The word *Pending* appears between the Bill To and Ship To areas on an invoice you mark as pending.

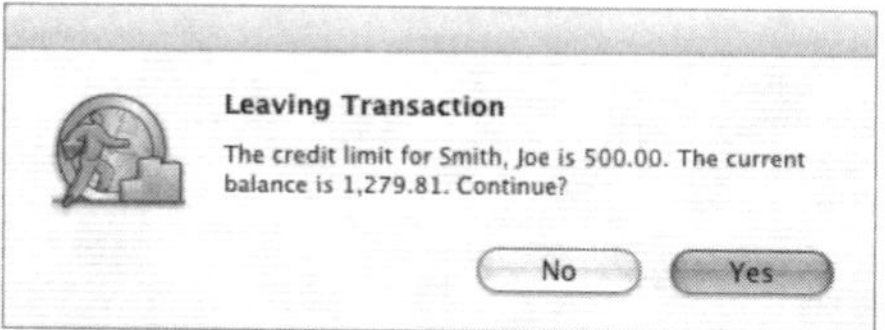

Figure 19 This dialog appears if an invoice would cause a customer to exceed its credit limit.

- You can mark an invoice or sales receipt as Pending if you want to create it but not post it. Choose Edit > Mark Invoice As Pending (**Figure 16**) or Edit > Mark Sales Receipt As Pending. The word *Pending* appears on the invoice (**Figure 18**) or sales receipt. To finalize and post a pending invoice or sales receipt, choose Edit > Mark Invoice As Final or Edit > Mark Sales Receipt As Final.
- If entering an invoice causes a customer to exceed its credit limit, a dialog like the one in **Figure 19** appears. You have two choices:
  - ▲ **No** returns you to the invoice so you can modify it.
  - ▲ **Yes** accepts the invoice, thus putting the customer over its credit limit.

  You could also open the Customer:Job List and modify the customer's record to increase its credit limit before accepting the invoice.

To include billable items, expenses, and time in an invoice or sales receipt

1. Follow steps 1 through 10 in the previous section to create an invoice or enter a sales receipt.
2. Click the Time/Costs button. The Choose Billable Time and Costs dialog appears. This window has three panes that display billable time and costs for the customer.
3. To include billable items in the invoice or sales receipt, click the Items button (**Figure 20**). Click in the Use column to place a check mark beside each item you want to include.
4. To include billable expenses in the invoice or sales receipt, click the Expenses button (**Figure 21**). Click in the Use column to place a check mark beside each expense you want to include. To apply a markup amount or percentage to the expense, enter a value or percentage in the Markup Amount or % box and choose an account from the Markup Account drop-down list. If the expenses are taxable, be sure to turn on the Selected expenses are taxable check box.
5. To include billable time in the invoice or sales receipt, click the Time button (**Figure 22**). Click in the Use column to place a check mark beside each activity you want to include.

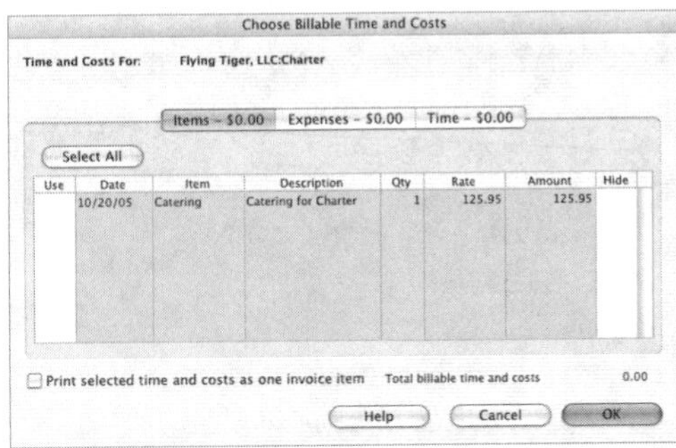

Figure 20 The Items pane of the Choose Billable Time and Costs dialog lists all items you have purchased for a specific customer.

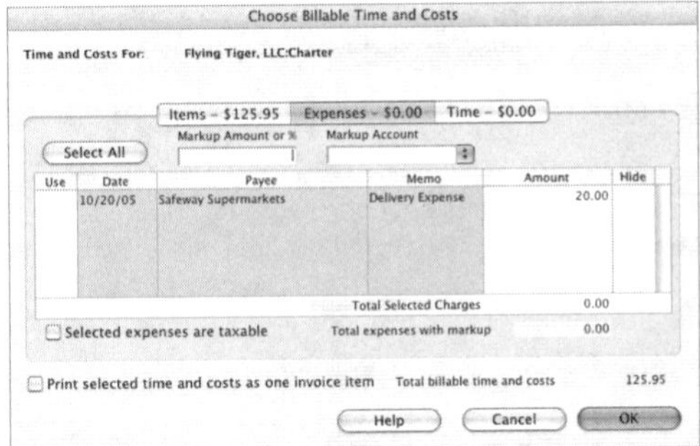

Figure 21 The Expenses pane of the Choose Billable Time and Costs dialog lists all expenses you have incurred for a specific customer.

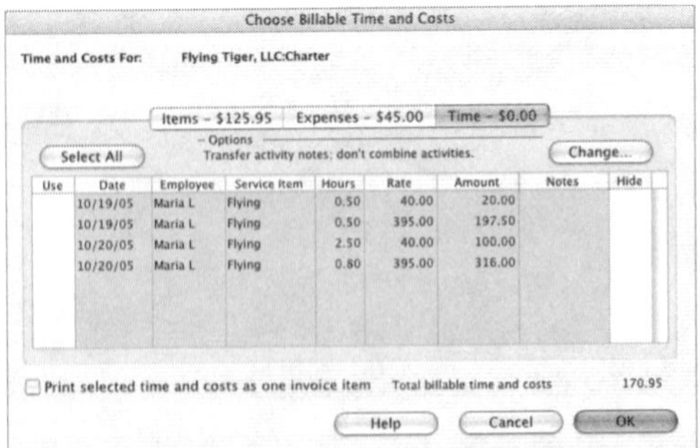

Figure 22 The Time pane of the Choose Billable Time and Costs dialog lists all time spent on service items for a specific customer.

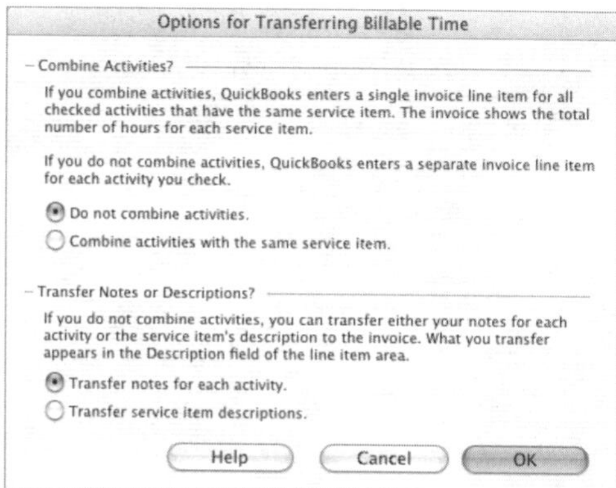

Figure 23 The Options for Transferring Billable Time dialog.

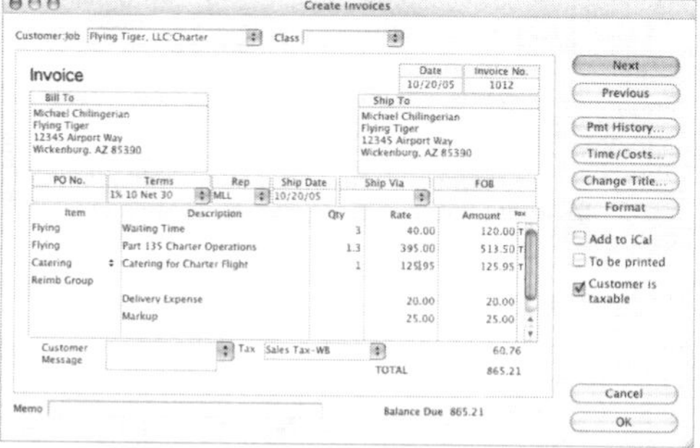

Figure 24 The billable items, expenses, and time in Figures 20, 21, and 22 added to an invoice.

6. To set options for how billable time will appear on the invoice or sales receipt, click the Change button in the Time tab to display the Options for Transferring Billable Time dialog (**Figure 23**). Select one of the Combine Activities? radio buttons and click OK:
   - ▲ **Do not combine activities** enters a separate line item for each activity. If you choose this option, you can then select one of the Transfer Notes or Descriptions? options: **Transfer notes for each activity** includes an activity's notes in the line item and **Transfer service item descriptions** includes an activity's service item description in the line item.
   - ▲ **Combine activities with the same service item** creates a single line item for all checked activities with the same service item. **Figure 24** shows an example of an invoice with this option set.
7. To include all selected time and costs as one line item on the invoice or sales receipt, turn on the Print selected time and costs as one invoice item check box.
8. Click OK. The item(s) you selected are added to the invoice or sales receipt (**Figure 24**).
9. Follow steps 11 and 12 in the previous section to complete the entry of the invoice or sales receipt.

Continued on next page...

Continued from previous page.

✔ Tips

- When you begin creating an invoice or sales receipt for a customer for which there are outstanding transactions for billable time or costs, a dialog like the one in **Figure 25** appears, making it difficult to forget to bill for these items.
- The Billable Time and Costs window displays only those items, expenses, or times that have already been entered and associated with a customer but have not yet been billed to the customer.
- I explain how to enter items in **Chapter 7**, expenses in **Chapter 4**, and time in **Chapter 6**.
- In steps 3, 4, and 5, you can click the Select All button to select all items in a list quickly.
- As you select items, expenses, or time in steps 3, 4, and 5, the amount to be billed for each type appears on the button. You can see this in **Figures 21 and 22**.
- To remove a billable item, expense, or time from the Choose Billable Time and Costs dialog, click in the Hide column beside the item. This does not delete the item from QuickBooks or remove the association between the item and the customer.

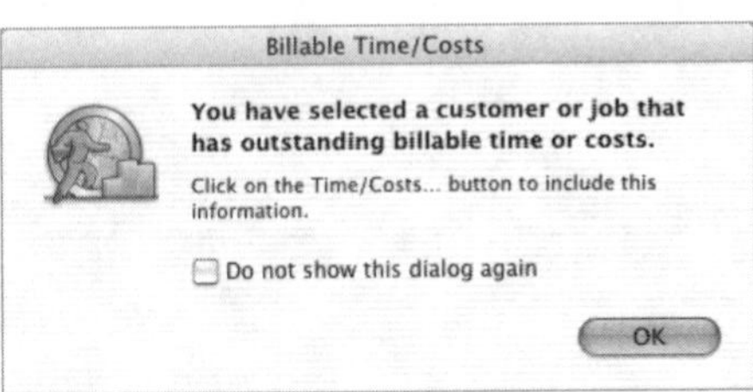

Figure 25 It's hard to forget to bill a customer when a dialog like this reminds you.

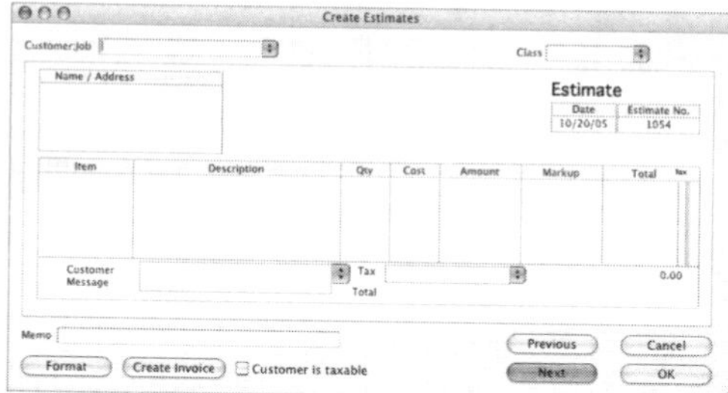

Figure 26 The Create Estimates window for a product or job estimate.

Using Estimates

Some businesses utilize estimates to give customers an idea of what a product or job will cost them. When the customer makes a purchase decision, all of the information for the purchase is already available.

With QuickBooks, it's just as easy to create an estimate as it is to create an invoice or sales receipt. Best of all, when the customer gives you the green light, you can quickly and easily convert an estimate to an invoice for billing purposes.

This part of the chapter explains how to create an estimate and how to turn an estimate into an invoice.

✔ Tip

- There can be only one outstanding estimate for each Customer:Job. To create more than one estimate for a customer, that customer must have more than one job. I explain how to add jobs for a customer in **Chapter 2**.

To create an estimate

1. Choose Customers > Create Estimates (**Figure 2**). The Create Estimates window appears (**Figure 26**).
2. Choose a customer from the Customer: Job drop-down list. The Name/Address field should fill in automatically with information for that customer.
3. If desired, choose a class from the Class drop-down list.
4. Enter information or change the entries in the following fields if necessary:
   - ▲ **Name/Address** is the customer's billing name and address.

Continued on next page...

Continued from previous page.

- **Date** is the estimate date. By default, the current date is automatically entered, but you can change the date if you need to.
- **Estimate No.** is the estimate number. This field is automatically incremented by one from the previous estimate.

5. Choose the name of an item to be included in the estimate from the Item drop-down list (**Figure 27**). The Description, Cost, Amount, Markup, and Total fields fill in automatically (**Figure 28**), but you can change any of them except Amount if desired. Enter a quantity in the Qty field for the line to update the amount (**Figure 29**).
6. Repeat step 5 for each item you want to include on the estimate.
7. If the customer is required to pay sales tax, turn on the Customer is Taxable check box and choose the correct tax item or tax group from the Tax drop-down list. QuickBooks calculates the sales tax and total (**Figure 30**).
8. If desired, choose a message from the Customer Message drop-down list.
9. If desired, enter a note in the Memo field. Notes do not print on estimates.
10. To save the estimate and create another new one, click Next.

    Or

    To save the estimate without creating another new one, click OK.

    QuickBooks makes an entry sound and saves the estimate.

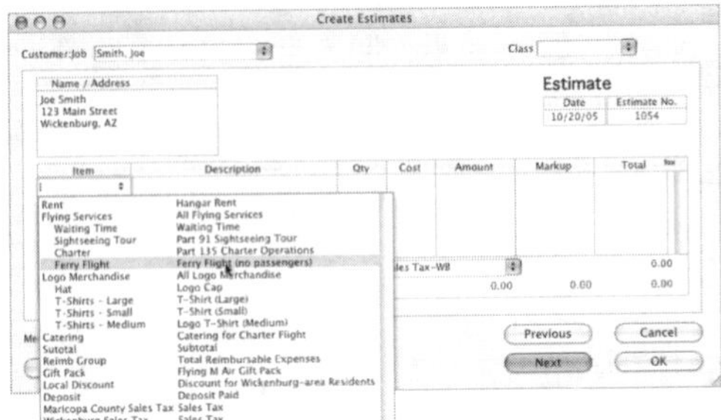

Figure 27 Choose an item to include in the estimate from the Item drop-down list.

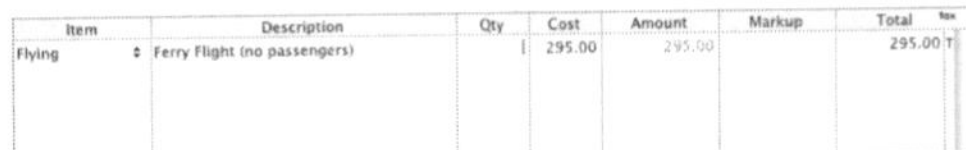

Figure 28 Details for the item appear in the estimate line.

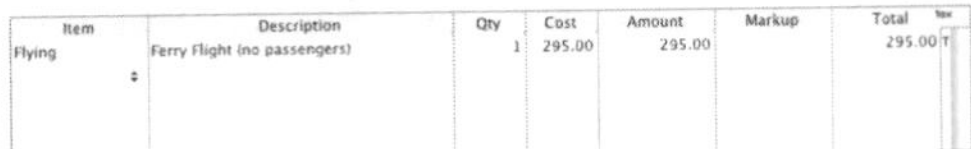

Figure 29 When you enter a quantity, QuickBooks updates the line total.

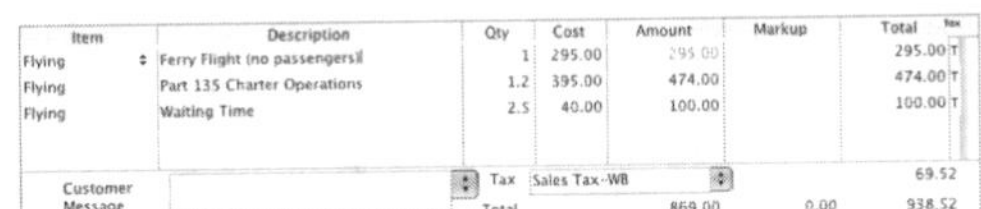

Figure 30 When you choose a tax item, QuickBooks calculates sales tax and an estimate total.

✔ Tips

- The exact appearance of the Create Estimates window depends on whether you have customized the estimate format. If a field mentioned in these instructions does not appear on the form you see, don't worry about it. I explain how to create custom estimates in **Chapter 11**.
- In step 5, QuickBooks displays cost and markup values from information you entered for the item when you added it to the Item list. If an item does not have a cost—for example, a service item that is performed by an employee rather than a subcontractor—the markup column may be blank (**Figures 28** through **30**).
- A *T* appears in the Tax column beside each taxable item (**Figure 30**). You can change the taxability of an item for that estimate by clicking in the Tax column beside the item to toggle the *T* on or off.
- To insert a line item above the currently selected line item, choose Edit > Insert Line (**Figure 16**) or press ⌘Y. Then enter information on the new line that appears.
- To delete a line item, position the insertion point anywhere in the line and choose Edit > Delete Line (**Figure 16**) or press ⌘B. The line is removed.
- To include a subtotal beneath line items, insert a subtotal item. QuickBooks automatically calculates a subtotal of all items above the subtotal item. To use a subtotal item, it must exist in the Item List; I explain how to work with the Item List in **Chapter 2**.

To create an invoice based on an estimate

1. Choose Customers > Create Estimates (**Figure 2**) to display the Create Estimates window (**Figure 26**).
2. Click the Previous button to scroll through existing estimates until you see the one you want to turn into an invoice (**Figure 31**).
3. Click the Create Invoice button.
4. A dialog like the one in **Figure 32** appears. Click OK.
5. Make changes as necessary to information in the Create Invoices window that appears (**Figure 33**).

✔ Tips

- If you're not sure what to do in step 5, consult the section titled "To create an invoice or enter a cash sale" earlier in this chapter.
- When you create an invoice based on an estimate, the original estimate remains in QuickBooks. You can use it to create additional invoices—for example, for recurring services—or you can delete it if you need to create a new estimate for the Customer:Job.

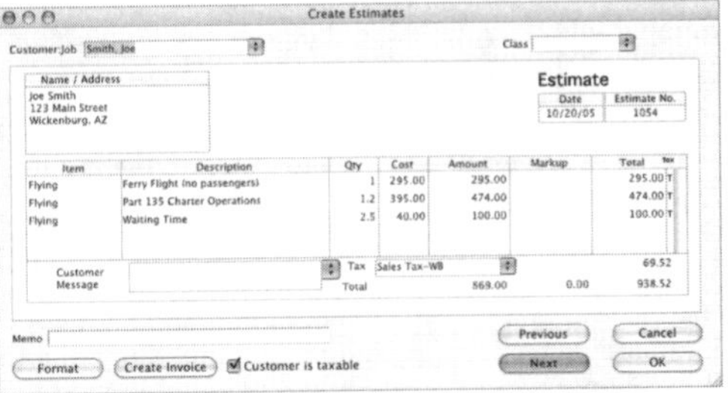

Figure 31 A completed estimate can be modified or used as the basis of an invoice.

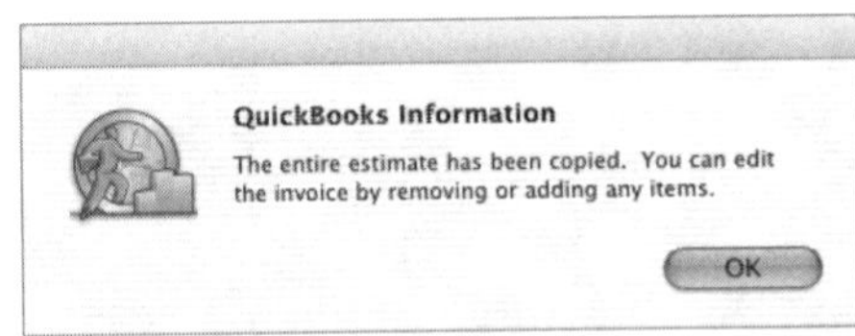

Figure 32 When you click the Create Invoice button, QuickBooks tells you that it has copied all information to an invoice form.

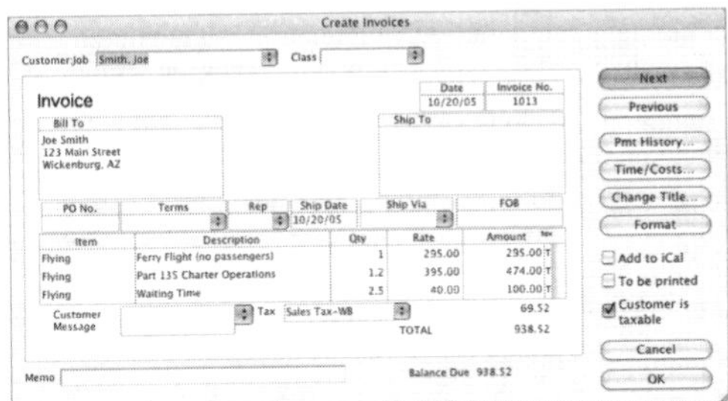

Figure 33 An invoice based on the estimate in **Figure 31**.

Working with Invoices, Sales Receipts, & Estimates

When you create an invoice, sales receipt, or estimate, it isn't engraved in stone. You can modify or delete it at any time. QuickBooks automatically makes all the necessary changes to affected accounts and balances.

✔ Tip

- I explain how to print invoices, sales receipts, and estimates in **Chapter 10**.

To view an invoice, sales receipt, or estimate

1. Choose a command from the Customers menu (**Figure 2**) to display the appropriate window:
   - **Create Invoices** displays the Create Invoices window (**Figure 3**).
   - **Enter Sales Receipts** displays the Enter Sales Receipt window (**Figure 4**).
   - **Create Estimates** displays the Create Estimates window (**Figure 26**).
2. Click the Previous button to scroll through existing invoices, sales receipts, or estimates until you see the one you want to view.

To modify or delete an invoice, sales receipt, or estimate

1. Display the invoice, sales receipt, or estimate you want to modify or delete.
2. Make changes as desired to the information in the form and click OK. The changes are saved.

   Or

   Choose Edit > Delete Invoice (**Figure 16**), Edit > Delete Sales Receipt (**Figure 34**), or Edit > Delete Estimate (**Figure 35**), or press ⌘D. Then click OK in the Delete Transaction confirmation dialog that appears (**Figure 36**).

✔ Tip

- Choosing Edit > Void Invoice, Edit >Void Sales Receipt, or Edit > Void Estimate in step 2 marks the transaction as void (**Figure 37**) but does not remove a record of it from QuickBooks.

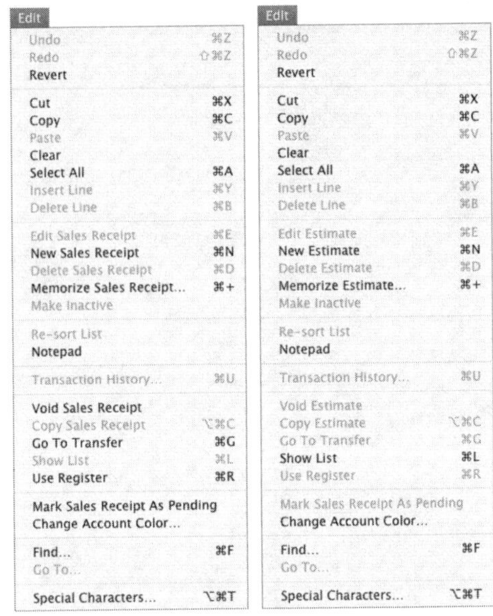

Figures 34 & 35 The Edit menu when a cash sale is displayed (left) and when an estimate is displayed (right).

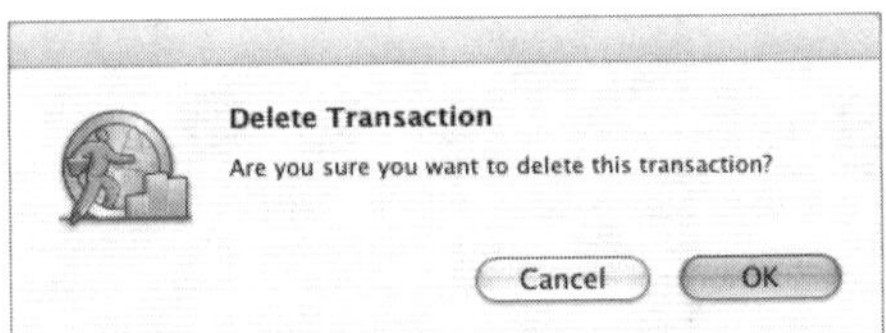

Figure 36 The Delete Transaction dialog confirms that you really do want to delete a transaction.

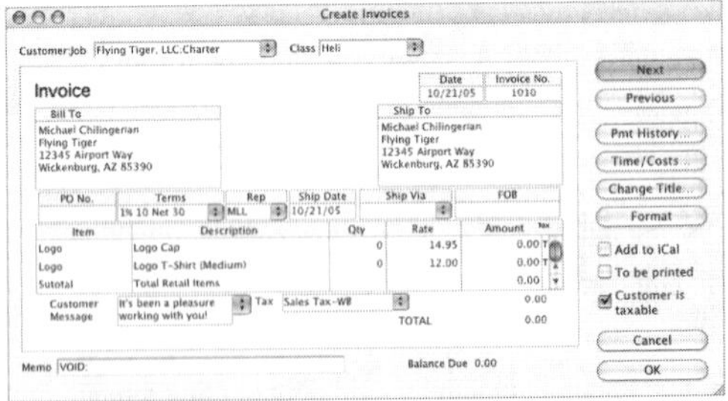

Figure 37 When you mark a transaction as void, the values change to zeros and the word *VOID* appears in the Memo field.

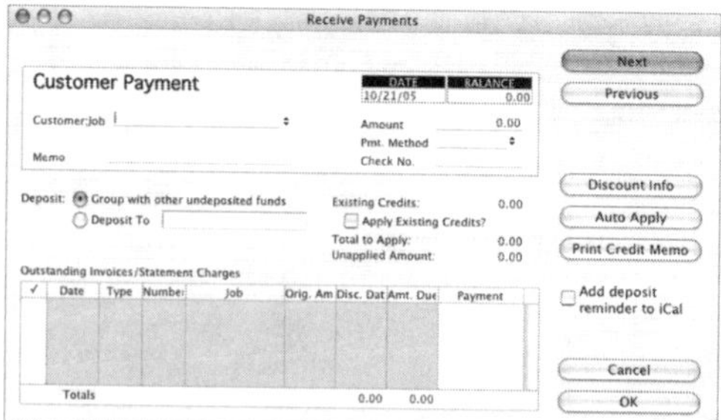

Figure 38 The Receive Payments window.

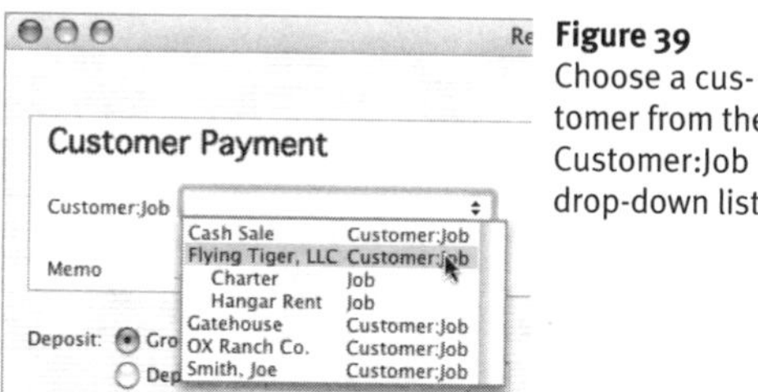

Figure 39 Choose a customer from the Customer:Job drop-down list.

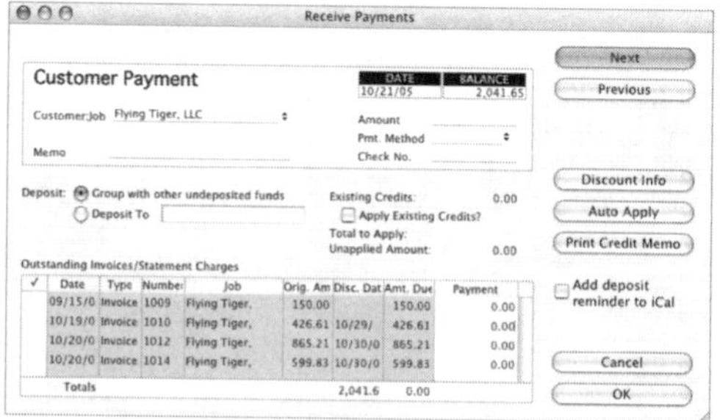

Figure 40 All open invoices for the customer you chose appear in the bottom of the window.

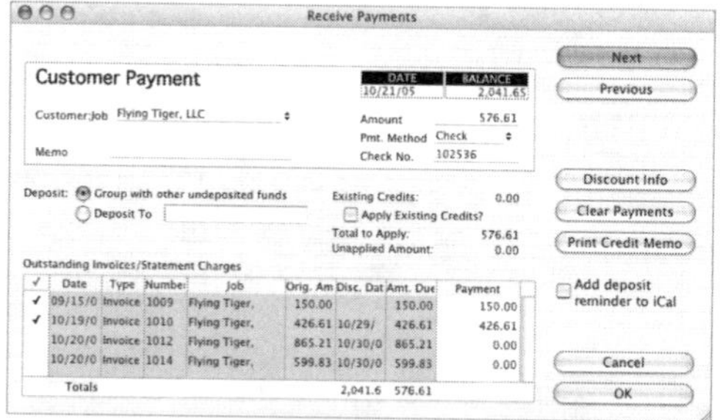

Figure 41 Enter payment information at the top of the window.

Receiving Payments

When you receive payments from a customer, you must apply those payments to outstanding invoices. This reduces the accounts receivable balance for the customer's account to accurately reflect what the customer owes you after making payments.

This part of the chapter explains how to use the Receive Payments window to apply payments to invoices. It also explains how to apply existing credits and discounts for early payments.

To apply a payment to open invoices

1. Choose Customers > Receive Payments (**Figure 2**) to display the Receive Payments window (**Figure 38**).
2. Choose the name of the customer or job from the Customer:Job drop-down list (**Figure 39**). A list of open invoices appears at the bottom of the window (**Figure 40**).
3. Fill in fields at the top of the window (**Figure 41**):
   - ▲ **Date** is the date payment receipt date.
   - ▲ **Amount** is the amount of the payment. This amount also appears in the Total to Apply area in the middle of the window.
   - ▲ **Pmt. Method** is payment method. Choose an option from the drop-down list, which includes all items on the Payment Method List.
   - ▲ **Check No.** is the number of the check used for payments made by check.
   - ▲ **Memo** is an optional note you can include about the payment.

Continued on next page...

Continued from previous page.

4. Select one of the Deposit radio buttons:
   - ▲ **Group with other undeposited funds** records the amount of the payment in the Undeposited Funds account for depositing into another account later.
   - ▲ **Deposit To** enables you to choose an account from a drop-down list.
5. If the customer has existing credits and you want to apply them to open invoices, turn on the Apply Existing Credits check box. This increases the Total to Apply amount in the middle of the window.
6. If necessary, click in the ✓ column at the bottom of the window to toggle check marks beside invoices you want to apply the payment to. QuickBooks distributes the payment among invoices and displays amounts in the Payment column (**Figure 41**). You can modify amounts if necessary to redistribute payments.
7. If the customer is eligible for a discount on an early payment of an invoice, click the Discount Info button. The Discount Information dialog appears (**Figure 42**). Check or change information in two fields and click OK:
   - ▲ **Discount** is the discount amount. QuickBooks automatically calculates applicable discounts based on payment terms and the payment date, but you can override this amount by entering a different amount.
   - ▲ **Discount Account** is the account the discount should be recorded in.

   Figure 43 shows what the Receive Payments window might look like if a customer paid more than the amount due after a discount was applied.
8. Click OK to save the payment info.

Figure 42 The Discount Information dialog enables you to enter a discount amount and account for the customer.

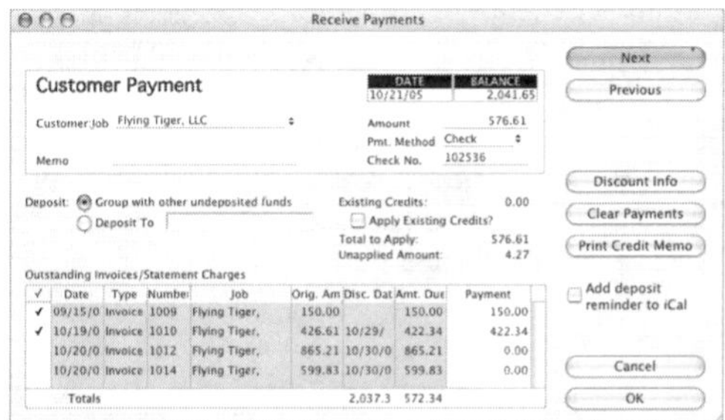

Figure 43 When a customer pays more than it owes, an unapplied amount appears in the middle of the window.

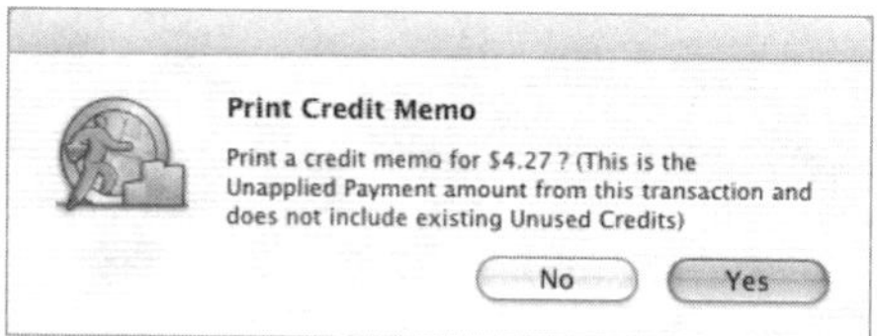

Figure 44 Click Yes in this dialog to print a credit memo.

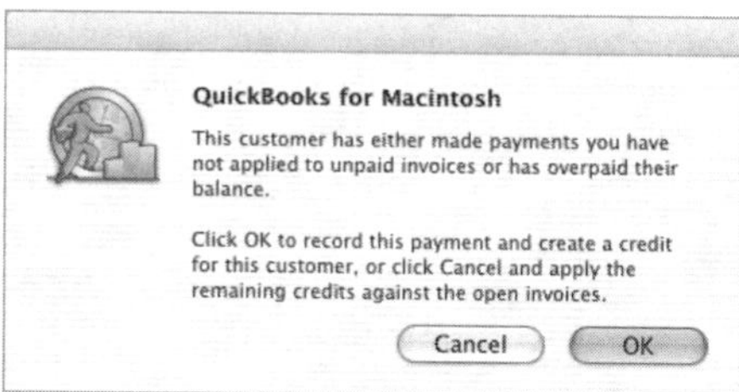

Figure 45 If a payment includes unapplied credits, QuickBooks tells you. You can click OK to create a credit for the customer.

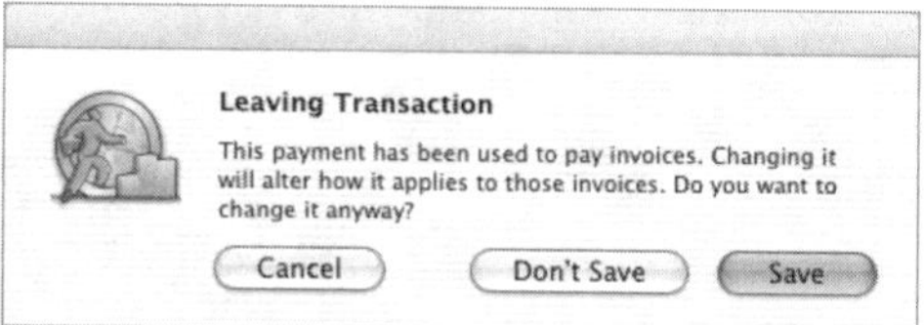

Figure 46 QuickBooks warns you when a change to a transaction will affect other transactions.

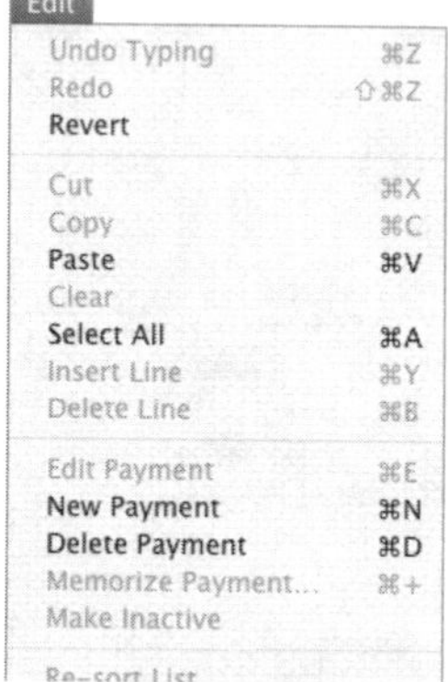

Figure 47 The Edit menu when the Receive Payments window is open.

✔ Tips

- After step 7, you can print a credit memo for an overpayment. Click the Print Credit Memo button and click Yes in the dialog that appears (**Figure 44**). Then follow the instructions in **Chapter 10** to finish printing the credit memo.
- After step 8, if the Receive Payments window included unapplied credits (**Figure 43**), a dialog like the one in **Figure 45** appears. Click OK to generate a credit for the customer.

To modify or delete a payment

1. Choose Customers > Receive Payments (**Figure 2**) to display the Receive Payments window (**Figure 38**).
2. Click the Previous button to scroll through existing payments until you see the one you want to modify or delete.
3. To modify the payment, make changes as desired and click OK. If a dialog like the one in **Figure 46** appears, click Yes. The changes are saved.

   Or

   To delete the payment, choose Edit > Delete Payment (**Figure 47**), or press ⌘D. If a dialog like the one in **Figure 48** appears, click OK. The payment is deleted.

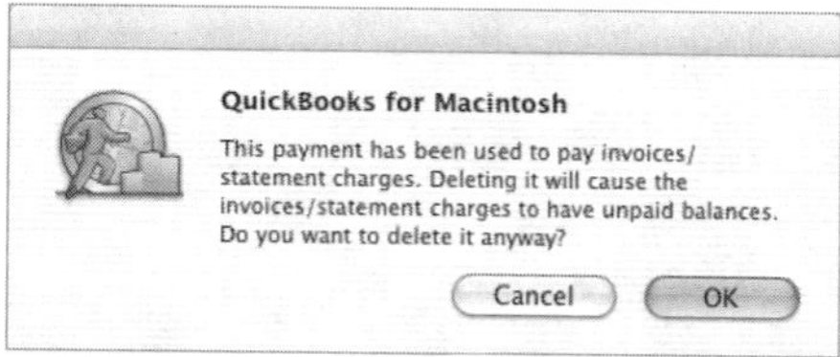

Figure 48 QuickBooks also warns you when deleting a payment will affect other transactions.

To view an invoice's payment history

1. Choose Customers > Create Invoices (**Figure 2**) or press ⌘ I to display the Create Invoices window (**Figure 3**).
2. Click the Previous button to scroll through existing invoices until you see the one you want to view payment history for (**Figure 49**).
3. Click the Pmt History button.
4. The Transaction History – Invoice dialog appears (**Figure 50**). It displays information about payments made on the invoice. Click a button to proceed:
   - ▲ **Print** prints the transaction history. I tell you more about printing reports in **Chapter 10**.
   - ▲ **Edit Invoice** displays the invoice so you can make changes to it. I explain how to modify invoices earlier in this chapter.
   - ▲ **Close** closes the Transaction History – Invoice window.
   - ▲ **Go To** displays the Receive Payments window for the payment selected in the bottom half of the window.

✔ Tip

- If the invoice you selected in step 2 does not have any payment history, a dialog like the one in **Figure 51** appears when you click the Pmt History button. Click OK to dismiss it.

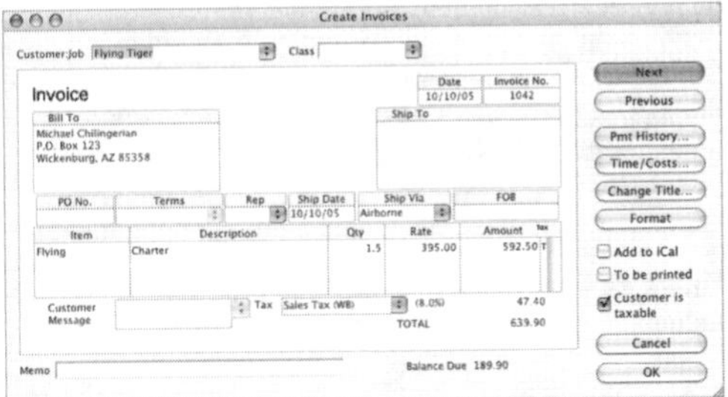

Figure 49 You can identify an invoice that has a payment history by comparing the invoice total to the balance due at the bottom of the invoice. If they're different, payments have been made.

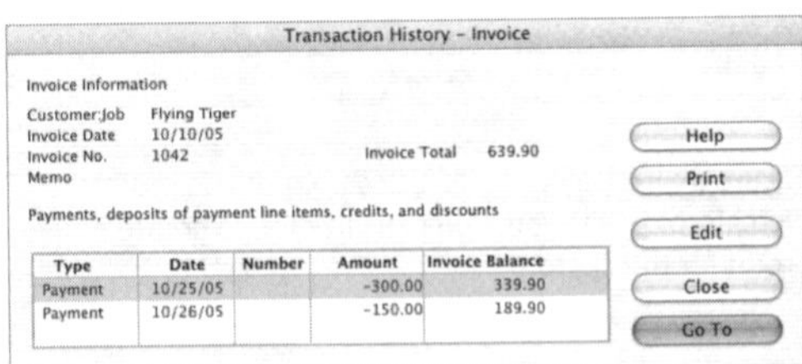

Figure 50 The Transaction history for an invoice.

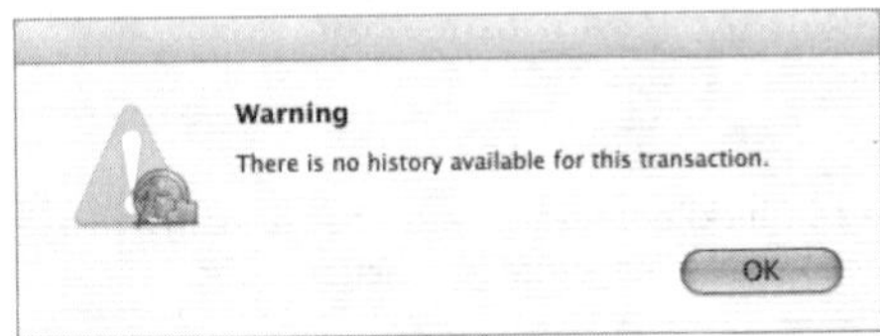

Figure 51 If an invoice has no payment history, this dialog appears.

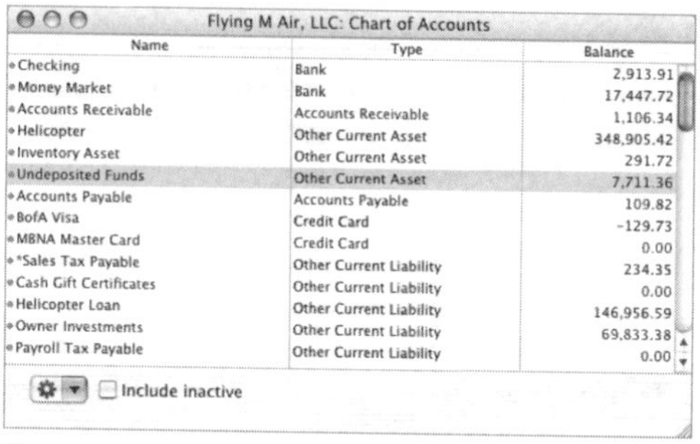

Flying M Air, LLC: Chart of Accounts

Name	Type	Balance
Checking	Bank	2,913.91
Money Market	Bank	17,447.72
Accounts Receivable	Accounts Receivable	1,106.34
Helicopter	Other Current Asset	348,905.42
Inventory Asset	Other Current Asset	291.72
Undeposited Funds	Other Current Asset	7,711.36
Accounts Payable	Accounts Payable	109.82
BofA Visa	Credit Card	-129.73
MBNA Master Card	Credit Card	0.00
*Sales Tax Payable	Other Current Liability	234.35
Cash Gift Certificates	Other Current Liability	0.00
Helicopter Loan	Other Current Liability	146,956.59
Owner Investments	Other Current Liability	69,833.38
Payroll Tax Payable	Other Current Liability	0.00

Include inactive

Figure 52 This example of the Chart of Accounts list window shows over $7,700 of Undeposited Funds.

Making Deposits

Chances are, you don't run to the bank to make a deposit every time a customer gives you money. Instead, you probably accumulate cash and check receipts and make deposits on a daily basis. Similarly, if your business accepts credit cards, funds from credit card transactions are likely to be deposited to your bank account every day or so.

As you accept payments, either through cash sales or the receipt of payments on customer accounts, you can use the Group with other undeposited funds radio button (**Figures 4 and 38**) to group payments in a sort of "holding account" within QuickBooks. This account, which is called the Undeposited Funds account (**Figure 52**), keeps track of money you receive until you actually deposit it.

When you take cash and checks to the bank, you can use the Make Deposits command to record them within QuickBooks as a deposit to your bank account. Likewise, when credit card receipts appear on your bank statement, you can record them within QuickBooks as deposits for the date they appear on the statement.

This part of the chapter explains how to use the Make Deposits command to record items in the Undeposited Funds account as deposits to a bank account.

✔ Tip

- Making deposits as instructed in this part of the chapter should make reconciling your bank statement to QuickBooks easy since each deposit on your bank statement should correspond to one in QuickBooks for the same bank account.

To deposit checks & cash

1. Gather together the cash and checks you want to deposit and prepare a deposit slip for your bank.
2. In QuickBooks, choose Banking > Make Deposits (**Figure 53**). The Payments to Deposit window appears. It lists all undeposited funds in order of payment method and date (**Figure 54**).
3. Click in the ✓ column to toggle check marks beside each item included in the deposit. **Figure 55** shows all items checked off except one.
4. Click OK. The Make Deposits window appears. It lists all of the items you checked in step 3 (**Figure 56**).
5. Choose the bank account that the deposit will be made to from the Deposit To drop-down list.
6. Enter the date of the deposit in the Date box.
7. Click OK. QuickBooks creates an entry that transfers the amount of the deposit from the Undeposited Funds account to the bank account you chose. The items you selected do not appear in the Payments to Deposit window the next time it is displayed (**Figure 57**).
8. Make the deposit at the bank.

✓ Tip

- After step 4, the Deposit Total amount at the bottom of the Make Deposits window (**Figure 56**) should match the amount of the deposit on the deposit slip you created in step 1.

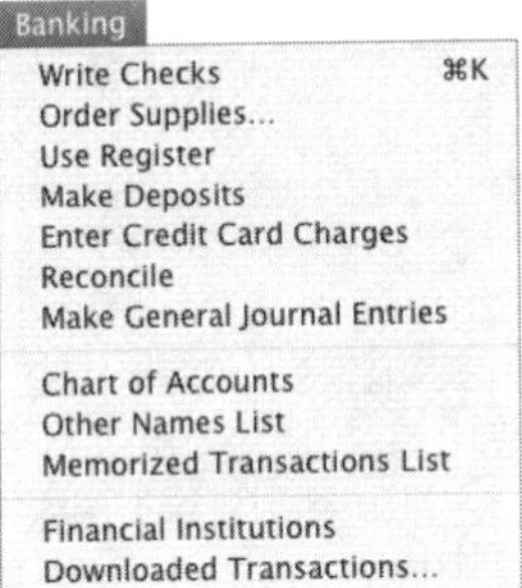

Figure 53 The Banking menu includes commands for banking activities.

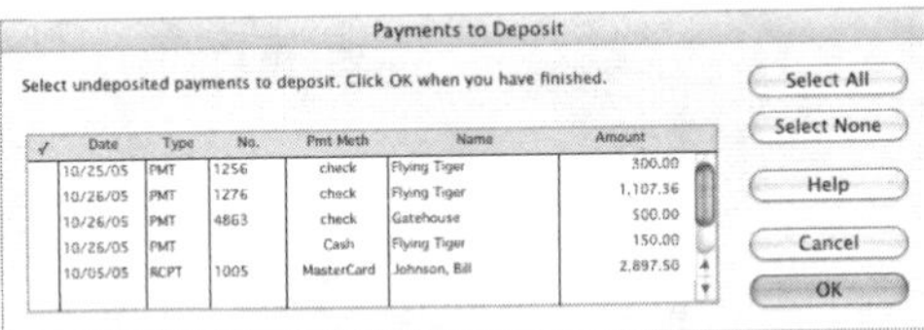

Figure 54 The Payments to Deposit window shows all undeposited funds.

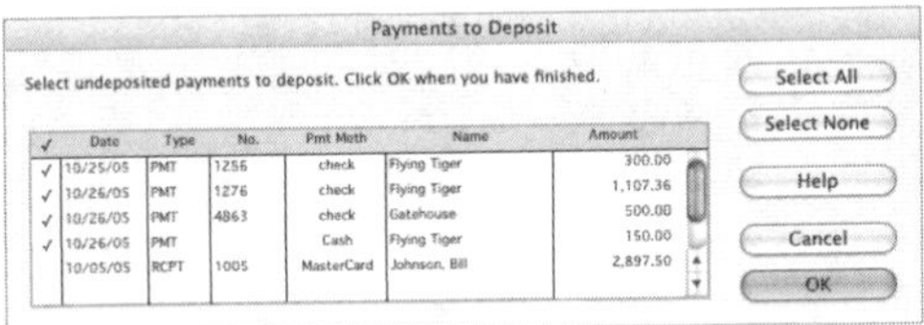

Figure 55 Check off the items you want to include in your deposit.

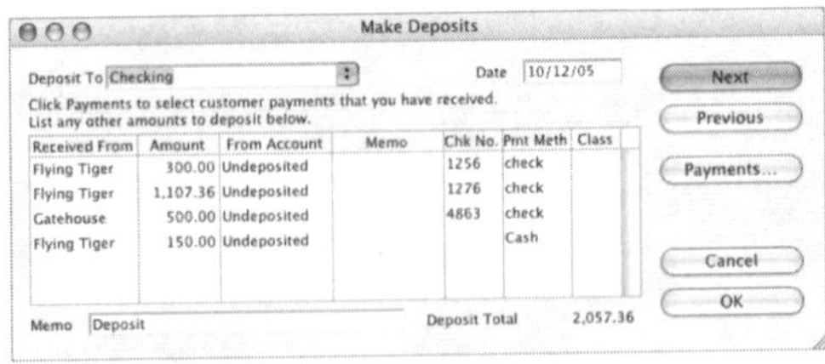

Figure 56 The items you checked appear in the Make Deposits window.

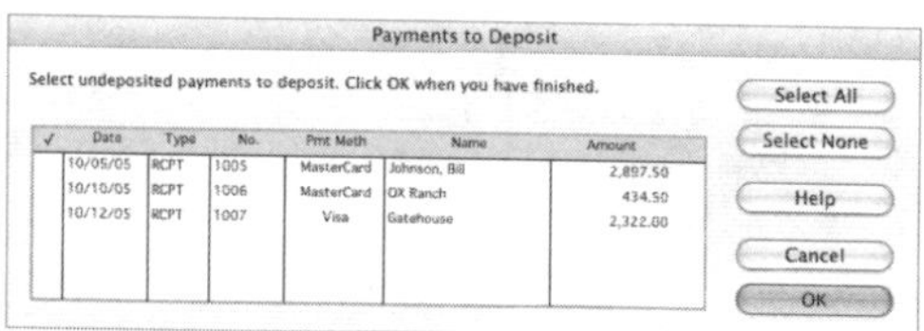

Figure 57 Here's the Payments to Deposit window from **Figures 54 and 55** after making the deposit shown in **Figure 56**.

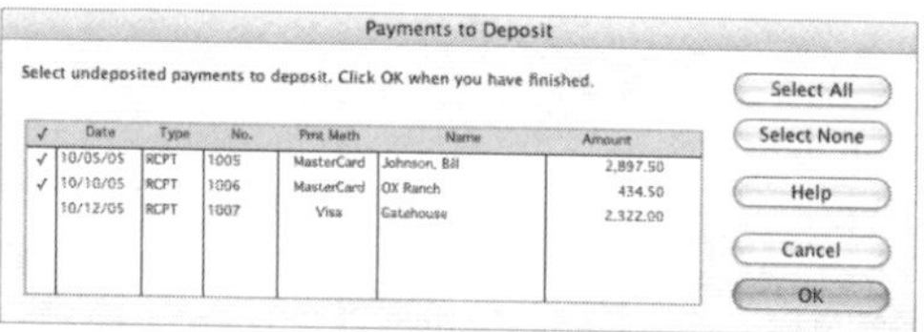

Figure 58 In this example, two credit card payments are selected for deposit.

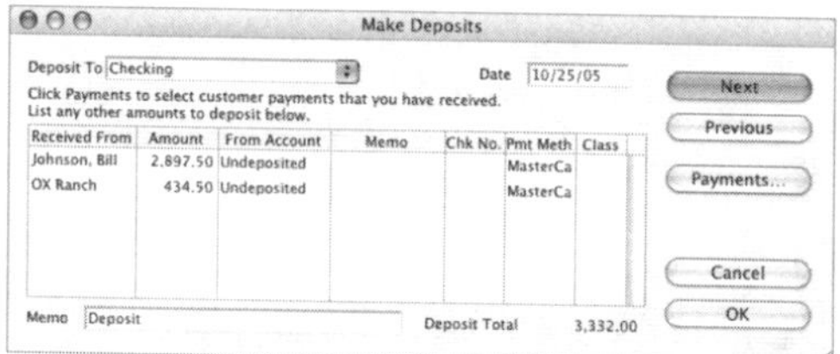

Figure 59 The payments appear in the Make Deposits window.

To record credit card deposits

1. Obtain the daily credit card statement or batch report listing all credit card deposits made for a specific date.
2. In QuickBooks, choose Banking > Make Deposits (**Figure 52**). The Payments to Deposit window appears. It lists all undeposited funds in order of payment method and date (**Figure 57**).
3. Click in the ✓ column to toggle check marks beside each item included in the deposit. **Figure 58** shows two credit card transactions checked off.
4. Click OK. The Make Deposits window appears. It lists all of the items you checked in step 3 (**Figure 59**).
5. Choose the bank account that the deposit was made to from the Deposit To drop-down list.
6. Enter the date of the deposit in the Date box.
7. Click OK. QuickBooks creates an entry that transfers the amount of the deposit from the Undeposited Funds account to the bank account you chose. The items you selected do not appear in the Payments to Deposit window the next time it is displayed.

✔ Tip

- After step 4, the Deposit Total amount at the bottom of the Make Deposits window (**Figure 59**) should match the amount of the deposit on the credit card statement or batch report you obtained in step 1.

To modify or delete a deposit

1. Choose Banking > Make Deposits (**Figure 52**).
2. If the Payments to Deposit window appears, click Cancel.

   The Make Deposits window appears, but without any payments listed (**Figure 60**).
3. Choose the account the deposit you want to modify or delete was made to from the Deposit To drop-down list.
4. Click the Previous button to scroll through existing deposits until you see the one you want to modify or delete.
5. To modify the deposit, make changes as desired and click OK. If a dialog like the one in **Figure 61** appears, click Yes. The changes are saved.

   Or

   To delete the deposit, choose Edit > Delete Deposit (**Figure 62**), or press ⌘ D. If a dialog like the one in **Figure 63** appears, click OK. The deposit is deleted.

✔ Tips

- In step 5, you can use commands under the Edit menu (**Figure 62**) to insert or remove deposit line items.
- Choosing Edit > Void Deposit in step 5 marks the deposit as void but does not remove a record of it from QuickBooks.

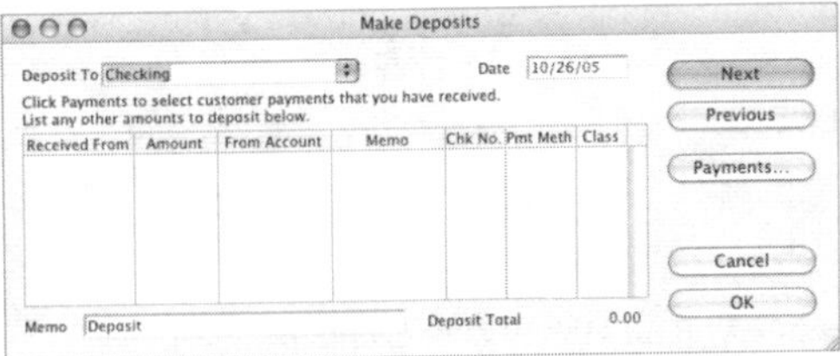

Figure 60 The Make Deposits window without any payments listed.

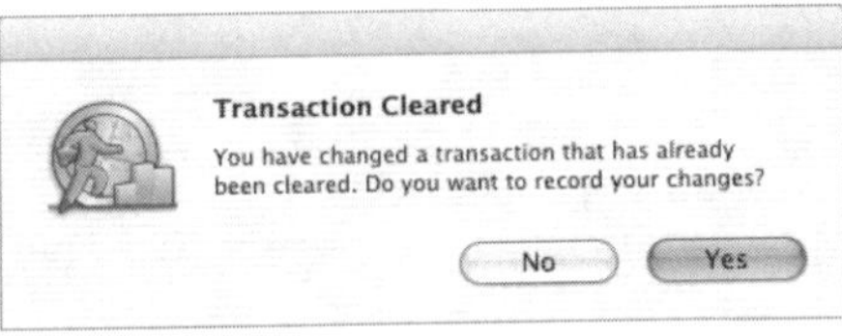

Figure 61 This dialog may appear if you modify a deposit and save your changes.

Figure 62 The Edit menu when a Deposit is selected.

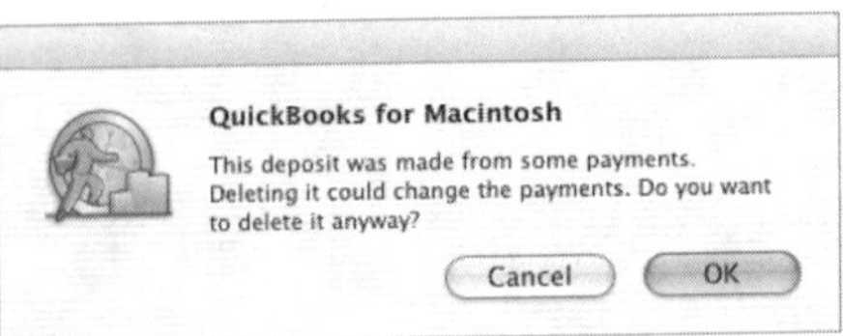

Figure 63 This dialog appears when you delete a deposit.

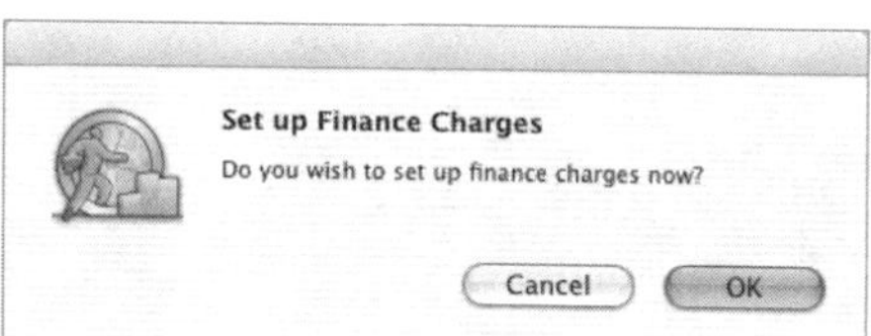

Figure 64 This dialog appears the first time you use the Assess Finance Charges command if finance charges have not already been set up.

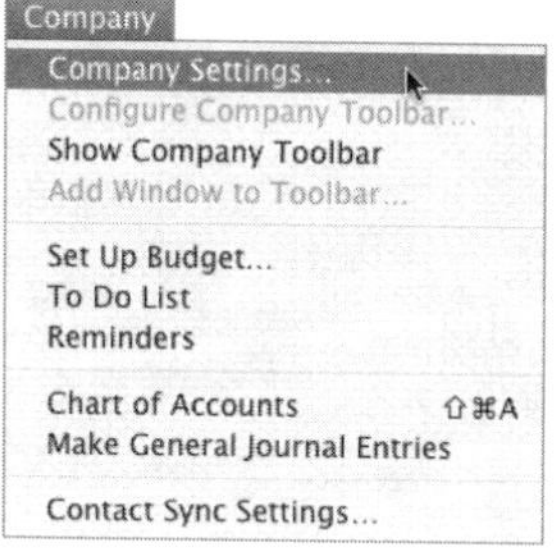

Figure 65 Choose Company Settings from the Company menu.

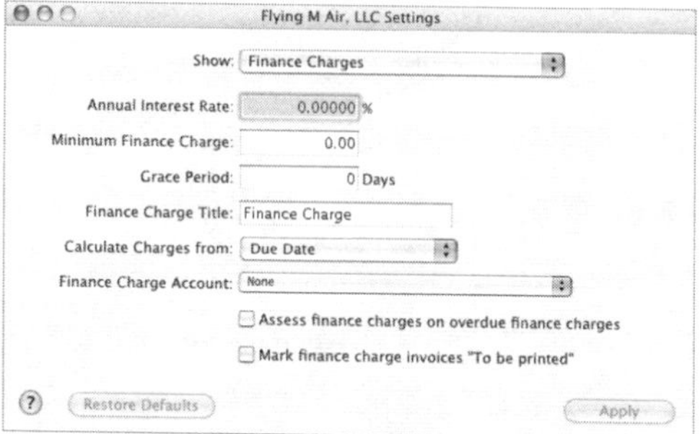

Figure 66 Finance Charges settings.

Assessing Finance Charges

Many businesses assess finance charges on unpaid invoice balances. This encourages customers to pay in a timely manner and compensates businesses for the cost of extending credit.

QuickBooks can calculate finance charges for you based on criteria you enter. It can apply charges to customer accounts, thus increasing account balances.

This part of the chapter explains how to set up and assess finance charges with QuickBooks.

To set up finance charges

1. If you have never set up finance charges, choose Customers > Assess Finance Charges (**Figure 2**) and click OK in the dialog that appears (**Figure 64**).

   Or

   If you have already set up finance charges but want to check or change them, choose Company > Company Settings (**Figure 65**). Then choose Finance Charges from the Show pop-up menu in the settings dialog that appears.

   QuickBooks displays Finance Charges settings (**Figure 66**).

2. Set options as desired:

   ▲ **Annual Interest Rate** is the annual interest rate you want to apply, stated as a percentage.

   ▲ **Minimum Finance Charge** is the minimum amount of finance charge that should be applied, stated in dollars and cents.

Continued on next page...

Continued from previous page.

- **Grace Period** is the number of days between the invoice due date and the date on which finance charges are assessed. For example, if an invoice is due on the 15th and you allow a 3-day grace period, QuickBooks will not assess finance charges until the 18th.
- **Finance Charge Title** is the text that appears on the customer statement to identify finance charges.
- **Calculate Charges from** enables you to choose the date from which finance charges should be calculated. **Due Date** is the date payment is due as indicated on the invoice. **Invoice/ Billed Date** is the date of the invoice.
- **Finance Charge Account** is the account that income from finance charges should be recorded into. The pop-up menu (**Figure 67**) lists all accounts in your Chart of Accounts. Choosing New enables you to create a new account.
- **Assess finance charges on overdue finance charges** tells QuickBooks to include the balance of unpaid finance charges when calculating new finance charges due.
- **Mark finance charge invoices "To be printed"** includes invoices for finance charges in a list of invoices to be printed.

3. Click Apply.
4. Click the Settings window's close button to dismiss it.

✔ Tip

- If you have already set up finance charges, the dialog in **Figure 64** will not appear.

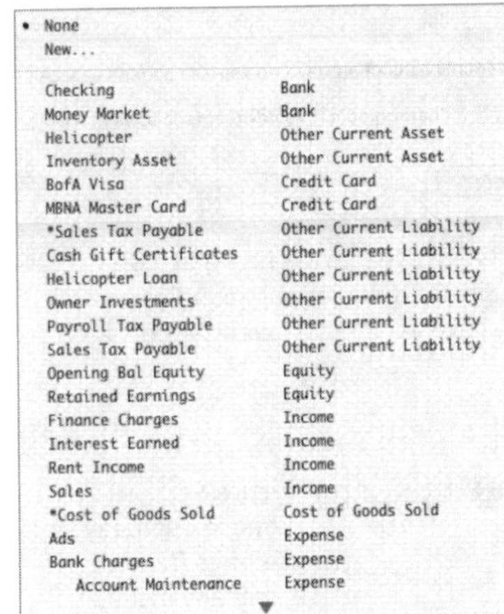

Figure 67 The Finance Charge Account pop-up menu includes all accounts created for your company.

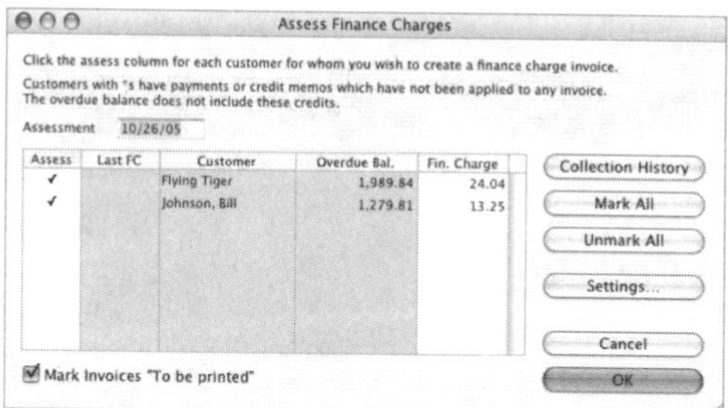

Figure 68 The Assess Finance Charges dialog.

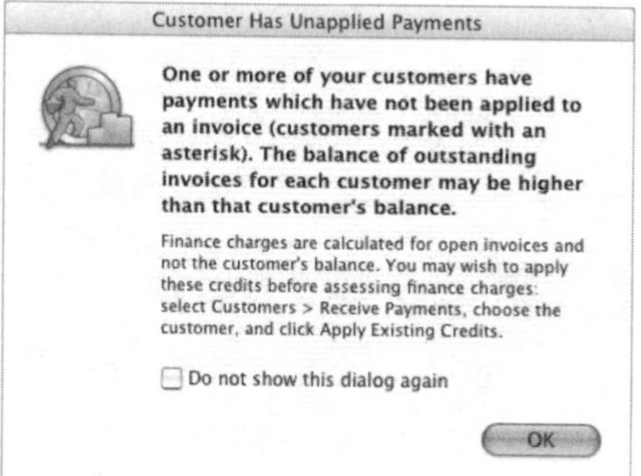

Figure 69 This dialog appears if one or more payments have not been properly applied to invoices.

To assess finance charges

1. Choose Customers > Assess Finance Charges (**Figure 2**).

   The Assess Finance Charges dialog appears (**Figure 68**). It summarizes overdue invoices on which finance charges should be assessed.

2. Enter the date for which you want to assess finance charges in the Assessment box.
3. Click in the Assess column to place a check mark beside each overdue invoice for which you want to assess finance charges.
4. If desired, edit any of the calculated amounts in the Fin. Charge column to change the amount of the finance charge.
5. To print finance charge invoices with other invoices you print, turn on the Mark Invoices "To be printed" check box.
6. Click OK. QuickBooks creates finance charge invoices for each charge it calculated and adds the amount of the finance charge to the customer's account balance.

✔ Tips

- If a dialog like the one in **Figure 64** appears after step 1, you have not yet set up finance charges. Follow the instructions in the section titled "To set up finance charges" earlier in this section.
- If a dialog like the one in **Figure 69** appears after step 1, some of the payments you recorded may not have been applied to a customer's invoice. If an asterisk appears beside any customer name, you should review payments you recorded for that customer to make sure they are properly applied to invoices.

Adjusting Customer Accounts

Invoices, payments, and finance charges, all of which are discussed earlier in this chapter, are three ways to affect the balance of a customer's account. But there are other ways:

- **Credit Memos**, which are normally issued when merchandise is returned or errors are made in an invoice, reduce the balance of a customer's account. **Refunds** work the same way, but instead of changing an account balance, they result in a check issued to the customer to refund amounts already paid.
- **Statement Charges** make it possible to add items to a customer's statement without creating an invoice. Statement charges are entered using QuickBooks's register window, which isn't quite as intuitive as its Create Invoices window.

This part of the chapter explains how to adjust a customer's account balance by creating credit memos and entering statement charges. Along the way, it explains how to issue refunds for amounts already paid.

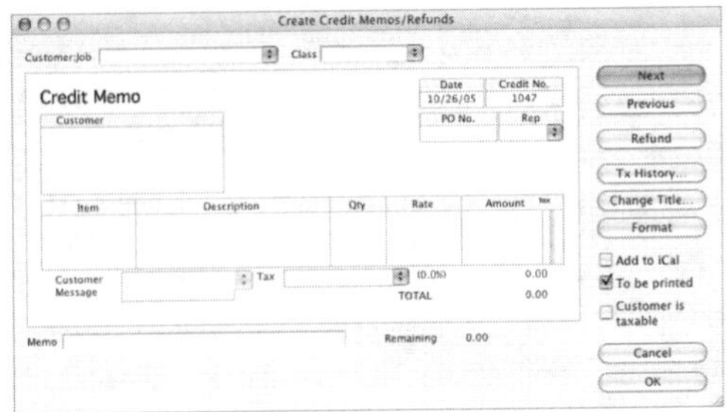

Figure 70 The Create Credit Memos/Refunds window.

To create a credit memo or refund

1. Choose Customers > Create Credit Memos/Refunds (**Figure 2**). The Create Credit Memos/Refunds window appears (**Figure 70**).
2. Choose a customer from the Customer: Job drop-down list. The Customer, Rep, and Tax fields should fill in automatically with information for that customer.
3. If desired, choose a class from the Class drop-down list.

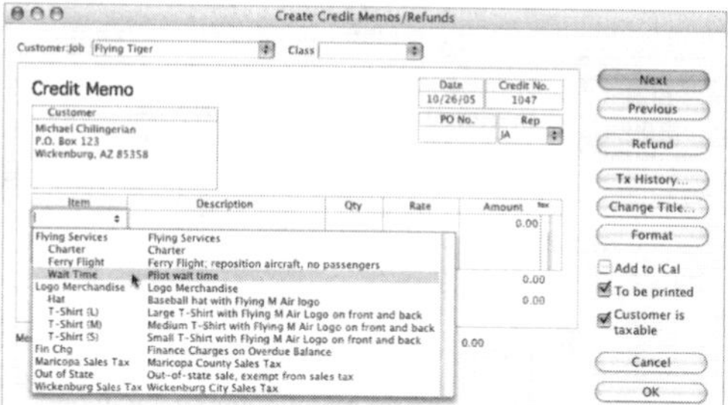

Figure 71 Choose an item to issue a credit or refund for from the Item drop-down list.

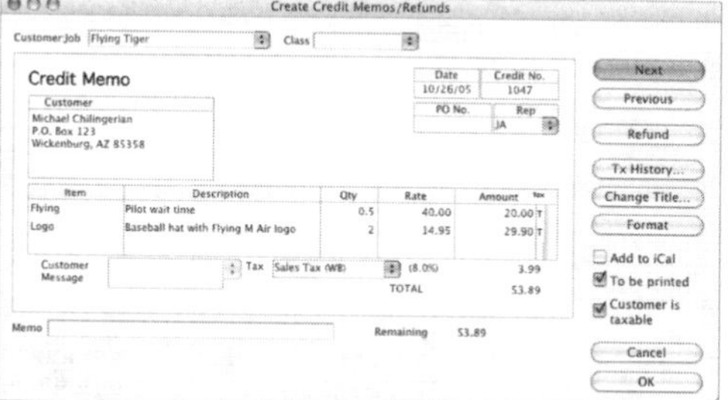

Figure 72 An example of a completed credit memo.

4. Enter information or change the entries in the following fields if necessary:
   - ▲ **Date** is the credit or refund date. By default, the current date is automatically entered, but you can change the date if you need to.
   - ▲ **Credit No.** is the credit or refund number. This field is automatically incremented by one from the previous form, so you should not need to change the number.
   - ▲ **PO No.** is the customer's purchase order number, if one was provided for the original sale.
   - ▲ **Rep** is the sales representative. This drop-down list displays initials for your employees.
   - ▲ **Customer** is the customer name and address.
5. Choose the name of an item you are issuing a credit or refund for from the Item drop-down list (**Figure 71**). The Description, Rate, and Amount fields fill in automatically, but you can change them if desired. Enter a quantity in the Qty field for the line to update the amount.
6. Repeat step 5 for each item you want to include on the credit memo or refund. **Figure 72** shows an example with two line items.
7. If the customer paid sales tax on any of the items, turn on the Customer is taxable check box and choose the correct tax item or tax group from the Tax drop-down list. QuickBooks calculates the sales tax and total.
8. If desired, choose a message from the Customer Message drop-down list.

Continued on next page...

Continued from previous page.

9. If you want to print a refund check for the amount of the credit memo, click the Refund button. QuickBooks displays the Write Checks window with the refund information already entered **(Figure 73)**. Select the correct account from the Bank Account drop-down list, turn on the To be printed check box, and click OK. QuickBooks makes an entry sound and dismisses the Write Checks window, returning you to the Create Credit Memos/Refunds window.

10. To print the credit memo with other items, turn on the To be printed check box.

11. Click OK. QuickBooks makes an entry sound and saves the transaction.

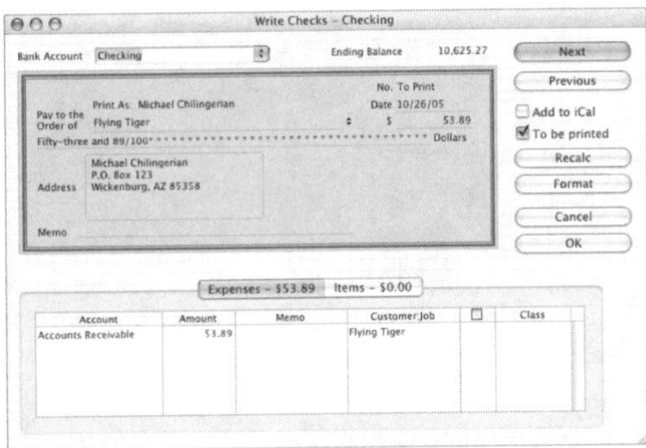

Figure 73 The Write Checks window with a check all prepared for a refund.

✔ Tips

- The exact appearance of the Create Credit Memos/Refunds window depends on options you set when you used the New Company Setup Assistant, as discussed in **Chapter 1**, as well as whether you have customized the credit memo format. **Figure 72** shows a Product credit memo form. The other built-in credit memo formats are Professional **(Figure 74)** and Service **(Figure 75)**. I explain how to create custom credit memos in **Chapter 11**.

- Most of the tips in the section titled "To create an invoice or enter a sales receipt" apply to creating credit memos. Review those tips to learn more about working with the Create Credit Memos/Refunds window and its options.

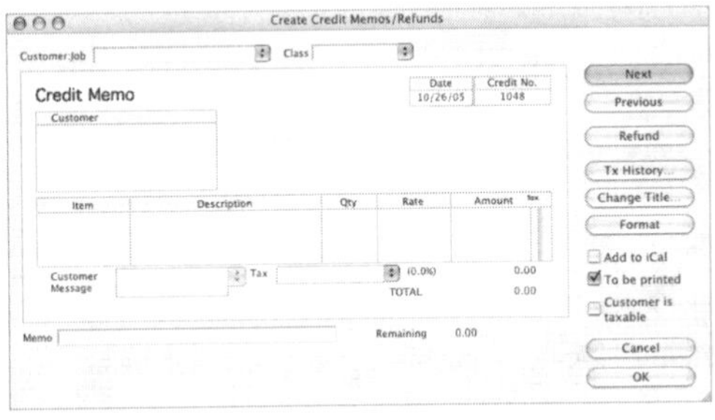

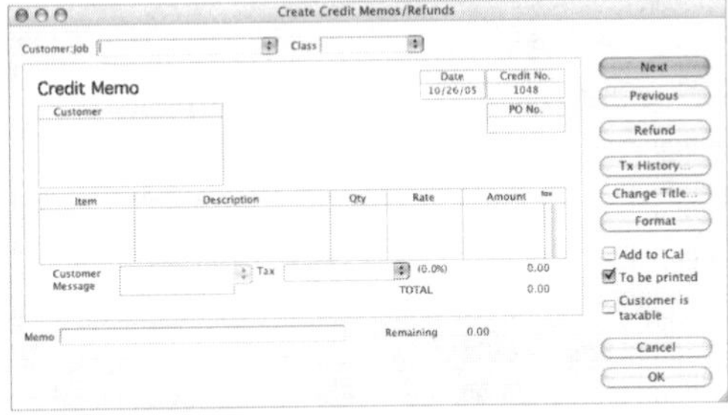

Figures 74 & 75 Two other versions of the Create Credit Memos/Refunds window: Professional (top) and Service (bottom).

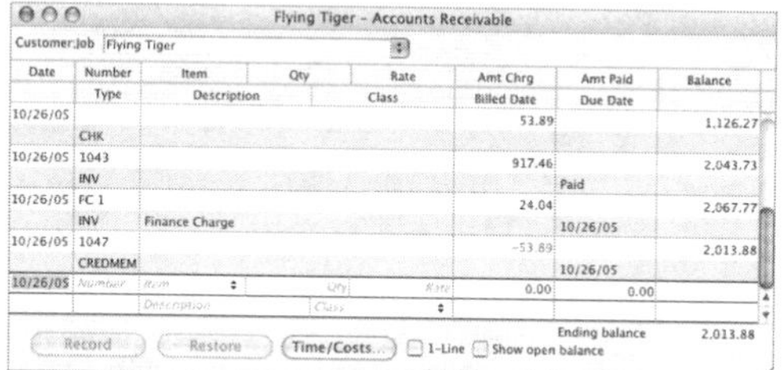

Figure 76 The Accounts Receivable register window.

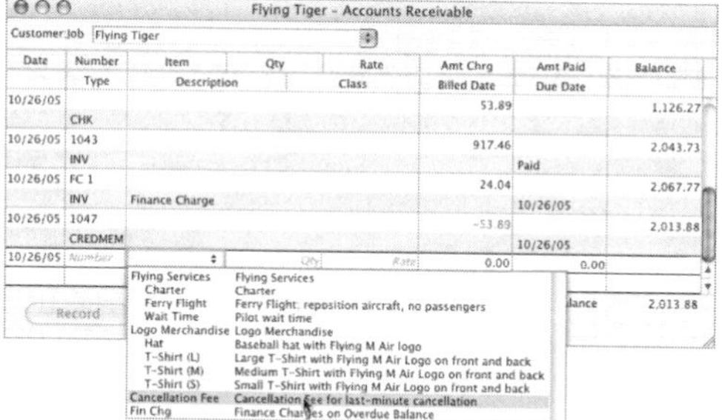

Figure 77 Choose an item from the drop-down list.

Figure 78 Choosing an item automatically enters its description and rate.

To enter statement charges

1. Choose Customers > Enter Statement Charges (**Figure 2**). The Accounts Receivable register window appears (**Figure 76**).
2. Choose the customer you want to enter statement charges for from the Customer: Job drop-down list. That customer's account activity appears in the window (**Figure 76**).
3. If necessary, click in the Date field in the first empty line in the register window and enter the date of the transaction.
4. Press Tab to advance to the Item field.
5. Choose an item from the drop-down list (**Figure 77**). QuickBooks fills in the Description and Rate (**Figure 78**).
6. Press Tab to advance to the Qty field.
7. Enter the item quantity.
8. Click Record. QuickBooks makes an entry sound and records the transaction.

✔ Tips

- You can make changes to other fields in the account register window for a statement charge. Simply click in the field and make the change.
- To include billable items, expenses, or time, click the Time/Costs button before step 8. Then follow the instructions in the section titled "To include billable items, expenses, and time in an invoice or sales receipt" to include these items in the entry.

Making Payments

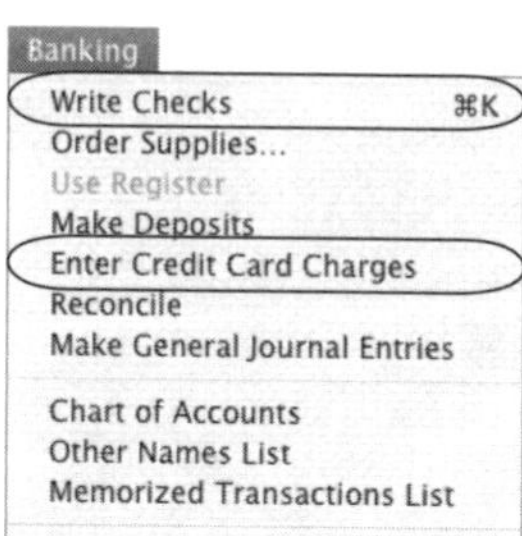

Figures 1 & 2
The Banking (top) and Vendors (bottom) menus include commands for recording amounts due and making payments.

Making Payments

One of the less pleasant parts of owning or operating a business is making payments to the people your company owes money to.

QuickBooks' Banking (**Figure 1**) and Vendors (**Figure 2**) menus offer several commands for recording amounts due to others and for making payments:

- **Write Checks** (**Figure 1**) enables you to write checks using a familiar check-like interface. Once a check is written in QuickBooks, you can print it on compatible check stock. You can use this feature to record checks you write, even if you don't print checks from within QuickBooks.
- **Enter Credit Card Charges** (**Figure 1**) enables you to record amounts charged to a credit card account. This increases the balances of credit card accounts so they accurately reflect what you owe.
- **Enter Bills** (**Figure 2**) enables you to enter details for amounts billed to you. You can then have QuickBooks remind you to pay bills when they're due.
- **Pay Bills** (**Figure 2**) enables you to prepare checks to pay bills you already entered.

Continued on next page...

Continued from previous page.

- **Pay Sales Tax (Figure 2)** enables you to pay tax agencies the amount owed for sales tax collected for a specific period.

As you enter transaction details, the information you provide automatically updates related accounts and balances. Properly using QuickBooks' payment features does two main things for you:

- Account balances are kept up-to-date so you can generate accurate financial reports.
- Transactions for billable items and expenses are recorded so they can be used for invoicing and recording sales.

This chapter explains how to use all of QuickBooks' features for recording amounts due and payments made.

✔ Tip

- I explain how to include billable items and expenses in sales transactions in **Chapter 3**.

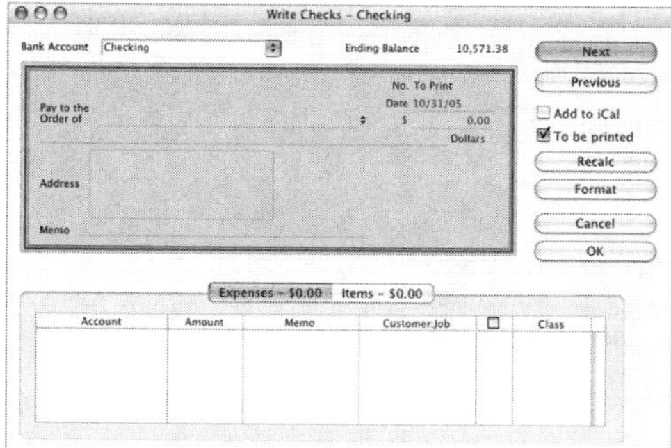

Figure 3 The Write Checks window.

Writing Checks

Writing checks is probably the easiest and most intuitive task you can perform with QuickBooks. After all, you probably already know how to use your checkbook to write a check. QuickBooks' Write Checks window (**Figure 3**) uses the same interface to get the job done.

Writing a check with the Write Checks window does three things:

- ◆ It records the amount of the check and deducts it from the balance in the appropriate checking account.
- ◆ It records what the check was written for, by debiting the appropriate account.
- ◆ It enables you to print the check on compatible check stock, saving you the bother of having to manually write the check.

This part of the chapter explains how to use the Write Checks window to write a check and how to get started printing the checks you write.

✔ Tip

- ■ Even if you do not print checks from within QuickBooks, you should use the Write Checks window to record the checks you write.

To write a check

1. Choose Banking > Write Checks (**Figure 1**), or press [⌘ K]. The Write Checks window appears (**Figure 3**).
2. Choose the account from which the check will be paid from the Bank Account drop-down list. This list includes all of your bank accounts.
3. If you are entering a handwritten check, turn off the To be printed check box and enter the check number in the No. box (**Figure 4**).
4. Enter the date of the check in the Date box.
5. Choose a payee name from the Pay to the Order of drop-down list (**Figure 5**). This list includes all names you have already defined in various QuickBooks lists. QuickBooks automatically enters address information on file for the payee, as well as details for that payee's most recent transaction (**Figure 6**). This is QuickBooks' "QuickFill" feature in action.
6. Make changes in other fields in the top half of the form as desired:
   - ▲ $ is the amount of the payment. Enter a numerical value; QuickBooks automatically converts it to words in the Dollars field below it.
   - ▲ **Address** is the payee's name and address. If you print the check, you can use a compatible window envelope to mail it if this is filled in.
   - ▲ **Memo** is a note that will appear on the face of the check.
7. If the check is to pay for expenses, click the Expenses button at the bottom of the window (**Figure 6**). Then enter information for each expense, one per line:

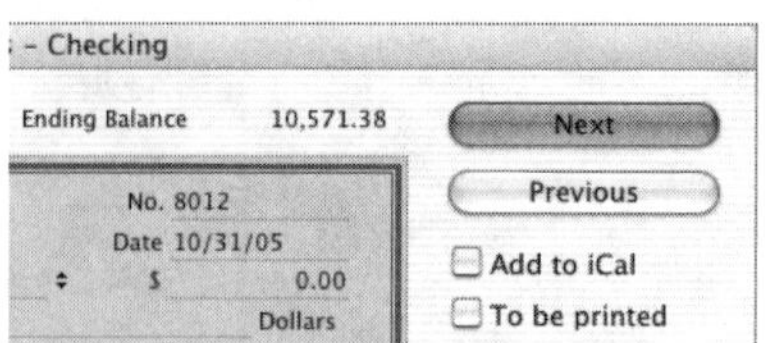

Figure 4 If you are recording a handwritten check, turn off the To be printed check box so you can enter the check number.

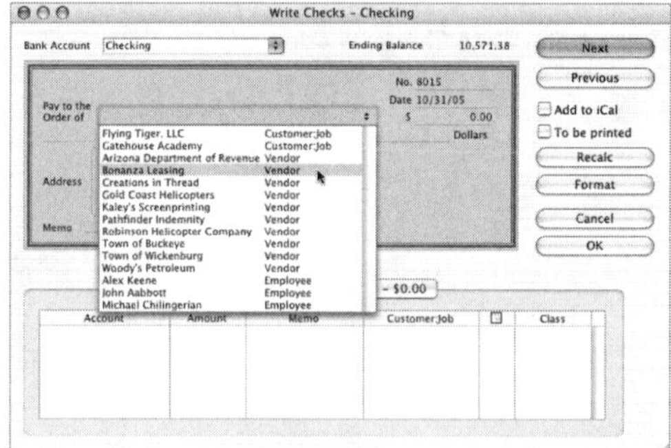

Figure 5 Choose a payee from a drop-down list of all names recorded in QuickBooks.

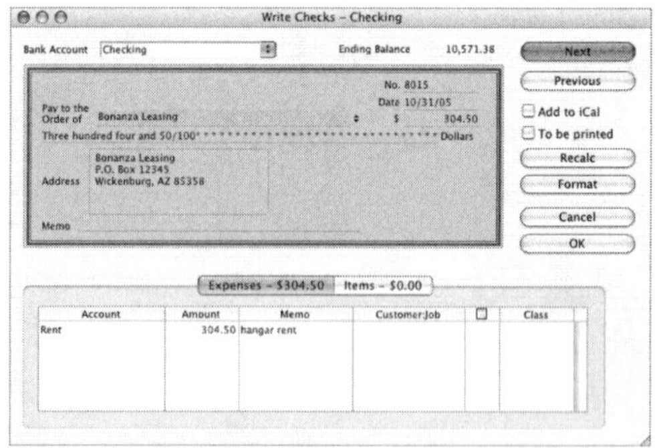

Figure 6 QuickBooks automatically enters information from the last check you wrote for that payee.

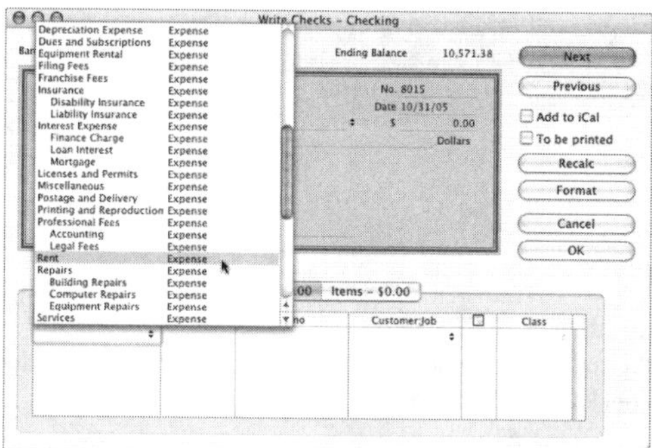

Figure 7 Use the Account drop-down (or in this case, "drop-up") list to choose an account.

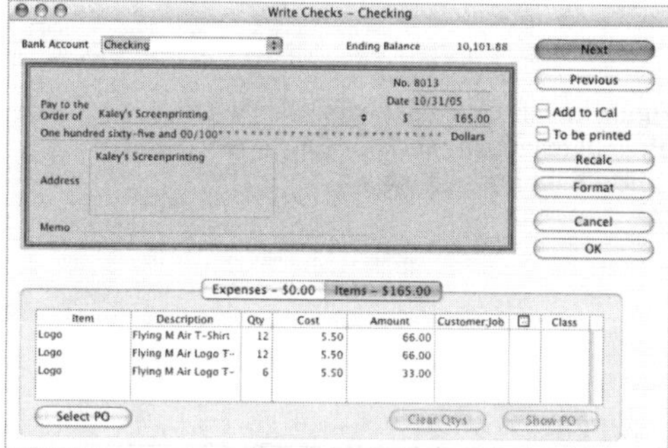

Figure 8 You can use the Items pane to record items purchased.

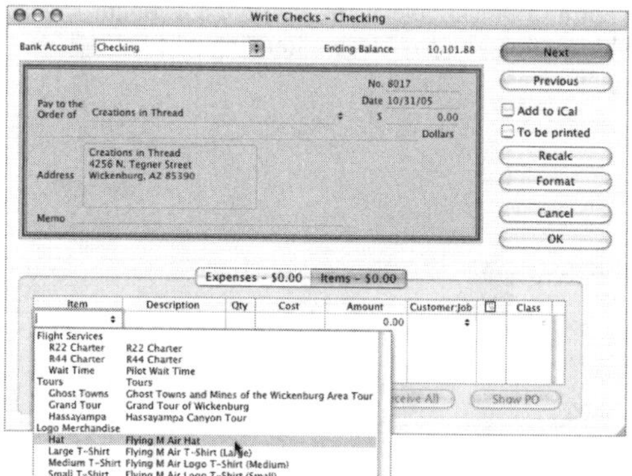

Figure 9 The Item drop-down list includes all items entered into QuickBooks.

- **Account** is the account the expense should be recorded in. Click in the field to display and choose from a drop-down list (**Figure 7**).
- **Amount** is the amount of that particular expense.
- **Memo** is an optional note to describe what the expense is for.
- **Customer:Job** is the customer or job the expense is for. Choosing an option from this drop-down list makes it possible to bill the customer for the expense as discussed in **Chapter 3**. This field is optional.
- **Class** is the class you want to assign for this expense. This field is optional.

8. If the check is to pay for items, click the Items button at the bottom of the window (**Figure 8**). Then enter information for each item, one per line:
   - **Item** is the item you are paying for. Click in the field to display and choose from a drop-down list (**Figure 9**). The item's Description and Cost fill in automatically.
   - **Description** is the item description.
   - **Qty** is the quantity of the item purchased.
   - **Cost** is the unit cost of the item.
   - **Amount** is the total amount of the item. This value is calculated automatically based on quantity and cost.
   - **Customer:Job** is the customer or job the item is for. Choosing an option from this drop-down list makes it possible to bill the customer for the item as discussed in **Chapter 3**. This field is optional.
   - **Class** is the class you want to assign for this item. This field is optional.

Continued on next page...

Continued from previous page.

9. To add the check to iCal as an event (**Figure 10**), turn on the Add to iCal check box.
10. To print the check with other checks, make sure the To be printed check box is turned on.
11. To save the check and write another one, click Next.

    Or

    To save the check without writing another one, click OK.

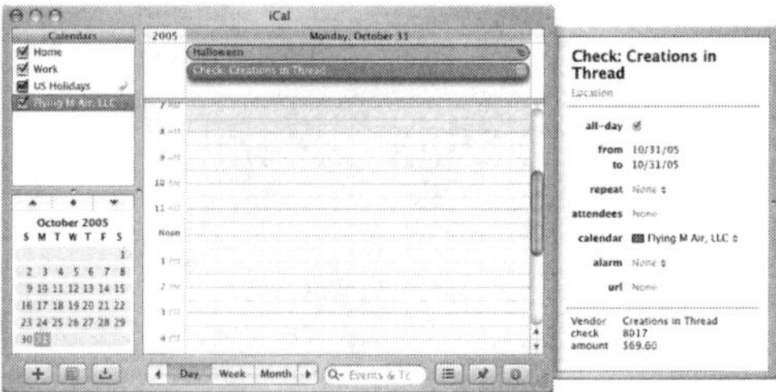

Figure 10 If you use Mac OS X 10.4 or later, you can add checks to iCal as events.

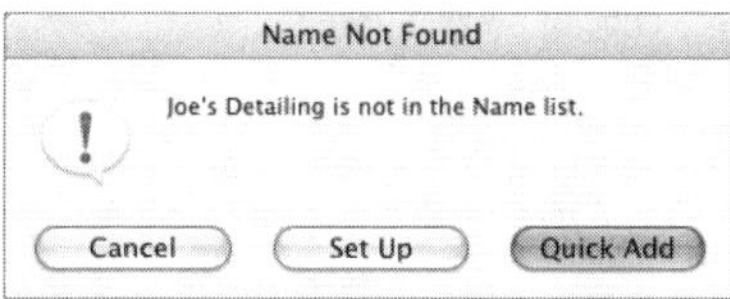

Figure 11 This dialog appears when you attempt to write a check for someone QuickBooks doesn't know.

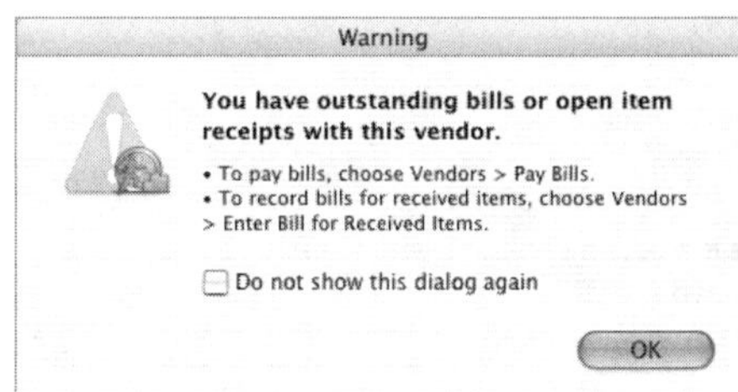

Figure 12 QuickBooks warns you when a vendor you are trying to pay has outstanding bills or open items.

✔ Tips

- I explain how to set up lists, such as the Vendor List, Item List, and Other Names List in **Chapter 2**.
- When the To be printed check box is turned on, you cannot manually assign a check number to a check. QuickBooks automatically assigns check numbers to checks when it prints them.
- In step 5, if you want to write a check to a person or company that does not appear in the drop-down list, enter the name in the Pay to the Order of box and press Tab, then click Set Up in the Name Not Found dialog that appears (**Figure 11**). Follow the prompts that appear onscreen and instructions in **Chapter 2** to add the name to the appropriate QuickBooks list.
- After step 5, if the name you chose has outstanding bills or open item receipts, a dialog like the one in **Figure 12** appears. Read the instructions in the dialog and click OK to dismiss it. I tell you how to pay bills later in this chapter and how to enter items received in **Chapter 7**.

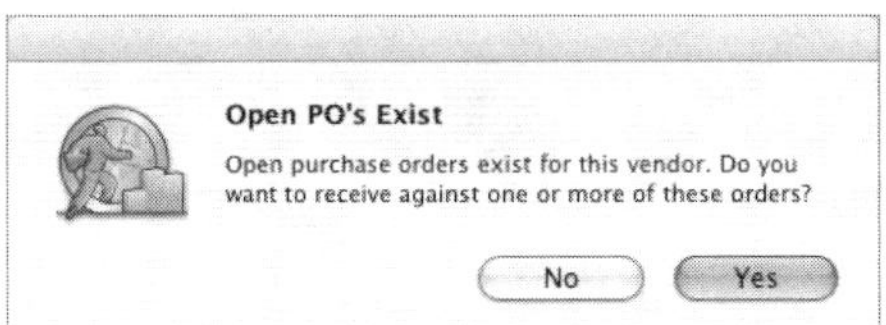

Figure 13 QuickBooks also tells you if a vendor you are trying to pay has open purchase orders.

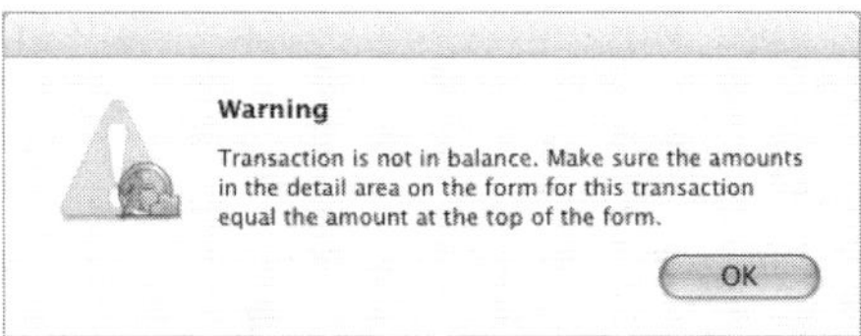

Figure 14 QuickBooks does not allow you to enter an out-of-balance transaction.

- After step 5, if the name you chose has open purchase orders, a dialog like the one in **Figure 13** appears. Click a button:
  - **No** tells QuickBooks that you are not making a payment for items listed on an open purchase order. The dialog disappears.
  - **Yes** tells QuickBooks that you are making a payment for items listed on an open purchase order. The dialog is replaced by the Open Purchase Orders dialog, which I illustrate and explain in **Chapter 7**.
- After step 11, if the amount you entered in step 6 does not equal the total of the amounts entered in steps 7 and 8, the transaction is out of balance and a dialog like the one in **Figure 14** appears. Click OK to dismiss the dialog and then either change the amounts entered or click the Recalc button in the Write Checks window to recalculate a total payment based on the amounts entered in steps 7 and 8.

Entering Bills & Credits

QuickBooks enables you to track and pay bills two ways:

- Use the Write Checks window, which I discuss in the previous section, to enter bills and related payment information when you pay the bills.
- Enter your bills as you receive them, specifying each bill's due date and amount due.

The second method, which I discuss in this part of the chapter, enables you to more accurately track your company's financial situation. When you enter a bill, you indicate that you owe money to someone; this increases your company's liabilities for accounts payable while recording related expenses. As a result, any reports you create will accurately reflect account balances and activity as of the creation date.

You enter bills with the Enter Bills window (**Figure 15**). This window prompts you for all information QuickBooks needs to enter a bill or a credit. QuickBooks keeps track of your unpaid bills and reminds you when it's time to pay them. You can use the Pay Bills window, which I discuss later in this chapter, to pay bills when they're due.

In this part of the chapter, I explain how to enter bills in the Enter Bills window.

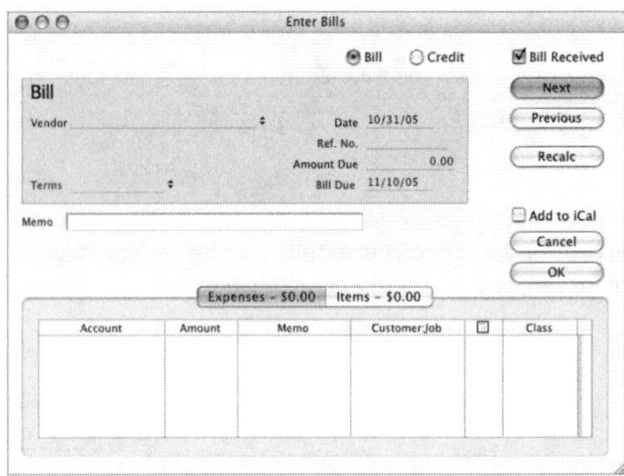

Figure 15 The Enter Bills window.

✔ Tips

- You also use the Enter Bills window to enter bills that you receive with items you purchased. I tell you more about receiving items in **Chapter 7**.
- Do not use the Enter Bills window to enter a bill for received items that have already been entered into QuickBooks. Instead, use the Select Item Receipt dialog, which I discuss in **Chapter 7**.

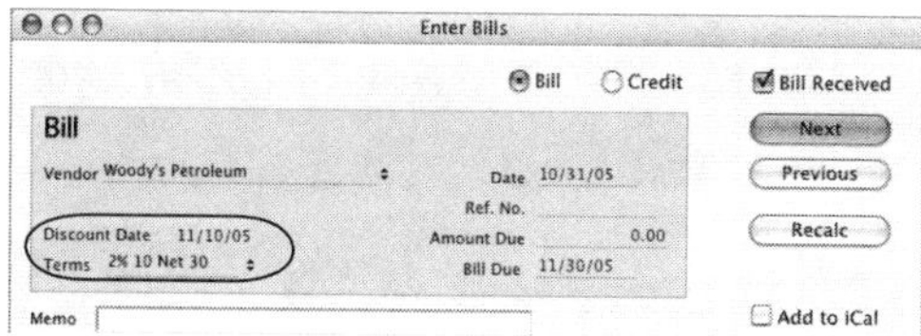

Figure 16 When you choose payment terms that include a discount, the discount date appears in the Enter Bills window.

To enter a bill

1. Choose Vendors > Enter Bills (**Figure 2**). The Enter Bills window appears (**Figure 15**).
2. Make sure the Bill radio button is selected and the Bill Received check box is checked near the top of the window.
3. Enter basic bill information in the top half of the window:
   - **Vendor** is the vendor who sent you the bill. Choose a name from the drop-down list.
   - **Date** is the bill date.
   - **Ref. No.** is a reference number for the bill, such as an invoice number.
   - **Amount Due** is the amount of the bill.
   - **Terms** refers to the payment terms for the bill. Choose an option from the drop-down list. If you choose an option that includes a discount, a discount date appears above the Terms field (**Figure 16**).
   - **Bill Due** is the bill's due date. This date should be filled in automatically when you choose Terms, but can be modified if necessary.
   - **Memo** is an optional note about the bill.
4. If the bill is for expenses, click the Expenses button at the bottom of the window (**Figure 15**). Then enter information for each expense, one per line:
   - **Account** is the account the expense should be recorded in. Click in the field to display and choose from the drop-down list.
   - **Amount** is the amount of that particular expense.

Continued on next page...

Continued from previous page.

- **Memo** is an optional note to describe what the expense is for.
- **Customer:Job** is the customer or job the expense is for. Choosing an option from this drop-down list makes it possible to bill the customer for the expense as discussed in **Chapter 3**. This field is optional.
- **Class** is the class you want to assign for this expense. This field is optional.

5. If the bill is for items, click the Items button at the bottom of the window (**Figure 17**). Then enter information for each item, one per line:
   - **Item** is the item you are being billed for. Click in the field to display and choose from the drop-down list. The item's Description and Cost fill in automatically.
   - **Description** is the item description.
   - **Qty** is the quantity of the item purchased.
   - **Cost** is the unit cost of the item.
   - **Amount** is the total amount of the item. This value is calculated automatically based on quantity and cost.
   - **Customer:Job** is the customer or job the item is for. Choosing an option from this drop-down list makes it possible to bill the customer for the item as discussed in **Chapter 3**. This field is optional.
   - **Class** is the class you want to assign for this item. This field is optional.
6. To add the bill to iCal as an event (**Figure 18**), turn on the Add to iCal check box.

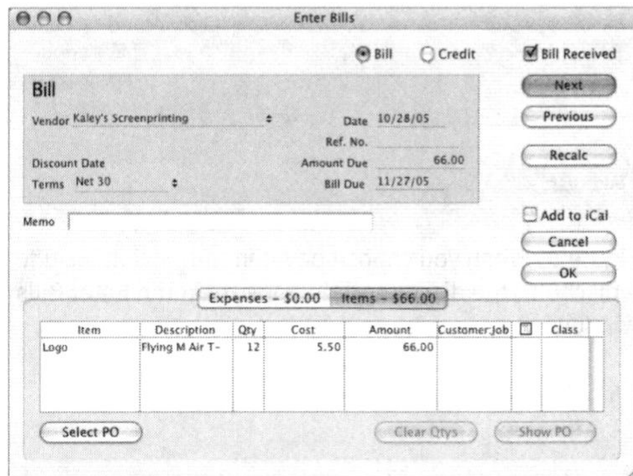

Figure 17 If a bill is for items you purchased, click the Items button in the bottom half of the dialog to enter the items.

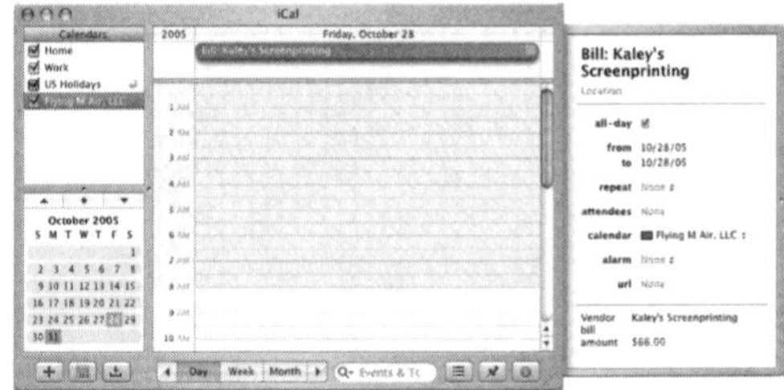

Figure 18 If you're using Mac OS X 10.4 or later, QuickBooks can create an iCal event for the bill.

7. To save the bill and enter another one, click Next.

   Or

   To save the bill without entering another one, click OK.

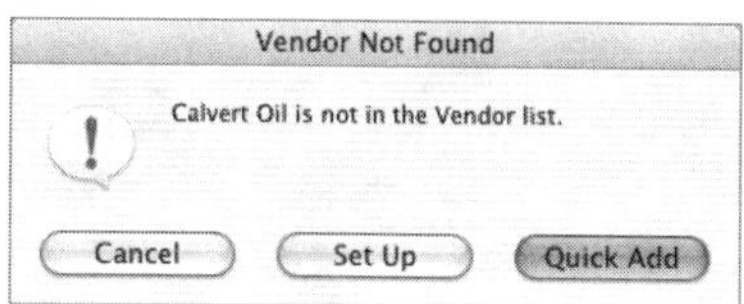

Figure 19 QuickBooks gives you a chance to enter a new vendor's information.

✔ Tips

- I explain how to set up lists, such as the Vendor List and Item List, in **Chapter 2**.
- Removing the check mark from the Bill Received check box in step 2 tells QuickBooks that you want to record items received that you have not yet been billed for. I explain how to do this in **Chapter 7**.
- In step 3, if you want to enter a bill from a person or company that does not appear in the drop-down list, enter the name in the Vendor box and press Tab, then click Set Up in the Vendor Not Found dialog that appears (**Figure 19**). Follow the prompts that appear onscreen and instructions in **Chapter 2** to add the vendor to the Vendor List.
- In step 3, if the vendor you chose has open purchase orders, a dialog like the one in **Figure 13** appears. Click a button:
  - **No** tells QuickBooks that you are not entering a bill for items listed on an open purchase order. The dialog disappears.
  - **Yes** tells QuickBooks that you are entering a bill for items listed on an open purchase order. The dialog is replaced by the Open Purchase Orders dialog, which I illustrate and explain in **Chapter 7**.
- After step 6, if the amount you entered in step 3 does not equal the total of the amounts entered in steps 4 and 5, the transaction is out of balance and a dialog like the one in **Figure 14** appears. Click OK to dismiss the dialog and then either change the amounts entered or click the Recalc button in the Enter Bills window to recalculate a total amount based on the amounts entered in steps 4 and 5.

To enter a credit

1. Choose Vendors > Enter Bills (**Figure 2**). The Enter Bills window appears (**Figure 15**).
2. Select the Credit radio button at the top of the window (**Figure 20**).
3. Enter basic credit information in the top half of the window:
   - ▲ **Vendor** is the vendor who sent you the credit. Choose a name from the drop-down list.
   - ▲ **Date** is the credit date.
   - ▲ **Ref. No.** is a reference number for the credit, such as a credit number.
   - ▲ **Credit Amount** is the amount of the credit.
   - ▲ **Memo** is an optional note about the credit.
4. Follow steps 4 and 5 in the section titled "To enter a bill" to enter details about expenses and items the credit is for.
5. To add the bill to iCal as an event, turn on the Add to iCal check box.
6. To save the credit and enter another one, click Next.

   Or

   To save the credit without entering another one, click OK.

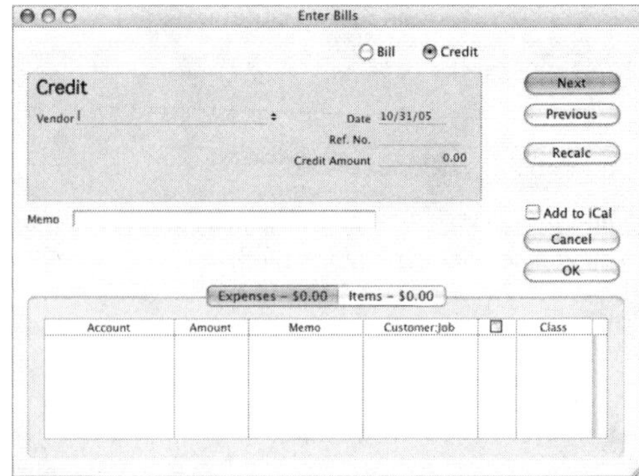

Figure 20 Selecting the Credit radio button turns a bill form into a credit form.

✔ Tips

- Most of the tips on the previous page also apply to entering credits.
- Credits reduce your accounts payable balance for a vendor, thus reducing your company's total liabilities.

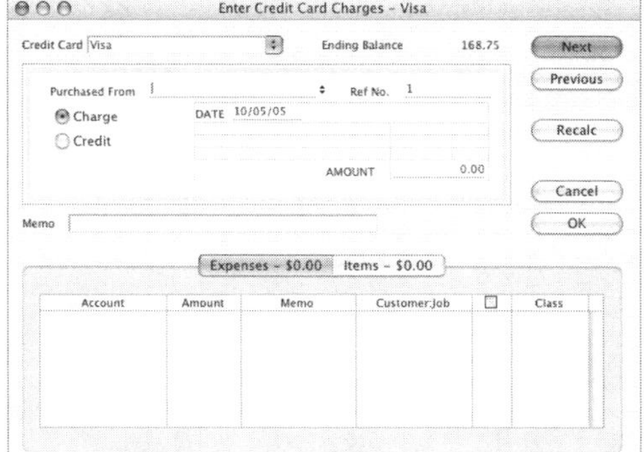

Figure 21 Use this window to enter details for credit card transactions.

Entering Credit Card Charges & Credits

Credit card charges are similar to bills in that they increase your company's total liabilities. Tracking credit card expenditures as they occur is a good way to keep account balances and financial activity up-to-date.

In QuickBooks, you can enter credit card activity in the Enter Credit Card Charges window (**Figure 21**). This window enables you to enter details for each credit card transaction, including the vendor where the credit card was used, the date of the transaction, the amount, and what the transaction was for.

This part of the chapter explains how to enter credit card charges and credits.

✔ Tip

- You can also enter credit card charges when you receive your monthly credit card bill. This, however, does not enable you to keep your financial records as up-to-date as entering charges soon after they are made.

To enter a credit card charge or credit

1. Choose Banking > Enter Credit Card Charges (**Figure 1**). The Enter Credit Card Charges window appears (**Figure 21**).
2. Choose the name of the credit card account from the Credit Card drop-down list. This list includes all credit card accounts set up within QuickBooks. The balance for that account appears at the top of the window (**Figure 21**).

Continued on next page...

Continued from previous page.

3. Select one of the radio buttons:
   - ▲ **Charge (Figure 21)** is for credit card charges—for example, when you buy something.
   - ▲ **Credit** is for credit card credits—for example, when you return something.
4. Enter basic transaction information in the top half of the window:
   - ▲ **Purchased From** is the name of the business where you made the credit card charge or received the credit. Choose a name from the drop-down list.
   - ▲ **Ref No.** is a reference number for the credit card charge or credit.
   - ▲ **Date** is the charge or credit date.
   - ▲ **Amount** is the amount of the charge or credit.
   - ▲ **Memo** is an optional note about the charge or credit.
5. If the charge or credit is for expenses, click the Expenses button at the bottom of the window (**Figure 21**). Then enter information for each expense, one per line:
   - ▲ **Account** is the account the expense should be recorded in. Click in the field to display and choose from a drop-down list.
   - ▲ **Amount** is the amount of that particular expense.
   - ▲ **Memo** is an optional note to describe what the expense is for.
   - ▲ **Customer:Job** is the customer or job the expense is for. Choosing an option from this drop-down list makes it possible to bill the customer for the expense as discussed in **Chapter 3**. This field is optional.

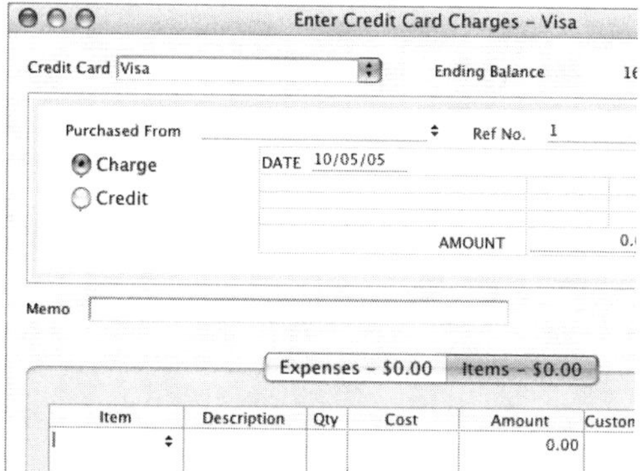

Figure 22 A credit card charge or credit can be for items in the Item List.

- **Class** is the class you want to assign for this expense. This field is optional.

6. If the charge or credit is for items, click the Items tab at the bottom of the window (**Figure 22**). Then enter information for each item, one per line:
   - **Item** is the item you bought or returned. Click in the field to display and choose from a drop-down list. The item's Description and Cost fill in automatically.
   - **Description** is the item description.
   - **Qty** is the quantity of the item purchased or returned.
   - **Cost** is the unit cost of the item.
   - **Amount** is the total amount of the item. This value is calculated automatically based on quantity and cost.
   - **Customer:Job** is the customer or job the item is for. Choosing an option from this drop-down list makes it possible to bill the customer for the item as discussed in **Chapter 3**. This field is optional.
   - **Class** is the class you want to assign for this item. This field is optional.
7. To save the credit card charge or credit and enter another one, click Next.

   Or

   To save the credit card charge or credit without entering another one, click OK.

Continued on next page...

Continued from previous page.

✔ Tips

- I explain how to set up lists, such as the Vendor List, Item List, and Other Names List, in **Chapter 2**.
- In step 4, if you want to enter a credit card charge from a company that does not appear in the drop-down list, enter the name in the Purchased From box and press Tab, then click Set Up in the Name Not Found dialog that appears (**Figure 11**). Follow the prompts that appear onscreen and instructions in **Chapter 2** to add the name to the appropriate list.
- In step 4, if the company you chose has open purchase orders, a dialog like the one in **Figure 13** appears. Click a button:
  - **No** tells QuickBooks that you are not entering a charge for items listed on an open purchase order. The dialog disappears.
  - **Yes** tells QuickBooks that you are entering a charge for items listed on an open purchase order. The dialog is replaced by the Open Purchase Orders dialog, which I illustrate and explain in **Chapter 7**.
- After step 7, if the amount you entered in step 4 does not equal the total of the amounts entered in steps 5 and 6, the transaction is out of balance and a dialog like the one in **Figure 14** appears. Click OK to dismiss the dialog and then either change the amounts entered or click the Recalc button in the Enter Credit Card Charges window to recalculate a total amount based on the amounts entered in steps 5 and 6.

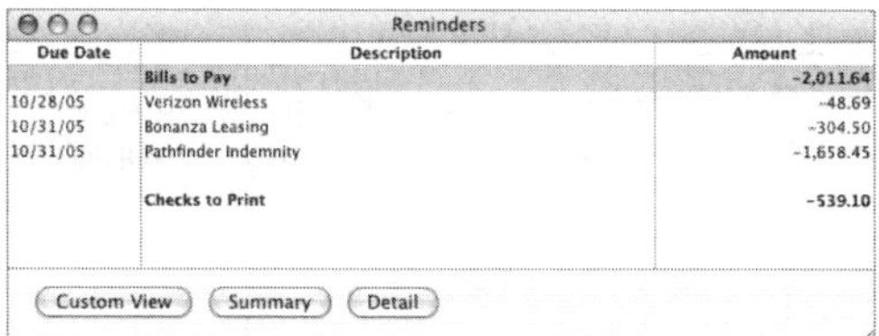

Figure 23 The Reminders list window lists all invoices that are due or overdue.

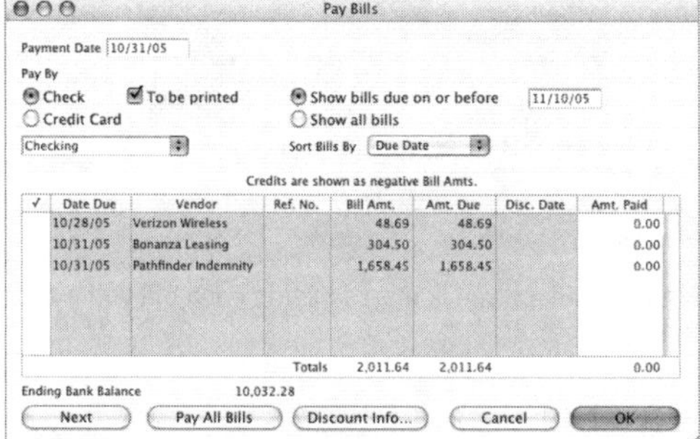

Figure 24 The Pay Bills window can list all invoices due before a certain date...

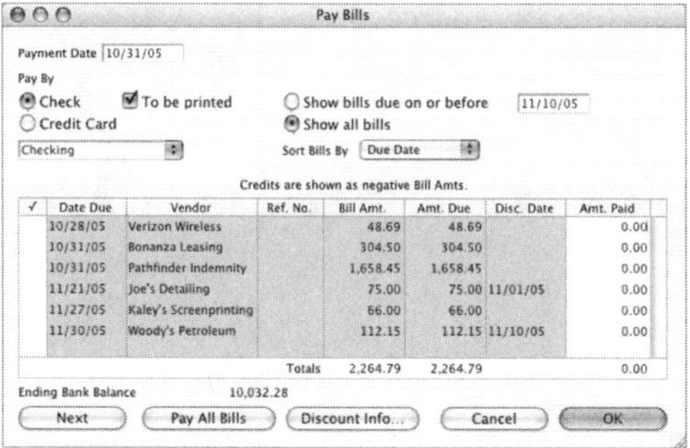

Figure 25 ...or all bills that have not yet been paid.

Paying Bills

QuickBooks keeps track of the bills you enter in two different places:

- The Reminders list (**Figure 23**) displays a list of all the bills that are currently due or overdue under the Bills to Pay heading. If necessary, double-click the heading or click the Detail button to display the list of bills.
- The Pay Bills window displays a list of all of the bills due before a certain date (**Figure 24**) or all bills that have not yet been paid (**Figure 25**).

QuickBooks enables you to pay a bill by check or credit card. If you elect to pay by check, QuickBooks automatically writes the check for you. You can then print it with your other checks. If you elect to pay by credit card, QuickBooks enters the credit card charge transaction; you still have to contact the vendor and arrange for the credit card payment.

When you pay a bill, QuickBooks reduces your company's liabilities for accounts payable by recording the payment transaction as a debit to the appropriate account. At the same time, it decreases the balance in the bank account or increases the balance in the credit card account used to pay the bill. Thus, it keeps your company's financial information accurate and up-to-date.

This part of the chapter explains how to pay the bills you enter in QuickBooks.

✔ Tip

- Do not use the Write Checks window to pay bills already entered into QuickBooks. Doing so displays a Warning dialog like the one in **Figure 12**. Instead, follow the instructions in this section to pay your bills.

To pay a bill

1. Choose Vendors > Pay Bills **(Figure 2)**. The Pay Bills window appears **(Figure 24)**.
2. Enter the date of the payment in the Payment Date box.
3. Select a Pay By option:
   - ▲ **Check** tells QuickBooks you are paying by check. If you choose this option, you can turn on the To be printed check box to print the check with other checks waiting to be printed.
   - ▲ **Credit Card** tells QuickBooks you are paying by credit card.
4. Choose the account you are using to pay the bill from the drop-down list.
5. Set options to specify which bills should be shown in the window:
   - ▲ **Show bills due on or before (Figure 24)** enables you to specify a date on or before which bills must be due to appear in the window. If you select this option, be sure to enter the date in the box beside the option.
   - ▲ **Show all bills** displays all unpaid bills **(Figure 25)**.
6. If desired, choose an option from the Sort Bills By pop-up menu **(Figure 26)**.
7. In the list of bills that are due, click in the ✓ column beside each bill you want to pay **(Figure 27)**.
8. To pay a different amount than the amount due, change the amount in the Amt. Paid column for the bill.

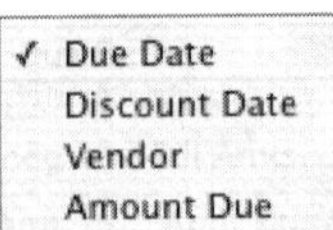

Figure 26 Use this pop-up menu to choose a sort order for the bills that appear in the Pay Bills window.

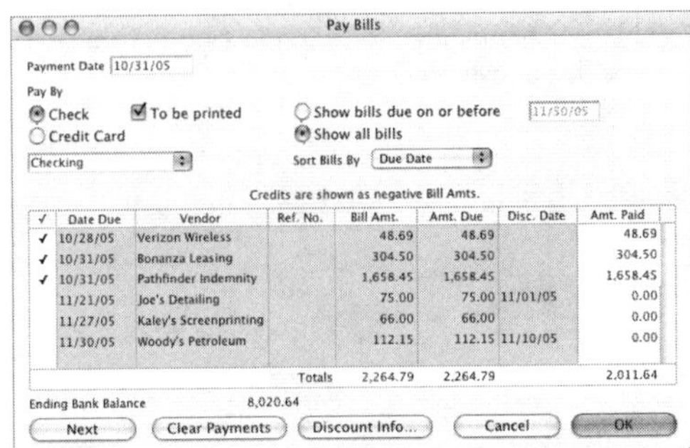

Figure 27 Place check marks beside each bill you want to pay.

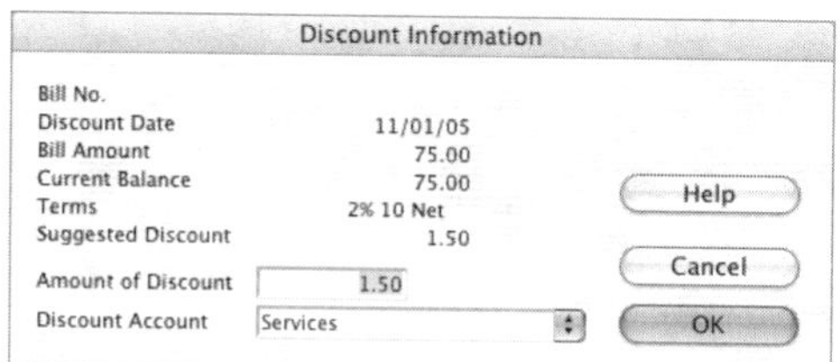

Figure 28 The Discount Information dialog calculates available discounts and enables you to choose an account in which to record the discount amount.

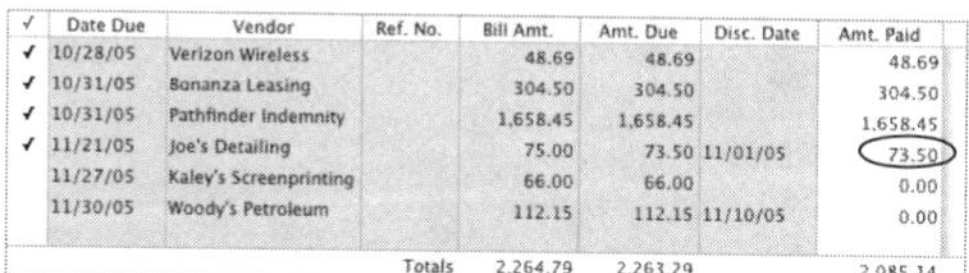

✓	Date Due	Vendor	Ref. No.	Bill Amt.	Amt. Due	Disc. Date	Amt. Paid
✓	10/28/05	Verizon Wireless		48.69	48.69		48.69
✓	10/31/05	Bonanza Leasing		304.50	304.50		304.50
✓	10/31/05	Pathfinder Indemnity		1,658.45	1,658.45		1,658.45
✓	11/21/05	Joe's Detailing		75.00	73.50	11/01/05	73.50
	11/27/05	Kaley's Screenprinting		66.00	66.00		0.00
	11/30/05	Woody's Petroleum		112.15	112.15	11/10/05	0.00
			Totals	2,264.79	2,263.29		2,085.14

Figure 29 The amount of the payment is automatically reduced by the amount of the discount.

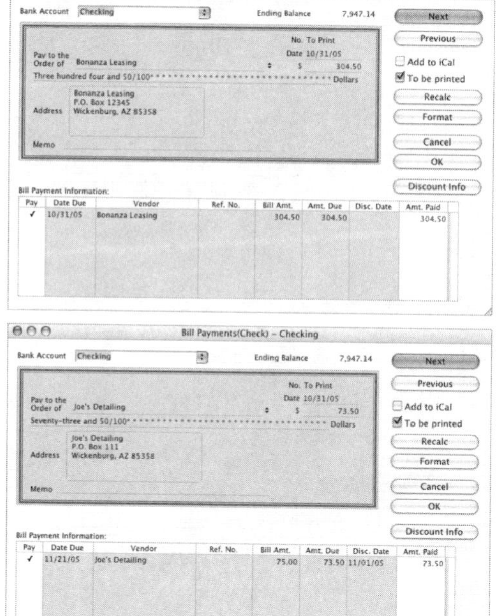

Figures 30a & 30b Two checks prepared for bill payments.

9. To take advantage of a discount for early payment, click in the Amt. Paid column for the bill and then click the Discount Info button. In the Discount Information dialog that appears (**Figure 28**), choose an account for the discount from the Discount Account drop-down list and click OK. The amount of the payment is adjusted accordingly (**Figure 29**).
10. Click OK. QuickBooks enters the transaction(s). If you indicated that you were paying by checks to be printed, it adds the checks to the list of checks to print. **Figures 30a and 30b** show two of the checks prepared for bills checked in **Figure 29**.

✔ Tips

- Selecting the Show all bills option in step 5 guarantees that you won't miss out on any bills offering a discount for early payment. This can save your company money.
- In step 9, you can also change the value in the Amount of Discount box in the Discount Information dialog (**Figure 28**). This overrides the amount of the discount calculated by QuickBooks.

Paying Sales Tax

As you record sales transactions using the Create Invoices and Enter Sales Receipts commands under the Customers menu, QuickBooks is working hard in the background, calculating sales tax and keeping track of what's owed to each taxing agency. When it's time to submit your sales tax returns and payments, QuickBooks is all ready to write the check for you.

When you use QuickBooks' Pay Sales Tax dialog (**Figure 31**) to pay sales tax, QuickBooks does several things:

- It calculates the amount of unpaid sales tax through a date you specify—normally the end of the previous month.
- It prepares payment transactions for sales tax payment. If you indicate that the checks should be printed, it adds the resulting checks to the list of checks to be printed.
- It reduces the balance of the payment account, as well as the balances in the liability accounts for sales tax, thus keeping your financial records up-to-date.

In this part of the chapter, I explain how to pay sales tax using the Pay Sales Tax dialog.

✔ Tip

- I explain how to set up sales tax items and related names in **Chapter 2** and how to enter sales transactions in **Chapter 3**.

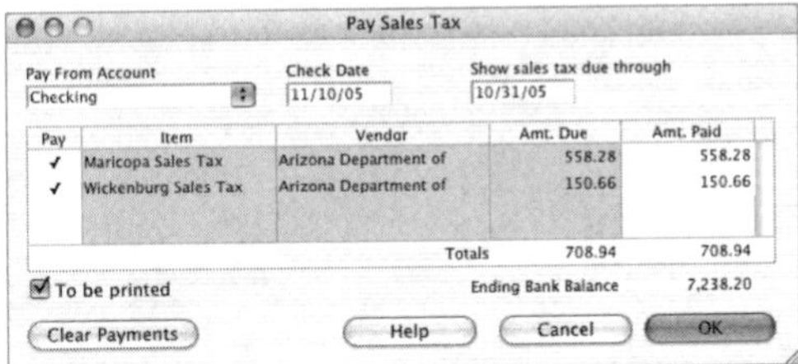

Figure 31 The Pay Sales Tax dialog calculates sales tax for you based on sales tax items you created.

To pay sales tax

1. Choose Vendors > Pay Sales Tax (**Figure 2**). The Pay Sales Tax dialog appears (**Figure 31**).
2. Set options at the top of the dialog:
   - ▲ **Pay From Account** is the account you want to use to pay sales tax. The drop-down list includes all bank accounts you have set up in QuickBooks.
   - ▲ **Check Date** is the date of the check for paying the sales tax.
   - ▲ **Show sales tax due through** is the date you want to calculate sales tax through. Normally, this date will be at the end of a month or quarter.
3. Turn on the check box beside each type of sales tax you want to pay.
4. To change the amount of tax you want to pay for a taxing agency, modify the amount in the Amt. Paid column for that agency.
5. To print sales tax checks with other checks, turn on the To be printed check box.
6. Click OK. QuickBooks creates the payment transactions and, if necessary, adds checks to the list of checks to be printed.

✔ Tip

- The amount QuickBooks calculates should equal the amount due on your sales tax return. You should check to make sure the amounts match before clicking OK in step 6. If the amounts do not match, modify the amount of the payment as instructed in step 4 so you pay the amount actually due.

Downloading Transactions

Downloading Transactions

For QuickBooks Pro 2006, Intuit added a brand new feature: the ability to download transactions from participating financial institutions into your QuickBooks company file.

What does this mean to you? If your bank or credit card company is one of the hundreds that support downloading transactions in QuickBooks Web Connect format, you can import transactions you download from the Internet directly into QuickBooks. This can save you hours of data entry time and help prevent data entry errors.

This chapter explains how you can find out whether your financial institutions support transaction download and, if they do, how you can sign up. It also tells you how you can download transactions from your bank or credit card company and accept them into your QuickBooks company file.

✔ Tips

- Although QuickBooks now supports transaction download, it does not directly support all of the online banking features offered by some banks. Consult your bank's Web site for information about online banking features it offers.
- You must have an Internet connection to use QuickBooks' transaction download feature.

Signing Up for Transaction Download

Before you can use QuickBooks' Web Connect transaction download feature, you must confirm that it is supported by your bank or credit card company and sign up to access it. Although the sign-up process may take a few days, the good news is that most financial insitutions offer transaction download for free on their Web sites.

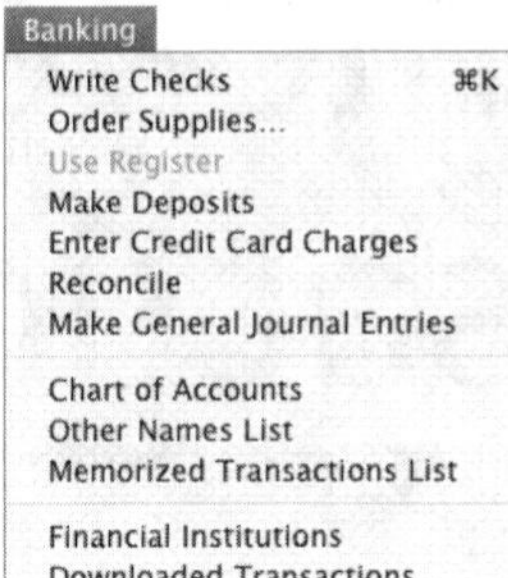

Figure 1 The Banking menu.

To determine whether your financial institution supports QuickBooks Web Connect

1. Choose Banking > Financial Institutions (**Figure 1**). QuickBooks accesses the Internet to update its list of compatible financial institutions, then displays it in the Financial Institution window (**Figure 2**).
2. Scroll through the alphabetical list to find your bank or credit card company and select it. Contact information appears at the top of the Financial Institutions window (**Figure 3**).

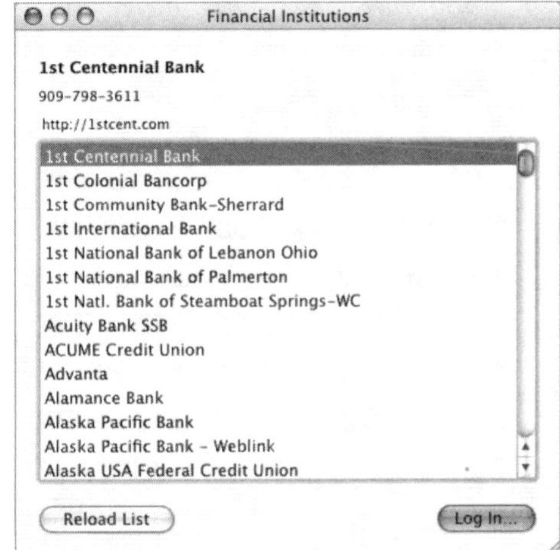

Figure 2 The Financial Institutions window lists banks and credit card companies that support transaction download.

✔ Tip

- If your bank or credit card company doesn't appear in the Financial Institutions window, don't panic. It may still support transaction download. Visit its Web site and look for a QuickBooks Web Connect or QuickBooks download feature. Or call your financial institution and ask for it.

Figure 3 In this example, I've selected my bank.

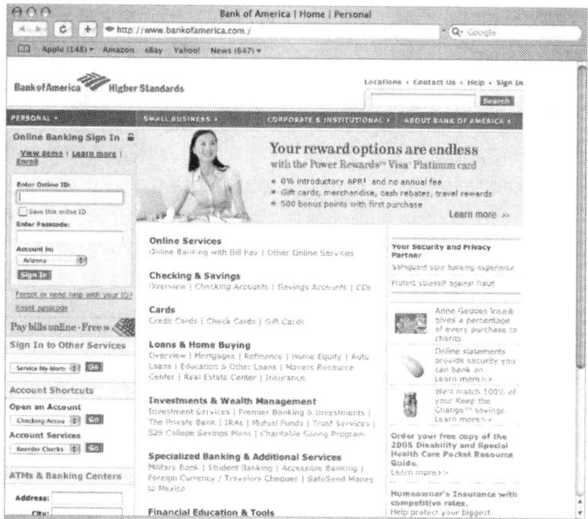

Figure 4 The login screen for the bank selected in Figure 3.

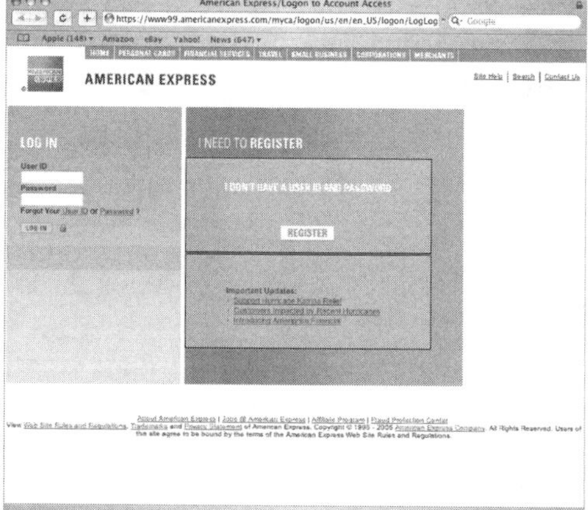

Figure 5 The login screen for one of my credit card companies, American Express.

To sign up for transaction download

1. Use the information in the Financial Institution window (**Figures** 2 and 3) to contact your bank by phone or visit its Web site.

2. Request access information for QuickBooks Web Connect transaction download. You may need to specify which accounts should be enabled. In most cases, your bank will mail a user ID and password or PIN to you, but some financial institutions enable you to set up online access on their Web sites.

To log into your bank or credit card company's Web site

1. Select your bank or credit card company in the Financial Institutions list (**Figure** 3).

2. Click the Log In button.

3. Wait while your Web browser launches and opens the Home page for your financial institution. **Figures** 4 and 5 show two examples.

4. Enter your user ID or login name and password or PIN in the appropriate login boxes and click the button to log in. (These boxes and buttons are labeled differently on every Web site, so I can't provide exact labels.)

   If login is successful, you'll see information about your accounts or go directly to a screen where you can initiate a download. You now have everything you need from your financial institution to download transactions into QuickBooks.

Downloading QuickBooks Transactions

Setting up a QuickBooks account for transaction download is easy. Just complete a QuickBooks Web Connect download and import the downloaded file into QuickBooks. Follow the instructions that appear to complete the setup.

In this section, I explain how to complete your first transaction download for an account, which should enable the corresponding account for all future QuickBooks transaction downloads. I also explain how to download subsequent transactions for QuickBooks.

✔ Tip

- You can only use transaction download with existing QuickBooks accounts. If your account is not already set up in QuickBooks, set it up now. You'll find instructions for setting up accounts in **Chapter 2**.

To complete the first transaction download for an account

1. Log into your financial institution's online banking feature.
2. Navigate through the system to find download options for the account you want to download. **Figures 6** and **7** show examples.
3. If given an option for the download format (**Figure 6**), choose QuickBooks or QuickBooks Web Connect.
4. Set other options, including transaction period, as desired for the download.

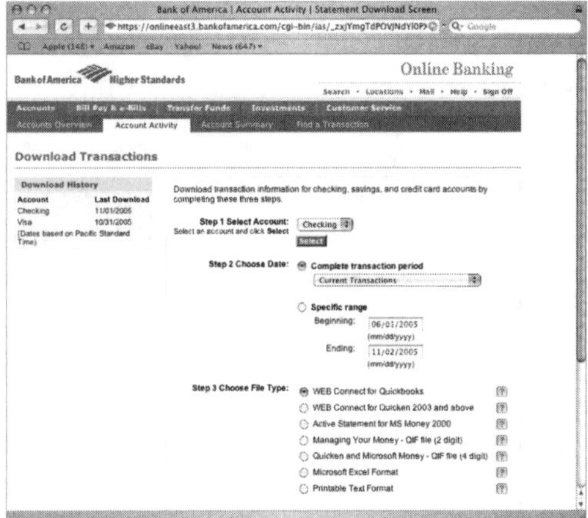

Figure 6 Here's what the download page looks like for my Bank of America checking account.

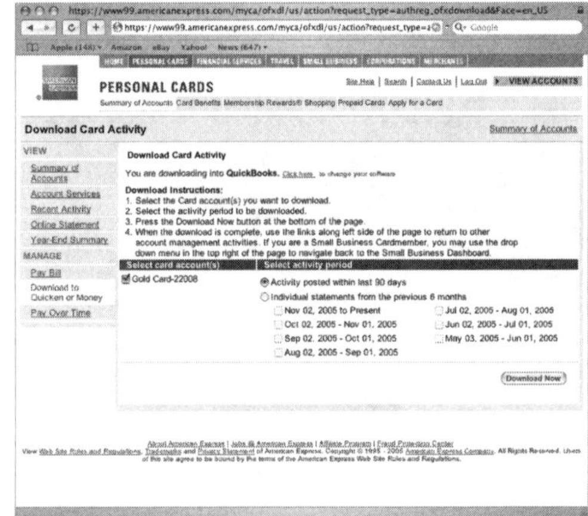

Figure 7 American Express offers these options on its QuickBooks Web Connect download page.

Figure 8 Two downloaded QuickBooks Web Connect files in my Desktop folder.

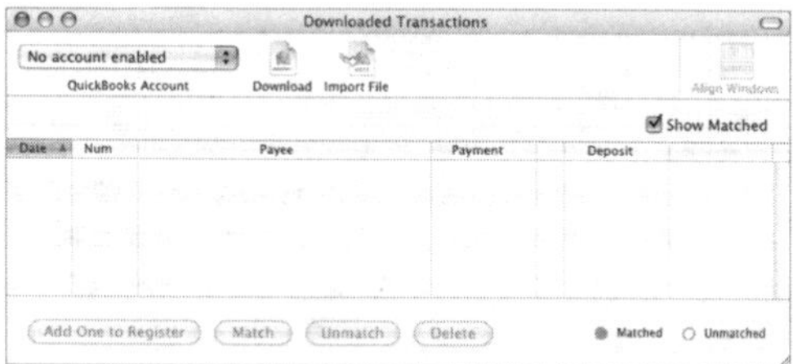

Figure 9 The Downloaded Transactions window before any transactions have been downloaded.

Figure 10 Use a standard Open dialog to locate, select, and open a QuickBooks Web Connect file.

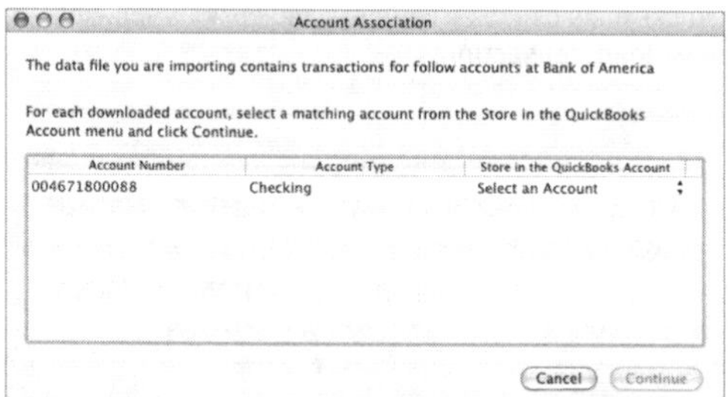

Figure 11 The first time you download transactions for an account, you'll have to match the downloaded account to a QuickBooks account.

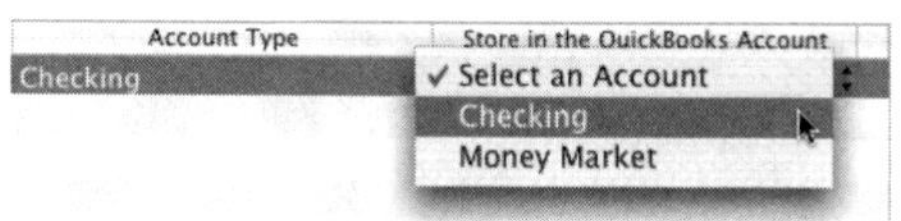

Figure 12 Choose the appropriate QuickBooks account from a pop-up menu.

5. Click the Download button.

   The transaction download file is downloaded to your computer and saved to your Web browser's default download location—most likely your Desktop, if you haven't changed it. **Figure 8** shows two Web Connect files downloaded to my computer's desktop.

6. Open or switch back to QuickBooks.

7. Choose Banking > Downloaded Transactions (**Figure 1**).

8. The first time you open the Downloaded Transaction window, a dialog sheet with information about the download and import process appears. After reading it, click OK to dismiss it.

9. Click the Import File button in the Downloaded Transaction window's toolbar (**Figure 9**).

10. An Open dialog appears (**Figure 10**). Use it to locate, select, and open a QuickBooks Web Connect file.

11. In the Account Association dialog that appears (**Figure 11**), use the Select an Account pop-up menu (**Figure 12**) to choose the account you want to associate with the downloaded transactions.

12. Click Continue.

13. Wait while the transactions are imported into QuickBooks. A dialog sheet tells you how many transactions were imported. Click OK.

    The newly imported transactions appear in the Downloaded Transactions window (**Figure 13**).

14. Repeat these steps for each account you want to download and import into QuickBooks.

Continued on next page...

Continued from previous page.

✔ Tips

- It is *very important* that you specify QuickBooks or QuickBooks Web Connect in step 3. If you download transactions in a different format, they cannot be imported into QuickBooks.
- If you don't see an option to download to QuickBooks or QuickBooks Web Connect format, call your bank's online customer support number and ask about it. This is something I needed to do for my Bank of America accounts even though it was listed in the Financial Institutions window (**Figure 3**).
- Some Web browsers are smart enough to figure out or ask (**Figure 14**) what program should open a downloaded transaction file. If you set up your browser to open the downloaded file with QuickBooks, you can skip steps 6 through 10.
- After step 5, you can double-click the icon for a downloaded transaction file. This enables you to skip steps 6 and 7.

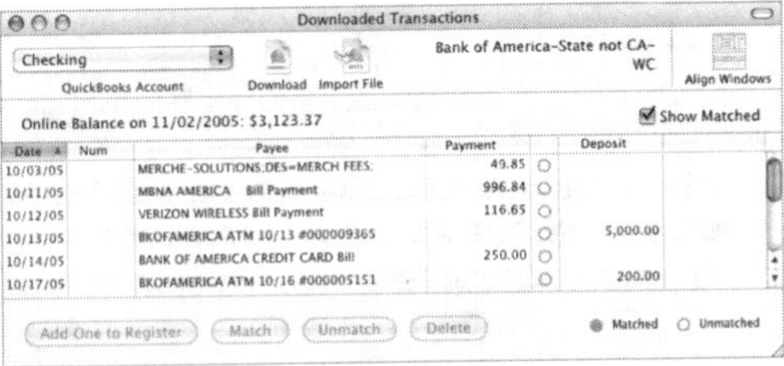

Figure 13 The transactions you import appear in the Downloaded Transactions list window until you review and accept them.

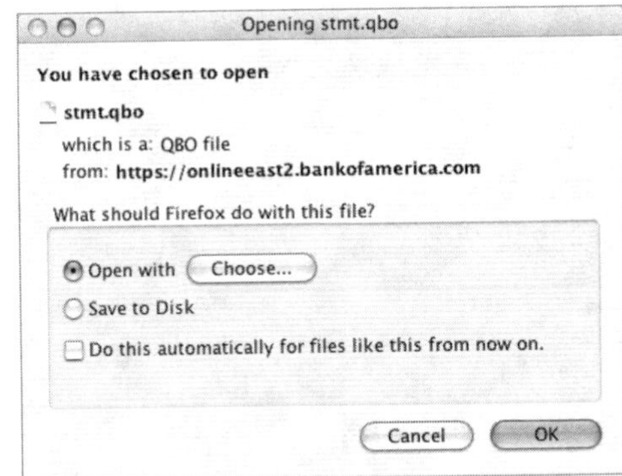

Figure 14 The Firefox Web browser is smart enough to ask what it should do with a downloaded file. Setting it up to automatically open a Web Connect file with QuickBooks can save you time and effort when you download transactions.

To complete subsequent transaction downloads for an account

1. Follow the steps earlier in this section to log into your financial institution and download transactions in a QuickBooks Web Connect format file.
2. Open or switch back to QuickBooks.
3. Choose Banking > Downloaded Transactions (**Figure 1**).
4. Click the Import File button in the Downloaded Transaction window's toolbar.
5. An Open dialog appears (**Figure 10**). Use it to locate, select, and open the QuickBooks Web Connect file you downloaded.
6. Wait while the transactions are imported into QuickBooks. A dialog sheet tells you how many transactions were imported. Click OK.

   The newly imported transactions appear in the Downloaded Transactions window (**Figure 13**).

✔ Tip

- If your Web browser is set up to automaticaly open a downloaded transaction file with QuickBooks, you can skip steps 2 through 5.

Reviewing Downloaded Transactions

When you import downloaded transactions into QuickBooks, they're held in the Downloaded Transactions window until you review them. The review process enables you to match a downloaded transaction to a trasnsaction already entered into QuickBooks or add the downloaded transaction to the account's register in QuickBooks.

You can easily tell the status of a transaction in the Downloaded Transactions window by looking at the orange bullet beside it:

- A filled in orange bullet appears beside matched transactions. These are downloaded transactions that match transactions already entered into the account.
- A hollow orange bullet—or circle, depending on how you look at it—appears beside unmatched transactions. These are downloaded transactions that do not match any transactions entered into the account. A transaction can be unmatched because it has not yet been entered in QuickBooks or some part of the transaction's information does not match the corresponding transaction that has been entered—for example, the amount or check number.

This part of the chapter explains how to review, match, and enter downloaded transactions into your QuickBooks company file.

Figure 15 Clicking the Align Windows button displays the Downloaded Transactions window with its corresponding account register window.

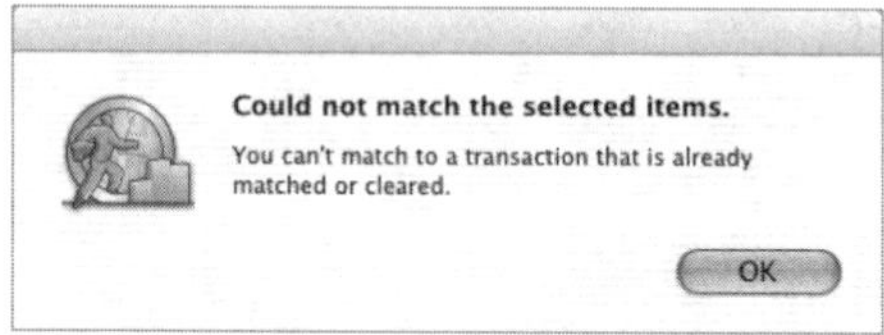

Figure 16 QuickBooks displays this dialog if it can't match a selected downloaded transaction.

To review downloaded transactions

1. If necessary, choose Banking > Downloaded Transactions to display the Downloaded Transactions window (**Figure 13**).

2. Use the pop-up menu to choose the name of the QuickBooks account you want to review transactions for.

3. To open and view the account register for the account, click the Align Windows button in the Downloaded Transaction window's title bar. The register window appears above the Downloaded Transactions window onscreen (**Figure 15**) so you can see inside both.

4. To check a matched transaction, select it. The transaction is selected in the account register. Then:

   ▲ If the transaction is properly matched, continue reviewing other transactions.

   ▲ If the transaction is not properly matched, click the Unmatch button. The transaction status changes to Unmatched.

5. To match an unmatched transaction, select the transaction in the Downloaded Transactions window and click the Match button. If a dialog like the one in **Figure 16** appears, click OK. Then, in the account register window, modify the transaction that should match a downloaded transaction and click Record. The transaction status should change to Matched; if it doesn't, click the Match button again.

Continued on next page...

Continued from previous page.

6. To enter a downloaded transaction into its account register, select the transaction in the Downloaded Transactions window and click the Add One to Register button. The transaction appears, partially completed, in the account register window (**Figure 17**). Enter the missing information and click Record. The downloaded transaction is marked as Matched (**Figure 18**).
7. To delete a downloaded transaction without matching or entering it, select it in the Downloaded Transactions window and click Delete. The transaction is removed.
8. Repeat steps 4, 5, and 6 to check and match all transactions in the Downloaded Transactions window.
9. To review transactions for another account, choose the account from the pop-up menu at the top of the Downloaded Transactions window, Then follow steps 3 through 8 to review those transactions.
10. When you are finished reviewing transactions, you can close the Downloaded Transactions and account register windows.

✔ Tips

- When a transaction is matched, a black check mark appears beside it in the account register window. You can see this in **Figures 17** and **18** on this page. This indicates that it has cleared the bank. I tell you about reconciling accounts in **Chapter 6**.
- If a transaction is not matched, it will not appear in the account register window.

Figure 17 When you click the Add One to Register button, QuickBooks begins entering the transaction in the account register.

Figure 18 When you complete the transaction, it is marked as Matched in the Downloaded Transactions window.

Working with Transactions

Working with Transactions

Most of the transactions you enter into QuickBooks are created using relatively intuitive forms that you fill in when you sell goods and services, pay bills, and write checks. Using these forms creates standard double-entry accounting entries in ledgers maintained by QuickBooks.

For example, when you use an Invoice form to invoice a customer for merchandise he purchased, QuickBooks automatically debits a cost of goods sold account and credits an inventory account for the value of the items sold. At the same time, it debits an accounts receivable account and credits an income account for the item purchase price. And if the customer was billed for sales tax, QuickBooks debits an accounts receivable account and credits a sales tax payable account for the amount of the sales tax due.

In this chapter, I explain how you can work directly with account registers to view entries and enter special transactions. I tell you how you can search for, modify, delete, and void transactions already entered into QuickBooks. I also explain how you can memorize and schedule transactions, track time, and reconcile accounts.

Viewing Account Registers

If you have a strong accounting background, you may not feel entirely comfortable letting QuickBooks make accounting entries for you without being able to check them. Although there really isn't any need to worry, you can assure yourself that QuickBooks is doing its job by checking ledger entries for yourself.

In QuickBooks, a ledger is referred to as an *account register*. QuickBooks maintains account registers for all asset, liability, and equity accounts. You can open these registers to see how QuickBooks recorded a transaction. And, as I discuss later in this chapter, you can use account registers to add, modify, delete, and void transactions.

✔ Tips

- I tell you more about account types and subtypes in the **Introduction** of this book.
- As shown in **Figure 4** and elsewhere throughout this chapter, an account register is very much like the paper check register that came with your check book.

To view an account register

1. Choose Lists > Chart of Accounts (**Figure 1**) to display the Chart of Accounts list window (**Figure 2**).
2. Scroll through the list to find the account you want to view.
3. Double-click the name of the account you want to view.

   Or

   Select the name of the account you want to view and choose Use Register from the Action pop-up menu (**Figure 3**).

   The account register window for the account appears (**Figure 4**).

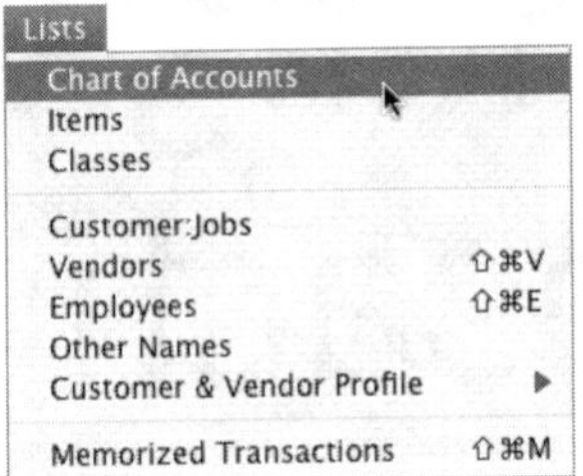

Figure 1 Choose Chart of Accounts from the Lists menu.

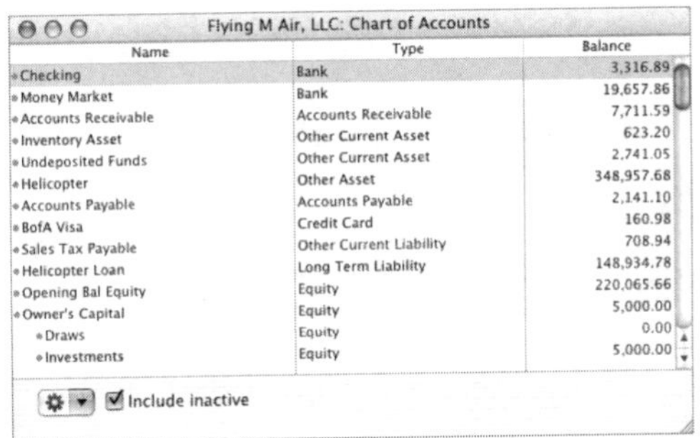

Figure 2 The Chart of Accounts list window with an asset account selected.

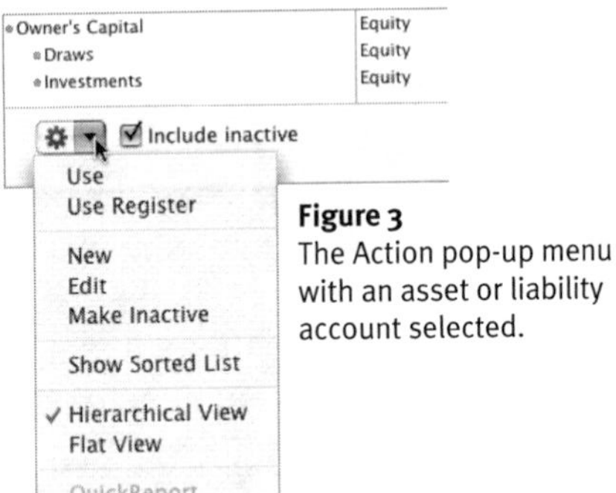

Figure 3 The Action pop-up menu with an asset or liability account selected.

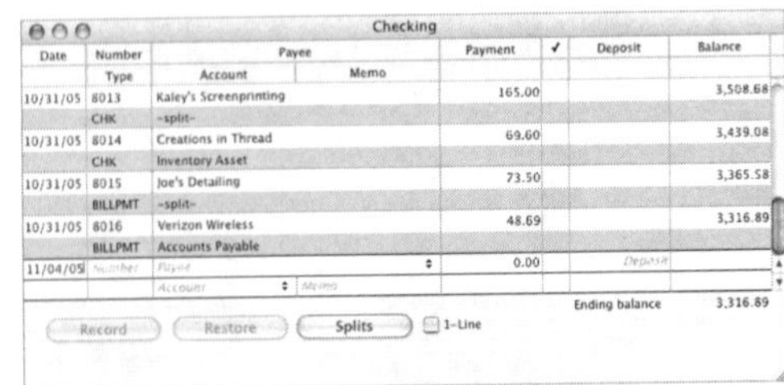

Figure 4 The account register for a bank account.

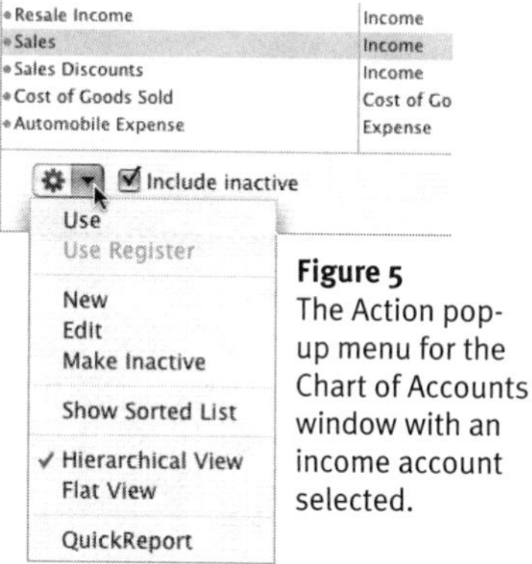

Figure 5 The Action pop-up menu for the Chart of Accounts window with an income account selected.

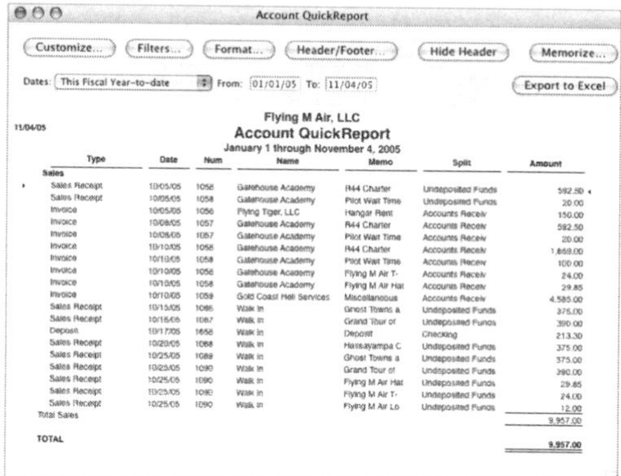

Flying M Air, LLC
Account QuickReport
January 1 through November 4, 2005

Type	Date	Num	Name	Memo	Split	Amount
Sales						
Sales Receipt	10/05/05	1056	Gatehouse Academy	R44 Charter	Undeposited Funds	592.50
Sales Receipt	10/05/05	1056	Gatehouse Academy	Pilot Wait Time	Undeposited Funds	20.00
Invoice	10/05/05	1056	Flying Tiger, LLC	Hangar Rent	Accounts Receiv	150.00
Invoice	10/08/05	1057	Gatehouse Academy	R44 Charter	Accounts Receiv	592.50
Invoice	10/08/05	1057	Gatehouse Academy	Pilot Wait Time	Accounts Receiv	20.00
Invoice	10/10/05	1058	Gatehouse Academy	R44 Charter	Accounts Receiv	1,669.00
Invoice	10/10/05	1058	Gatehouse Academy	Pilot Wait Time	Accounts Receiv	100.00
Invoice	10/10/05	1058	Gatehouse Academy	Flying M Air T-	Accounts Receiv	24.00
Invoice	10/10/05	1058	Gatehouse Academy	Flying M Air Hat	Accounts Receiv	29.85
Invoice	10/10/05	1059	Gold Coast Heli Services	Miscellaneous	Accounts Receiv	4,585.00
Sales Receipt	10/15/05	1086	Walk In	Ghost Towns a	Undeposited Funds	375.00
Sales Receipt	10/16/05	1087	Walk In	Grand Tour of	Undeposited Funds	390.00
Deposit	10/17/05	1656	Walk In	Deposit	Checking	213.30
Sales Receipt	10/20/05	1088	Walk In	Hassayampa C	Undeposited Funds	375.00
Sales Receipt	10/25/05	1089	Walk In	Ghost Towns a	Undeposited Funds	375.00
Sales Receipt	10/25/05	1090	Walk In	Grand Tour of	Undeposited Funds	390.00
Sales Receipt	10/25/05	1090	Walk In	Flying M Air Hat	Undeposited Funds	29.85
Sales Receipt	10/25/05	1090	Walk In	Flying M Air T-	Undeposited Funds	24.00
Sales Receipt	10/25/05	1090	Walk In	Flying M Air Lo	Undeposited Funds	12.00
Total Sales						9,957.00
TOTAL						9,957.00

Figure 6 A QuickReport for an income account.

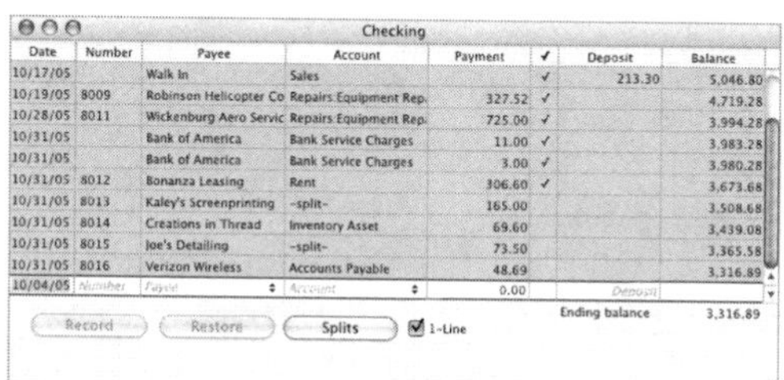
Checking

Date	Number	Payee	Account	Payment	✓	Deposit	Balance
10/17/05		Walk In	Sales		✓	213.30	5,046.80
10/19/05	8009	Robinson Helicopter Co	Repairs:Equipment Rep.	327.52	✓		4,719.28
10/28/05	8011	Wickenburg Aero Servic	Repairs:Equipment Rep.	725.00	✓		3,994.28
10/31/05		Bank of America	Bank Service Charges	11.00	✓		3,983.28
10/31/05		Bank of America	Bank Service Charges	3.00	✓		3,980.28
10/31/05	8012	Bonanza Leasing	Rent	306.60	✓		3,673.68
10/31/05	8013	Kaley's Screenprinting	-split-	165.00			3,508.68
10/31/05	8014	Creations in Thread	Inventory Asset	69.60			3,439.08
10/31/05	8015	Joe's Detailing	-split-	73.50			3,365.58
10/31/05	8016	Verizon Wireless	Accounts Payable	48.69			3,316.89
10/04/05	Number	Payee	Account	0.00		Deposit	

Ending balance 3,316.89

Figure 7 Turning on the 1-Line check box displays each entry in just one line.

✔ Tips

- If you select an income or expense account in step 3, the Use Register command on the Action pop-up menu is gray and the QuickReport command appears (**Figure 5**). Double-clicking an income or expense account name or choosing QuickReport from the Action pop-up menu displays a report of all activity for that account within a certain date range (**Figure 6**). I tell you about reports in **Chapter 9**.
- The exact appearance of an account register varies by account type. In general, however, most account registers appear like the one in **Figure 4**.
- By default, each account register entry consists of two lines (**Figure 4**). You can display entries in a single line (**Figure 7**) by turning on the 1-Line check box at the bottom of the account register window.
- The last entry in an account register is actually a blank form for creating a new register entry. I explain how to enter transactions in an account register later in this chapter.

Entering Special Transactions

As discussed in **Chapters 3 and 4**, QuickBooks uses intuitive forms for entering sales, cash receipts, deposit, payment, and billing transactions. For most businesses, these forms will handle the vast majority of transactions that need to be entered.

There are some instances, however, when you may need to enter transactions that are not covered by forms. For example, you may need to adjust the balance of an asset account to account for depreciation or a change in market value. That's where QuickBooks' Make General Journal Entries command comes in. But you can also enter special transactions directly into account registers.

In this part of the chapter, I explain how to enter special transactions with the General Journal Entry window (**Figure 9**) and directly into an account register window (**Figure 17**).

✔ Tips

- I discuss inventory-related transactions in **Chapter 7**.
- Making journal entries using the techniques in this part of the chapter requires a good knowledge of accounting practices and a complete understanding of how double-entry accounting works. If you're an accounting novice, it's best not to enter special transactions unless you have specific instructions from a knowledgeable bookkeeper or accountant.

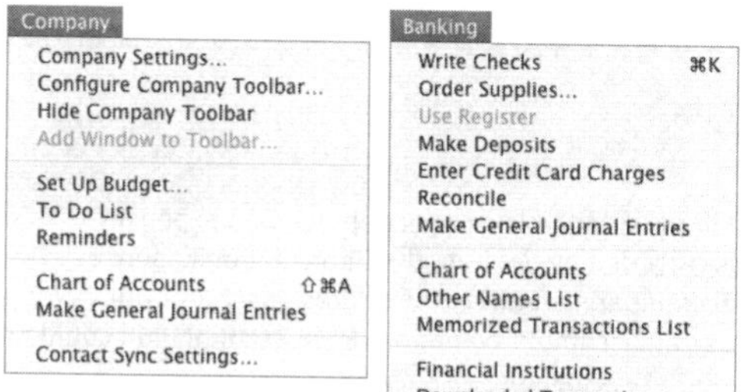

Figures 8a & 8b The Make General Journal Entries command appears on two of QuickBooks's menus: Company (left) and Banking (right).

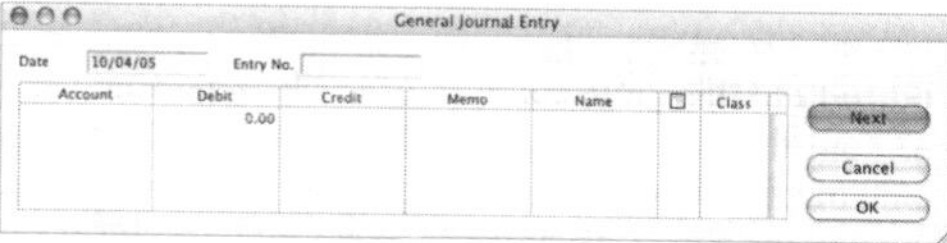

Figure 9 The General Journal Entry window is a form for entering good, old-fashioned debits and credits.

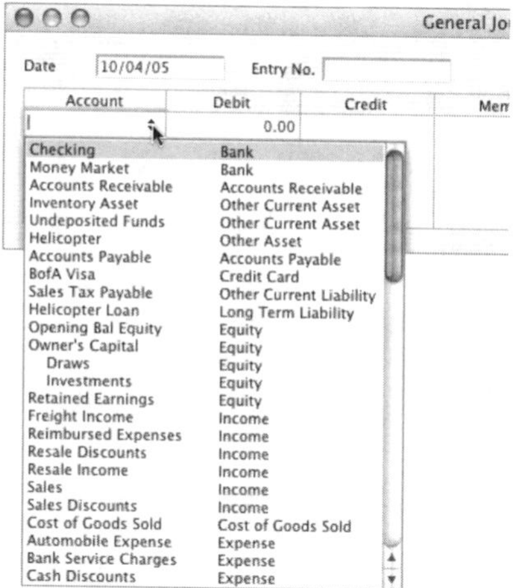

Figure 10 Choose an account from the drop-down list.

To enter a transaction in the General Journal Entry window

1. Choose Company > Make General Journal Entries (**Figure 8a**) or Banking > Make General Journal Entries (**Figure 8b**) to display the General Journal Entry window (**Figure 9**).
2. Enter the transaction date in the Date box.
3. If desired, enter a reference number for the transaction in the Entry No. box.
4. Fill out the first line of the transaction detail area with debit information:
   - **Account** is the name of the account you want to debit. Choose an account from the drop-down list (**Figure 10**).
   - **Debit** is the amount of the debit.
   - **Memo** is an optional memo to appear with the debit part of the transaction.
   - **Name** is the name associated with the account debit. This is optional and may not apply.
   - **Class** is the name of the class associated with the debit. This is optional.
5. If another account should be debited as part of the transaction, enter its information in the next line of the transaction detail area. Repeat this process for each account to be debited for the transaction.
6. Fill out the next line of the transaction detail area with credit information:
   - **Account** is the name of the account you want to credit. Choose an account from the drop-down list.
   - **Credit** is the amount of the credit.
   - **Memo** is an optional memo to appear with the credit part of the transaction.

Continued on next page...

Continued from previous page.

- ▲ **Name** is the name associated with the account credit. This is optional and may not apply.
- ▲ **Class** is the name of the class associated with the credit. This is optional.

7. If another account should be credited as part of the transaction, enter its information in the next line of the transaction detail area. Repeat this process for each account to be credited for the transaction.

8. To save the transaction and enter another one, click Next.

   Or

   To save the transaction without entering another one, click OK.

   QuickBooks makes an entry sound and enters the transaction into appropriate registers.

Figure 11 shows an example of a simple entry to record depreciation. **Figure 12** shows a more complex example to record an owner's contribution of assets to the business.

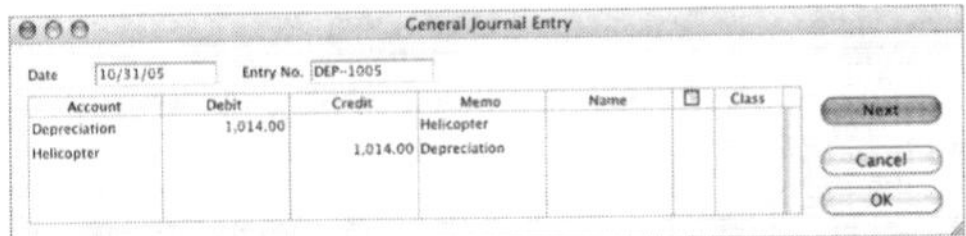

Figure 11 In this example, depreciation expense is recorded by debiting the Depreciation Expense account and crediting the related asset account. If you use an accumulated depreciation account, you could credit that instead.

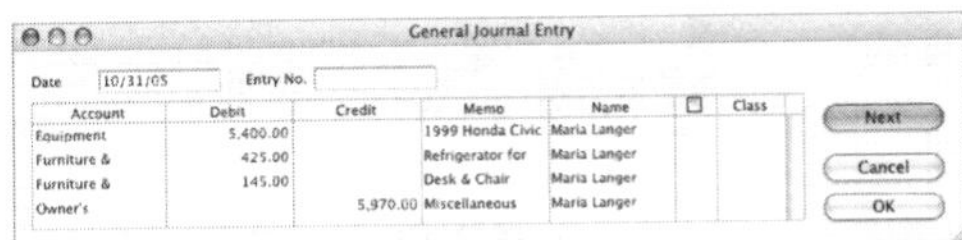

Figure 12 In this more complex example, an owner has contributed various assets to the business. The value of each asset is debited to the appropriate asset account and the total value of the contribution is credited to the owner's investments account. Note that a cash contribution could be recorded using the Make Deposits command (as discussed in **Chapter 4**) instead of a General Journal Entry.

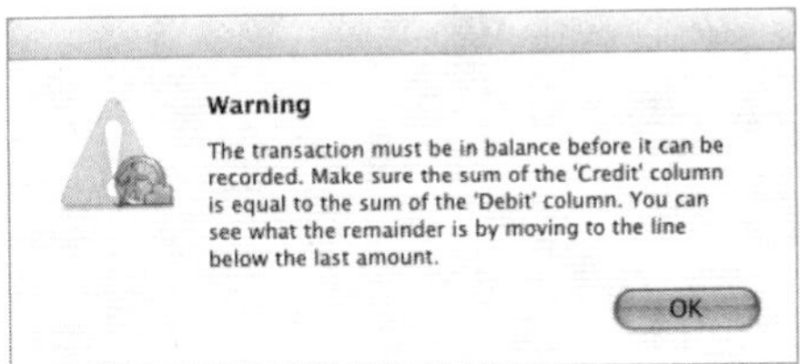

Figure 13 If a transaction's debits and credits don't balance, you'll see this dialog when you try to save the entry.

✔ Tips

- It isn't really necessary to enter all debits before all credits in a transaction. You can enter them in any order, as long as the transaction balances. In other words, you can perform steps 4 through 7 in any order.
- After step 8, if a transaction's debits do not equal its credits, a Warning dialog like the one in **Figure 13** appears. Click OK, then correct the appropriate debit or credit amount to balance the transaction before trying to save the transaction again.
- If you enter a Name for a transaction debit or credit, that name may appear in the Payee field of the transaction. Take a look at **Figures 12, 15,** and **16** for an example.

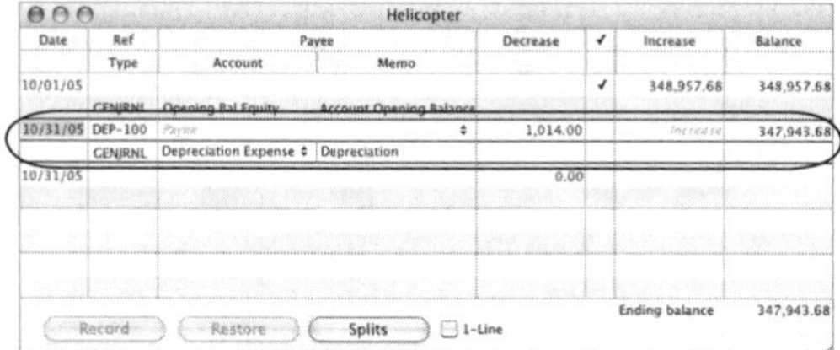

Figure 14 The account register for an asset account, showing the credit side of a transaction to record depreciation.

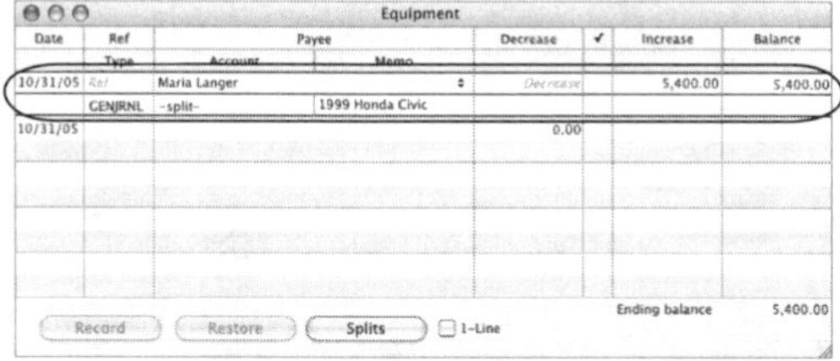

Figure 15 The account register for an asset account, showing the debit side of a transaction to record a partner's investment in the company.

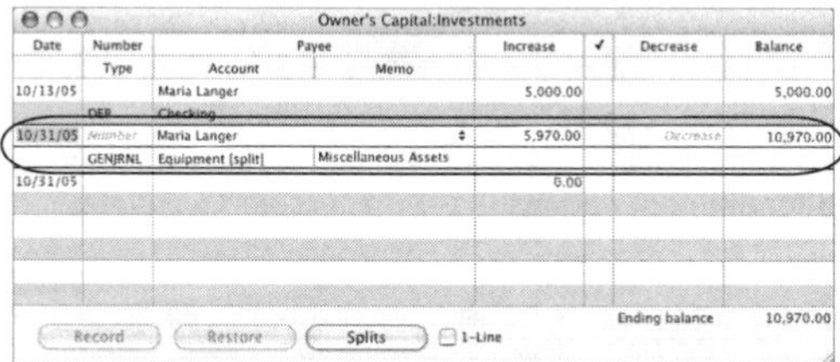

Figure 16 The account register for an owner's equity investment account, showing the credit side of a transaction to record the owner's investment in the company.

To modify a General Journal entry

1. Open the account register for either the debit or credit part of the transaction and scroll to the transaction (**Figures 14, 15, and 16**).
2. Double-click the transaction. The General Journal Entry window for the transaction appears (**Figures 11 and 12**).
3. Make changes to the transaction as desired.
4. Click OK. The changes are saved.

✔ Tips

- You can only use this technique with transactions that display GENJRNL as the transaction type in the ledger window. Double-clicking other types of transactions may display other forms or messages indicating that they cannot be edited.
- A potentially annoying thing about QuickBooks is its backwards presentation of debits and credits. I don't know about you, but when I learned accounting, debits appeared on the left and credits appeared on the right. QuickBooks reverses this in its account registers, as shown in **Figures 14, 15, and 16**.

To enter a transaction in an account register window

1. Open the account register for the account you want to enter a transaction into. The account can be either the debit or credit side of the transaction, but it must be an asset, liability, or equity account.
2. Click in the date field in the empty transaction in the window to activate that transaction (**Figure 17**).
3. Enter information in each field of the transaction. The field names are identified with gray italic labels:
   - ▲ **Date** is the date of the transaction. The date is automatically filled in with the current date or the date of the last transaction entered, but you can override the date by entering a different one.
   - ▲ **Ref (Figures 14, 15,** and **17)** or **Number (Figure 16, 18,** and **19)** is a reference number for the transaction. This field is optional.
   - ▲ **Payee**, **Customer**, or **Vendor** is the name associated with the transaction. Although this field is optional, you should not leave it blank when entering a transaction affecting an accounts receivable (**Figure 18**) or accounts payable (**Figure 19**) balance.
   - ▲ **Item** is the item sold. This field appears for accounts receivable accounts only (**Figure 18**).
   - ▲ **Account** is the account on the other side of the transaction. For example, to enter depreciation expense in an asset account's account register, you'd choose Depreciation Expense from the Account drop-down list. This option does not appear in accounts receivable account registers (**Figure 18**).

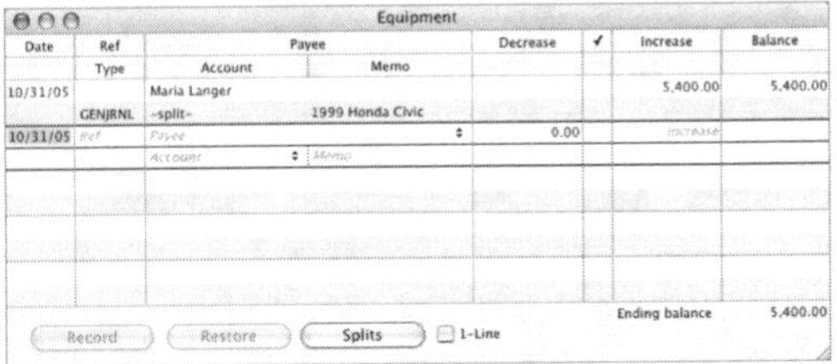

Figure 17 Clicking anywhere in a transaction activates the transaction so you can enter or edit contents.

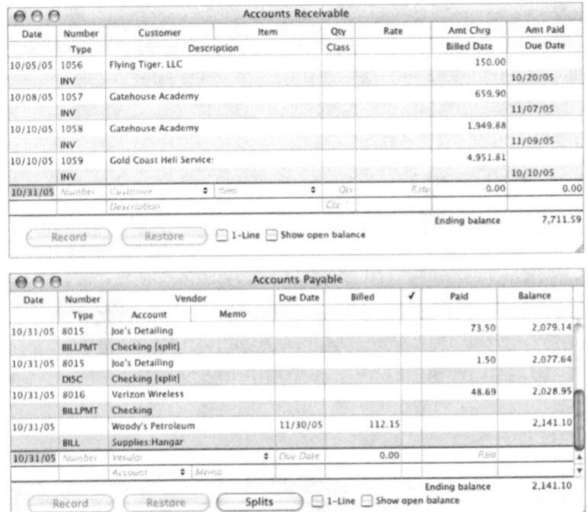

Figures 18 & 19 Accounts receivable (top) and accounts payable (bottom) account register windows offer different options than other account registers.

- **Memo** is an optional note about the transaction. This field does not appear in all account registers.
- **Description** is a description of the item sold. This optional field appears only in accounts receivable account registers (**Figure 18**).
- **Qty** is the number of items sold. This field appears only in accounts receivable account registers (**Figure 18**).
- **Class** is the class associated with the transaction. This optional field appears only in accounts receivable account registers (**Figure 18**).
- **Rate** is the per unit price of items sold. This field appears only in accounts receivable account registers (**Figure 18**).
- **Due Date** is the date the amount of the transaction is due. This field appears only in accounts receivable (**Figure 18**) and accounts payable (**Figure 19**) account registers.
- **Increase**, **Decrease**, **Payment**, **Deposit**, **Billed**, **Amt Chrg**, **Paid**, or **Amt Paid** is the amount of the transaction for that account. It is vital to enter the amount in the correct column to make a debit or credit. QuickBooks automatically uses the same amount for the account on the other side of the transaction.
- **Billed Date** is the date the amount was billed. This field only appears in accounts receivable account registers (**Figure 18**).
- **Balance** is calculated by QuickBooks and cannot be modified.

4. Click Record. QuickBooks makes a sound and records the transaction.

Continued on next page...

Continued from previous page.

✔ Tips

- Entering transactions directly into account registers can be tricky. My advice: don't do it. Use the General Journal Entry window or other forms within QuickBooks to enter all transactions.
- If the transaction amount needs to be split between two or more other accounts, you can click the Splits button that appears in certain account register windows to expand the window and offer more options (**Figure 20**). Simply enter the account and amount for each line in the split in the bottom half of the form. You can enter as many lines as necessary before clicking Record to enter the transaction.

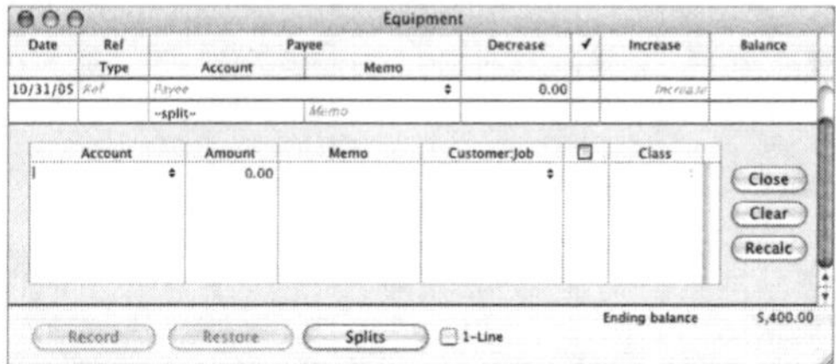

Figure 20 Clicking the Splits button offers additional lines for transaction details. This is a relatively advanced feature of QuickBooks that requires a solid understanding of double-entry accounting.

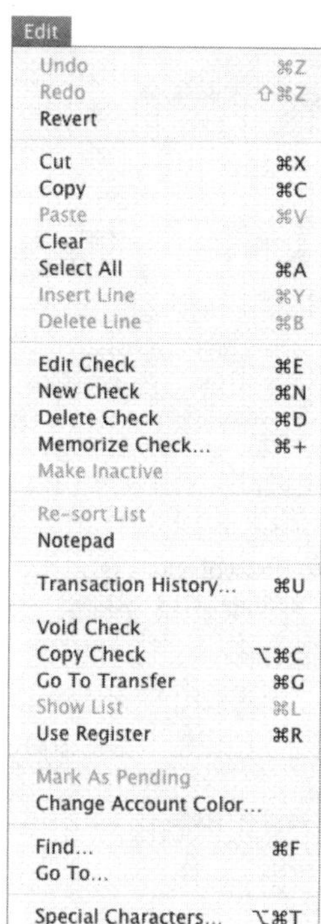

Figure 21
The Edit menu.

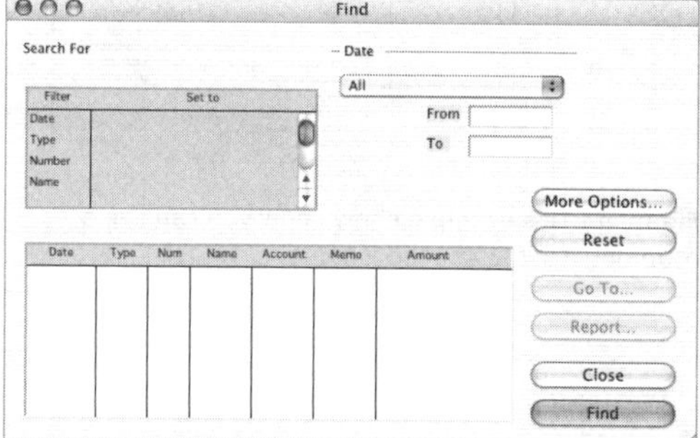

Figure 22 The Find window before any criteria has been set.

Searching for Transactions

Suppose you get a phone call from one of your customers. His company's internal auditors are in his office, questioning a payment he made for $63.78 in February of last year. Although he can find the cancelled check, he can't find the invoice identifying what it was for. He needs a copy faxed to him right away.

Your company has been using QuickBooks for years now and has hundreds—if not thousands—of transactions recorded. How can you quickly find just that one?

The answer is simple: use QuickBooks' built-in searching feature. This feature enables you to search through all QuickBooks records to find transactions based on criteria you specify. Just create *filters* that detail your search criteria and click a button. QuickBooks instantly displays a list of all transactions that match the search criteria.

✔ Tip

- QuickBooks finds transactions that match *all* search criteria you enter. The more filters you include in the Find dialog, the fewer transactions QuickBooks will find.

To search for a transaction

1. Choose Edit > Find (**Figure 21**), or press ⌘F. The Find window appears (**Figure 22**).
2. In the Filter list, select the type of criteria you want to search by. Your options are Date, Type, Number, Name, Source, Account, Memo, and Amount. The top center of the window changes to display options for setting that criteria.

Continued on next page...

Continued from previous page.

3. Set filter criteria as desired, using the pop-up menu, drop-down list, or boxes that appear (**Figures 23 and 24**).
4. To set more than one filter, repeat steps 2 and 3. **Figure 25** shows an example with two filters set. Remember, QuickBooks will find records that match all search criteria.
5. Click Find. QuickBooks displays a list of matches in the bottom half of the Find window (**Figure 26**).

✔ Tips

- Clicking the More Options button in the Find dialog (**Figure 22**) displays the Report Filters dialog, which offers more filtering options. I explain how to use this feature in **Chapter 9**.
- Clicking the Report button in the Find dialog (**Figure 26**) displays a report of the search results (**Figure 27**). I tell you more about working with QuickBooks reports in **Chapter 9**.
- The list of matches that appears includes both bold and regular text. Entries that appear in bold text are transactions. Entries that appear in regular text are entries within a transaction.

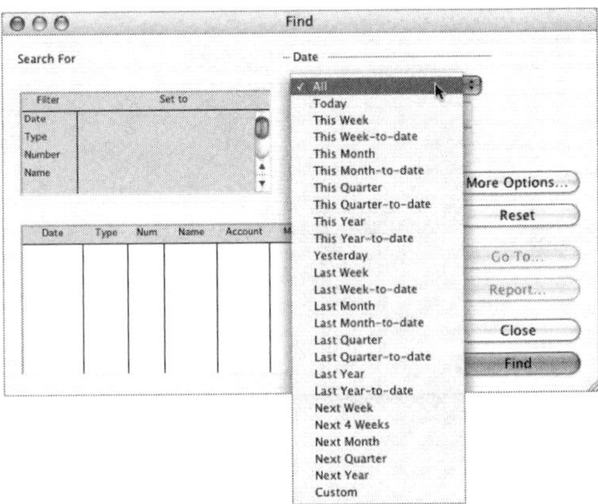

Figure 23 This example shows how you can use a pop-up menu to choose a date range.

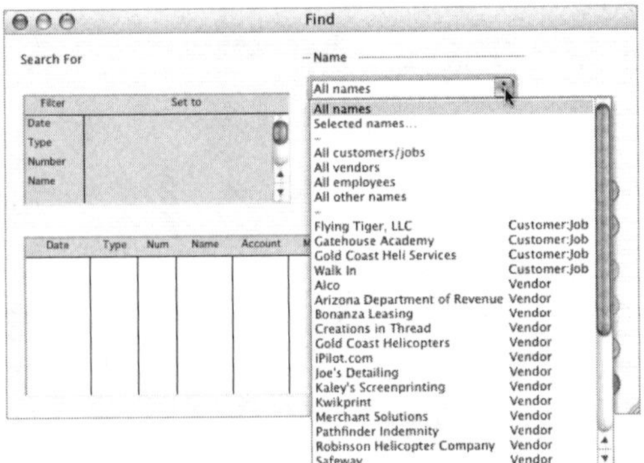

Figure 24 This example shows how you can use a drop-down list to choose a name.

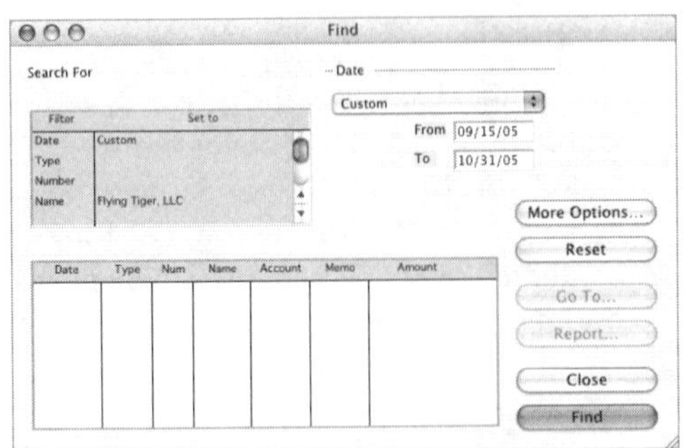

Figure 25 The Find window with two filters set.

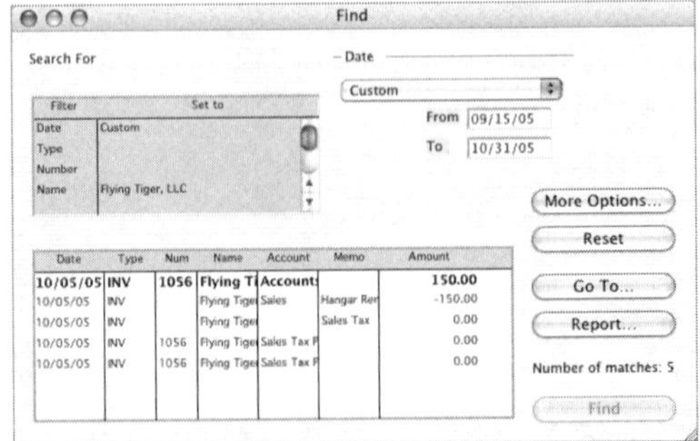

Figure 26 The search results based on two filters.

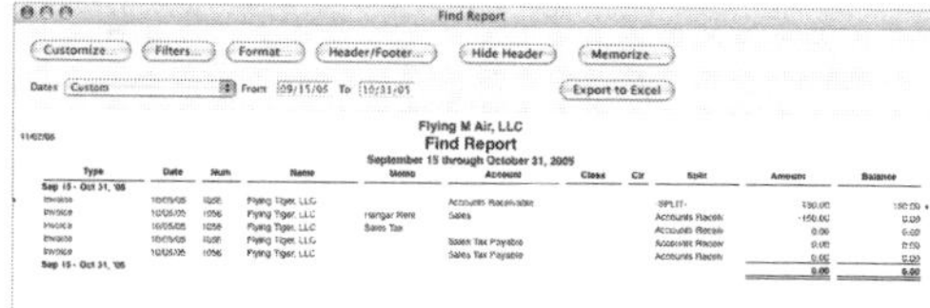

Figure 27 Clicking the Report button in the Find dialog displays a report of search results.

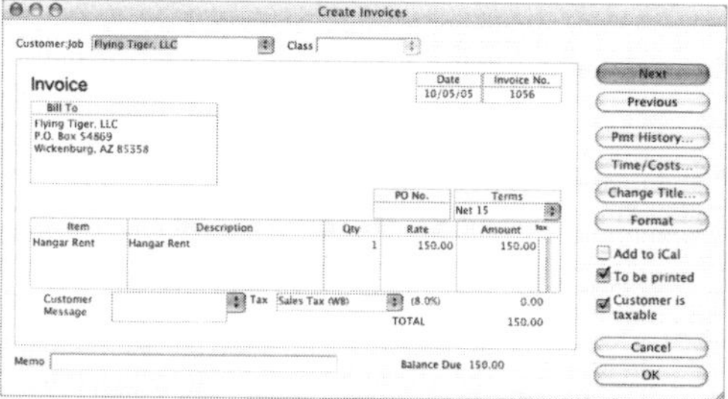

Figure 28 Double-clicking a found transaction opens it in its own window. You can then modify, delete, void, or print it.

To perform another search

1. In the Find window (**Figure 26**), click the Reset button. All filters are cleared and the search results disappear (**Figure 22**).
2. Follow steps 2 through 5 in the previous section to create filters and perform the search.

To work with a found transaction

1. In the bottom half of the Find window, double-click the transaction you want to work with (**Figure 26**). The transaction opens in its own window (**Figure 28**).
2. When you are finished working with the transaction, click the close button in its window to dismiss it.

Working with Transactions

One of the best features of QuickBooks is that when a transaction is created, its details are not carved in stone. At any time, you can open a transaction to modify, delete, or void it. This part of the chapter explains how.

To open a transaction

1. Open the form that created the transaction. For example, if the transaction is an invoice, choose Customers > Create Invoices.
2. Click the Previous or Next button to scroll through transactions until you find the one you want to work with.

Or

1. Use QuickBooks's search feature, as discussed earlier in this chapter, to search for the transaction.
2. In the list of search results (**Figure 26**), double-click the transaction you want to work with.

Or

In a QuickBooks report window (**Figure 27**), double-click the transaction you want to work with.

No matter which method you use, the transaction you want to work with appears in a window you can use to view its details and work with it (**Figure 28**).

✔ Tips

- I explain how to open various data entry forms throughout this book.
- In many cases you can double-click an entry in an account register window to view and work with the entry in the appropriate form. This technique, however, does not work for all types of entries.

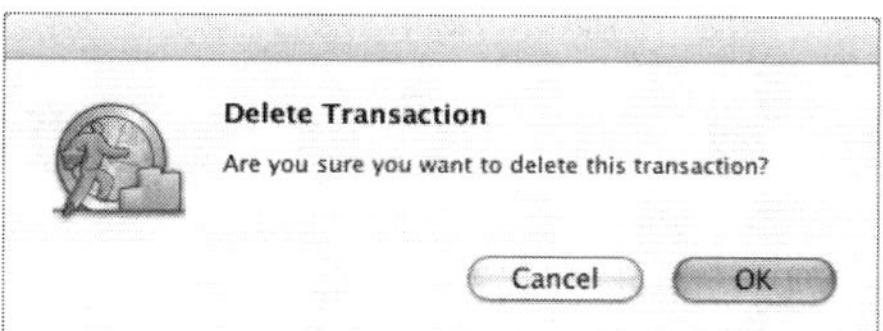

Figure 29 This dialog appears when you choose Delete from the Edit menu.

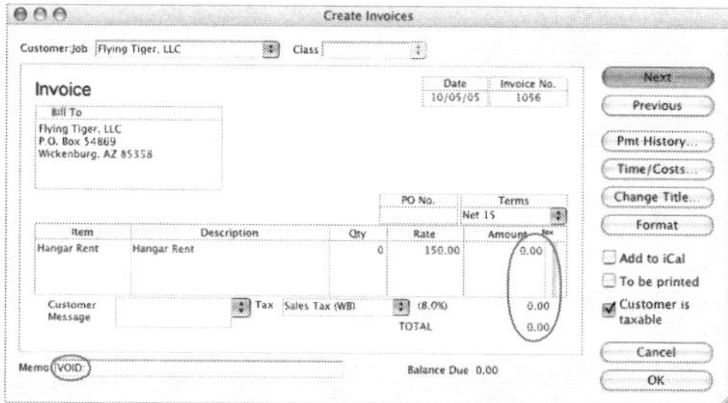

Figure 30 The transaction in **Figure 28** after being voided. Note how the amounts are changed to zero and the word *VOID* appears in the Memo field.

To modify a transaction

1. Follow the instructions on the previous page to view the transaction you want to modify.
2. Make changes as desired in the transaction window.
3. Click OK to save your changes.

✖ Warning!

- Use caution when modifying reconciled transactions! Changing the value of a transaction that has been reconciled can cause account balances to be incorrect. I tell you more about reconciling accounts later in this chapter.

To delete or void a transaction

1. Follow the instructions on the previous page to view the transaction you want to work with.
2. Choose the appropriate option from the Edit menu (**Figure 21**):
   - **Delete *Item Type*** deletes the item. This removes all record of it from QuickBooks. When you choose this option, a confirmation dialog like the one in **Figure 29** appears. Click OK to delete the transaction.
   - **Void *Item Type*** voids the item. This marks the item as void, thus preventing its amounts from affecting journal and ledger balances. The transaction remains in QuickBooks and can be consulted if necessary. When you choose this option, the amount of the transaction is zeroed out and the word *VOID* appears in the memo field (**Figure 30**).

Memorizing & Scheduling Transactions

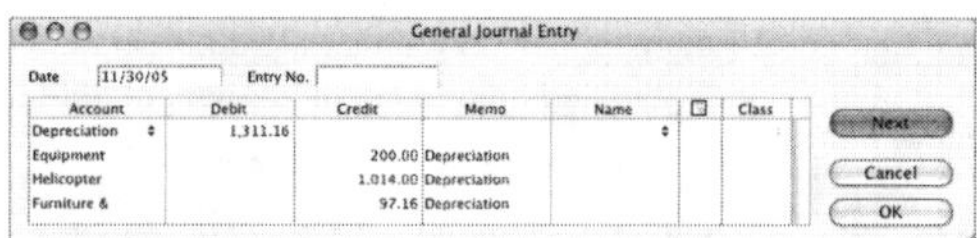

Figure 31 An example of an entry to record monthly depreciation for several assets.

Suppose that every month, at month-end, you prepare an entry that records depreciation for a bunch of assets your company has owned for several years. The transaction is cumbersome because it includes a separate line item for each asset's depreciation amount (**Figure 31**), which remains the same each month.

You can automate much of the entry process by memorizing the transaction. Then, when you need to record depreciation, simply recall the memorized transaction and enter it.

If you want to make your job even easier, however, you can take the memorized transactions feature one step further by scheduling transactions to be entered automatically at a predetermined time. Imagine how much time this could save you if you set up a scheduled transaction for an asset's depreciation so it automatically enters every month for the entire life of the asset!

In this part of the chapter, I explain how to memorize transactions and how to work with the Memorized Transaction List. I also explain how to schedule transactions so QuickBooks either reminds you to enter them when they're due or enters them automatically for you.

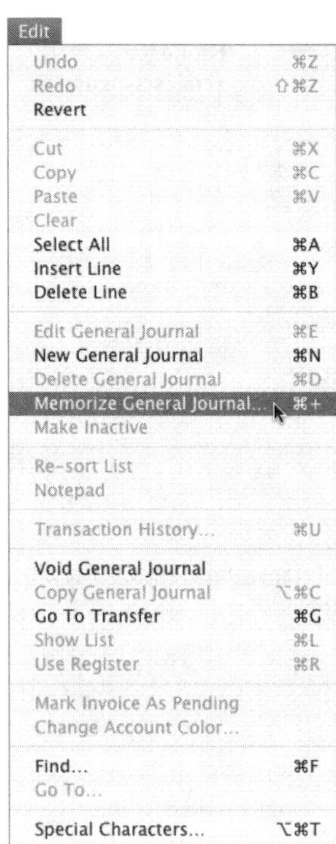

Figure 32 The exact wording of the Memorize command varies depending on the type of transaction window that is active. In this example, the command is referring to the General Journal entry in **Figure 31**.

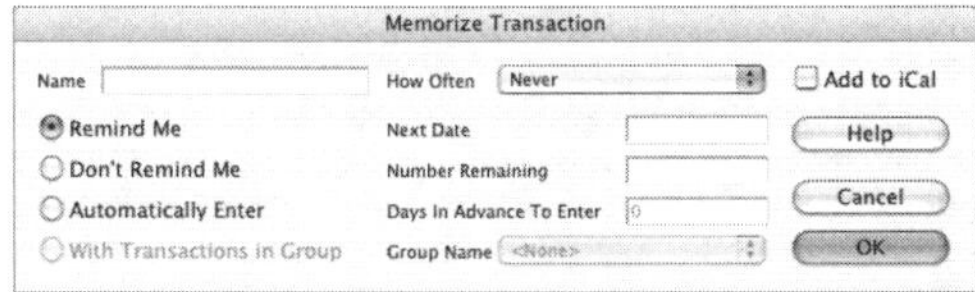

Figure 33 The Memorize Transaction dialog.

To memorize a transaction

1. Create an entry you want to memorize, but do not click OK or Next to save it (**Figure 31**).

   Or

   Follow the instructions earlier in this chapter to view the transaction you want to memorize.

2. Choose Edit > Memorize *Transaction Type* (**Figure 32**) or press ⌘+. The Memorize Transaction dialog appears (**Figure 33**).

3. Enter a name for the transaction in the Name box.

4. Click OK. QuickBooks makes a sound to indicate that the transaction has been memorized and the dialog disappears.

5. If you have not yet saved the transaction you memorized—for example, if you just created it—click OK to save and enter it.

✔ Tip

- I explain how to set other options in the Memorize Transaction dialog (**Figure 33**) later in this part of the chapter.

To open the Memorized Transaction List window

Choose Lists > Memorized Transactions (**Figure 34**) or press Shift ⌘ M. The Memorized Transaction List window appears (**Figure 35**).

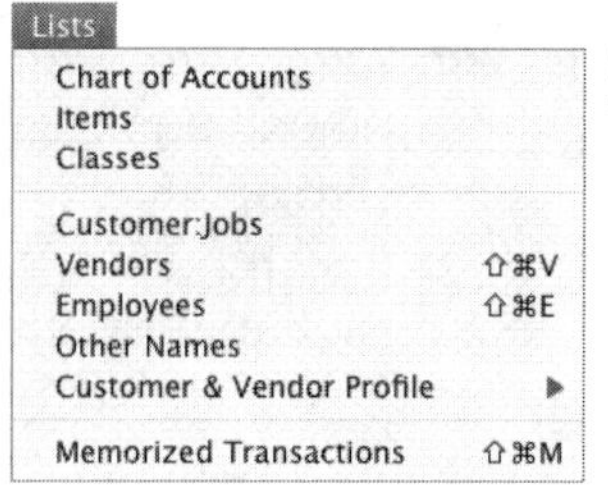

Figure 34 The Lists menu.

To use a memorized transaction

1. In the Memorized Transaction List window (**Figure 35**), select the transaction you want to use.
2. Choose Use from the Action pop-up menu.
3. The transaction appears in the appropriate window (**Figure 31**). Make changes if necessary to transaction details.
4. Click OK. The transaction is entered.

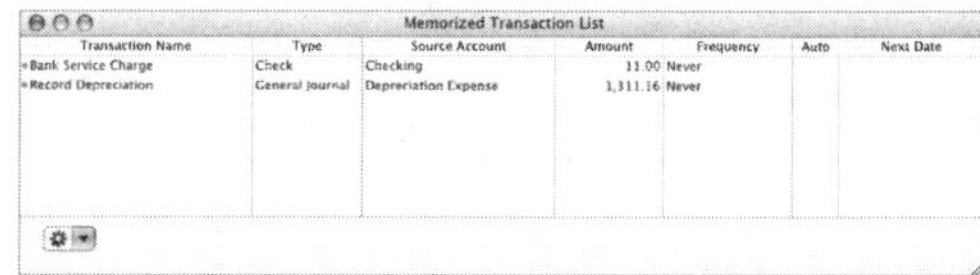

Figure 35 The Memorized Transaction List window with two memorized transactions.

✔ Tip

- Following these instructions makes a copy of the original transaction—it does not actually open the original transaction. As a result, making changes as suggested in step 3 does not modify the original transaction.

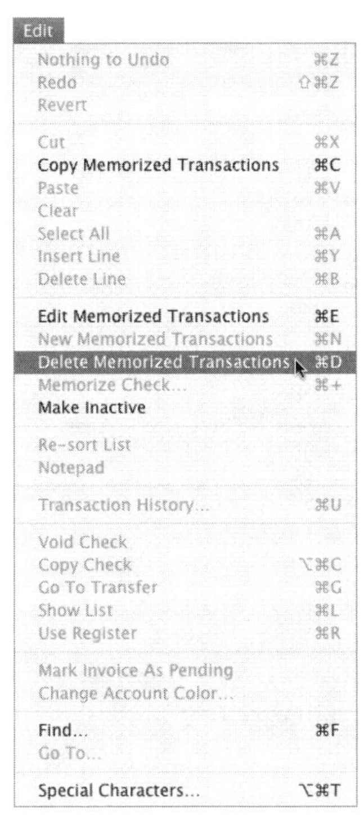

Figure 36 Choose Delete Memorized Transaction from the Edit menu.

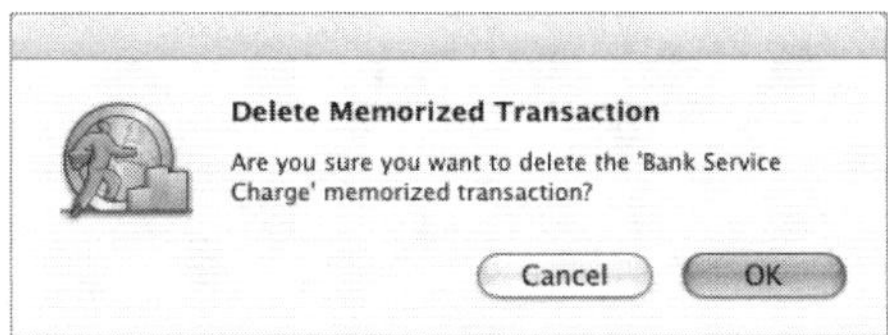

Figure 37 Click OK in this dialog to delete the memorized transaction.

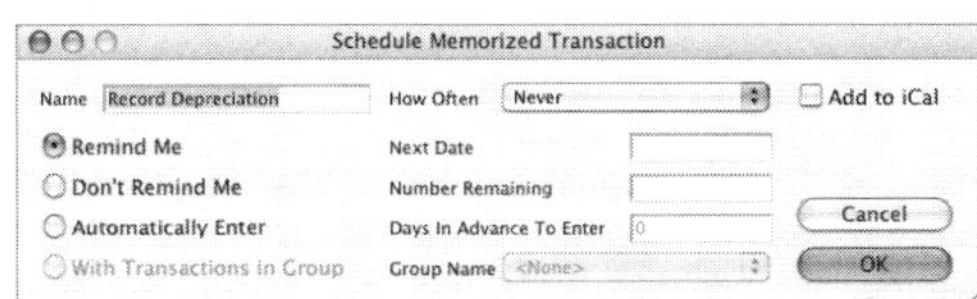

Figure 38 Use this window to set options for a memorized transaction.

To delete a memorized transaction

1. In the Memorized Transaction List window (**Figure 35**), select the transaction you want to delete.
2. Choose Edit > Delete Memorized Transaction (**Figure 36**) or press ⌘D.
3. A confirmation dialog like the one in **Figure 37** appears. Click OK. The transaction is removed from the Memorized Transaction List window.

✔ Tip

- Deleting a memorized transaction does not delete any transactions that have already been entered into QuickBooks. It simply removes the transaction from the Memorized Transaction List and prevents it from being used or automatically entered again.

To modify the settings for a memorized transaction

1. In the Memorized Transaction List window (**Figure 35**), select the transaction you want to modify settings for.
2. Choose Edit from the window's Action pop-up menu. The Schedule Memorized Transaction window appears (**Figure 38**).
3. Make changes to settings as desired.
4. Click OK.

To set reminder & scheduling options for a memorized transaction

1. Display the Memorize Transaction dialog (**Figure 33**) or Schedule Memorized Transaction window (**Figure 38**) for a transaction.
2. Select one of the radio buttons:
   - ▲ **Remind Me** tells QuickBooks to add the transaction to the Reminders window (**Figure 39**) when scheduled.
   - ▲ **Don't Remind Me** tells QuickBooks not to remind you about the transaction. If you choose this option, skip ahead to step 8.
   - ▲ **Automatically Enter** tells QuickBooks to automatically enter the transaction when scheduled.
   - ▲ **With Transactions in Group** enables you to associate the transaction with a predefined group, which can then be scheduled. A discussion of the transaction group feature is beyond the scope of this book.
3. Choose one of the options from the How Often pop-up menu (**Figure 40**).
4. Enter the date of the next reminder or entry in the Next Date box. If you chose Remind Me in step 2, skip ahead to step 8.
5. Enter the remaining number of transactions in the Number Remaining box.
6. Use the Days in Advance To Enter box to set the number of days before the transaction date to enter the transaction into QuickBooks.
7. To add the scheduled transaction to iCal as an event, turn on the Add to iCal check box.
8. Click OK.

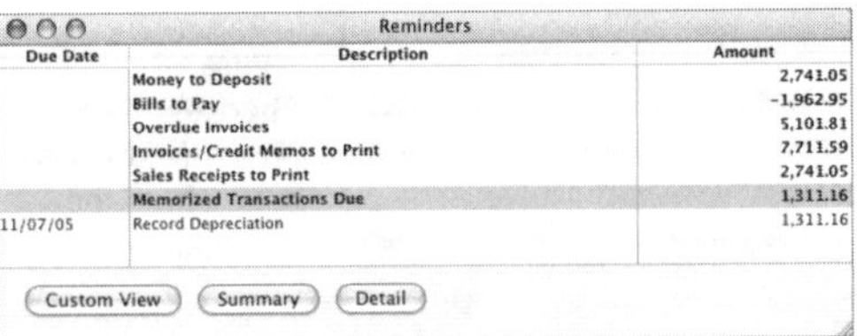

Figure 39 You can add a memorized transaction to the Reminders list window.

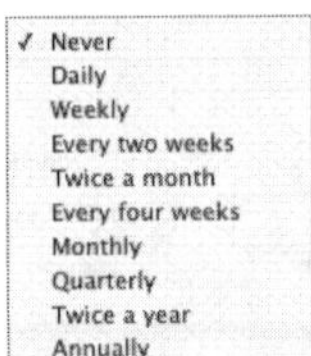

Figure 40 Use the How Often pop-up menu to set the frequency for reminders or automatic entries.

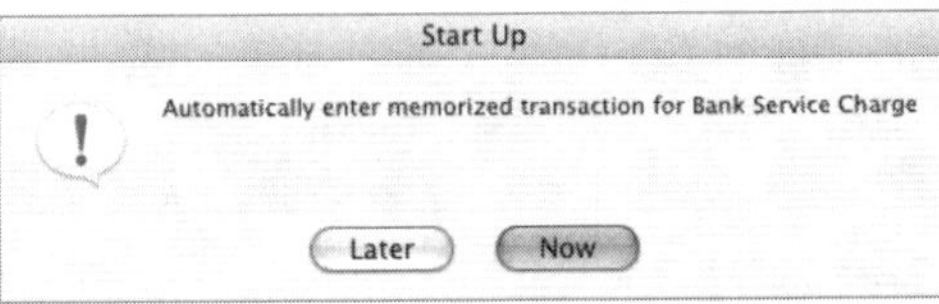

Figure 41 QuickBooks displays a dialog like this one when it's time to automatically enter a transaction.

✔ Tip

- When you set up a memorized transaction to be entered automatically, QuickBooks displays a dialog like the one in **Figure 41** when you start up QuickBooks and the entry is due. Click Later to enter the transaction at another time or click Now to enter it immediately.

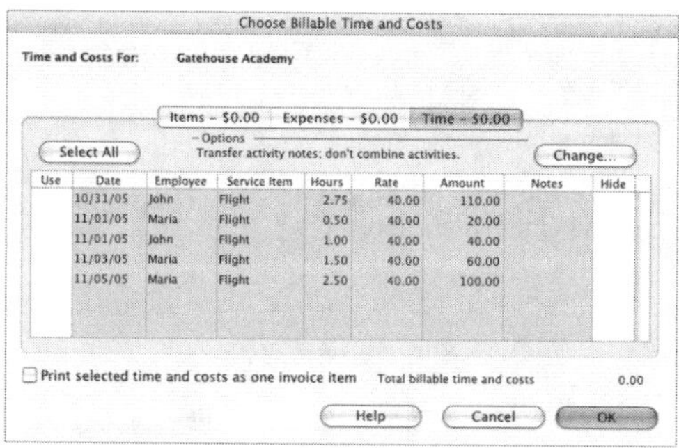

Figure 42 The Time pane of the Choose Billable Time and Costs dialog lists all service items billable for a specific customer or job.

Tracking Time

QuickBooks' built-in time tracking feature makes it easy to keep track of time spent by employees on specific jobs. Simply enter the name of the employee who performed the service, the name of the customer the service was for, the service that was performed, and the amount of time spent. At the same time, you can indicate whether the time is billable or not billable. QuickBooks stores this information in its data file.

Billable time information that has been entered in QuickBooks appears in the Time pane of the Choose Billable Time and Costs dialog for the related customer (**Figure 42**). You can select the items you want to bill to include them on invoices and sales receipts.

In this part of the chapter, I explain how to enter time information using two different onscreen forms: the Enter Single Activity form and the Weekly Timesheet form.

✔ Tips

- I explain how to use the Choose Billable Time and Costs dialog to charge customers for service items in **Chapter 3**.
- Tracking time works with service items. I explain how to create service items in **Chapter 2**.
- Although you may pay your employees based on billable time worked, QuickBooks' time tracking feature is entirely separate from its payroll feature. I tell you how to process payroll in **Chapter 8**.
- Although you can use QuickBooks' time tracking features to track time spent by subcontractors on services, that time cannot be marked as billable. Instead, to record billable time spent by subcontractors, be sure to enter the customer name for the service rendered when entering the subcontractor's bill for the service. The item the contractor billed you for will appear in the Items pane of the Choose Billable Time and Costs dialog for the customer or job.

To enter a single activity

1. Choose Employees > Time Tracking > Enter Single Activity (**Figure 43**). The Enter Single Activity window appears (**Figure 44**).
2. Fill in the form's fields:
   - ▲ **Date** is the date of the activity.
   - ▲ **Name** is the name of the employee or vendor who performed the activity.
   - ▲ **Customer:Job** is the name of the customer or job the activity was performed for.
   - ▲ **Service Item** is the name of the service item that was performed.
   - ▲ **Duration** is the amount of time spent performing the activity. Use decimal places to enter fractions.
   - ▲ **Class** is the class you want to assign to the activity. This field is optional.
   - ▲ **Notes** is notes about the activity performed. This field is optional.
3. If the activity is billable, turn on the Billable check box. Remember, services performed by vendors cannot be marked billable using the time tracking feature.
4. To save the activity and enter another one, click Next.

   Or

   To save the activity without entering another one, click OK.

Figure 45 shows an example of an entry for a single activity.

✔ Tip

- If you attempt to enter information that does not appear on the corresponding list for that field, QuickBooks displays a dialog offering to let you set up that name, customer or job, service item, or class.

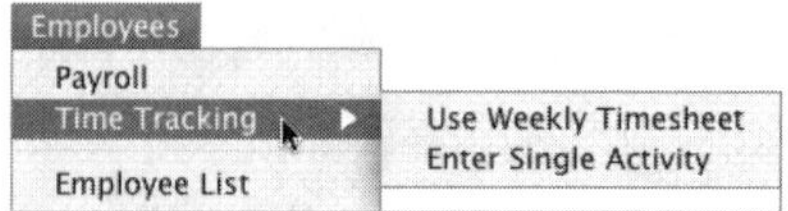

Figure 43 The Time Tracking submenu under the Employees menu.

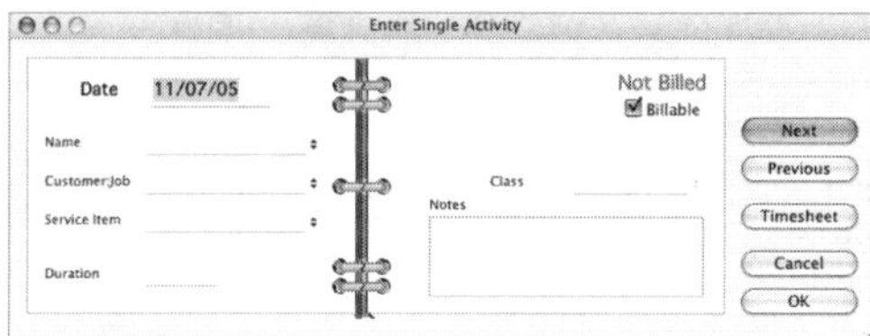

Figure 44 Use this form to enter information about a single activity.

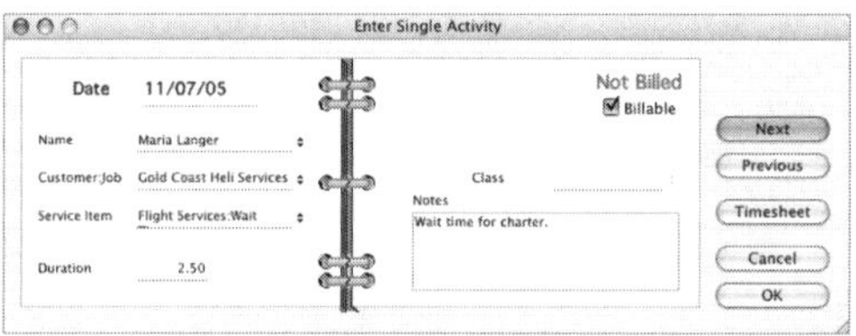

Figure 45 Here's an example of what an activity might look like when entered.

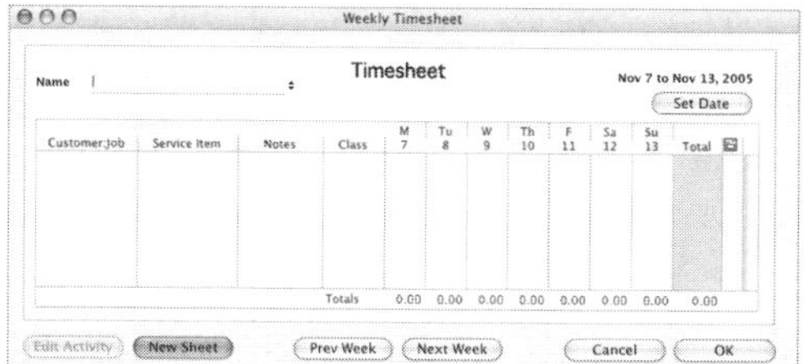

Figure 46 The Weekly Timesheet window enables you to enter a whole week's worth of activities for an employee or vendor.

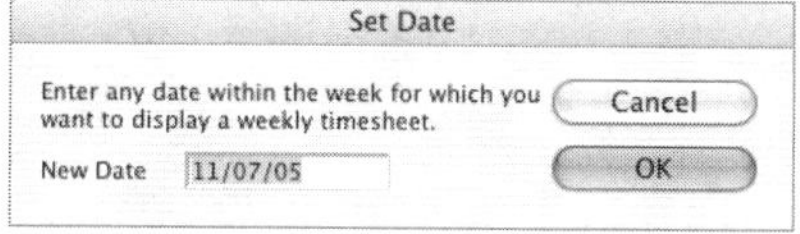

Figure 47 You can use this dialog to quickly display a specific week.

To enter multiple activities on a weekly timesheet

1. Choose Employees > Time Tracking > Use Weekly Timesheet (**Figure 43**). The Weekly Timesheet window for the current week appears (**Figure 46**).
2. Choose the name of the employee or vendor for which you want to record time from the Name drop-down list.
3. Click the Prev Week or Next Week button to display the week for which you want to enter activities.

   Or

   Click the Set Date button to display the Set Date dialog (**Figure 47**). Then enter any date within the week you want to enter activities for and click OK.
4. In the middle of the form, enter information for services performed during the week. Use one line per customer or job and service item:
   - **Customer:Job** is the name of the customer or job the activity was performed for.
   - **Service Item** is the name of the service item that was performed.
   - **Notes** is for notes about the service performed for the customer or job. This field is optional.
   - **Class** is the class you want to assign to the service for the customer or job. This field is optional.
   - **M**, **Tu**, **W**, **Th**, **F**, **Sa**, and **Su** are the amount of time spent performing the service for that customer or job on each day of the week. Use decimal places to enter fractions.

Continued on next page...

Continued from previous page.

- **Total** is automatically calculated by QuickBooks.

  Figure 48 shows an example with several line items.

5. If an activity is not billable, click on the little invoice icon on the far-right end of its line to place a red X there (**Figure 48**). Remember, services performed by vendors cannot be marked as billable using the time tracking feature so those items will already have red Xs.

6. To save the timesheet and create another one, click New Sheet.

   Or

   To save the timesheet without creating another one, click OK.

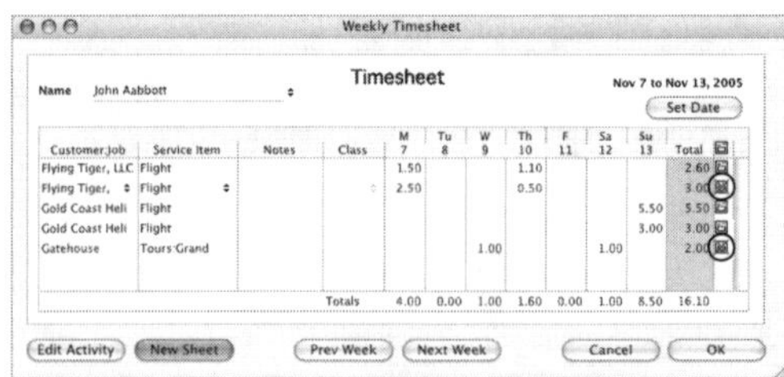

Figure 48 An example of a timesheet for a busy employee. Invoice icons with a red X are not billable.

Reconciling Accounts

Throughout the month, you enter transactions into QuickBooks. You write checks, pay bills, record sales, and make deposits. You enter credit card charges, record the receipt of inventory items, and enter bills for items and services received. QuickBooks faithfully keeps track of all of this information, recording your transactions and maintaining account balances.

But what if you made a mistake? Or if a deposit you mailed to the bank was never received? Or a check was never cashed? Chances are, your QuickBooks data file would not have accurate information. Worse yet, unless you checked the information you recorded, you'd have no way of knowing about inaccuracies.

That's where reconciling accounts comes in. When you reconcile an account, you check its balance against the balance in the corresponding account elsewhere. For example, you can check a bank statement against the activity in the corresponding bank account within QuickBooks. Transactions that don't appear in both records could indicate problems.

Manually reconciling a bank or credit card account is a boring, tedious task that requires a calculator and a bank-provided form. Fortunately, QuickBooks makes reconciling accounts easy since it does all the math for you. You simply enter balances and related information, check off the transactions that match, and let QuickBooks tell you whether the balances match.

In this part of the chapter, I explain how to reconcile a checking account. The process, however, works the same for other types of bank accounts and credit card accounts.

To reconcile an account

1. Choose Banking > Reconcile (**Figure 8b**) to display the Reconcile window.
2. Choose the name of the account you want to reconcile from the Account To Reconcile drop-down list. That account's activity appears in the Reconcile window (**Figure 49**).
3. Check the amount in the Opening Balance box to verify that it matches the account statement's opening balance. This amount comes from the last time you reconciled the account, but it may need to be changed if this is the first time you are reconciling the account.
4. Enter the ending balance from the account statement in the Ending Balance box.
5. If the account had a service charge, enter the amount, date, and account in which to record the charge in the appropriate boxes on the Service Charge line.
6. If the account earned interest, enter the amount, date, and account in which to record the interest in the appropriate boxes on the Interest Earned line.
7. In the Deposits and Other Credits area, click in the first column to place a check mark beside each deposit that appears on the statement. At the same time, use a pen to check off each matched transaction on the bank statement.
8. In the Checks and Payments area, click in the first column to place a check mark beside each check or other payment that appears on the statement. At the same time, use a pen to check off each matched transaction on the bank statement.

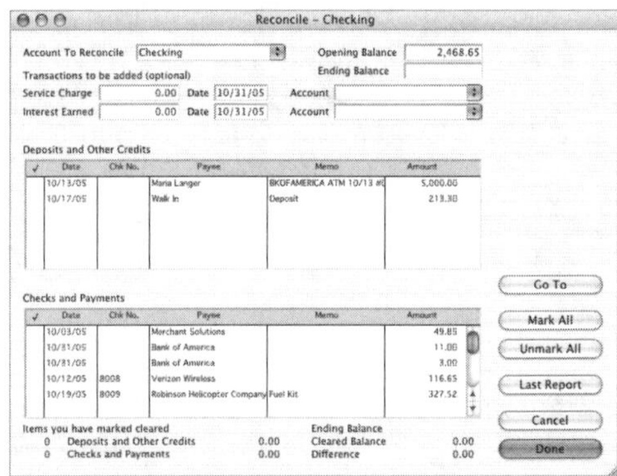

Figure 49 The Reconcile window for a checking account, before any items have been entered or checked off.

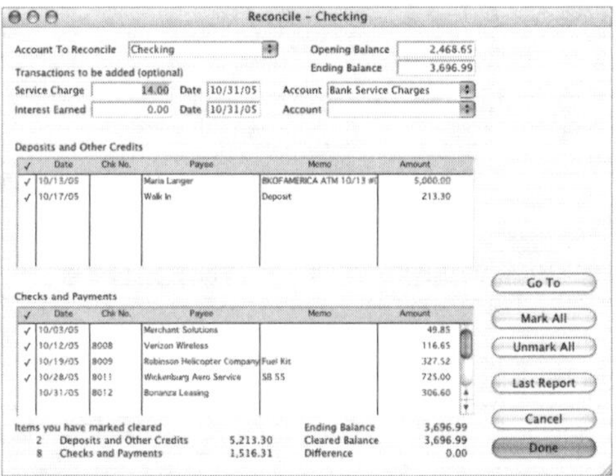

Figure 50 In this example, the account has been successfully reconciled. The Difference amount is 0.00.

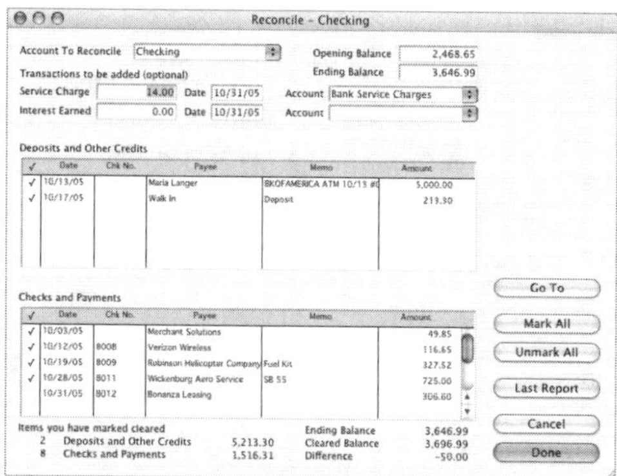

Figure 51 In this example, the difference is a negative number, indicating that I probably forgot to enter a check or withdrawal.

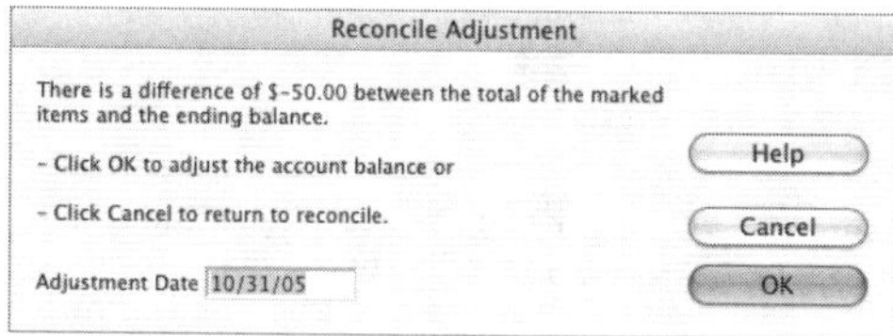

Figure 52 If you can't reconcile the account, use the Reconcile Adjustment dialog to create an adjusting entry in the account.

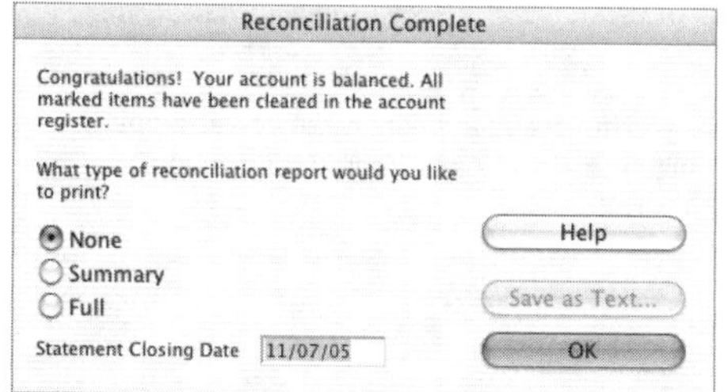

Figure 53 When the reconciliation is complete, QuickBooks offers to prepare a reconciliation report.

9. Check the amount in the Difference line at the bottom of the statement:
   - ▲ If the Difference is 0.00 (**Figure 50**), the account has been successfully reconciled. Click Done. Skip ahead to step 13.
   - ▲ If the Difference is a positive number, you may have forgotten to enter a deposit that appears on the bank statement. Check the statement and look for deposits that don't have inked check marks beside them from step 7.
   - ▲ If the Difference is a negative number (**Figure 51**), you may have forgotten to enter a payment that appears on the bank statement. Check the statement and look for payments that don't have inked check marks beside them from step 8.
10. Use the appropriate command within QuickBooks to enter any transactions that appear on the bank statement but do not appear in the Reconcile window.
11. Switch back to the Reconcile window and repeat steps 7 through 10 until the Difference is 0.00.
12. If you cannot resolve the Difference amount and want to give up—shame on you!—click Done. A dialog like the one in **Figure 52** appears. Enter a date for the adjusting entry and click OK.
13. The Reconciliation Complete dialog appears (**Figure 53**). If you want to print a reconciliation report, select the Summary or Full radio button. Enter the statement closing date in the box and click OK. Then use the Print dialog that appears to set print options and print the report.

Continued on next page...

Continued from previous page.

✔ Tips

- To reconcile a credit card account, open the account's register window and choose Banking > Reconcile Credit Card **(Figure 54)**. Then follow steps 2 through 13 on the previous pages to complete the reconcilation. Step 6 will not apply.
- If you use QuickBooks's transaction download feature, some items may already be checked off as cleared when you first open the Reconcile window as described in step 2. I explain how to download transactions in **Chapter 5**.
- I tell you more about printing in **Chapter 10**.
- When a transaction has been reconciled, QuickBooks places a bold check mark beside it in its account register (**Figure 55**) to mark it as cleared. If you attempt to change the amount of a cleared transaction, QuickBooks displays a dialog like the one in **Figure 56**. My advice: click No. Changing the amounts of cleared transactions can cause accounts to be out of balance and prevent future reconciliations from being completed properly.

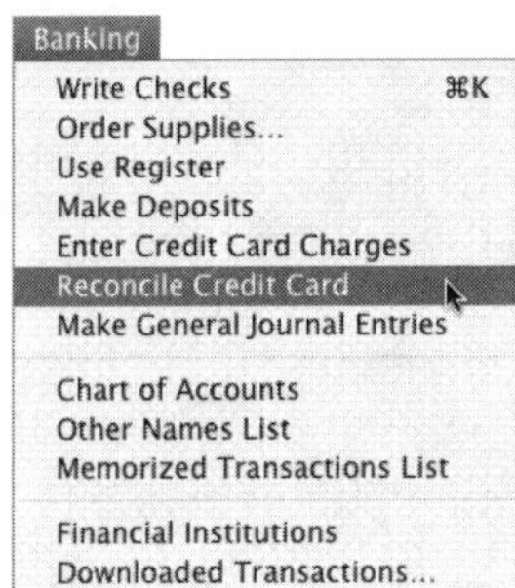

Figure 54 The Reconcile Credit Card command appears on the Banking menu when a credit card register window is active.

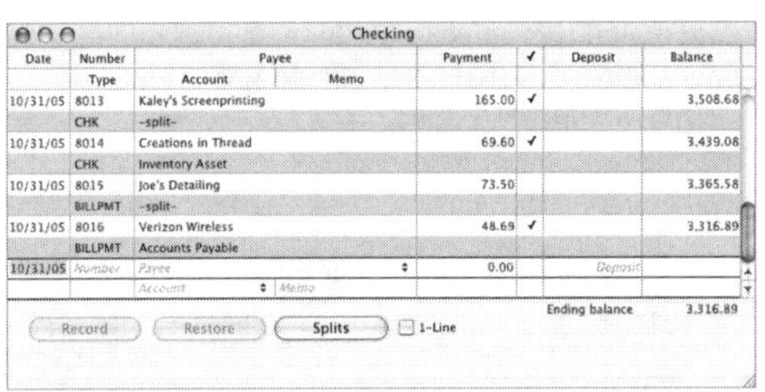

Figure 55 A bold check mark beside a transaction indicates that it has been reconciled or cleared.

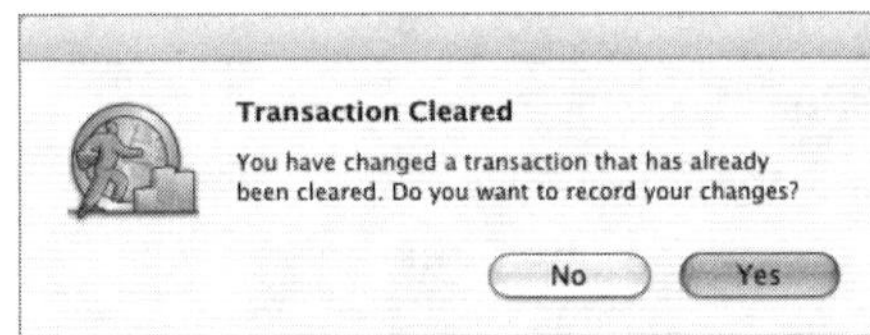

Figure 56 This dialog appears when you attempt to change the amount in a cleared transaction. Just click No!

Tracking Inventory

Figure 1 The Item List window includes all types of items, including inventory parts.

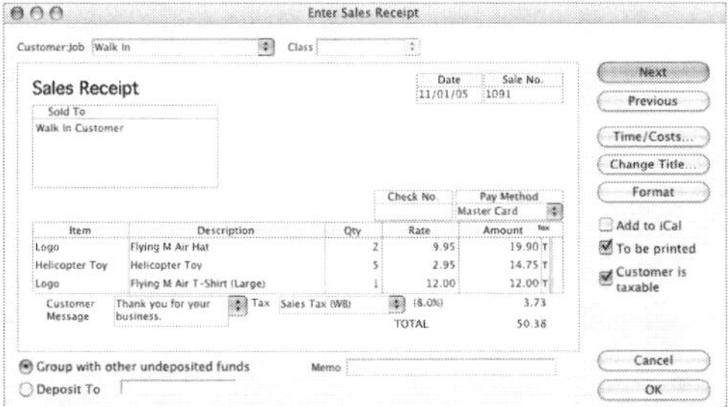

Figure 2 A sales receipt showing the sale of three different inventory items. Item price is stored with the rest of the item information.

Tracking Inventory

QuickBooks's inventory tracking features help you keep track of inventory items that you buy and sell. These features are well thought out and fully integrated with the rest of its accounting features.

You start by creating inventory part items, as discussed in **Chapter 2**. For each inventory item, you specify the item name or number, description, cost, supplier, resale price, and other details. QuickBooks stores this information in its Item List (**Figure 1**).

To order inventory items, you fill in a Purchase Order form, using the inventory item and vendor information you already entered. When the items arrive, you enter them as received. QuickBooks adds received items to inventory balances and updates account balances accordingly. You can enter the bill for received items when the items are received or when the bill is received. QuickBooks updates the accounts payable balances accordingly.

As you sell inventory items, using an invoice or sales receipt form (**Figure 2**) as discussed in **Chapter 3**, QuickBooks automatically updates inventory and account balances for the items sold. It also uses price information already entered to calculate sales totals that affect accounts receivable or other asset account balances.

Continued on next page...

Continued from previous page.

QuickBooks won't let you sell more items than you have on hand (**Figure 3**) and, if you use the reorder point feature, it reminds you to order more stock (**Figure 4**). And, if somewhere along the line, inventory items have been lost or destroyed, you can always use QuickBooks to adjust the balance or value of the items on hand.

In this chapter, I explain how to use QuickBooks to order and receive inventory items, as well as how to adjust inventory balances when necessary.

✔ Tips

- Before you read this chapter, follow the instructions in **Chapter 2** to set up the inventory items you plan to track.
- Purchase orders and sales forms use cost and price information stored in the Item List. You can change information in the Item List at any time; **Chapter 2** explains how.
- I explain how to record sales in **Chapter 3**.

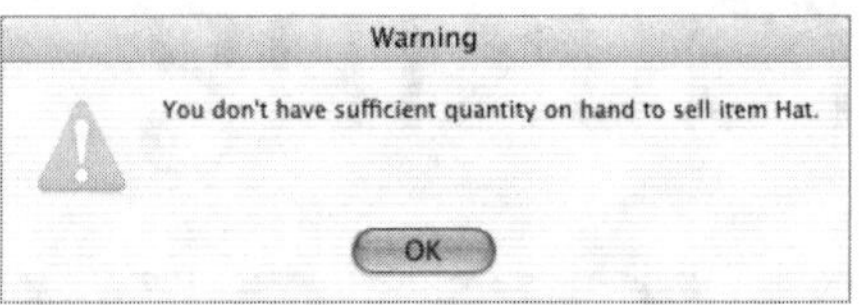

Figure 3 QuickBooks displays a warning dialog like this one when you try to record the sale of more items than you have on hand.

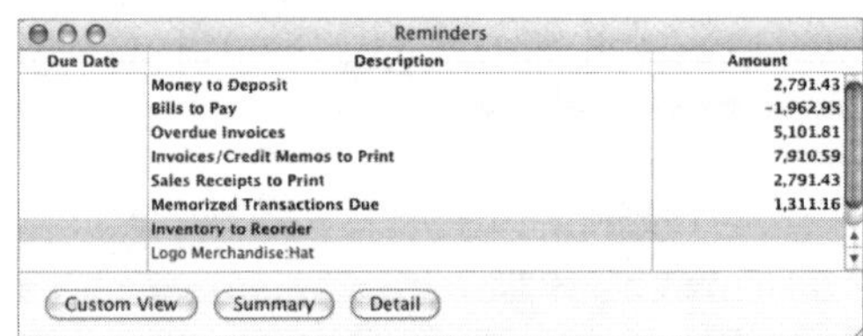

Figure 4 The Reminders window includes a list of inventory items you need to reorder.

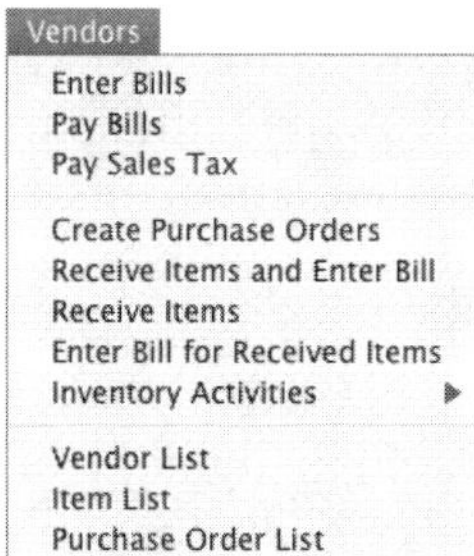

Figure 5 The Vendors menu.

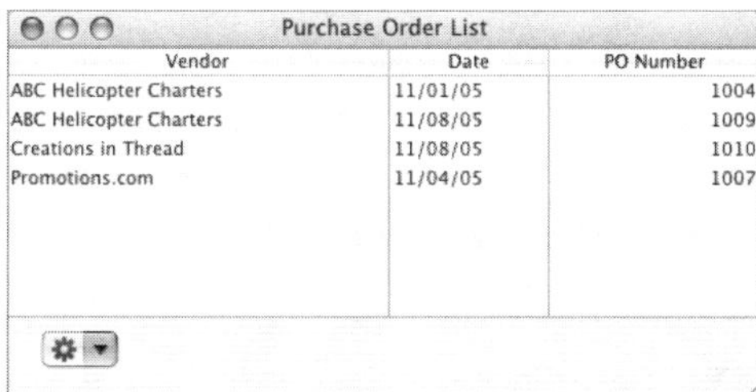

Figure 6 The Purchase Order List window can display only open purchase orders...

Purchase Order List

Vendor	Date	PO Number
ABC Helicopter Charters	11/01/05	1004
ABC Helicopter Charters	11/08/05	1009
Creations in Thread	11/01/05	1006
Creations in Thread	11/08/05	1010
Kaley's Screenprinting	11/07/05	1008
Promotions.com	11/04/05	1007

New
Edit
Show Only Open Purchase Orders

Figure 7 ...or all purchase orders.

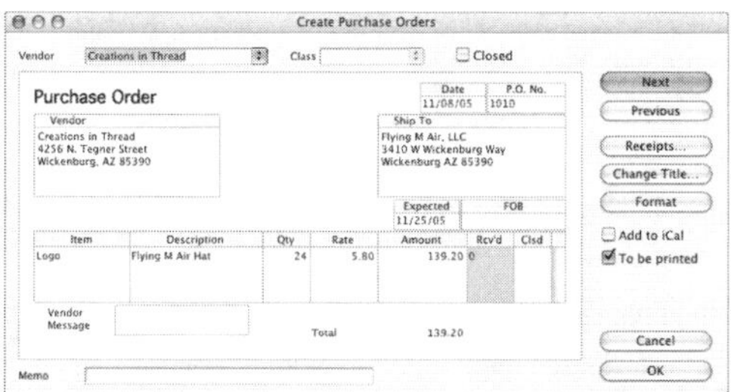

Figure 8 Double-click a purchase order in the list to view its details.

Creating Purchase Orders

A purchase order is a document you use to order inventory items from a vendor. Although some vendors may provide their own forms for placing orders or accept orders over the phone or on the Internet, it's a good idea to document all orders within QuickBooks using its Purchase Order form.

When you create a purchase order, you tell QuickBooks that certain inventory part items are on order. Then, when items and related bills are received, it's easy to add them to your QuickBooks data file.

✔ Tips

- Purchase orders aren't just for inventory items. You can create purchase orders for service items, too.
- Before creating a purchase order, be sure you have added the vendor you want to order from to the Vendor list as discussed in **Chapter 2**.

To view the Purchase Order list

Choose Vendors > Purchase Order List (**Figure 5**). The Purchase Order List window appears (**Figures 6** and **7**).

✔ Tip

- The Purchase Order list can display all purchase orders (**Figure 7**) or only open purchase orders (**Figure 6**). To toggle the display, choose Show Only Open Purchase Orders from the window's Action pop-up menu (**Figure 7**).

To view a specific purchase order

In the Purchase Order list (**Figure 6** or **7**), double-click the purchase order you want to view. The Create Purchase Orders window for that purchase order appears (**Figure 8**).

To create a purchase order

1. Choose Vendors > Create Purchase Orders (**Figure 5**).

   Or

   Choose New from the Action pop-up menu at the bottom of the Purchase Order List window (**Figure 7**).

   The Create Purchase Orders window appears (**Figure 9**).
2. Choose the name of the vendor from which you want to purchase the items from the Vendor drop-down list (**Figure 10**). The vendor's name and address appear in the Vendor part of the form (**Figure 11**).
3. If desired, choose a class from the Class drop-down list.
4. Enter information in the top half of the form:
   - ▲ **Date** is the date of the order.
   - ▲ **P.O. No.** is the purchase order number. QuickBooks automatically increments the number from the previous purchase order.
   - ▲ **Vendor** is the name and address of the vendor, which should have been filled out automatically when you chose a vendor name in step 2. You can make changes as necessary in this field.
   - ▲ **Ship To** is the shipping address for the order. This should be filled in automatically with shipping information you provided when you installed and configured QuickBooks as instructed in **Chapter 1**. You can make changes to this field if necessary.
   - ▲ **Expected** is the date you expect to receive the order.
   - ▲ **FOB** is the FOB (*free on board*) information for the order.

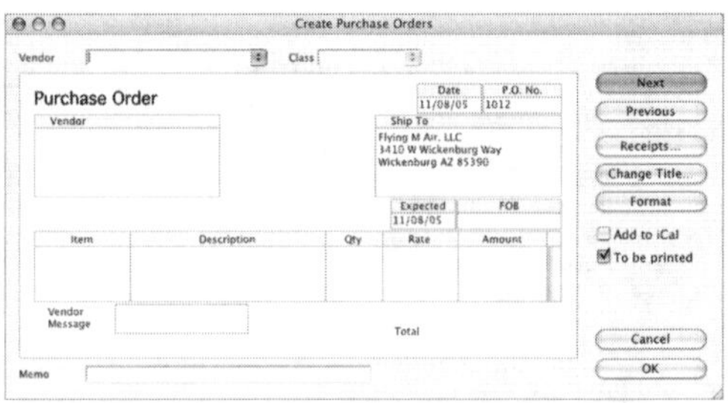

Figure 9 A blank purchase order form.

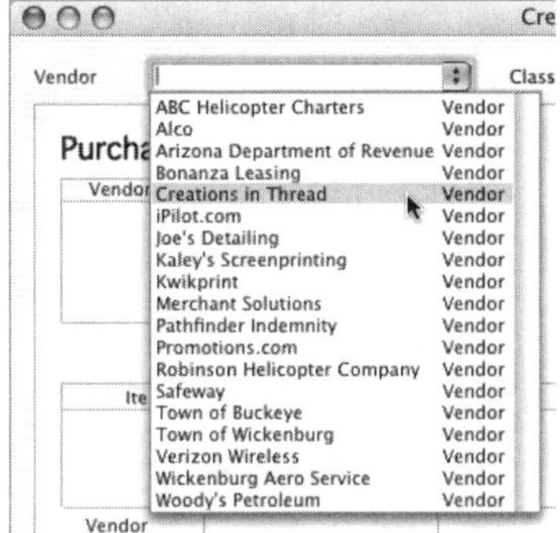

Figure 10 Choose a vendor from the Vendor drop-down list.

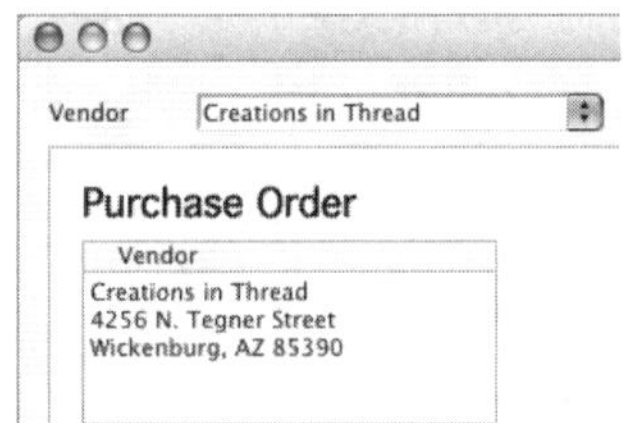

Figure 11 The vendor's name and address appear in the Vendor area.

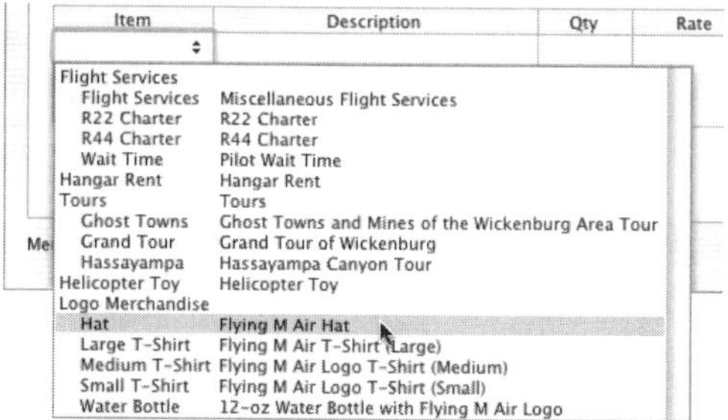

Figure 12 Choose an item from the Item drop-down list.

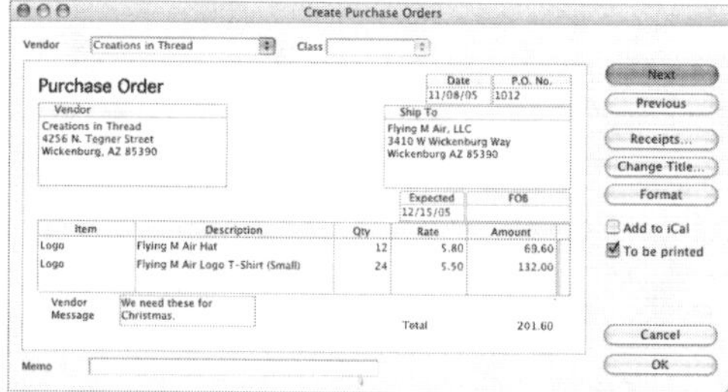

Figure 13 A completed purchase order for two different items.

5. Enter item information in a line in the bottom half of the form:
   - ▲ **Item** is the item name. Choose an option from the drop-down list (**Figure 12**).
   - ▲ **Description** is the item description. This information should be filled in automatically when you choose the item name, but you can change it if you need to.
   - ▲ **Qty** is the number of items you want to order.
   - ▲ **Rate** is the purchase price for the item. This information should be filled in automatically when you choose the item name, but you can change it if you need to.
   - ▲ **Amount** is the total amount for that item. This value is calculated by QuickBooks.
6. Repeat step 5 in a new line for each item you want to order. **Figure 13** shows an example with two items entered.
7. If desired, enter a message to appear on the purchase order in the Vendor Message box.
8. If desired, enter a memo for your own records in the Memo box.
9. To add the purchase order to iCal as a QuickBooks event, turn on the Add to iCal check box.
10. To print the purchase order later, with other purchase orders, turn on the To be printed check box.

Continued on next page...

Continued from previous page.

11. To save the purchase order and create another one, click Next.

    Or

    To save the purchase order without creating another one, click OK.

✔ Tips

- If the entry you make in the Vendor, Class, or Item field does not already exist in the corresponding list, QuickBooks offers to add it. This makes it possible to add items to these lists on the fly as you create purchase orders.
- Note that the description for an item on a purchase order may not match the description on a sales form. That's because QuickBooks uses the purchase information description that you entered when you created the inventory item rather than the sales information description.

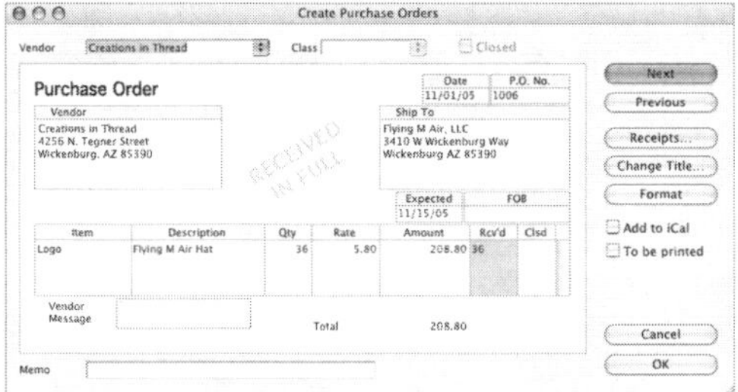

Figure 14 QuickBooks marks a purchase order "Received in Full" when you have received all items on it.

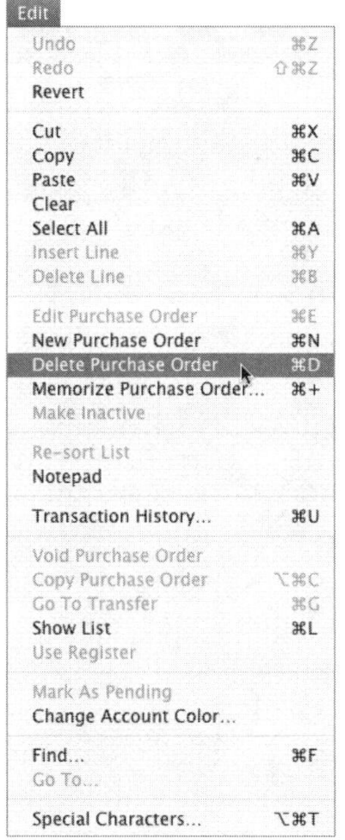

Figure 15 Choose Delete Purchase Order from the Edit menu.

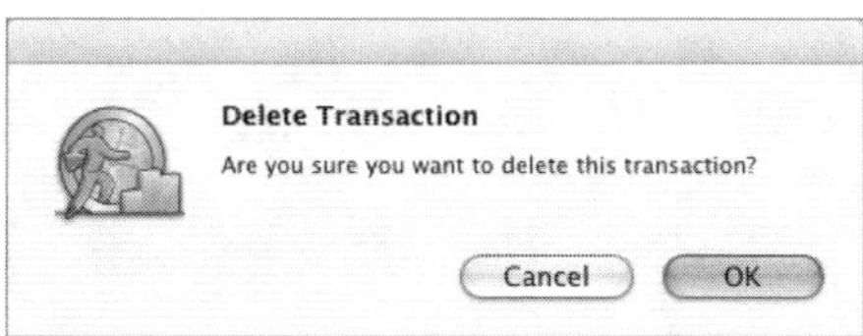

Figure 16 Click OK in this dialog to delete the purchase order.

To modify a purchase order

1. In the Purchase Order List window (**Figures 6 and 7**), double-click the purchase order you want to modify to display it.
2. Make changes as desired to the purchase order's details.
3. Click OK.

✔ Tip

- If the purchase order form indicates that the items have been Received in Full (**Figure 14**), modifying the purchase order could result in changes to other records, including inventory counts and account balances. I explain how to receive inventory items later in this chapter.

To delete a purchase order

1. In the Purchase Order List window (**Figures 6 and 7**), select the purchase order you want to delete.
2. Choose Edit > Delete Purchase Order (**Figure 15**) or press ⌘D.
3. A dialog like the one in **Figure 16** appears. Click OK.

✔ Tip

- To prevent possible account balance errors, don't delete purchase orders for items that have been Received in Full (**Figure 14**).

Receiving Items & Entering Bills

When inventory items you ordered arrive, they must be recorded as received in QuickBooks. You do this with one of the commands on the Vendors menu (**Figure 5**).

- **Receive Items and Enter Bill** enables you to record items as received and enter a bill for them at the same time.
- **Receive Items** enables you to record items as received without entering a bill.
- **Enter Bill for Received Items** enables you to enter a bill for items you have already recorded as received.

No matter which command you choose, some version of the Enter Bills (**Figure 17**) or Create Item Receipts window appears. I discuss how you can use this window to enter bills for expenses in **Chapter 4**. This part of the chapter explains how to use the Enter Bills window to receive items and enter corresponding bills.

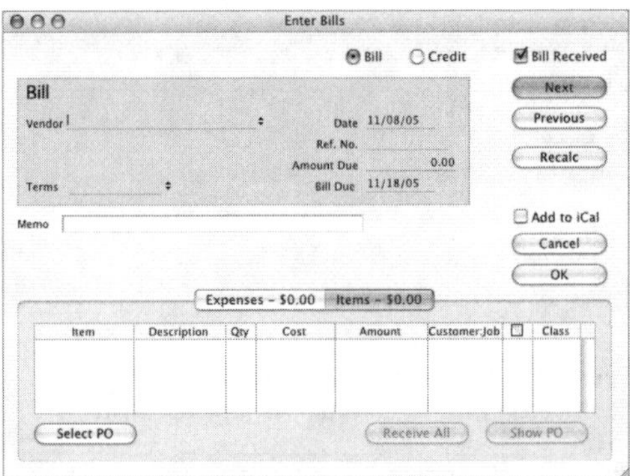

Figure 17 The Enter Bills window when you receive items and enter the corresponding bill at the same time.

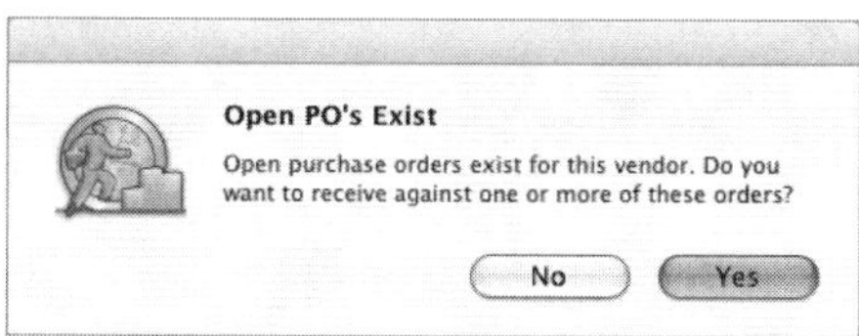

Figure 18 This dialog appears when the vendor you select has open purchase orders.

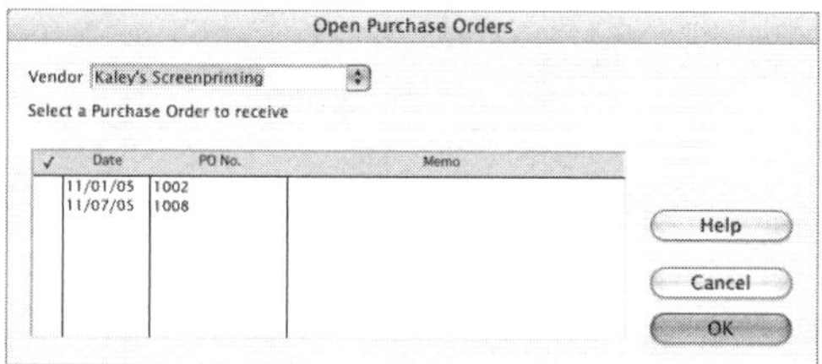

Figure 19 Click one or more of the purchase orders for a vendor to receive items on them.

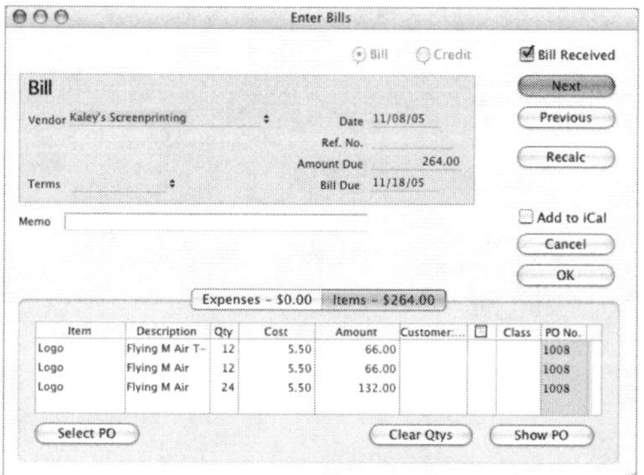

Figure 20 The details from the purchase order(s) you selected appear in the Enter Bills window.

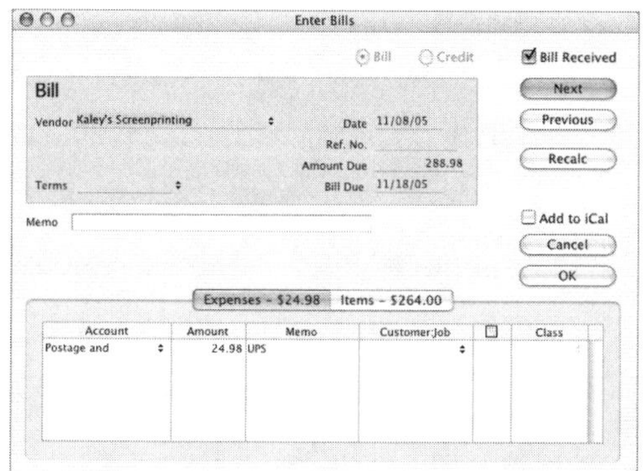

Figure 21 You can enter expenses related to the item receipt in the Expenses tab.

To receive items & enter a corresponding bill

1. Choose Vendors > Receive Items and Enter Bill (**Figure 5**). An Enter Bills window like the one in **Figure 17** appears.
2. Choose the name of the vendor who sent the items from the Vendor drop-down list.
3. A dialog like the one in **Figure 18** should appear. Click Yes.
4. The Open Purchase Orders dialog appears (**Figure 19**). It lists all open purchase orders for the vendor. Click a purchase order to place a check mark beside the appropriate order. Then click OK.
5. The details of the purchase order appear in the Items tab of the Enter Bills dialog (**Figure 20**). Check the items and quantities in the list against the items and quantities received. Make changes in the Item and Qty fields as necessary.
6. If your company was charged for shipping or other expenses related to the shipment, click the Expenses tab. Then enter expense information in the bottom half of the window. **Figure 21** shows an example of what it might look like.
7. Fill in other form fields to complete the basic billing information:
   - ▲ **Date** is the bill date.
   - ▲ **Ref. No.** is the packing slip or invoice number for the items.
   - ▲ **Amount Due** is calculated automatically by QuickBooks based on the total expenses and items. It should match the amount due on the bill that came with the items.

Continued on next page...

Continued from previous page.

- ▲ **Terms** refers to payment terms for the bill. Choose an option from the drop-down list.
- ▲ **Bill Due** is the bill's due date. This is calculated by QuickBooks based on the Date and Terms field contents, but you can override it by entering a different date.
- ▲ **Memo** is an internally-used memo regarding the item receipt or bill.

Figure 22 shows an example of a completed bill for received items.

8. To add the Bill to iCal as a QuickBooks event, turn on the Add to iCal check box.
9. Click OK. QuickBooks adjusts inventory and accounts payable account balances. It also marks the purchase order "Received in Full" **(Figure 14)**.

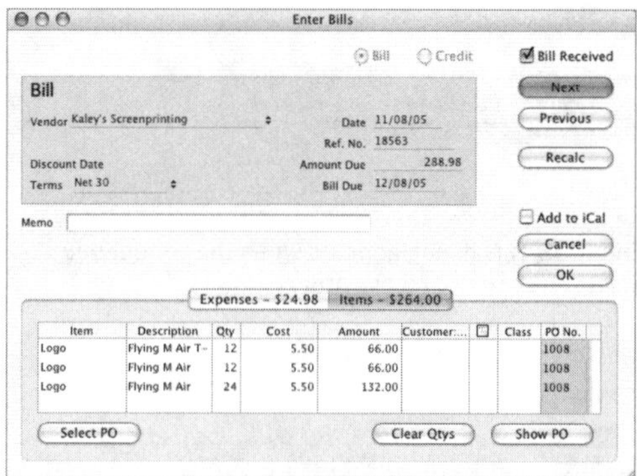

Figure 22 A completed bill for items received.

✔ Tips

- If the dialog in **Figure 18** does not appear in step 3, the vendor does not have any open purchase orders. Check to make sure you chose the correct vendor, then check to make sure you created a purchase order for the purchase. If the vendor is correct and no purchase order exists, you'll have to manually enter items and quantities in the Items tab of the Enter Bills window as discussed in **Chapter 4**.
- In step 4, you can select more than one purchase order to receive.

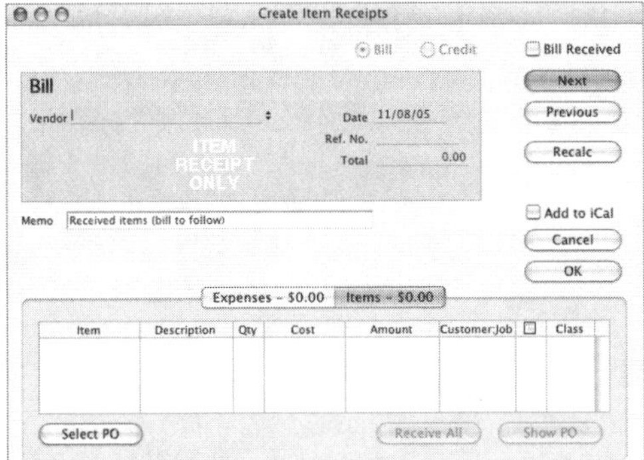

Figure 23 The Create Item Receipts window.

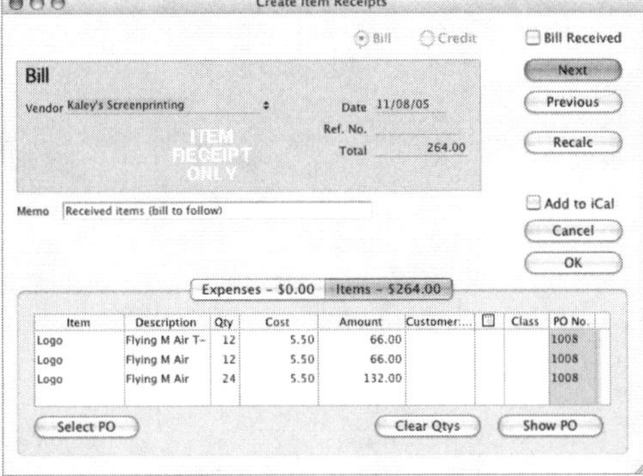

Figure 24 QuickBooks fills in the purchase order details.

To receive items without entering a corresponding bill

1. Choose Vendors > Receive Items (**Figure 5**). A Create Item Receipts window like the one in **Figure 23** appears.
2. Choose the name of the vendor who sent the items from the Vendor drop-down list.
3. A dialog like the one in **Figure 18** should appear. Click Yes.
4. The Open Purchase Orders dialog appears (**Figure 19**). It lists all open purchase orders for the vendor. Click a purchase order to place a check mark beside the appropriate order. Then click OK.
5. The details of the purchase order appear in the Items tab of the Create Item Receipts dialog (**Figure 24**). Check the items and quantities in the list against the items and quantities received. Make changes in the Item and Qty fields as necessary.
6. Fill in other form fields to complete the basic information:
   - ▲ **Date** is the date the items were received.
   - ▲ **Ref. No.** is the packing slip number for the items.
   - ▲ **Total** is calculated automatically by QuickBooks based on the total items.
   - ▲ **Memo** is an internally-used memo regarding the item receipt. Quick-Books enters a memo for you, but you can override it by entering something different.
7. To add the item receipt to iCal as a QuickBook event, turn on the Add to iCal check box.

Continued on next page...

Continued from previous page.

8. Click OK. QuickBooks adjusts inventory and accounts payable account balances. It also marks the purchase order "Received in Full" (**Figure 14**).

✔ Tips

- You can turn the Create Item Receipts window (**Figure 23**) into an Enter Bills window (**Figure 17**) by turning on the Bill Received check box.
- If the dialog in **Figure 18** does not appear in step 3, the vendor does not have any open purchase orders. Check to make sure you chose the correct vendor, then check to make sure you created a purchase order for the purchase. If the vendor is correct and no purchase order exists, you'll have to manually enter items and quantities in the Items tab of the Create Item Receipts window.
- In step 4, you can select more than one purchase order to receive.
- You can use the Expenses tab of the Create Item Receipts window to record expenses related to the items received. But if you haven't gotten the bill for the items yet, you're not likely to know what those expenses are!
- Although QuickBooks adjusts the accounts payable account balance to account for the cost of items received, it does not record a bill to be paid. The amount due can change when the bill is received.

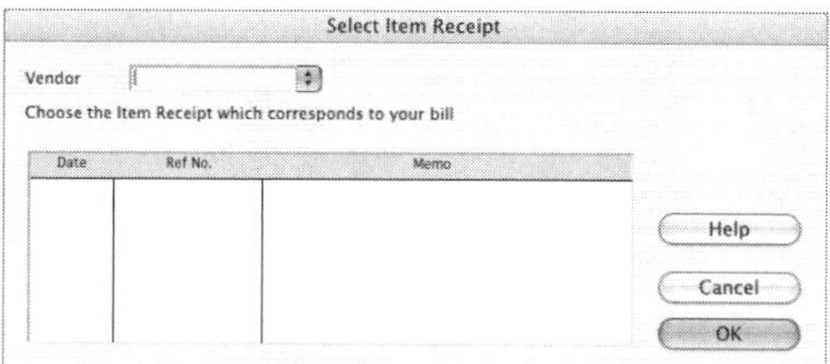

Figure 25 The Select Item Receipt dialog.

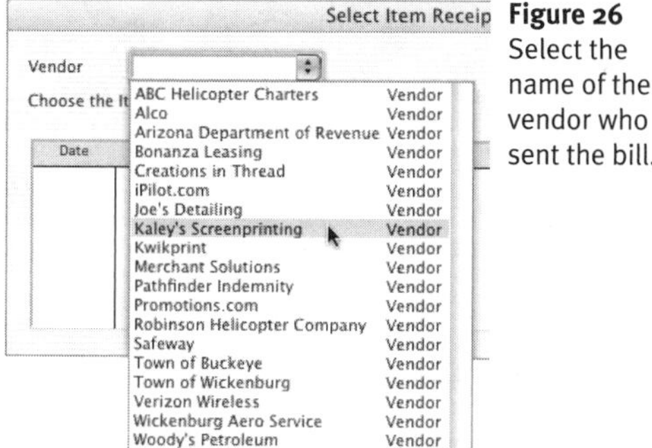

Figure 26 Select the name of the vendor who sent the bill.

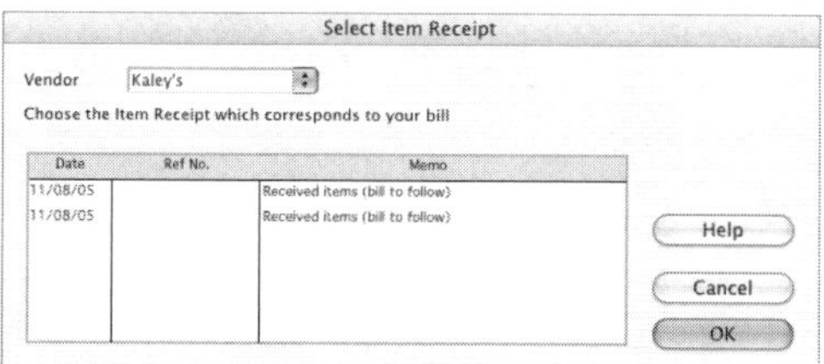

Figure 27 A list of item receipts appears in the dialog.

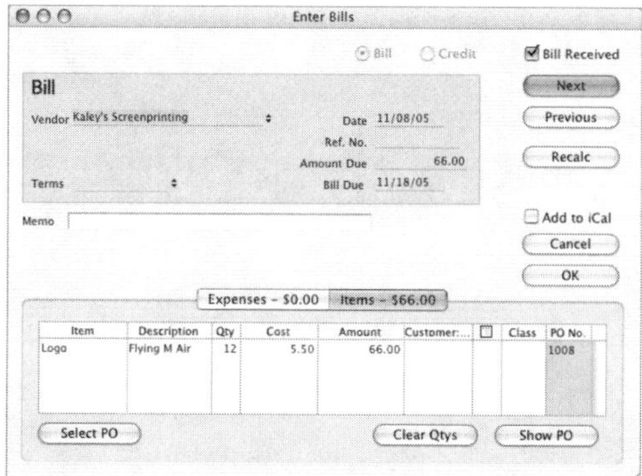

Figure 28 Use the Enter Bills window to enter billing information for the received items.

To enter a bill for received items

1. Choose Vendors > Enter Bill for Received Items (**Figure 5**). A Select Item Receipt dialog appears (**Figure 25**).
2. Choose the name of the vendor who billed you from the Vendor drop-down list (**Figure 26**).
3. A list of item receipts appears in the dialog (**Figure 27**). Select the receipt for which you want to enter a bill and click OK. The Enter Bills window with the details of the receipt appears (**Figure 28**).
4. If your company was charged for shipping or other expenses related to the shipment, click the Expenses tab. Then enter expense information in the bottom half of the window. **Figure 21** shows an example of what it might look like.
5. Fill in other form fields to complete the basic billing information:
   - **Date** is the bill date.
   - **Ref. No.** is the packing slip or invoice number for the items.
   - **Amount Due** is calculated automatically by QuickBooks based on the total expenses and items. It should match the amount due on the bill for the items.
   - **Terms** refers to payment terms for the bill. Choose an option from the drop-down list.
   - **Bill Due** is the bill's due date. This is calculated by QuickBooks based on the Date and Terms field contents, but you can override it by entering a different date.
   - **Memo** is an internally-used memo regarding the item receipt or bill.
6. Click OK. QuickBooks adjusts accounts payable account balances if necessary.

Adjusting Inventory Balances

Periodically, your company probably performs a physical inventory to count the inventory items that are actually on hand. This count is then compared to your accounting records in QuickBooks.

Although QuickBooks does a good job keeping track of what you bought and sold, it doesn't know anything about items lost due to damage or theft. At the same time, it doesn't know about count errors on incoming or outgoing items. As a result, there may be differences between the physical inventory count and the QuickBooks item balances.

QuickBooks' Inventory Activities submenu (**Figure 29**) offers two commands for helping you adjust inventory balances:

- **Adjust Quantity/Value on Hand** displays the Adjust Quantity/Value on Hand window (**Figure 31**), which you can use to adjust inventory counts, values, or both.
- **Physical Inventory Worksheet** prepares a printable report (**Figure 30**) you can use to perform a physical count of inventory items on hand. You can then use the completed report as the basis for inventory count or value adjustments.

This part of the chapter explains how to use QuickBooks' Inventory Activities commands to adjust inventory counts and balances.

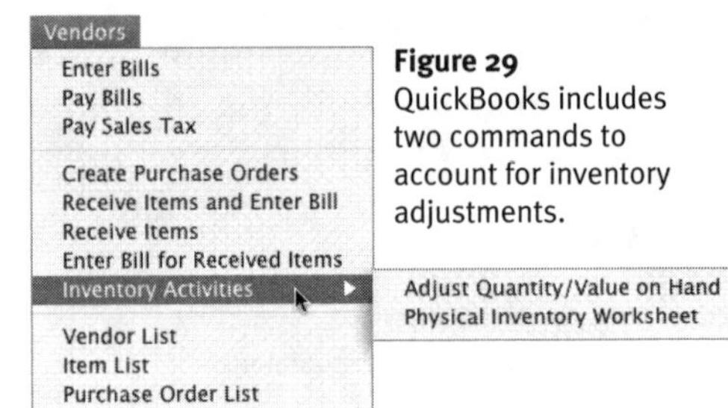

Figure 29 QuickBooks includes two commands to account for inventory adjustments.

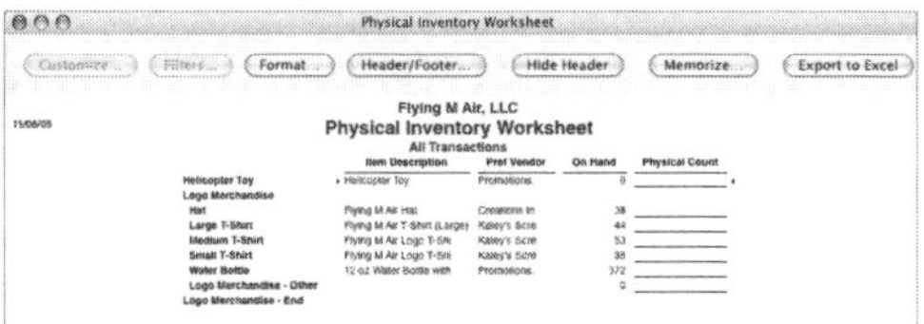

Figure 30 A Physical Inventory Worksheet report lists all inventory items that should be on hand.

To conduct a physical inventory

1. Choose Vendors > Inventory Activities > Phyiscal Inventory Worksheet (**Figure 29**). QuickBooks displays the Physical Inventory Worksheet report (**Figure 30**).
2. Print the report.
3. Go to the location in which inventory items are stored.
4. Count each item on hand and enter the corresponding value in the Physical Count column of the Physical Inventory Worksheet.

✔ Tips

- The Physical Inventory Worksheet report (**Figure 30**) includes all inventory items and subitems in the Items list.
- I explain how to print reports in **Chapter 10**.
- Physical inventory accounts are normally controlled or observed by a company's internal auditors or conducted under strict internal control procedures. Check to make sure you follow your company's procedures for inventory counts before making any adjustments based on counts.

To adjust inventory quantities

1. Choose Vendors > Inventory Activities > Adjust Quantity/Value on Hand (**Figure 29**). The Adjust Quantity/Value on Hand window appears (**Figure 31**).

2. Enter information in the top half of the window:

   ▲ **Adjustment Date** is the date of the adjustment entry.

   ▲ **Ref. No.** is a reference number for the transaction. This field is optional.

   ▲ **Adjustment Account** is the name of the account that the adjustment will be recorded in. Normally, the account you select will be an income or expense account.

   ▲ **Customer:Job** is the name of the customer or job the inventory change can be attributed to. This field is optional.

   ▲ **Class** is the name of the class the inventory adjustment can be attributed to. This field is optional.

3. Look down the list of inventory items and quantities. For each item with a wrong quantity, enter the correct quantity in the New Qty field. QuickBooks automatically calculates the difference and the value of the difference (**Figure 32**).

4. If desired, enter a memo about the adjustment in the Memo field at the bottom of the window.

5. Click OK. QuickBooks makes an entry that adjusts inventory counts and values.

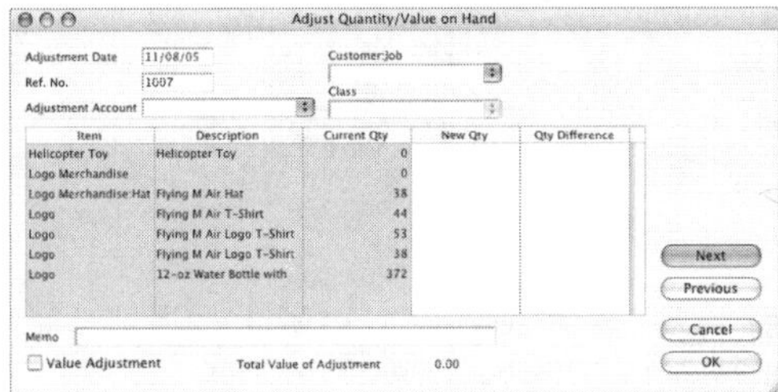

Figure 31 The Adjust Quantity/Value on Hand window.

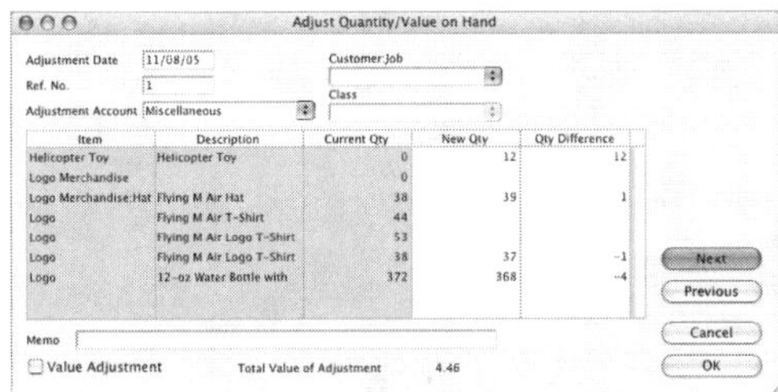

Figure 32 QuickBooks automatically calculates the value of inventory adjustments.

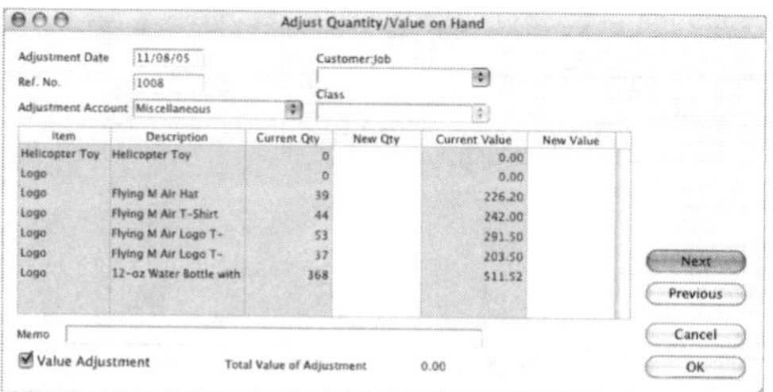

Figure 33 The window changes to add a New Value column.

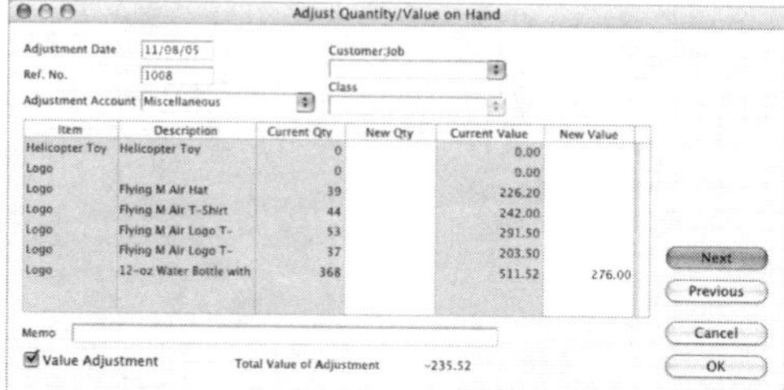

Figure 34 When you enter a new value, QuickBooks calculates the adjustment.

✔ Tip

■ With the Value Adjustment check box turned on, you can change both quantities and values.

To adjust inventory values

1. Choose Vendors > Inventory Activities > Adjust Quantity/Value on Hand (**Figure 29**). The Adjust Quantity/Value on Hand window appears (**Figure 31**).
2. Enter information in the top half of the window:
   - ▲ **Adjustment Date** is the date of the adjustment entry.
   - ▲ **Ref. No.** is a reference number for the transaction. This field is optional.
   - ▲ **Adjustment Account** is the name of the account that the adjustment will be recorded in. Normally, the account you select will be an income or expense account.
   - ▲ **Customer:Job** is the name of the customer or job the inventory change can be attributed to. This field is optional.
   - ▲ **Class** is the name of the class the inventory adjustment can be attributed to. This field is optional.
3. Turn on the Value Adjustment check box at the bottom of the window. The window changes to add a New Value field (**Figure 33**).
4. Look down the list of inventory items and values. For each item with a wrong value, enter the correct value in the New Value field. QuickBooks automatically calculates the total adjustment (**Figure 34**).
5. If desired, enter a memo about the adjustment in the Memo field at the bottom of the window.
6. Click OK. QuickBooks makes an entry that adjusts inventory values.

Processing Payroll

Processing Payroll with QuickBooks

An important—and extremely complex—part of any company's accounting records is payroll. Tracking employee payroll means keeping track of hours worked, vacation time accrued, and monies paid. It means deciphering tax laws for the Federal and state governments and making calculations for withholding, employer taxes, and other deductions and expenses. The more employees you have, the more trouble tracking payroll can be.

Although QuickBooks does not have a built-in payroll feature, it does work with two different payroll services:

- **QuickBooks Payroll for Mac** is a Web-based payroll service provided by PayCycle Inc. You subscribe to the PayCycle service that best meets your needs. Then, when it's time to do payroll, you log into your PayCycle account, enter payroll information, and let PayCycle do all the calculations for you. When you're finished, import PayCycle-generated payroll data directly into your QuickBooks company file.
- **Aatrix Top Pay** is a Macintosh application that was bundled with some previous versions of QuickBooks and still works with QuickBooks 2006. When you're ready

Continued on next page...

Continued from previous page.

to do payroll, you launch Top Pay and use it to perform payroll calculations and print checks. When you're finished, you can import payroll transactions into your QuickBooks company file.

In this chapter, I take a closer look at processing payroll using PayCycle's services. I'll show you how to set up your PayCycle account and walk you through a typical payroll processing. Although I won't go into great depth on PayCycle's many features, the information provided here should be enough to get your payroll system up and running with PayCycle and QuickBooks.

✔ Tips

- This chapter assumes you have or will set up a PayCycle account. You can learn more about PayCycle, its features, and its costs on the PayCycle Web site (**Figure 1**), `www.paycycle.com`.
- To use PayCycle and import its data into QuickBooks, the computer on which you use QuickBooks must have an Internet connection.
- For more information about using Aatrix Top Pay, consult the documentation that came with the Top Pay software.

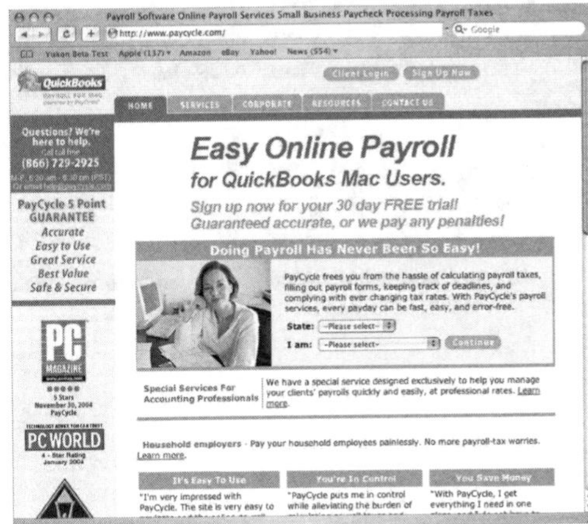

Figure 1 The PayCycle Web site provides more information about the services PayCycle offers.

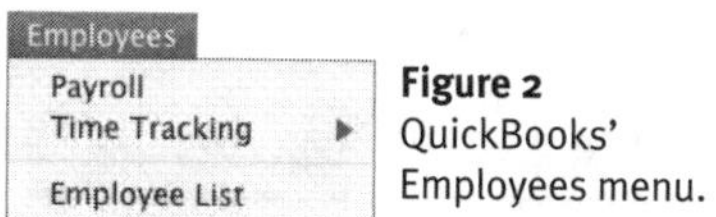

Figure 2 QuickBooks' Employees menu.

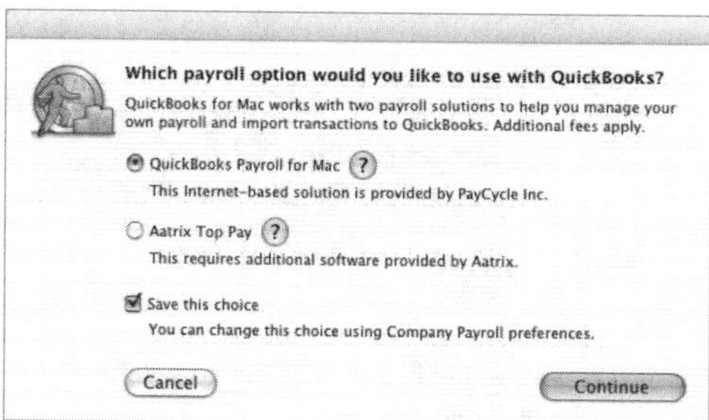

Figure 3 This dialog appears the first time you choose the Payroll command.

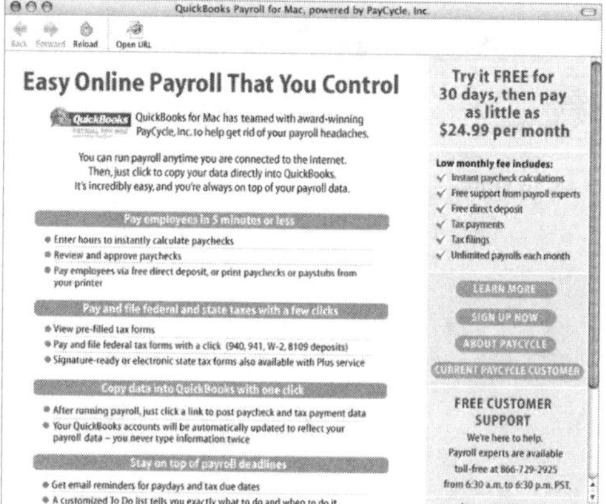

Figure 4 The first time you open PayCycle, it displays more information and links for you to sign up or log in.

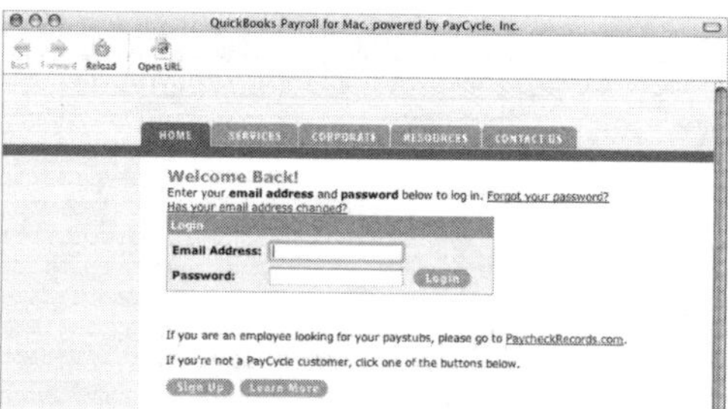

Figure 5 After opening PayCycle for the first time, the login screen appears.

Getting Started with PayCycle

Before you start using PayCycle to process your company's payroll, you must create a PayCycle account and configure it for your payroll needs.

Configuring PayCycle is easy because PayCycle provides a To Do List (**Figure 7**) full of tasks that need to be completed before you set up employees, process payroll, or pay taxes. This part of the chapter explains how to do many, but not all, of the setup tasks on your PayCycle To Do list. You can do the other tasks on your own, following instructions that appear onscreen.

To open PayCycle for the first time

1. Choose Employees > Payroll (**Figure 2**).

   A dialog like the one in **Figure 3** appears. It displays your two payroll options.

2. Select the QuickBooks Payroll for Mac option.

3. Turn on the Save this choice check box.

4. Click Continue.

   QuickBooks connects to the Internet and displays information about PayCycle in a QuickBooks Internet window (**Figure 4**).

5. If you do not yet have a PayCycle account, click the Sign Up Now button and follow the instructions that appear to set up a trial account.

   or

   If you already have a PayCycle account, click the Current PayCycle Customer button and use the login screen that appears (**Figure 5**) to log into your account.

To open PayCycle after the first time

1. Choose Employees > Payroll (**Figure 2**).
2. Enter your e-mail address and password in the login screen that appears (**Figure 5**) and click Login.

To open your To Do list

1. Open PayCycle and log in as instructed on the previous page.

   The Welcome to PayCycle screen appears (**Figure 6**).

2. Click the See My To Do List button. A list of setup options appears (**Figure 7**).

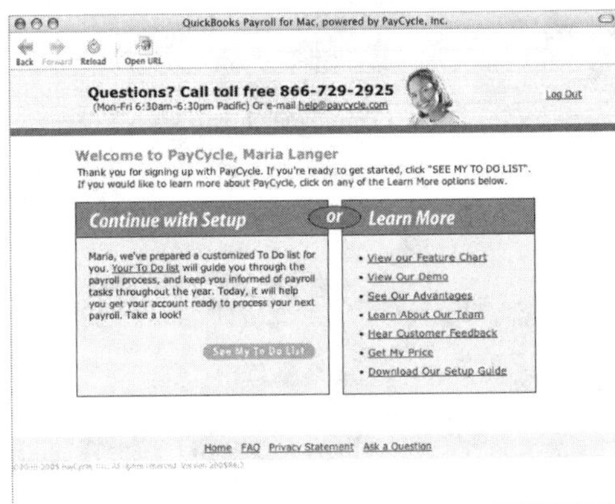

Figure 6 When you log in and have not completed setup, PayCycle displays these options.

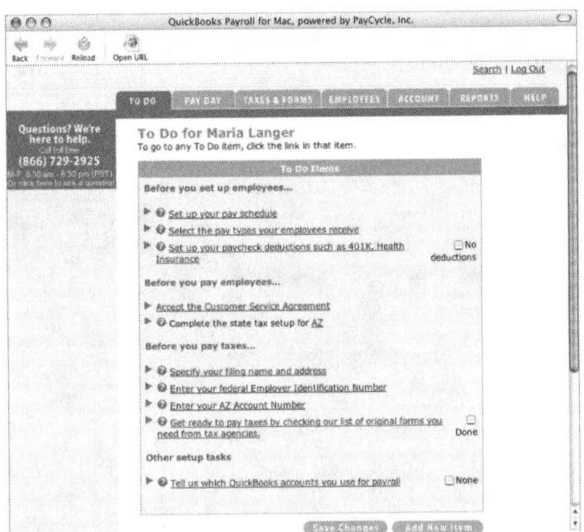

Figure 7 Use your To Do list to complete the setup tasks.

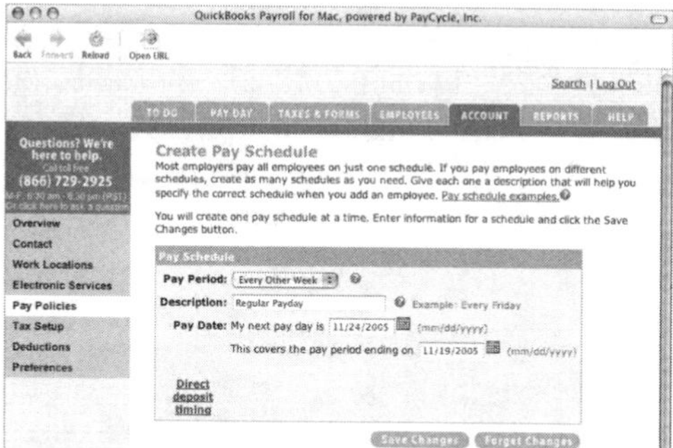

Figure 8 Use this screen to set up your pay schedules.

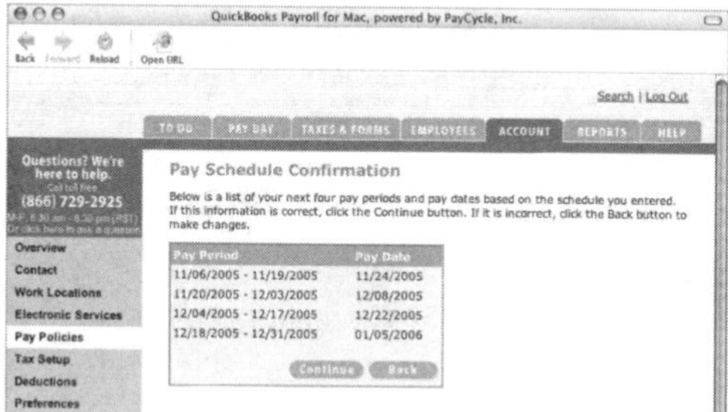

Figure 9 PayCycle asks you to confirm pay schedules.

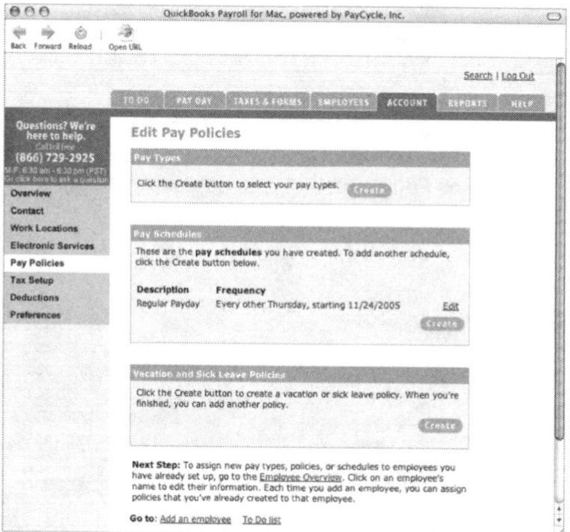

Figure 10 The Edit Pay Policies gives you access to pay policy options you must set before adding employees.

To set up your pay schedule & policies

1. In the PayCycle To Do list (**Figure 7**), click the Set up your pay schedule link.
2. Set options in the Create Pay Schedule screen that appears (**Figure 8**):
   - ▲ **Pay Period** is the frequency of your payroll. Your options are Every Week, Every Other Week, Twice a Month, or Every Month.
   - ▲ **Description** is an internal identifier for the pay schedule. This is especially useful if you have multiple pay schedules.
   - ▲ **Pay Date** has two parts. The first part is the date of your next pay day. The second part is the date of the end of that pay period. For example, if your pay day is Thursday, November 24, it might cover the pay period ending Saturday, November 19.
3. Click the Save Changes button.
4. Review the information in the Pay Schedule Confirmation screen that appears (**Figure 9**). If it is correct, click Continue; if not, click Back and repeat steps 2 through 4.
5. The Edit Pay Policies screen appears next (**Figure 10**). To create another Pay Schedule, click the Create button under Pay Schedules and follow steps 2 through 4 again.
6. Click the Create button under Pay Types.
7. In the Types of Pay screen (**Figure 11**), turn on the check boxes beside each type of pay your company uses.
8. Click Save Changes. The Edit Pay Policies screen reappears (**Figure 12**).

Continued on next page...

Continued from previous page.

9. Click the Create button under Vacation and Sick Leave Policies.
10. In the Create Vacation and Sick Leave Policies screen (**Figure13**), set options to define sick and/or vacation leave:
    - ▲ **Category** is the type of leave. Your options are Sick or Vacation.
    - ▲ **Description** is an identifier for the type of leave.
    - ▲ **Hours are accrued** specifies when leave begins accruing. Your options are at beginning of year, each pay period, and per hour worked.
    - ▲ **Employees earn** is the number of hours of leave time earned each year or hour of work time.
    - ▲ **Maximum Available** is the maximum amount of leave time an employee can have available at any one time. If your company requires all leave time to be taken in the year it is earned, enter the same value you entered for the Employees earn option.
11. Click Save Changes. The Edit Pay Policies screen reappears (**Figure 14**).
12. To add another sick or vacation leave policy, click the Create button under Vacation and Sick Leave Policies. Then follow steps 10 and 11.
13. Click the To Do list link at the bottom of the screen (**Figure 14**) to return to the To Do list (**Figure 15**).

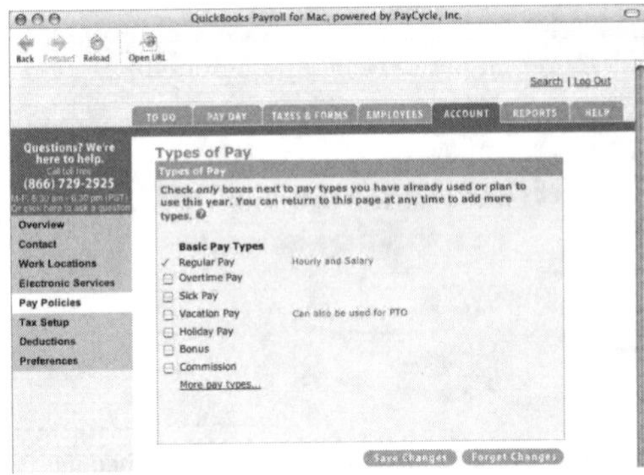

Figure 11 Use this screen to indicate the type of pay you process.

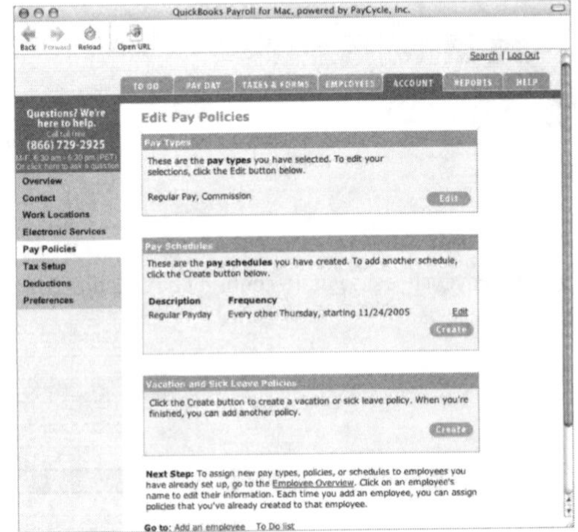

Figure 12 The Edit Pay Policies screen shows the policies you've set up.

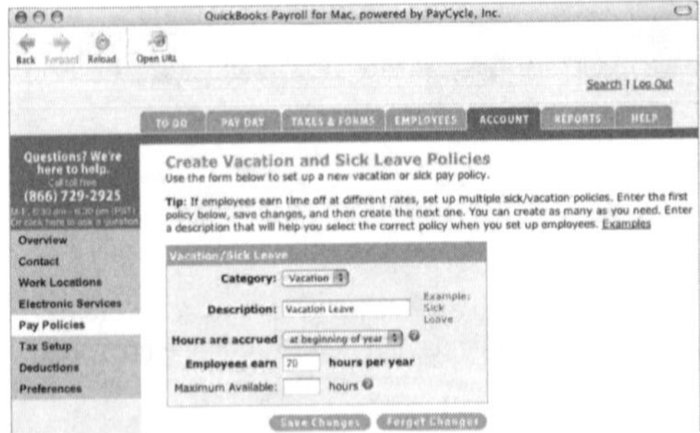

Figure 13 Use this screen to set up vacation and sick leave policies.

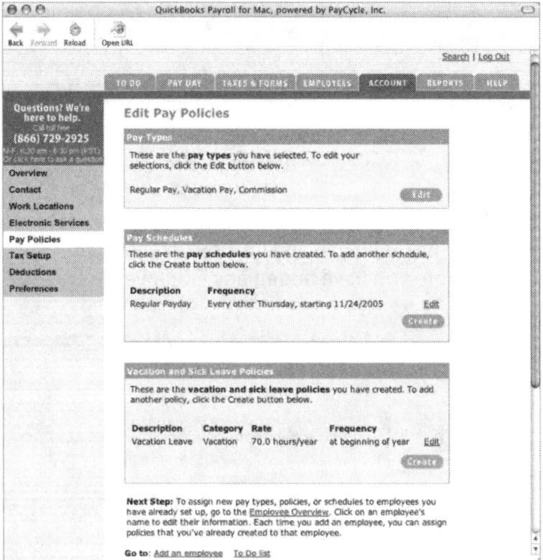

Figure 14 The Edit Pay Policies window shows all of your pay policy settings.

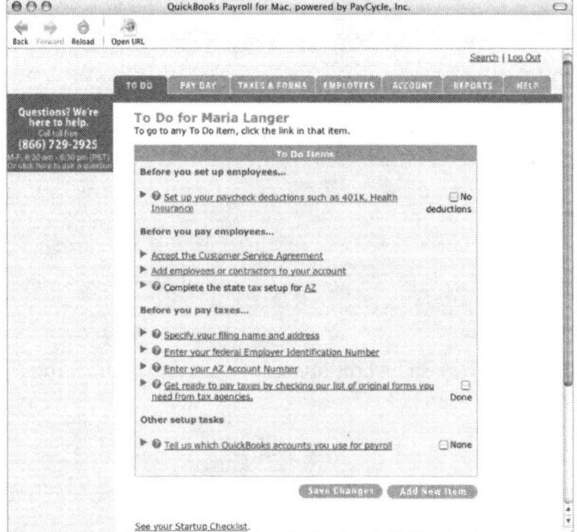

Figure 15 The To Do list after a number of items have been completed.

✔ Tips

- In step 2, you can click the Direct deposit timing link (**Figure 8**) to learn more about the amount of time between pay period end and pay day that is required for processing direct deposit.
- You might want to have multiple pay schedules if you have different types of pay checks. For example, your sales staff may get paid every two weeks with the rest of the company's employees, but they might also get paid once a month for sales commissions.
- You can have multiple vacation and sick leave policies. For example, new employees may only get two weeks paid vacation per year while long-time employees may get more.
- To modify any of the pay policies you created, click the Edit link beside the pay policy you want to change in the Edit Pay Policies screen (**Figure 14**). Then set new options in the screen that appears and click Save Changes to save them. Changes are in effect on a go-forward basis.
- The To Do list items you completed are automatically removed from the To Do list after they're done.
- To set up paycheck deductions, click the Set up your paycheck deductions such as 401K, Health Insurance link in the To Do list (**Figures 7** and **15**). Follow the instructions that appear to add deductions. When you're finished, return to the To Do list. If you don't have any deductions, you can turn on the No Deductions check box in the To Do list (**Figures 7** and **15**) to skip this item.

To add employees

1. In the To Do list (**Figure 15**), click the Add employees or contractors to your account link.
2. In the Employee and Contractor Overview screen that appears (**Figure 16**), click the Click here link beside If you are ready to add an employee.
3. In the Add Employee screen (**Figure 17**), click the Enter basic employee information link.
4. Fill in the form in the Basic Employee Information: Name and Address screen (**Figure 18**). The fields are self-explanatory.
5. Click Save Changes.
6. In the employee's Access Preferences screen (**Figure 19**), turn on the check box if you want the employee to be able to access his own payroll information at PaycheckRecords.com.
7. Click Save Changes.
8. If you turned on the check box in step 6, a screen appears, telling you PayCycle has sent an instructional e-mail to the employee. Click Continue.

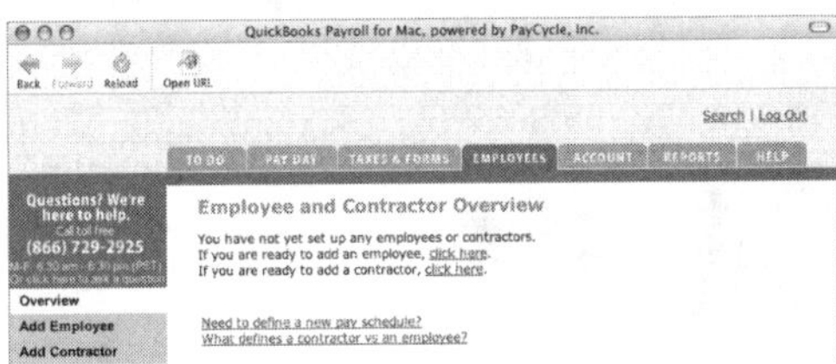

Figure 16 The Employee and Contractor Overview screen before you have added any employees.

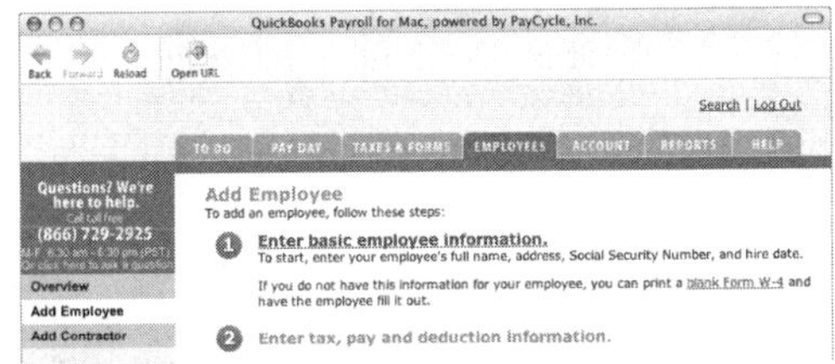

Figure 17 The Add Employee screen.

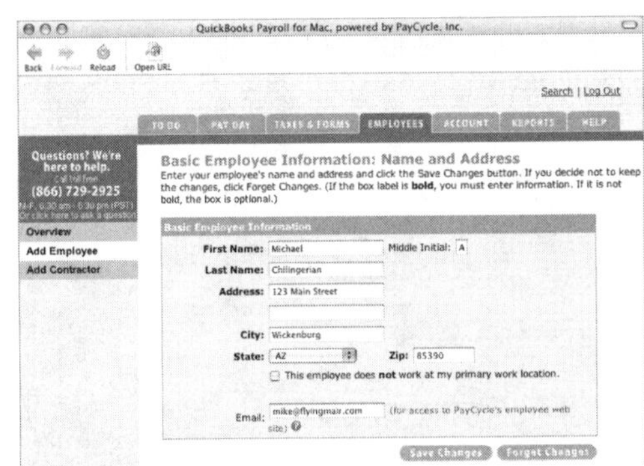

Figure 18 The Basic Employee Information: Name and Address screen.

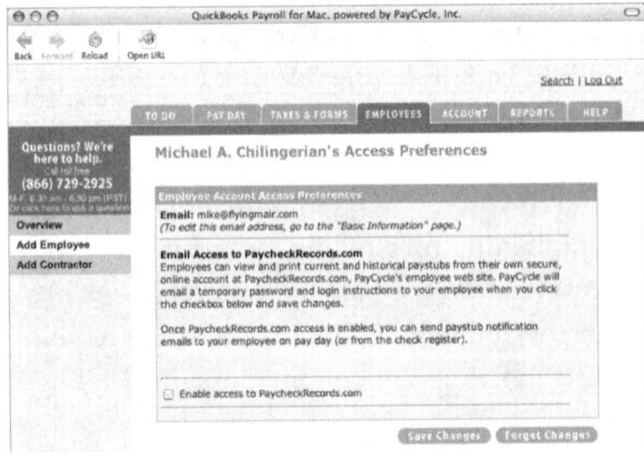

Figure 19 Use this screen to determine whether the employee should have access to his payroll information online.

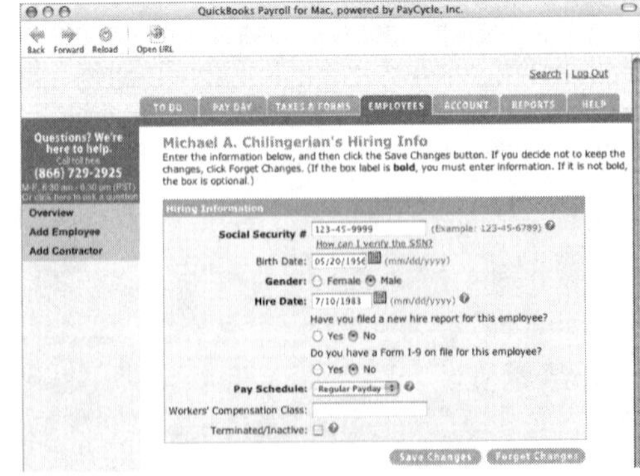

Figure 20 The employee's Hiring Info screen.

Figure 21 The Complete Employee Setup screen for an employee.

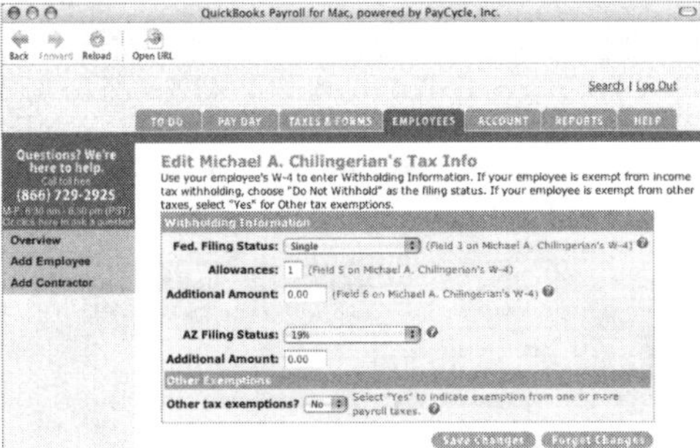

Figure 22 Enter information from the employee's W-4 form in this screen.

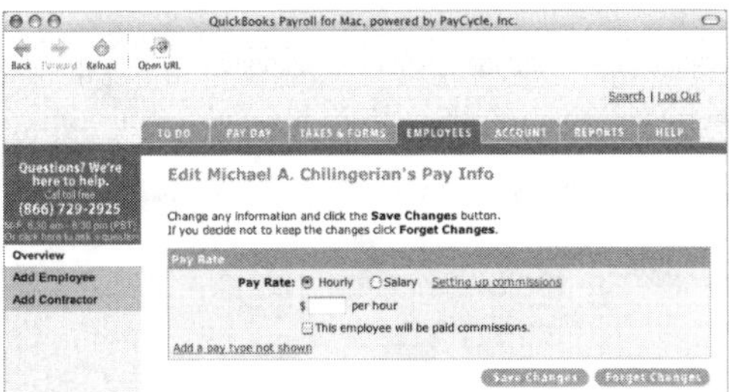

Figure 23a You can enter an employee's pay rate by hour...

9. In the employee's Hiring Info screen (**Figure 20**), enter information about the employee. Again, the fields are self-explanatory so I won't go into details.
10. Click Save Changes.
11. The Complete Employee Setup screen appears next (**Figure 21**). Click the Enter tax, pay and deduction information link.
12. In the Edit employee's Tax Info form (**Figure 22**), enter information from the employee's W-4 form.
13. Click Save Changes.
14. The Edit employee's Pay Info screen appears next. Select a Pay Rate option to specify whether the employee is paid hourly (**Figure 23a**) or on salary (**Figure 23b**). Then fill out the form for the rate and other options.
15. Click Save Changes.
16. In the Edit employee's Pay Info screen (**Figure 24**), choose a pay policy from the pop-up menu and enter the current balance in hours in the box.
17. Click Save & Next.

Continued on next page...

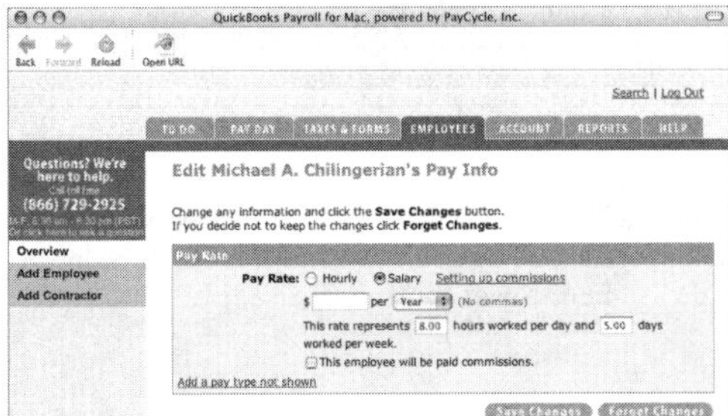

Figure 23b ...or by salary.

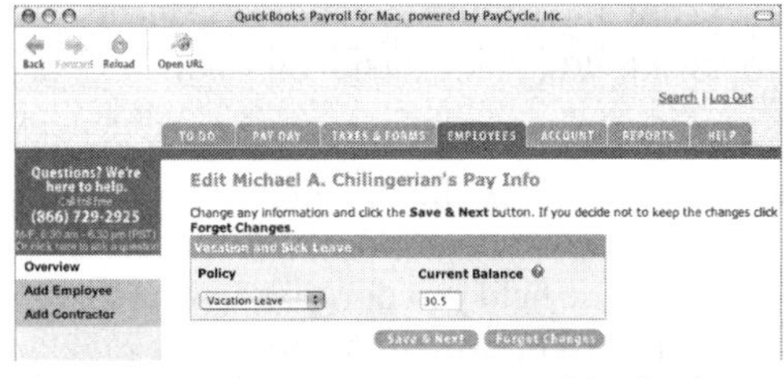

Figure 24 Use this screen to set pay policies for the employee.

Continued from previous page.

18. In the next Edit employee's Pay Info screen (**Figure 25**), select an option to indicate how you pay the employee.
19. Click Save Changes.
20. Depending on what you selected in step 18, the screen may expand to request additional information. Enter information as required and click Save Changes.
21. The Complete Employee Setup screen appears next (**Figure 26**). To add another employee, click the Add another Employee link and follow steps 3 through 20.
22. When you are finished adding employes, click the Return to To Do list link in the Complete Employee Setup screen (**Figure 26**).

✔ Tips

- Not all versions of PayCycle can pay contractors. If you subscribed for the basic service, the link for setting up contractors might not appear.
- While following these steps, you can click the Back (left arrow) button at the top of the window to go back to a previous screen and make changes.
- You can click the Blank Form W-4 link in the Add Employee screen (**Figure 17**) to print blank W-4 forms for employees to fill out and submit to you. These forms are required to be on file for each employee.
- If you need help filling out a PayCycle form, click the question mark button beside the field you don't understand. Additional information appears in a separate window.

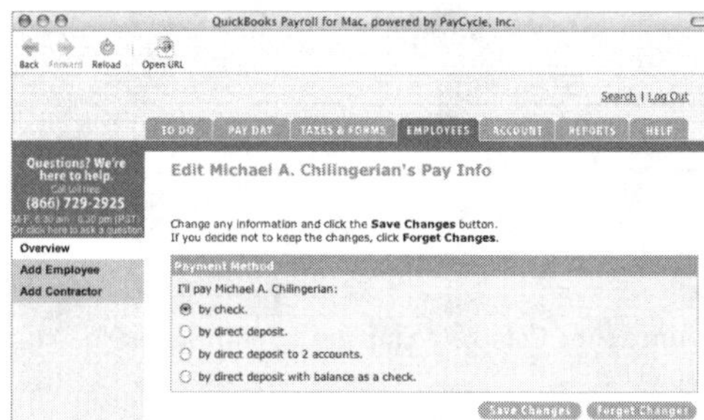

Figure 25 Use this screen to indicate how you pay this employee.

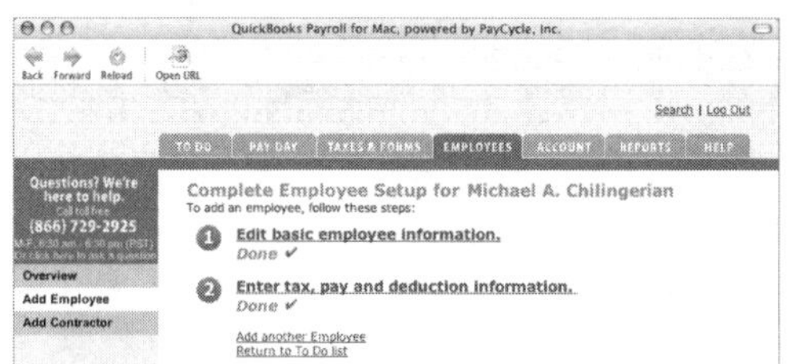

Figure 26 When you're finished setting up an employee, this screen appears.

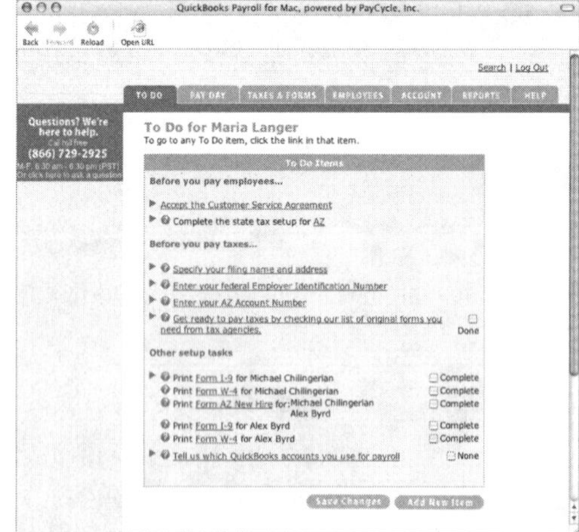

Figure 27 The To Do list changes to remove things you no longer have to do and to add new things. (Just like a to do list, huh? Never completely disappears.)

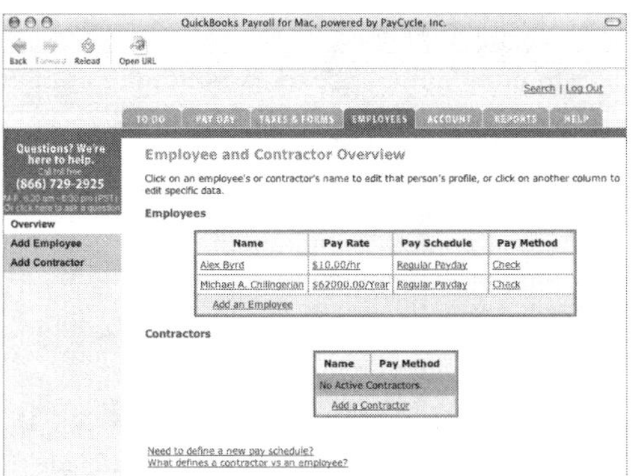

Figure 28 Clicking the Employees tab displays a list of all employees you've set up.

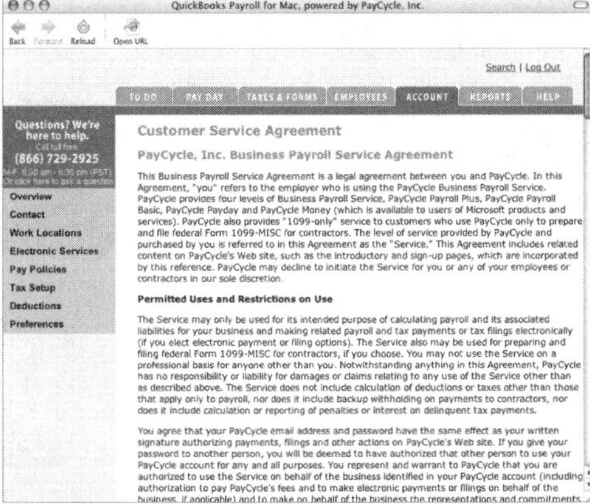

Figure 29 You must accept the Customer Service Agreement before you can pay employees.

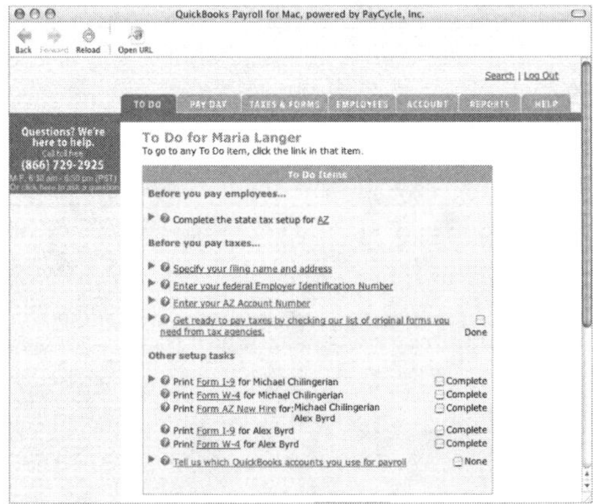

Figure 30 The revised To Do list.

- If you didn't enter an e-mail address for the employee in step 4 (**Figure 18**), you can skip steps 6 through 8; the screens will not appear.
- In step 16, if you have multiple pay policies set up, a pop-up menu will appear for each pay policy.
- After setting up employees, the To Do list changes to remove that item (**Figure 27**).
- To see a list of employees you have set up (**Figure 28**), click the Employees tab. You can then click links in the list to make changes to employee settings.
- To set up contractors, click the Add a Contractor link in the Employees screen (**Figure 28**) and follow the instructions that appear.

To accept the Customer Service Agreement

1. In the To Do list (**Figure 27**), click the Accept the Customer Service Agreement link.
2. Read the contents of the Customer Service Agreement screen that appears (**Figure 29**). You'll have to scroll down to read it all.
3. If you accept the terms of the agreement, click the I Accept button at the end of the agreement.

   A revised version of the To Do list appears (**Figure 30**).

✔ Tip

- As you've probably guessed, if you click the I Do NOT Accept button at the end of the agreement, you cannot use QuickBooks Payroll using PayCycle, Inc.

To complete state tax setup

1. In the To Do list (**Figure 30**), click the link for your state under Before you pay employees. For example, in **Figure 30**, you'd click *AZ*.
2. The Edit State Tax Information screen appears (**Figure 31**). Fill out the form for your business. The options on the form vary from state to state. **Figure 31** shows the form for Arizona.
3. Click Save Changes.

   The Revised To Do list appears (**Figure 32**).

✔ Tip

- You can follow links in the Common Questions area at the bottom of the Edit State Tax Information screen to get additional information that may help you complete the form.

To complete other setup tasks

1. Click a link in the To Do list screen (**Figure 32**) to view a setup item.
2. Provide information as required.
3. Click Save Changes.
4. Repeat this process for all setup tasks that appear on the To Do list.

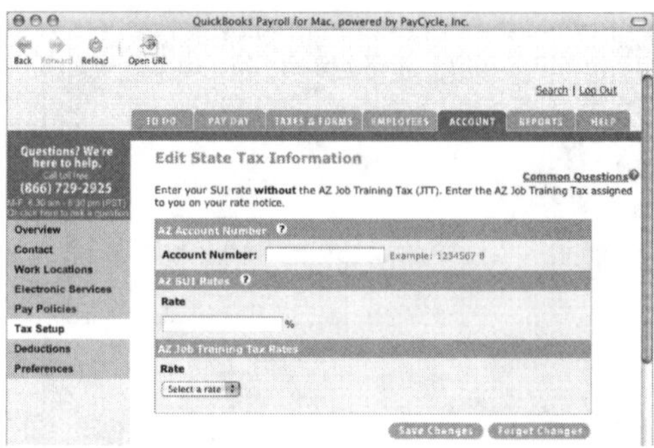

Figure 31 Fill out a form like this one to provide state tax information for your state.

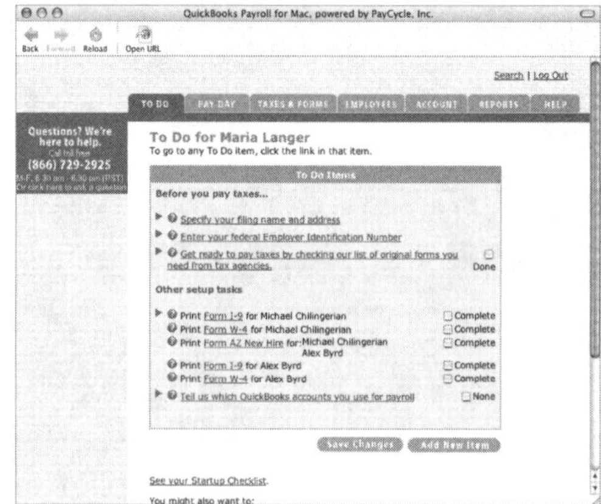

Figure 32 The To Do list might look something like this when you're ready to start paying employees.

Preparing QuickBooks for Payroll Processing

Before you use PayCycle for payroll processing with QuickBooks, you need to make sure QuickBooks is configured with the accounts you'll need to record payroll expenses and liabilities.

To prepare payroll checks, you need a bank account with check writing privileges. Normally, this will be your company's Checking account or a specially created payroll checking account.

To record payroll expenses, you need two expense accounts:

- **Wage Account** records expenses for wages paid.
- **Tax Account** records expenses for payroll taxes.

To record payroll liabities, you need at least four current liability accounts:

- **State Income Tax** is for recording withholding amounts for state income taxes.
- **State Unemployment Tax** is for recording state unemployment taxes payable.
- **Federal Taxes (941)** is for recording withholding amounts payable for all Federal taxes payable, as reported on form 941.
- **Federal Unemployment (940)** is for recording Federal unemployment taxes payable, as reported on form 940.

If you are missing any one of these accounts, now is the time to add them to QuickBooks. You can then tell PayCycle which QuickBooks accounts you use for Payroll.

To add payroll accounts to QuickBooks

1. Check your QuickBooks Chart of Accounts to make sure it includes all of the accounts listed on the previous page.
2. Add any missing accounts to your Chart of Accounts.

✔ Tip

- I explain how to add accounts to QuickBooks in **Chapter 2**.

To identify which QuickBooks accounts you use for Payroll

1. In the PayCycle To Do list **(Figure 32)**, click the Tell us which QuickBooks accounts you use for payroll link.
2. The Preferences - Accounting Software Integration screen appears **(Figure 33)**.
3. Choose QuickBooks for Mac from the Choose a program pop-up menu.
4. Click the menu button beside the Checking Account box to display a list of QuickBooks accounts **(Figure 34)**. Select the account you will use as the payroll checking account.
5. Click the menu button beside each of the Expense Accounts and Tax Liability Accounts boxes and use the list that appears **(Figure 34)** to select the corresponding account.
6. Click Save Changes.

✔ Tip

- These instructions assume that all radio buttons in the Preferences screen are set as shown in **Figure 33**. If you make changes to these options, additional configuration screens may appear.

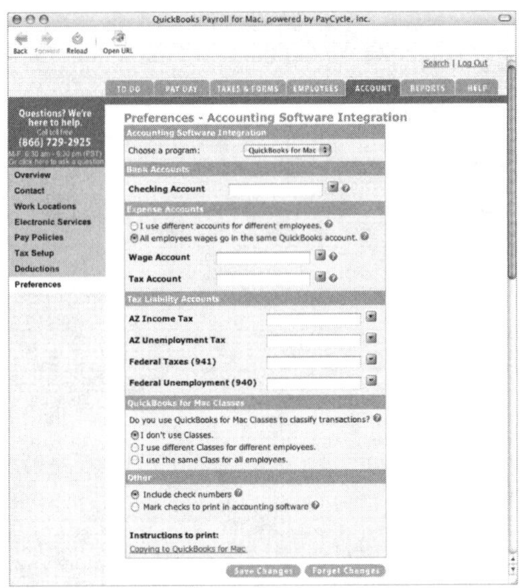

Figure 33 Use this screen to match PayCycle payroll items to QuickBooks accounts.

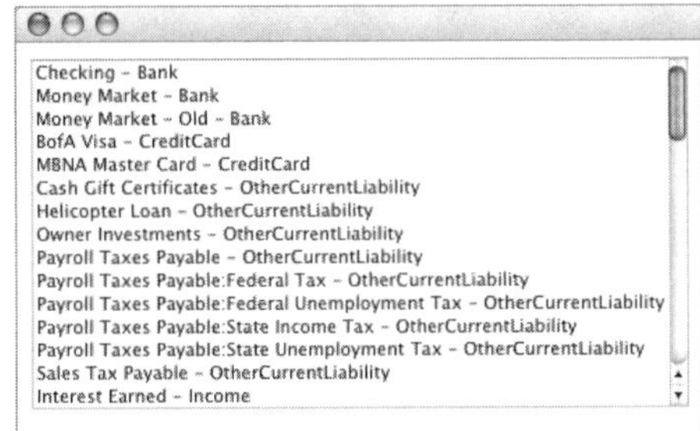

Figure 34 You can choose a matching account from a list like this one.

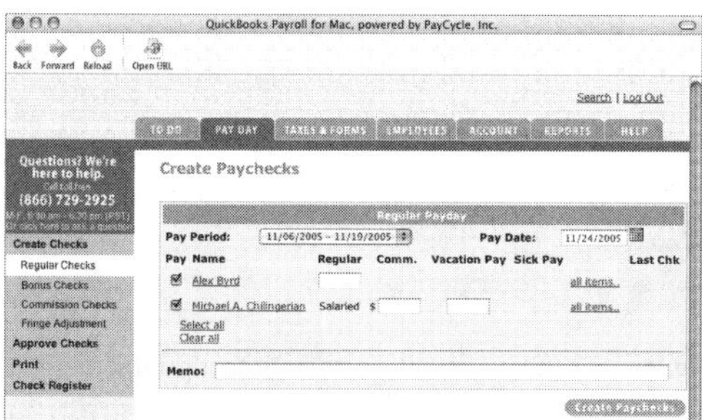

Figure 35 Use this form to enter pay day information for employees to be paid.

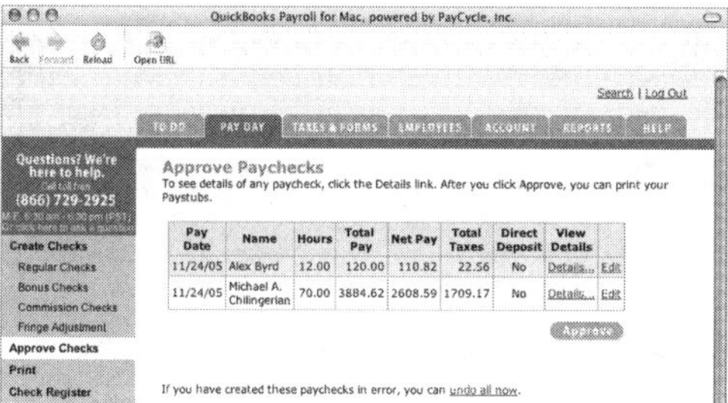

Pay Date	Name	Hours	Total Pay	Net Pay	Total Taxes	Direct Deposit	View Details
11/24/05	Alex Byrd	12.00	120.00	110.82	22.56	No	Details... Edit
11/24/05	Michael A. Chilingerian	70.00	3884.62	2608.59	1709.17	No	Details... Edit

Figure 36 You can review and approve a summary of paychecks in this screen.

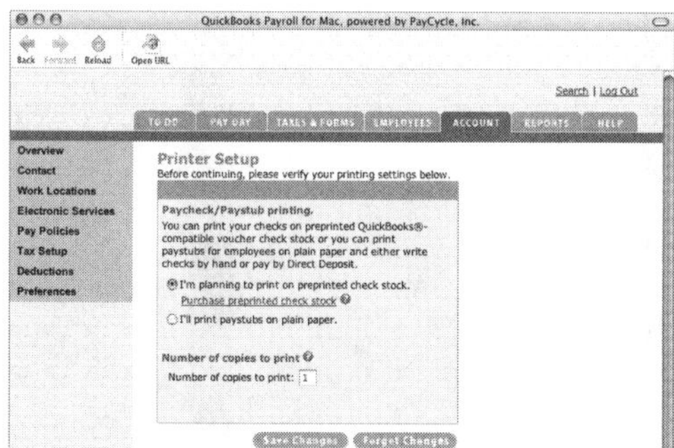

Figure 37 You may be prompted to set Printer Setup options.

Creating Paychecks

Once you've completed the setup process for PayCycle as discussed on the previous pages, you're ready to pay employees. Gather together the information you need to calculate the payroll. This may include, but is not limited to, the following information:

- For hourly employees, the number of hours worked.
- The amount of vacation or sick time used by each employee.
- The amount of any commissions due to employees.

This part of the chapter explains how to use PayCycle to calculate and print paychecks and to copy payroll transaction information into QuickBooks.

To create paychecks

1. From within QuickBooks, choose Employees > Payroll (**Figure 2**).
2. In the login screen (**Figure 5**), enter your e-mail address and password and click Login.
3. In the PayCycle window, click the Pay Day tab.
4. Fill out the form in the Create Paychecks window that appears (**Figure 35**).
5. Click Create Paychecks.
6. The Approve Paychecks window appears (**Figure 36**). Check the amounts due to each employee; if they look correct, click Approve.
7. The Printer Setup screen may appear next (**Figure 37**). Select a Paycheck/Paystub printing option, enter the number of copies to print, and click Save Changes.

Continued on next page...

Continued from previous page.

8. Another Printer Setup screen may appear (**Figure 38**). If options are correct, click Save Changes.
9. In the View and Print Paychecks window (**Figure 39**), turn on the check box beside each check you want to print. Then click the View & Print button.
10. QuickBooks opens the paycheck documents with Adobe Reader or Preview (**Figure 40**) and displays the first one on screen.
11. If you are printing checks on check stock, insert the check stock in your printer.
12. In Adobe Reader, click the Print button on the toolbar.

    Or

    In Preview (**Figure 40**), choose File > Print or press ⌘P.
13. If a Print dialog appears, click the Print button.
14. Examine the checks. If they have printed incorrectly, repeat steps 11 through 13. Otherwise, Choose Quit from the Adobe Reader or Preview menu.
15. Back in the View and Print Paychecks window (**Figure 39**), click Continue.
16. The Enter Check Numbers screen may appear (**Figure 41**). If you have printed a lot of checks, enter the first check number in the Starting Check # box and click the Auto-Fill button. Otherwise, you can enter each check number in the table at the bottom of the window. Then click Save Check #s.
17. In the Copy to QuickBooks for Mac screen (**Figure 42**), click the Copy to QuickBooks button.

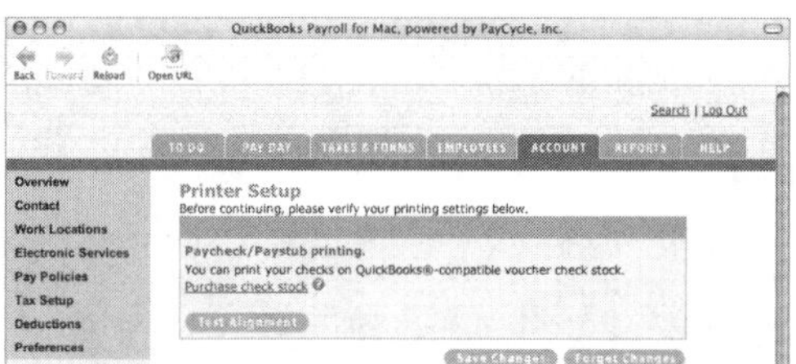

Figure 38 You can use this screen to test printer alignment for printing on check stock.

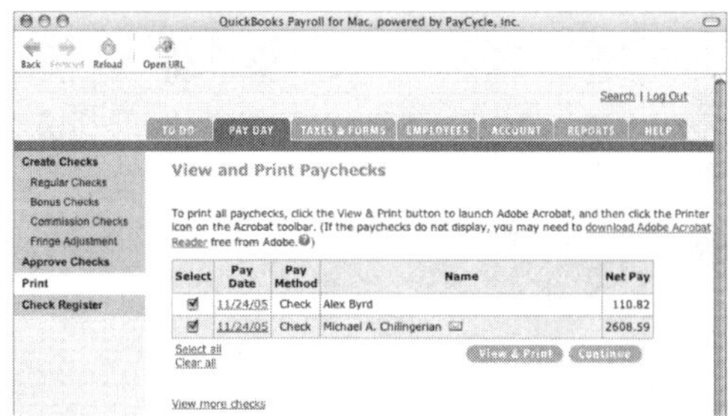

Figure 39 Use this screen to indicate which checks should print.

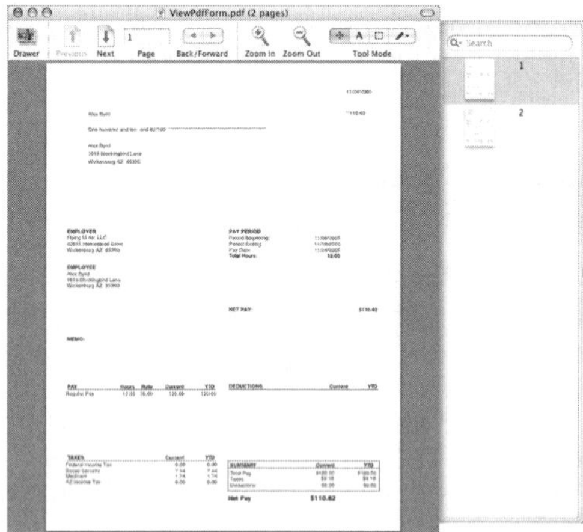

Figure 40 Here's what the paychecks for two employees might look like in Preview.

Figure 41 Use this screen to enter check numbers for the paychecks you printed.

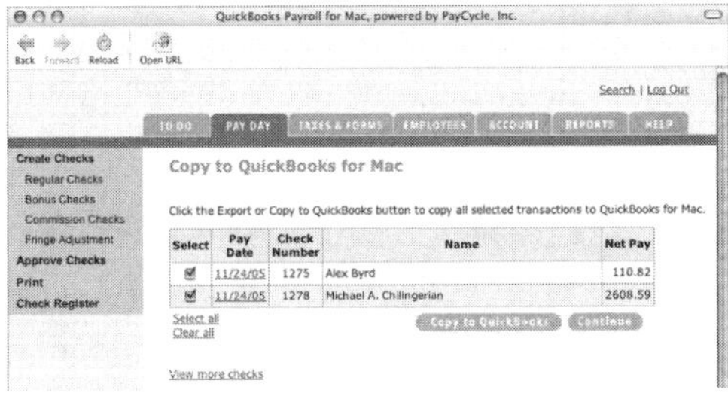

Figure 42 This screen enables you to send payroll information from PayCycle to QuickBooks.

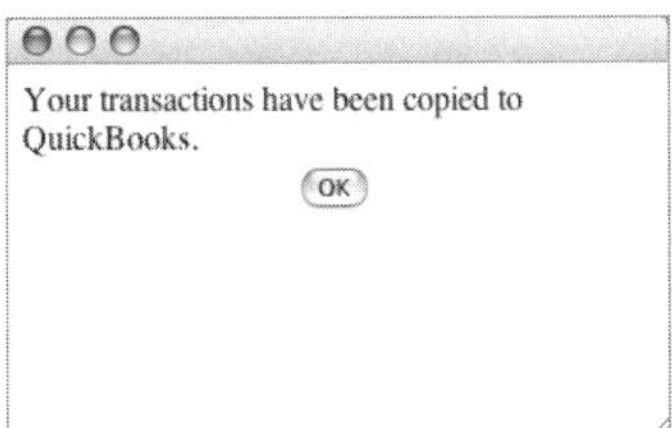

Figure 43 A dialog like this confirms that payroll information has been copied to QuickBooks.

18. You should hear a QuickBooks entry sound. A dialog like the one in **Figure 43** appears. Click OK.

19. In the Copy to QuickBooks for Mac window (**Figure 42**), click Continue.

20. In the Email Paystubs window (**Figure 44**):

    Turn on check boxes beside each employee you want to e-mail a paystub to. Then click Send E-mail.

    Or

    Click Skip Email.

21. In the Final Steps window (**Figure 45**):

    Click links to perform other payroll-related tasks with PayCycle.

    Or

    Close the PayCycle window to continue working with QuickBooks.

✔ Tips

- After step 3, a screen may ask if you have paid any wages this year. If you have,

Continued on next page...

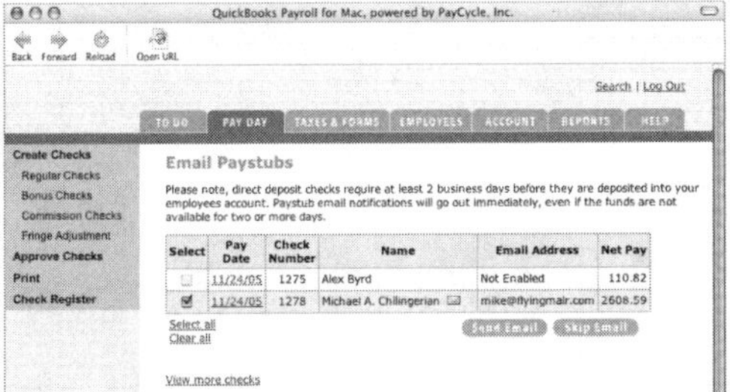

Figure 44 You can use this screen to send paystubs to employees by e-mail. This can save time and paper, especially for direct-deposit employees.

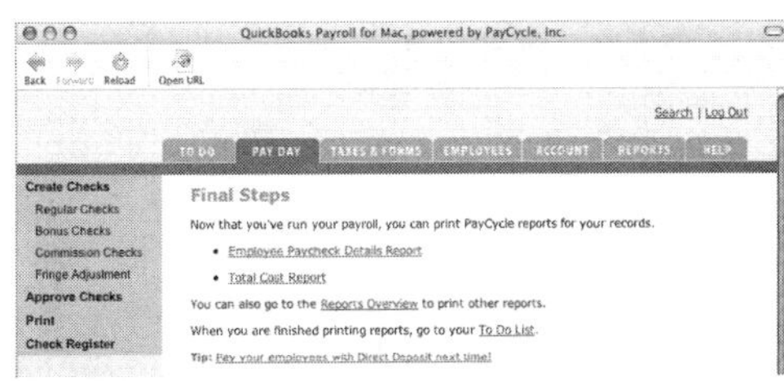

Figure 45 This screen suggest some other payroll-related tasks you might want to perform before returning to QuickBooks.

Continued from previous page.

click Yes and follow the instructions that appear to enter year-to-date amounts.

- The appearance of the Create Paychecks screen (**Figure 35**) varies depending on options you set for employees.
- In step 6, if the amount in the Approve Paychecks window (**Figure 36**) for an employee does not appear to be correct, click the Edit link for that employee. You can then check or change pay day information for that employee.
- After step 6, if you have not provided information for PayCycle services, you'll see a series of screens that enable you to enter it.
- You can print paychecks and paystubs on any QuickBooks-compatible voucher style check stock.
- If you prefer to hand-write your pay checks, print paychecks and paystubs to blank paper. You can then include the paystubs with your hand-written paychecks.
- When PayCycle copies payroll information to QuickBooks, it records paychecks in the checking account you indicated. **Figure 46** shows an example of a payroll transaction in the Write Checks window. I tell you more about writing checks in **Chapter 4**.

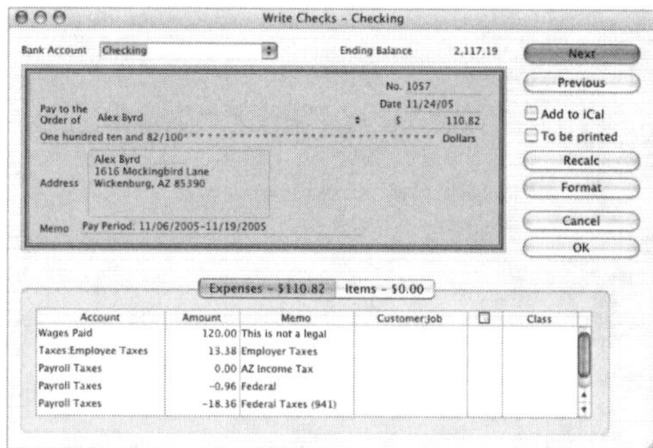

Figure 46 A paycheck in the QuickBooks Write Checks window.

Reporting Results

Reporting Results

If you use QuickBooks to track your business's finances, you'll probably want to generate reports that summarize financial activity. After all, what's the sense in taking the time to enter transactions if you can't see the income statements, balance sheets, and other financial statements you need to judge your business's health and well being?

QuickBooks has an extensive and flexible reporting system that can summarize just about any data entered into your accounting records. There are three types of reports, all of which can be customized in a wide variety of ways:

- **QuickReports** summarize activity in an account or provide supporting details for a value in another report. These reports can be created by clicking a button or double-clicking a report value.
- **Predefined reports** include the kinds of financial reports you'd find useful for running your business. These reports are listed on submenus under the Reports menu, as well as in the Report Finder window.
- **Memorized reports** are reports that you have customized and memorized. This makes it quick and easy to create and recreate reports to your specifications.

Continued on next page...

Continued from previous page.

QuickBooks also offers a number of standard graphs that can graphically portray financial results. Graphs can be customized to display information in a number of ways.

This chapter explains how to use QuickBooks' reporting features to report financial activity and results. It also explains how to use its simple but powerful budgeting feature so you can compare actual results to corresponding budgeted amounts.

✔ Tip

- QuickBooks can only report results for transactions that have been entered into your QuickBooks data file. If you began using QuickBooks in the middle of a fiscal year, the results QuickBooks reports for that year may not be complete.

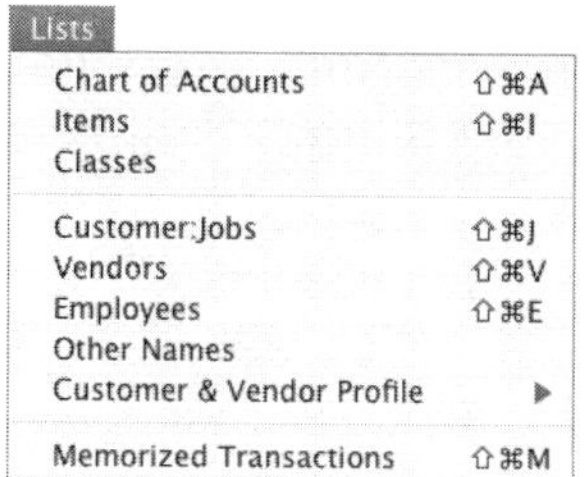

Figure 1 The Lists menu.

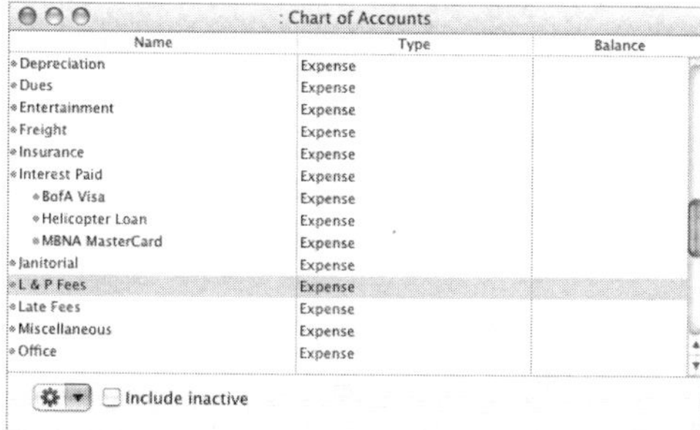

Figure 2 Select the account you want to create a QuickReport for.

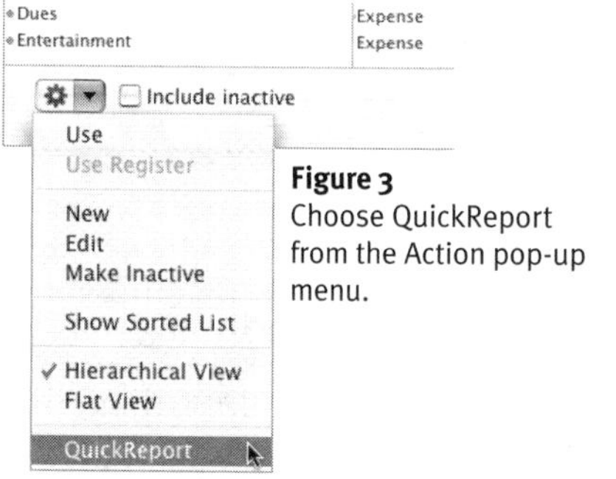

Figure 3 Choose QuickReport from the Action pop-up menu.

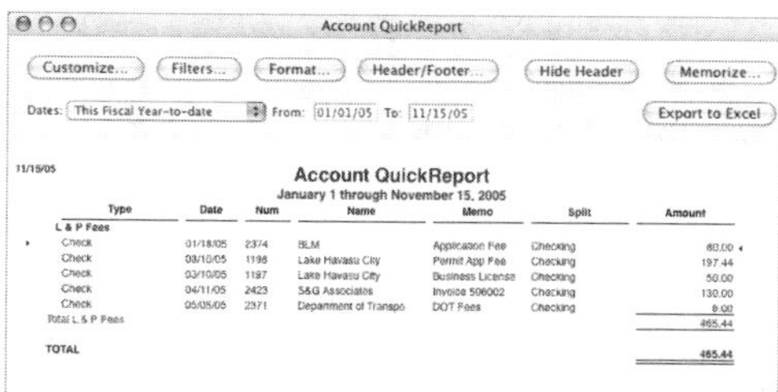

Figure 4 A QuickReport for an expense account.

Creating QuickReports & Using QuickZoom

A QuickReport (**Figure 4**) is just that: a quickly created report. QuickReports can be created in two ways:

- Click a QuickReport button or choose the QuickReport command from the Action menu (**Figure 3**) in a window or dialog.
- Double-click a value in another report. This is known as QuickBooks's *Quick-Zoom* feature.

This part of the chapter explains how to create QuickReports for accounts and how to use the QuickZoom feature to get additional information about a value in a report.

✔ Tip

- You can customize QuickReports. I explain how later in this chapter.

To create a QuickReport for an account

1. Choose Lists > Chart of Accounts (**Figure 1**) or press Shift ⌘ A to display the Chart of Accounts window.
2. Select the income or expense account you want to create a QuickReport for (**Figure 2**).
3. Choose QuickReport from the Action pop-up menu (**Figure 3**). An Account QuickReport window displaying the report appears (**Figure 4**).

✔ Tip

- You can only create a QuickReport for the following types of accounts: income, expense, other income, other expense.

To create a QuickReport from a list

1. Use the Lists menu (**Figure 1**) to display a list.
2. Select the list item for which you want to create a QuickReport (**Figure 5**).
3. Choose QuickReport from the Action pop-up menu (**Figure 3**). A QuickReport for that item appears (**Figure 6**).

✔ Tip

- You can use this technique to create QuickReports from most lists.

To use QuickZoom

1. In a report window, point to a value you want more information for. The mouse pointer turns into a magnifying glass icon with the letter *Z* inside it (**Figure 7**).
2. Double-click the value. One of two things happens:
   - ▲ If the value is the sum of other values, a detail report for the value appears (**Figure 8**).
   - ▲ If the value is the result of a single transaction, a form for that transaction appears (**Figure 9**).

✔ Tip

- I tell you about the various transaction forms in **Chapters 3**, **4**, **6**, and **7**.

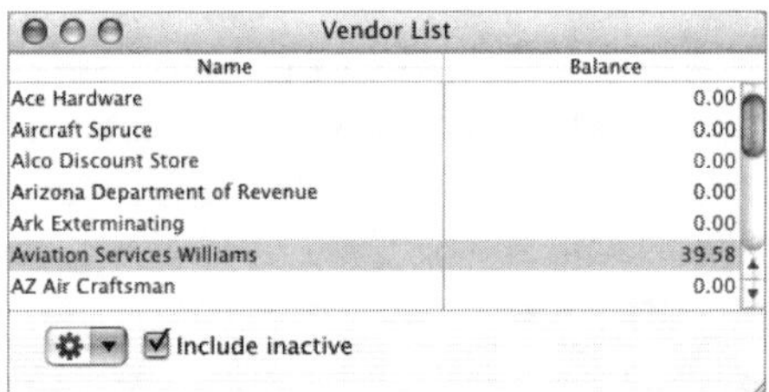

Figure 5 The Vendor List window.

Figure 6 A QuickReport for a vendor.

Amount

37.50
54.96
-92.46
39.54
67.20

Figure 7 The QuickZoom pointer looks like Zorro's magnifying glass.

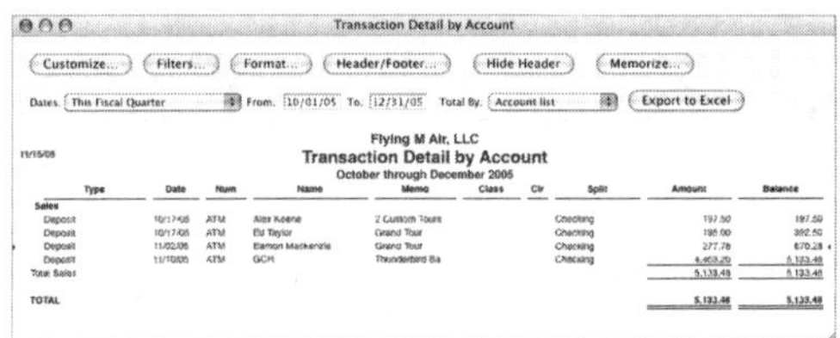

Figure 8 Double-clicking a value that is the sum of other values displays a transaction detail report.

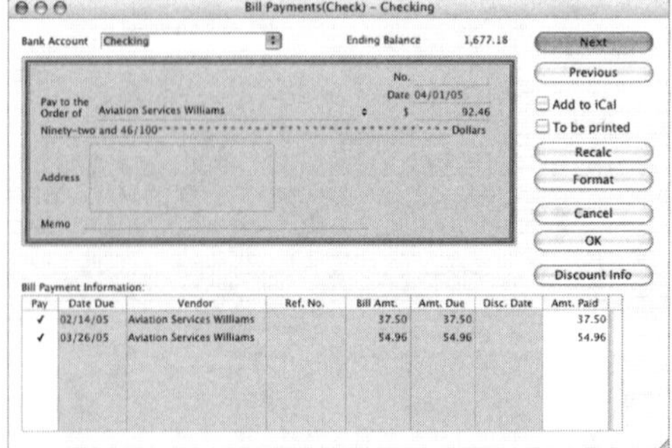

Figure 9 Double-clicking a value in a QuickReport displays the transaction the value is based on.

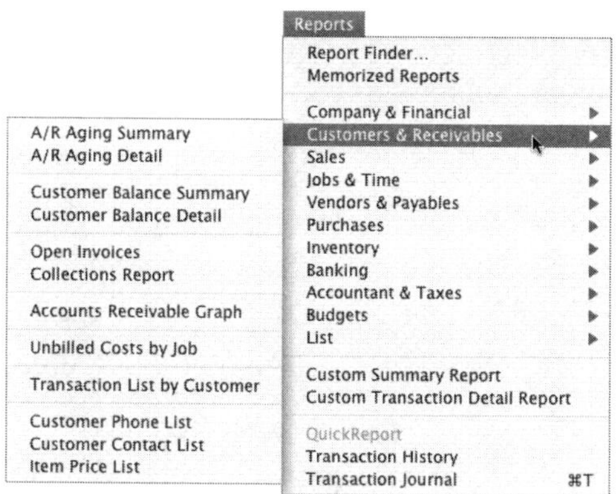

Figure 10 Submenus under the Reports menu offer many reporting options.

Creating Reports with the Reports Menu

The submenus in QuickBooks' Reports menu (**Figure 10**) offer a number of predefined reports, including many standard accounting reports. The Reports menu breaks reports down into several categories:

- **Company & Financial** offers a variety of standard financial reports and graphs, including profit and loss, income, expenses, balance sheet, net worth, and cash flow.
- **Customers & Receivables (Figure 10)** includes accounts receivable reports for aging, customer balances, invoices, collections, and customer contact information.
- **Sales** reports sales by customer, item, or sales rep. This category also includes a report of pending sales.
- **Jobs & Time** includes reports for jobs, items, time, and unbilled costs.
- **Vendors & Payables** includes reports for accounts payable aging, vendor balances, unpaid bills, 1099 form activity, sales tax liability, and vendor contact information.
- **Purchases** includes reports for purchases by item and vendor as well as open purchase orders.
- **Inventory** offers inventory valuation and status reports, as well as worksheets for completing physical inventories and a price list.
- **Banking** includes deposit detail, check detail, and missing checks reports.

Continued on next page...

Continued from previous page.

- **Accountant & Taxes** includes reports of interest to an accountant, such as trial balance, general ledger, and journal, as well as reports to make completing tax returns easier.
- **Budgets** includes reports that examine budgets and compare budgeted to actual results.
- **List** provides reports of each of QuickBooks' lists.

The Reports menu also includes commands for creating predefined and customized transaction reports.

No matter which report you choose, QuickBooks displays information accurate to the current date, based on transactions entered into your data file.

✔ Tips

- I explain how to set up a budget near the end of this chapter.
- The predefined reports on Reports menu submenus can be customized to meet your needs. I explain how later in this chapter.

To create a report with the Reports menu

Choose the name of the report you want to create from the appropriate submenu under the Reports menu (**Figure 10**). The report appears in a report window (**Figure 11**).

Figure 11 Choosing Open Invoices from the Customers & Receivables submenu displays the Open Invoices report for the current date.

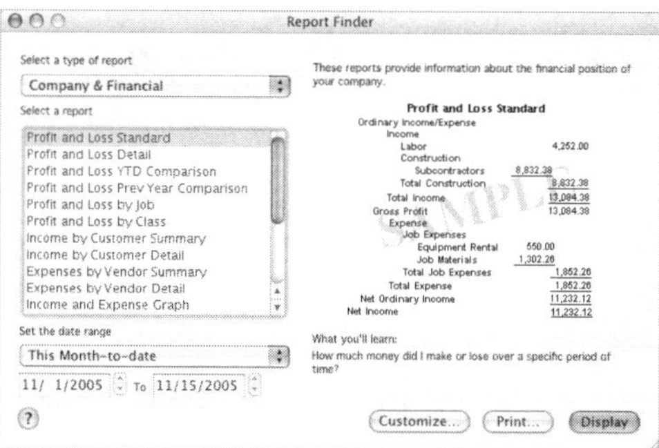

Figure 12 The Report Finder window, displaying Company & Financial reports.

✓ Company & Financial
Customers & Receivables
Sales
Jobs & Time
Vendors & Payables
Purchases
Inventory
Banking
Accountant & Taxes
Budgets
List

Figure 13 Use this pop-up menu to choose a type of report.

Creating Reports with the Report Finder

The Report Finder window (**Figure 12**) offers a more friendly interface for creating a specific report. Instead of knowing in advance what report you want to create, all you need to know is the type of report.

The Report Finder window includes a pop-up menu with several types of reports (**Figure 13**):

- **Company & Financial** offers a variety of standard financial reports and graphs, including profit and loss, income, expenses, balance sheet, net worth, and cash flow.
- **Customers & Receivables** includes accounts receivable reports for aging, customer balances, invoices, collections, and customer contact information.
- **Sales** reports sales by customer, item, or sales rep. This category also includes a report of pending sales.
- **Jobs & Time** includes reports for jobs, items, time, and unbilled costs.
- **Vendors & Payables** includes reports for accounts payable aging, vendor balances, unpaid bills, 1099 form activity, sales tax liability, and vendor contact information.
- **Purchases** includes reports for purchases by item and vendor as well as open purchase orders.
- **Inventory** offers inventory valuation and status reports, as well as worksheets for completing physical inventories and a price list.
- **Banking** includes deposit detail, check detail, and missing checks reports.

Continued on next page...

Continued from previous page.

- **Accountant & Taxes** includes reports of interest to an accountant, such as trial balance, general ledger, and journal, as well as reports to make completing tax returns easier.
- **Budgets** includes reports that examine budgets and compare budgeted to actual results.
- **List** provides reports of each of QuickBooks' lists.

Once you select a type of report, you can click specific report names in a list. A sample of the report appears on the right side of the window, making it easy to see exactly what the report will do for you.

When you see a report that looks like what you want, you have three options:

- **Customize** enables you to customize the report before you create it. This makes it possible to get the report right the first time you create it, rather than having to fine-tune it after it already exists.
- **Print** prints the report without displaying it onscreen.
- **Display** displays the report onscreen so you can work with it.

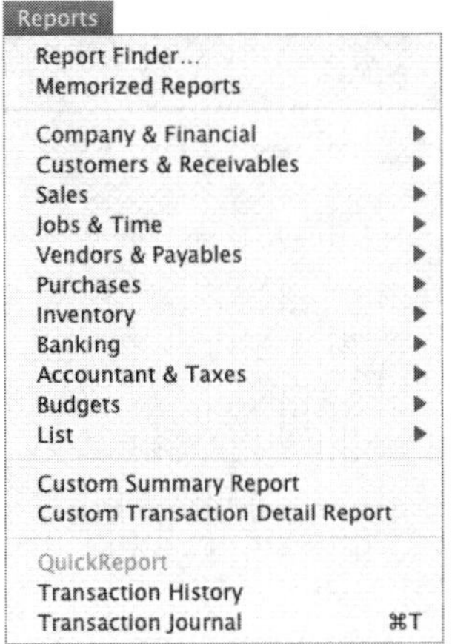

Figure 14
The Reports menu.

✔ Tips

- The Report Finder window also includes graphs. I explain how to create and modify graphs later in this chapter.
- The Report Finder includes all of the reports found on Reports menu submenus. They're just organized differently, probably to keep writers like me busy.
- I explain how to customize reports later in this chapter and how to print reports in **Chapter 10**.

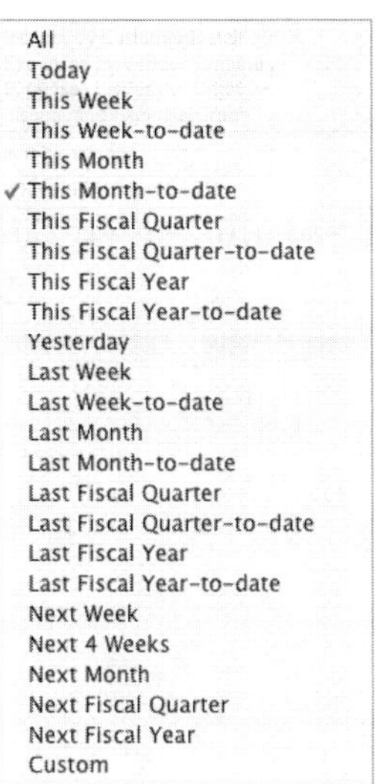

Figure 15 Use this pop-up menu to choose a date range for the report.

Figure 16 A Profit and Loss report.

To create a report with the Report Finder

1. Choose Reports > Report Finder (**Figure 14**) to display the Report Finder window (**Figure 12**).
2. Use the pop-up menu near the top of the window (**Figure 13**) to choose a type of report.
3. In the list of reports, click a report name to view a sample of it in the preview area on the right side of the window (**Figure 12**). Repeat this process until you select the report you want to create.
4. Choose a date option from the pop-up menu at the bottom of the window (**Figure 15**).

   Or

   Enter report starting and ending dates in the two boxes at the bottom of the window.
5. Click Display. The report appears in a report window (**Figure 16**).

✔ Tips

- If you're not sure what a report is for, check the area below the report preview for a "What you'll learn" tip (**Figure 12**).
- The default date range option varies depending on which report is selected.

Customizing Reports

Although QuickBooks' predefined reports might completely meet your needs, you may want to customize them to even better meet your needs.

QuickBooks offers many customization options that enable you to change both the content and the appearance of your reports onscreen and when printed. These options are available via buttons, pop-up menus, and boxes that appear at the top of each report window (**Figures 4**, **8**, **11**, and **16**):

- **Customize** enables you to change options that affect a report's content. The dialog that appears varies from one report to another, so options are report-specific.
- **Filters** enables you to change the content of what appears in a report by filtering out transactions that don't meet criteria you specify.
- **Format** enables you to change a report's number and font format.
- **Header/Footer** enables you to change the information that appears in the header and footer of a report, as well as its formatting.
- **Hide Header** removes the header from view. When the header is hidden, the Hide Header button turns into a **Show Header** button, which displays the header again.

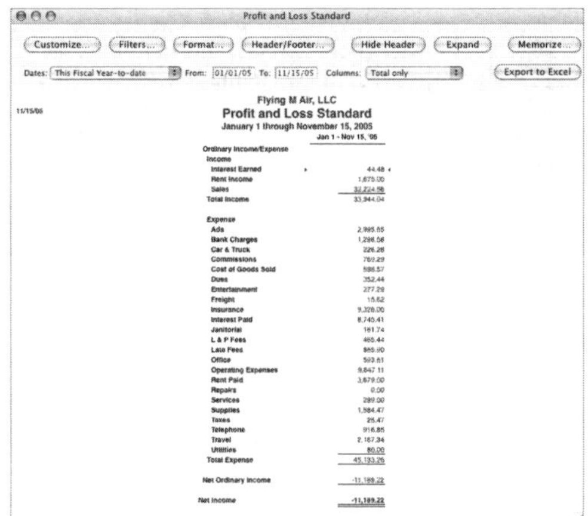

Figure 17 A Profit and Loss report, collapsed to hide subaccount detail.

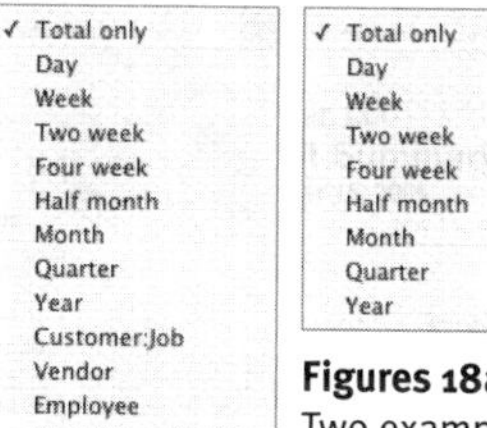

Figures 18a & 18b Two examples of how the Columns pop-up menu may appear in a report window: the menu for a Profit and Loss report (left) and the menu for a Balance Sheet (above).

Profit and Loss Standard.slk

Flying M Air, LLC	
Profit and Loss Standard 11/15/05	
January 1 through November 15, 2005	
	Jan 1 - Nov 15, '05
Ordinary Income/Expense	
Income	
Interest Earned	44.48
Rent Income	1,675.00
Sales	32,224.56
Total Income	33,944.04
Expense	
Ads	2,995.65
Bank Charges	
Account Maintenance	129.00
Credit Card Acceptance	509.58
Overdraft Protection	40.00
Bank Charges - Other	620.00
Total Bank Charges	1,298.58
Car & Truck	226.28
Commissions	769.29
Cost of Goods Sold	598.57
Dues	352.44
Entertainment	277.29
Freight	15.62
Insurance	9,328.00
Interest Paid	
BofA Visa	99.02
Helicopter Loan	8,532.39
MBNA MasterCard	114.00
Total Interest Paid	8,745.41
Janitorial	181.74
L & P Fees	465.44
Late Fees	885.90
Office	593.81
Operating Expenses	
Fuel	7,005.39
Maintenance	2,303.42
Oil	338.30
Total Operating Expenses	9,647.11
Rent Paid	3,679.00
Repairs	0.00
Services	299.00
Supplies	1,584.47
Taxes	
Adjustments	25.47

Figure 19 A Profit and Loss report, exported to Excel.

- **Collapse** displays only top-level information in a report—for example, in a Profit and Loss report (**Figure 16**), clicking Collapse hides all subaccount totals (**Figure 17**). When a report is collapsed, the Collapse button turns into an **Expand** button (**Figure 17**), which expands the report.
- **Memorize** memorizes the report so it can be quickly created again.
- **Dates** offers date range options (**Figure 15**). Only transactions that fall in the date range will be included in the report.
- **From** and **To** enable you to enter a custom date range for the report. Only transactions between the two dates you specify will be included in the report.
- **Columns** enables you to choose how the report's information will be broken down into columns. The options that appear on this menu vary depending on the report you are working with; **Figures 18a and 18b** show two examples.
- **Export to Excel** creates an SYLK format file of the report and opens it in Excel (**Figure 19**)—if Excel is installed on your computer.

In this part of the chapter, I explain how you can use the Customize Report, Report Filters, Format Report, and Format Header/Footer dialogs to fine-tune the appearance and content of your reports.

Continued on next page...

Continued from previous page.

✔ Tips

- Customization options differ from one type of report to another, so it's impossible to discuss all possible options in this chapter. Instead, I'll do my best to show you the kinds of options you can expect to find.
- You can set certain default report options in the *Company Name* Settings window. I explain how in **Chapter 11**.
- The Customize Report dialog, which appears when you click the Customize button, can also be accessed from within the Report Finder window (**Figure 12**). This enables you to set certain customization options before you create a report.
- QuickBooks' Find feature, which I discuss in **Chapter 6**, also works with filters.
- Clicking the Hide Header button does not remove the header and footer from printed reports.
- The Collapse button does not appear in all reports.
- I explain how to memorize reports later in this chapter and how to print reports in **Chapter 10**.
- Time for a shameless plug. If you use Excel and want to learn more about it, be sure to check out my *Microsoft Excel Visual QuickStart Guides*, which are also published by Peachpit Press. Hey, if your second business' bottom line looked as bad as the one in **Figure 17**, you'd be plugging away like this, too!

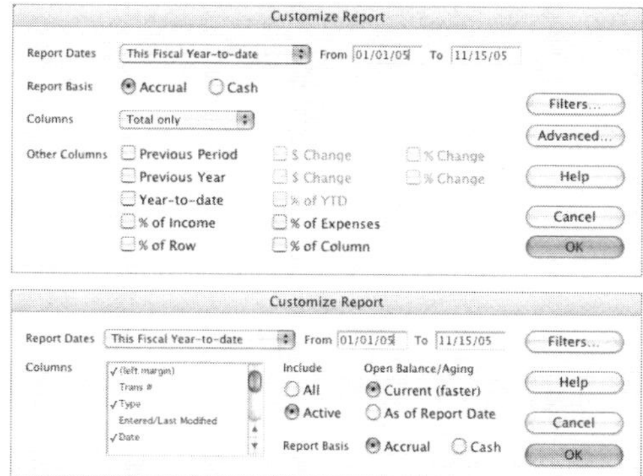

Figures 20a & 20b The Customize Report dialog for a Profit and Loss report (top) and for an Account Quick-Report (bottom).

To set report customization options

1. In a report window (**Figures 4, 8, 11, 16,** and **17**), click the Customize button.

   Or

   In the Report Finder window with the report you want to create selected (**Figure 12**), click the Customize button.

   The Customize Report dialog appears (**Figures 20a** and **20b**).

2. Set options as desired in the dialog. Here's an alphabetical listing of the options you might find:

   ▲ **Age through how many days** enables you to specify the highest aging to include in the report.

   ▲ **Columns** and **Other Columns** enable you to select columns of information to be included in the report. In some versions of the dialog, there's a pop-up menu and there may be a series of check boxes (**Figure 20a**). In other versions of the dialog, there's a scrolling list with column names you can check off (**Figure 20b**).

   ▲ **Customer:Job** enables you to specify a single customer or job for the report.

   ▲ **Days Past Due** enables you to specify how many days past due an invoice must be to appear on the report.

   ▲ **Days per aging period** enables you to specify how many days should be in each aging period in the report.

   ▲ **Delay receipts how many days** enables you to specify a delay time for cash receipts to provide a more realistic cash flow forecast.

Continued on next page...

Continued from previous page.

- **Formats** enables you to determine breakdown points for a job report.
- **Include** enables you to specify which subtotal headings appear in transaction detail reports. **All** includes all subtotal headings and **Active** includes only subtotal headings that have transactions.
- **Open Balance/Aging** enables you to specify how a customer's open balance appears on aging reports. **Current** shows the current open balance. **As of report date** shows the customer's open balance as of the report date.
- **Report Basis** enables you to select from Accrual or Cash basis reporting.
- **Report Dates** enables you to choose a date option from a pop-up menu (**Figure 15**) or enter one or more custom dates.
- **Reporting Periods** enables you to specify a time interval for columns in the report.
- **Row Axis** enables you to specify the row headings you want for the report.
- **Show Actuals**, **Difference**, and **% of Budget** enables you to specify whether you want the report to show actual amounts, the difference between budgeted and actual amounts, and the percent of the budgeted amount.
- **Sort By** enables you to specify how you want transactions sorted in a report.
- **Total By** enables you to specify how transactions in a report should be grouped and subtotaled.

3. Click OK. The report changes to your specifications.

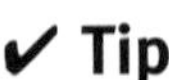

Tip

- After step 3, if you don't like what you see, you can always click the Customize button and change settings again.

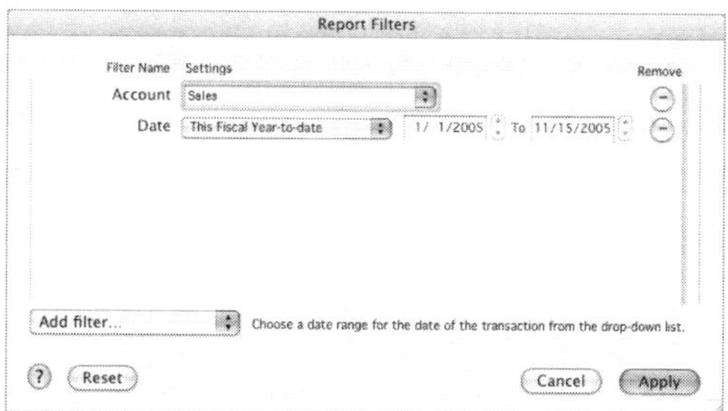

Figure 21 The Report Filters dialog with predefined filters for a Sales account QuickReport.

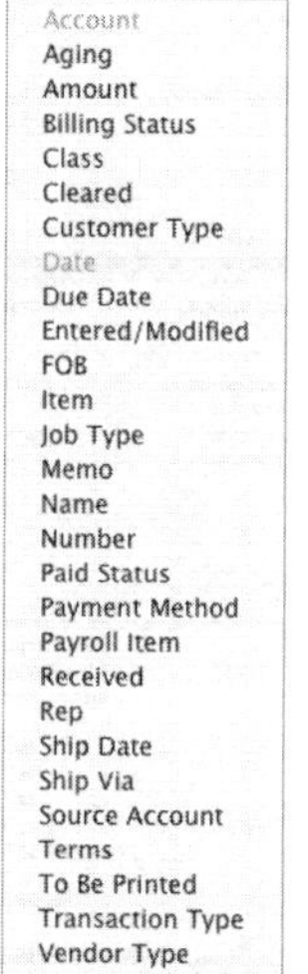

Figure 22 Use this pop-up menu to select a filter to add. Gray filters have already been added.

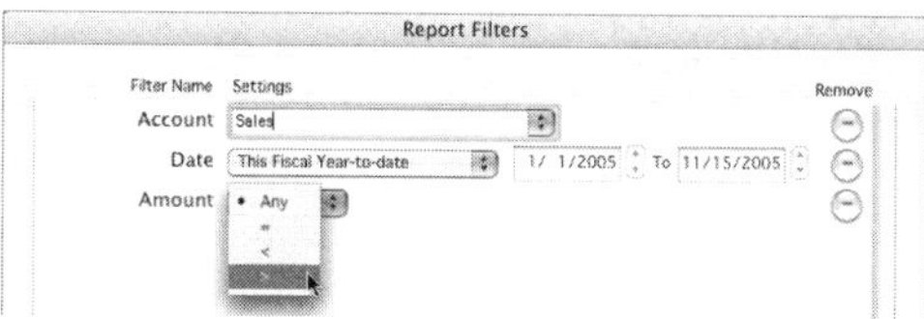

Figure 23 Setting options for an Amount filter.

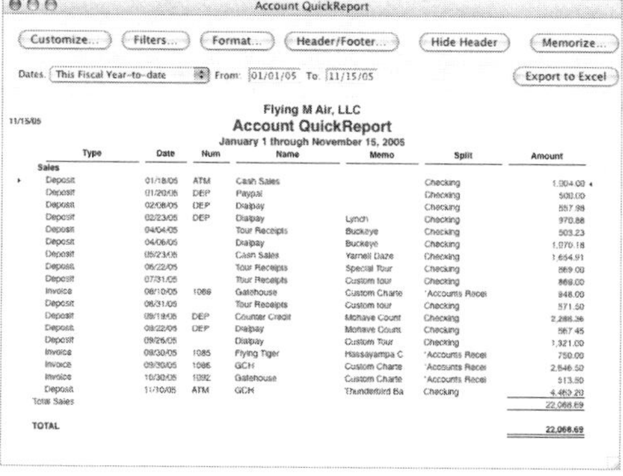

Figure 24 An Account QuickReport, filtered to show only the transactions over $500.

To set report filters

1. In a report window (**Figures 4, 8, 11, 16,** and **17**), click the Filters button. The Report Filters dialog appears (**Figure 21**).
2. Change, add, and remove filters as desired:
   - ▲ To change a filter, set different options in its line.
   - ▲ To add a filter, choose the name of the filter from the pop-up menu at the bottom of the dialog (**Figure 22**). Then set options in the new line that appears in the dialog. **Figure 23** shows an example with the Amount filter added to the two existing filters.
   - ▲ To remove a filter, click the – button at the far right end of its line.
   - ▲ To remove all filters that are not preset for the report, click the Reset button.
3. Click Apply. The report changes to include only those transactions that match the filters you set (**Figure 24**).

✔ Tips

- Transactions that appear in a report must match *all* filters set for the report. The more filters you set, the fewer transactions will be included.
- To learn more about how to set a filter, point to the filter after adding it to the Report Filters dialog (**Figure 23**). Instructions appear near the bottom of the dialog.

To set report formatting options

1. In a report window (**Figures 4, 8, 11, 16,** and **17**), click the Format button. The Format Report dialog appears (**Figure 25**).
2. Select a Show Negative Numbers option and toggle the check box to specify how negative numbers should appear:
   - ▲ **Normally** displays negative numbers with a minus sign before them.
   - ▲ **In Parentheses** displays negative numbers within parentheses.
   - ▲ **With a Trailing Minus** displays negative numbers with a minus sign after them.
   - ▲ **Show in Bright Red** displays negative numbers in red.
3. Toggle check boxes in the Show All Numbers area to specify how numbers should be formatted:
   - ▲ **Divide all numbers by 1,000** reports numbers in thousands. In other words, it removes the last three digits of the number. This option should not be used unless all numbers in the report are greater than 1,000.
   - ▲ **Display Cents** includes both dollars and cents.
   - ▲ **Display Zero Amounts** displays zero amounts. This option does not appear for all reports.
4. To change the font formatting of a report component, select the component in the Change Font For list and then click the Change Font button. Set options in the Select Font dialog that appears (**Figure 26**) and click OK. You can repeat this process for any combination of report components.
5. Click OK to save your settings. Your changes take effect immediately.

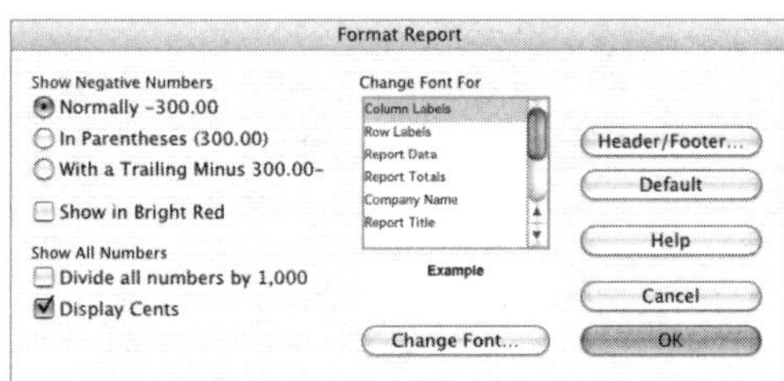

Figure 25 The Format Report dialog.

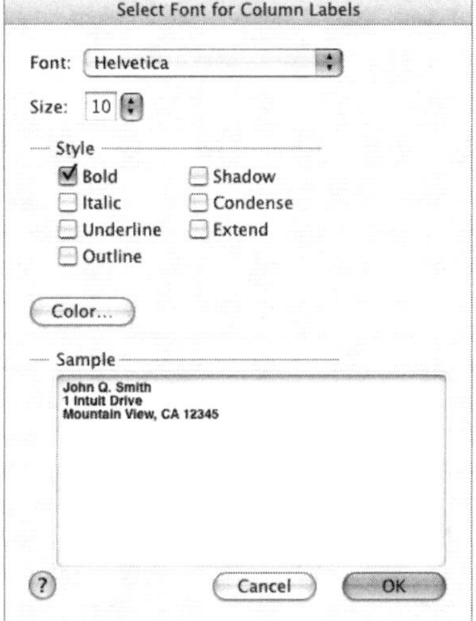

Figure 26 Use a dialog like this one to set font formatting options for report components.

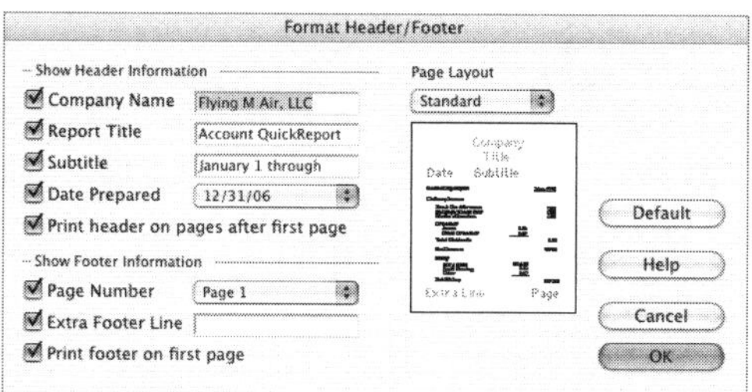

Figure 27 The Format Header/Footer dialog.

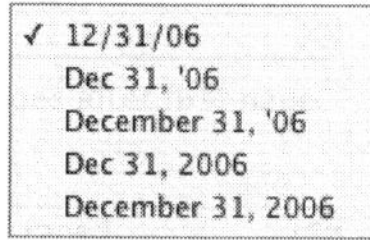

Figure 28 Use this pop-up menu to set a date format for the Date Prepared field.

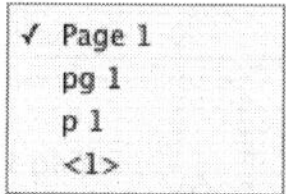

Figure 29 This pop-up menu enables you to set a page number format for page numbers in the footer.

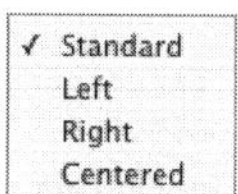

Figure 30 Use this pop-up menu to set the position of the header and footer on the page.

To format a report header & footer

1. In a report window (**Figures 4, 8, 11, 16,** and **17**), click the Header/Footer button. The Format Header/Footer dialog appears (**Figure 27**).
2. Toggle check boxes in the Show Header Information area to specify what should appear in the report header:
   - ▲ **Company Name** is the name of your company, as it appears in the text box.
   - ▲ **Report Title** is the name of the report, as it appears in the text box.
   - ▲ **Subtitle** is the subtitle of the report, as it appears in the text box.
   - ▲ **Date Prepared** is the current date, formatted using one of the options in the pop-up menu (**Figure 28**).
   - ▲ **Print header on pages after first page** tells QuickBooks to print the header on all pages of the report—not just the first page.
3. Toggle check boxes in the Show Footer Information area to specify what should appear in the footer:
   - ▲ **Page Number** is the number of the current page, formatted using one of the options in the pop-up menu (**Figure 29**).
   - ▲ **Extra Footer Line** is additional text to include in the footer, as it appears in the text box.
   - ▲ **Print footer on first page** tells QuickBooks to print the footer on all pages of the report, including the first page.
4. Choose an option from the Page Layout pop-up menu (**Figure 30**) to specify how the header and footer should be positioned on the page.
5. Click OK to save your settings.

Creating Graphs

QuickBooks includes a number of graphs you might find useful to graphically represent financial results. Most graphs include a column chart and a pie chart of related information. Customization options enable you to choose the breakdown of the pie chart options and to specify a custom date period.

QuickBooks offers six graphs:

- **Income & Expenses (Figure 31)** displays income and expense amounts by month and either income or expense amounts broken down by account, customer, or class.
- **Net Worth (Figure 32)** displays assets and liabilities as stacked columns and net worth as a line.
- **Accounts Receivable** displays accounts receivable amounts by age and by customer.
- **Sales** displays sales amounts by month and by item, customer, or sales rep.
- **Accounts Payable** displays accounts payable amounts by age and by vendor.
- **Budget vs. Actual** displays a comparison of budgeted amounts to actual results by month and by account.

In this part of the chapter, I explain how to create and customize graphs.

✔ Tips

- I explain how to set up budgets later in this chapter.
- You cannot memorize a graph.

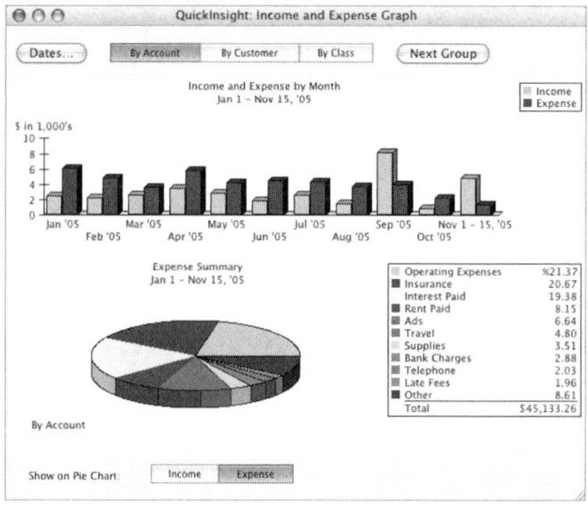

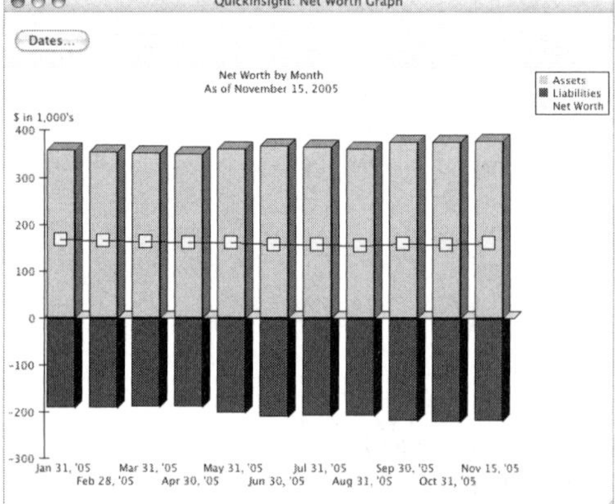

Figures 31 & 32 Two examples of QuickBooks graphs: An Income and Expense graph (top) and a Net Worth graph (bottom).

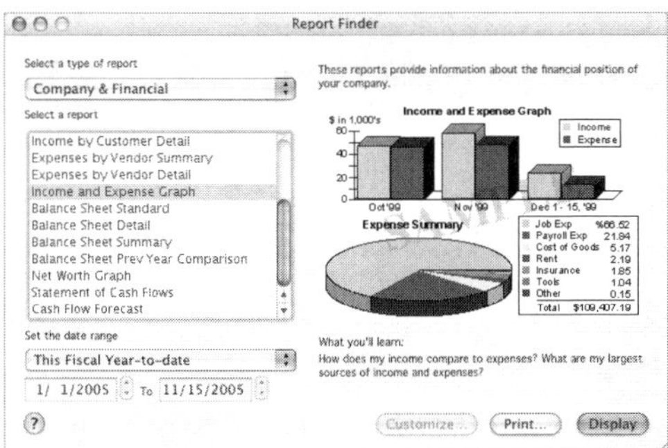

Figure 33 The Report Finder window with the Income and Expense Graph selected.

To create a graph with the Reports menu

Choose the name of the graph you want to create from the submenu on which it appears. **Figure 10** shows an example.

The graph appears in its own window (**Figure 31** or **32**).

To create a graph with the Report Finder

1. Choose Reports > Report Finder (**Figure 14**) to display the Report Finder window (**Figure 12**).
2. Use the pop-up menu near the top of the window (**Figure 13**) to choose a type of graph.
3. In the list of reports and graphs, click a graph name to view a sample of it in the preview area on the right side of the window (**Figure 33**). Repeat this process until you select the graph you want to create.
4. Choose a date option from the pop-up menu at the bottom of the window (**Figure 15**).

   Or

   Enter graph starting and ending dates in the two boxes at the bottom of the window.
5. Click Display. The graph appears in its own window (**Figure 31** or **32**).

To customize a graph

1. Display the graph you want to customize (**Figure 31** or 32).
2. To change the graph's date range, click the Dates button. The Change Graph Dates dialog appears (**Figure 34**). Choose an option from the pop-up menu or enter starting and ending dates in the boxes beneath it and click OK.
3. To change the organization and/or content of the graph(s), click buttons within the graph window. For example, clicking the By Class button in **Figure 31** changes the graphs to display information by class.

✔ Tip

- If a graph's pie chart has more slices than what can fit in the chart, a Next Group button appears in the graph window (**Figure 31**). Click this button to display the remaining information (**Figure 35**).

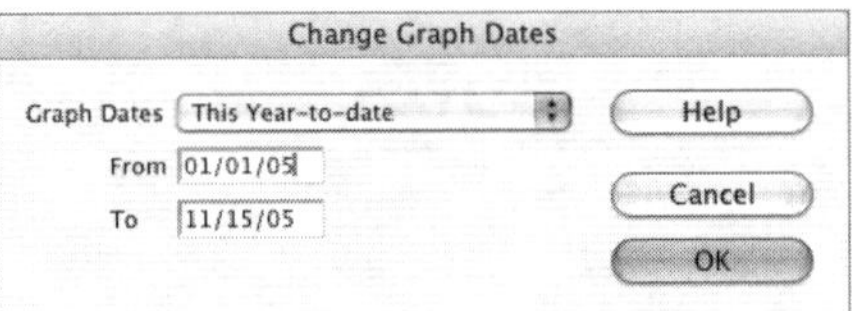

Figure 34 The Change Graph Dates dialog.

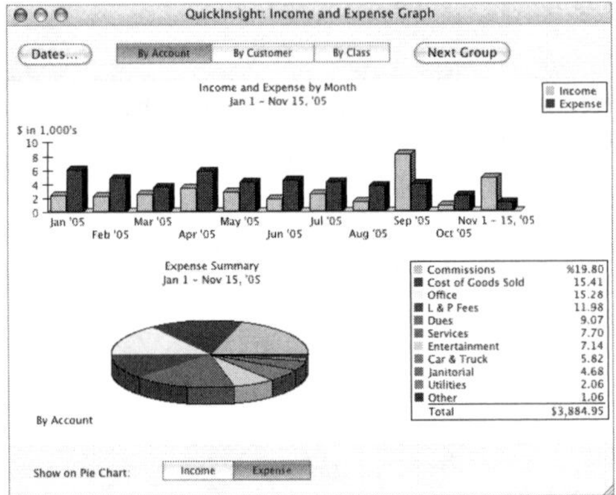

Figure 35 The Next Group button displays the next group of data in the pie chart.

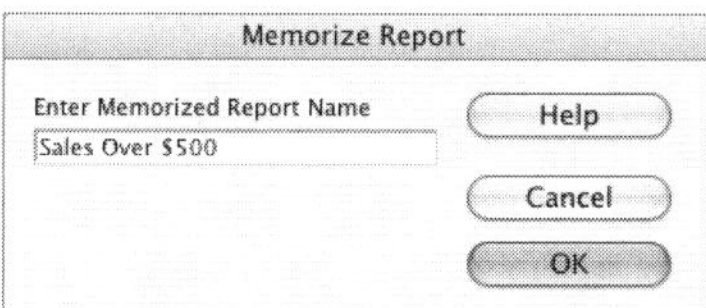

Figure 36 Use the Memorize Report dialog to enter a name for the report you want to memorize.

Memorizing Reports

Creating reports is easy, but customizing them can be a bit time consuming. Fortunately, you can memorize your favorite reports so you can recreate them as quickly as any other QuickBooks report.

✔ Tips

- When QuickBooks memorizes a report, it remembers the report settings—not the data in the report. As a result, the report will have up-to-date information each time it is created.
- QuickBooks recalls a report's date settings relative to the date it was memorized. For example, if you memorize a report with the settings "This Month," the report will always display the current month's data—no matter when you create it.

To memorize a report

1. Follow the instructions earlier in this chapter to create and customize a report so it's just the way you want it.
2. In the report window (**Figures 4**, **8**, **11**, **16**, and **17**), click the Memorize button.
3. In the Memorize Report dialog that appears (**Figure 36**), enter a name for the report and click OK. QuickBooks makes a sound and adds the report to the Memorized Report List.

To recreate a memorized report

1. Choose Reports > Memorized Reports (**Figure 14**) to display the Memorized Report List window (**Figure 37**).
2. Double-click the report you want to create.

   The report appears in a report window (**Figures 4, 8, 11, 16,** and **17**).

✔ Tip

- You can modify the name of a memorized report by selecting its name in the Memorized Report List window (**Figure 37**) and choosing Edit from the Action pop-up menu.

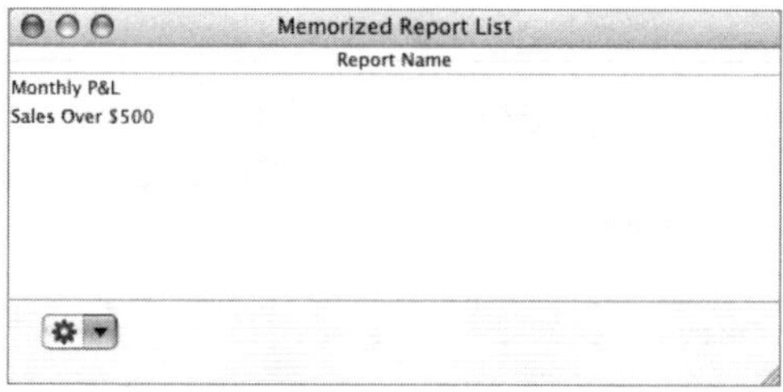

Figure 37 The Memorized Report List window includes all reports you have memorized.

To delete a memorized report

1. In the Memorized Report List window (**Figure 37**), select the report you want to delete.
2. Choose Edit > Delete Memorized Reports (**Figure 38**) or press [⌘ D].
3. A confirmation dialog like the one in **Figure 39** appears. Click OK.

   The report is deleted from the list.

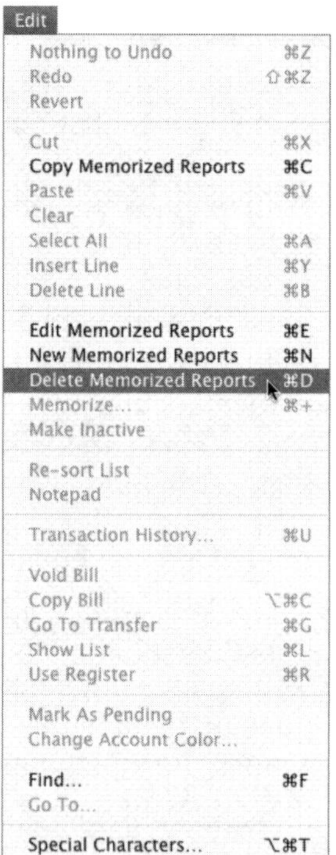

Figure 38 Choose Delete Memorized Reports from the Edit menu.

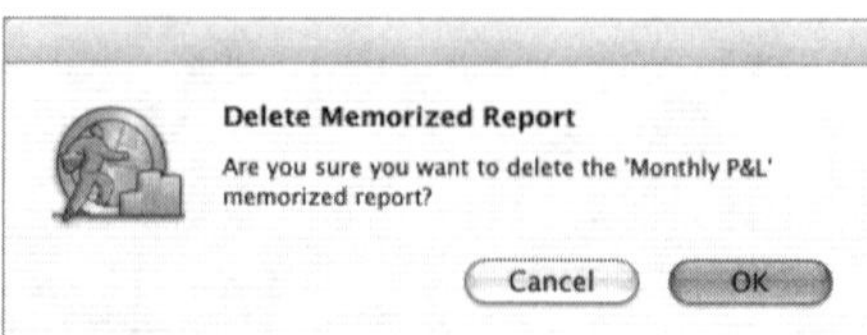

Figure 39 Confirm that you really do want to delete the memorized report.

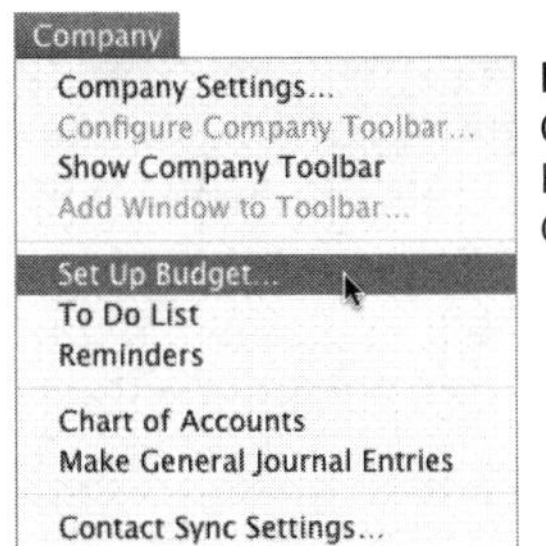

Figure 40 Choose Set Up Budget from the Company menu.

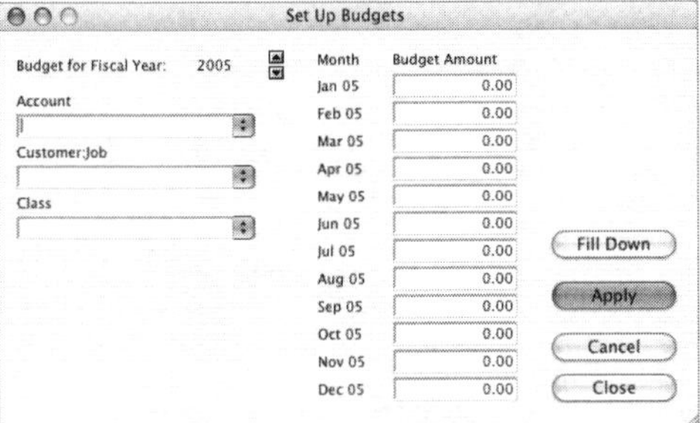

Figure 41 The Set Up Budgets window.

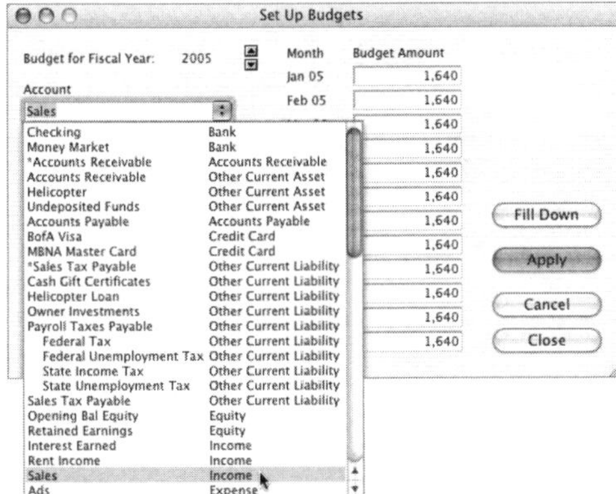

Figure 42 Choose an account from the drop-down list.

Setting Up Budgets

QuickBooks has a simple yet powerful budgeting feature that enables you to set up monthly budget amounts for each account. Once set up, you can use budget reports to compare budgeted amounts to actual results.

The budget feature enables you to set multiple criteria for budgeted amounts:

- **Account** is the account the budget is for. This option is required.
- **Customer:Job** is the customer or job the budgeted amount applies to. This option is optional.
- **Class** is the class the budgeted amount applies to. This option is only available if you have enabled QuickBooks' class feature.

In this part of the chapter, I explain how to set up budgets for your accounts.

✔ Tip

- Although creating a complete budget for your company can be time consuming and a bit tedious, a realistic budget can be an excellent tool for keeping your business profitable and on track.

To set up budgets

1. Choose Company > Set Up Budget (**Figure 40**). The Set Up Budgets window appears (**Figure 41**).
2. Use the tiny arrow buttons near the top of the window to set the fiscal year the budget is for.
3. Choose an account from the Account drop-down list (**Figure 42**).

Continued on next page...

Continued from previous page.

4. If desired, choose a customer or job from the Customer:Job drop-down list. If you do this, the amounts you enter will only apply to the account for that customer or job.
5. If desired, choose a class from the Class drop-down list. If you do this, the amounts you enter will only apply to the account for that class.
6. To enter a different amount for each month, enter the amounts you want in the appropriate boxes.

   Or

   To enter the same amount for each month or base each month's amount on the first month's entry, enter an amount in the top box, click the Fill Down button, enter the desired percent increase in the Fill Down dialog that appears (**Figure 43**), and click OK. QuickBooks fills in the months for you (**Figure 44**).
7. Click Apply.
8. Repeat steps 3 through 7 for each combination of account, customer or job, and class you want to set a budget for.
9. Click Close to dismiss the Set Up Budgets window.

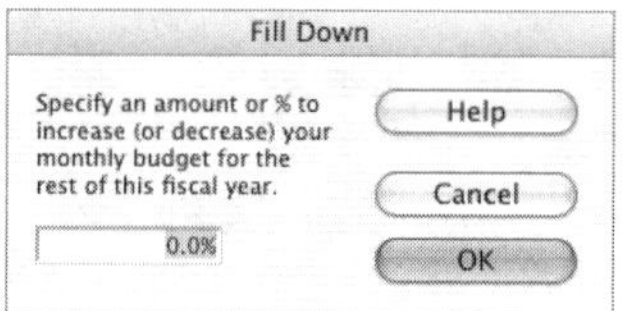

Figure 43 Use the Fill Down dialog to apply a percentage increase to each month's value.

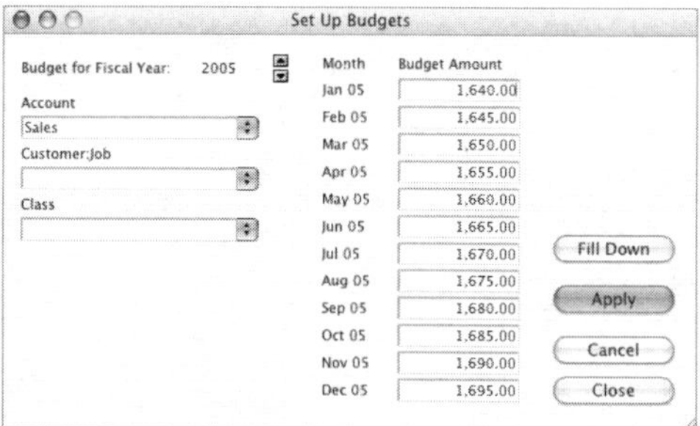

Figure 44 Here's what the Fill Down feature did with 5% entered.

✔ Tips

- To change a budget amount, repeat these steps. When you choose the appropriate combination of account, customer or job, and class, the budgeted amounts you already entered appear.
- To remove an account's budget, clear the values for the months you want to remove.

Printing

Printing

Throughout this book, I explain how to create documents: sales forms such as invoices, sales receipts, credit memos, and estimates; payment documents such as checks; purchase documents such as purchase orders; and a wide variety of highly customizable reports and graphs. In most cases, creating these documents is only half the job. The other half is printing them.

QuickBooks can handle printing different ways depending on what you're printing:

- **Invoices, statements, sales receipts, credit memos, and purchase orders** can be printed on QuickBooks-compatible preprinted forms, blank paper, or letterhead paper.
- **Checks** can be printed on QuickBooks-compatible check stock.
- **Mailing labels** can be printed on a variety of Avery and Rolodex brand labels or cards.
- **1099s** can be printed on preprinted IRS-approved forms.
- **Reports and graphs** can be printed on plain paper.

In this chapter, I explain how to print forms and reports from within QuickBooks. I think you'll agree that letting QuickBooks print these documents for you sure beats printing them by hand.

Setting Up to Print

Before you print a type of document for the first time, it's a good idea to set print options for it. This one-time task helps ensure that all of your documents print correctly the first time and every time.

✔ Tip

- In QuickBooks 2006, it is not necessary to use a Print Setup command before you print the corresponding document type for the first time. I highly recommend doing so, however, if you plan to print on preprinted forms, check stock, or labels.

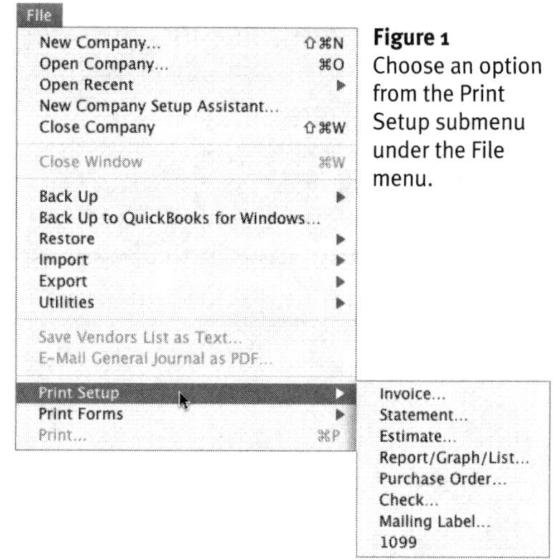

Figure 1 Choose an option from the Print Setup submenu under the File menu.

To set up for printing invoices, statements, estimates, or purchase orders

1. Choose the item you want to set up to print from the Print Setup submenu under the File menu (**Figure 1**).

   A dialog like the one in **Figure 2**, **3**, **4**, or **5** appears. As you can see, these dialogs are virtually identical.

2. Choose an option from the Print On pop-up menu (**Figure 6**):

   ▲ **Preprinted Form** prints on Quick-Books-compatible forms.

   ▲ **Blank Paper** prints on blank paper.

   ▲ **Blank Paper (w/ drawn in boxes)** prints on blank paper and draws boxes around various form fields to make it look more like a form.

   ▲ **Letterhead Paper** prints on letterhead paper. This option omits the name of the document—*Invoice, Estimate,* etc.—and starts printing about two inches from the top of the page.

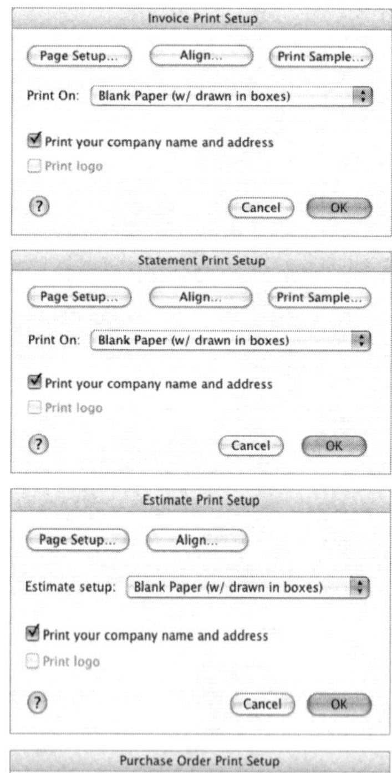

Figures 2, 3, 4, & 5 The Print Setup dialog for (top to bottom) invoices, statements, estimates, and purchase orders.

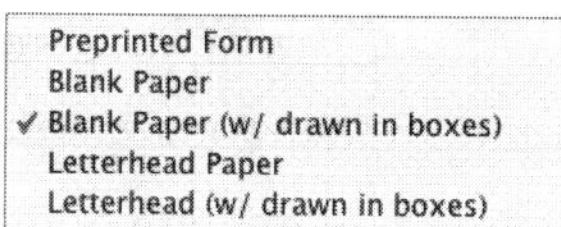

Figure 6 Choose the type of paper you will print on from this pop-up menu.

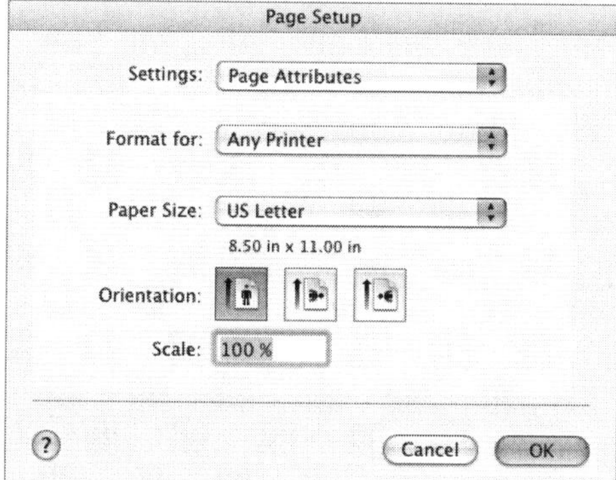

Figure 7 The Page Setup dialog in Mac OS X.

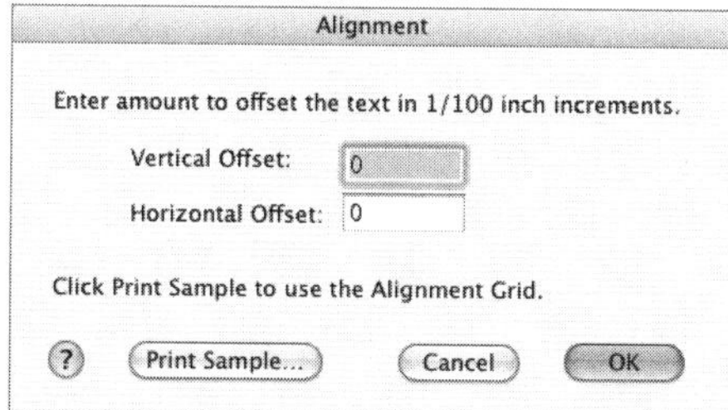

Figure 8 Use this dialog to set vertical and horizontal offsets for aligning the printout on the form or page.

- **Letterhead (w/ drawn in boxes)** is the same as Letterhead Paper, but also includes boxes drawn around various form fields to make it look more like a form.

3. Toggle check boxes to print additional information on the document:
   - **Print your company name and address** prints the company name and address information you provided for your company at the top of the form.
   - **Print logo** prints your company logo at the top of the form. This option is only available if you have added your logo to your company settings.
4. To set standard Mac OS page setup options, click the Page Setup button. Then use the Page Setup dialog that appears (**Figure 7**) to set printer, paper size, orientation, and scale options and click OK.
5. To adjust the horizontal and vertical offsets for printing on the form, click the Align button. Then use the Alignment dialog that appears (**Figure 8**) to enter offset amounts in 1/100ths of an inch and click OK.
6. To print a test document, click the Print Sample button in the Print Setup dialog. Then use the Print dialog that appears (**Figure 37**) to print a sample on the type of paper you selected.
7. Click OK to save your settings.

Continued on next page...

Continued from previous page.

✓ Tips

- Invoice setup options (**Figure 2**) also apply to sales receipt and credit memo forms.
- To order QuickBooks-compatible forms, choose Banking > Order Supplies or use your Web browser to visit `www.intuitmarket.com`.
- I explain how to add a logo to your company settings in **Chapter 11**.
- In step 5, if you click Print Sample in the Alignment dialog, you can use the Print dialog to print a sample document with a grid for alignment. This can help you know what values to enter in the Offset boxes of the Alignment dialog (**Figure 8**).
- In step 6, the Print Sample button may not be available, depending on the type of form you are setting up to print (**Figures 4** and **5**).

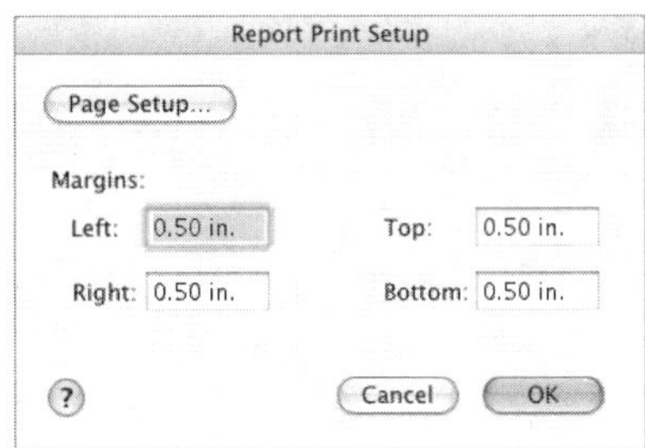

Figure 9 The Report Print Setup dialog.

To set up for printing reports, graphs, & lists

1. Choose File > Print Setup > Report/Graph/List (**Figure 1**). The Report Print Setup dialog appears (**Figure 9**).
2. To set margins for documents, enter values in each of the Margins boxes.
3. To set standard Mac OS page setup options, click the Page Setup button. Then use the Page Setup dialog that appears (**Figure 7**) to set printer, paper size, orientation, and scale options and click OK.
4. Click OK in the Report Print Setup dialog to save your settings.

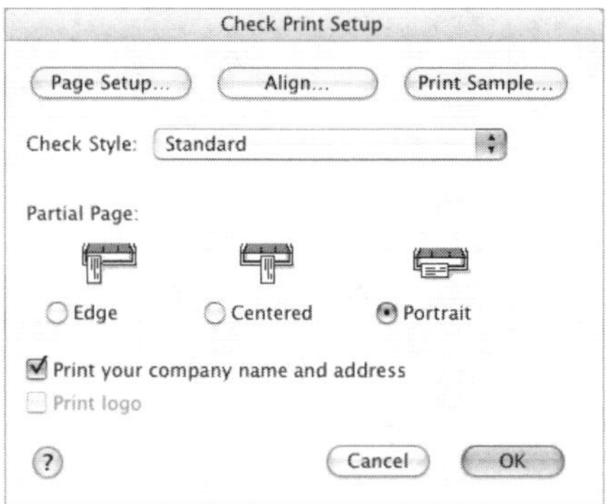

Figure 10 The Check Print Setup dialog.

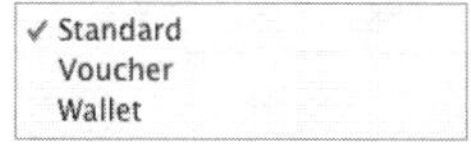

Figure 11 Choose the type of check on which you will print.

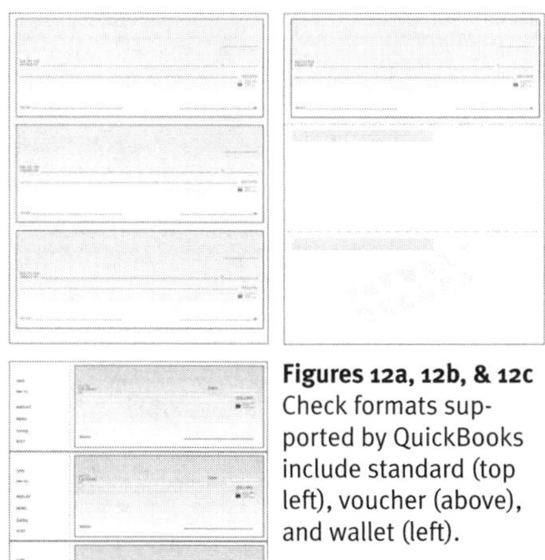

Figures 12a, 12b, & 12c Check formats supported by QuickBooks include standard (top left), voucher (above), and wallet (left).

To set up for printing checks

1. Choose File > Print Setup > Check (**Figure 1**). The Check Print Setup dialog appears (**Figure 10**).
2. Choose an option from the Check Style pop-up menu (**Figure 11**):
   - ▲ **Standard** (**Figure 12a**) has three checks on each sheet of paper.
   - ▲ **Voucher** (**Figure 12b**) has one check and two vouchers per sheet.
   - ▲ **Wallet** (**Figure 12c**) has three personal sized checks with stubs per sheet.
3. If you chose Standard or Wallet in step 2, select an option to determine how you will feed partial pages of checks with your printer's envelope feeder:
   - ▲ **Edge** positions the check on the left side, with the right or left side of the check feeding into the printer.
   - ▲ **Centered** positions the check in the center, with the right or left edge feeding into the printer.
   - ▲ **Portrait** positions the check in the center, with the top or bottom of the check feeding into the printer.
4. Toggle check boxes to print additional information on the document:
   - ▲ **Print your company name and address** prints the company name and address information you provided for your company at the top of the form.
   - ▲ **Print logo** prints your company logo at the top of the form. This option is only available if you have added your logo to your company settings.

Continued on next page...

Continued from previous page.

5. To set standard Mac OS page setup options, click the Page Setup button. Then use the Page Setup dialog that appears (**Figure 7**) to set printer, paper size, orientation, and scale options and click OK.
6. To adjust the horizontal and vertical offsets for printing on checks, click the Align button. One of two things happens:
   - ▲ If you chose Standard or Wallet in step 2, the Align Checks dialog appears (**Figure 13**). Click a button to display the Alignment dialog (**Figure 8**) and enter horizontal and vertical offsets for a specific check and click OK. Repeat this process for each check. Then click OK to dismiss the Align Checks dialog.
   - ▲ If you chose Voucher in step 2, use the Alignment dialog that appears (**Figure 8**) to set horizontal and vertical offset amounts for the first check. Then click OK.
7. To print a test check, click the Print Sample button. Then use the Print dialog that appears (**Figure 37**) to print a sample on your check stock.
8. Click OK to save your settings.

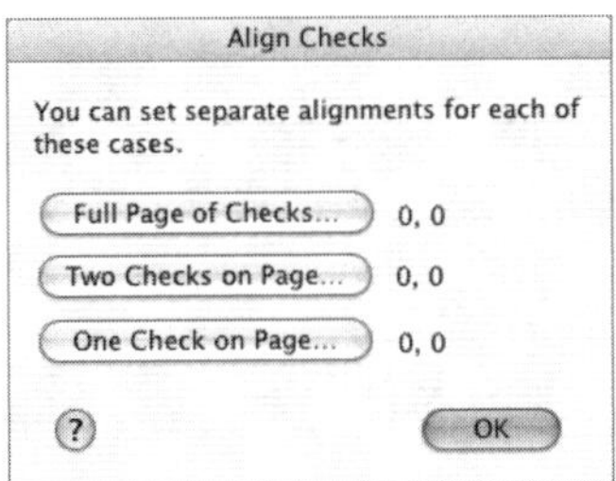

Figure 13 The Align Checks dialog appears for check styles with more than one check on a page.

✔ Tips

- You must follow the steps in this section to specify, in advance, what check stock you will use. Setting options in the Check Print Setup dialog (**Figure 10**) sets default options for printing all checks.
- In step 3, if you're not sure which option to pick, consult the recommendations in your printer manual.
- I explain how to add a logo to your company settings in **Chapter 11**.
- In step 6, if you click Print Sample in the Alignment dialog, you can use the Print dialog to print a sample check with a grid for alignment. This can help you enter values in the Offset boxes of the Alignment dialog (**Figure 8**).
- To order QuickBooks-compatible check stock and window envelopes, choose Banking > Order Supplies.

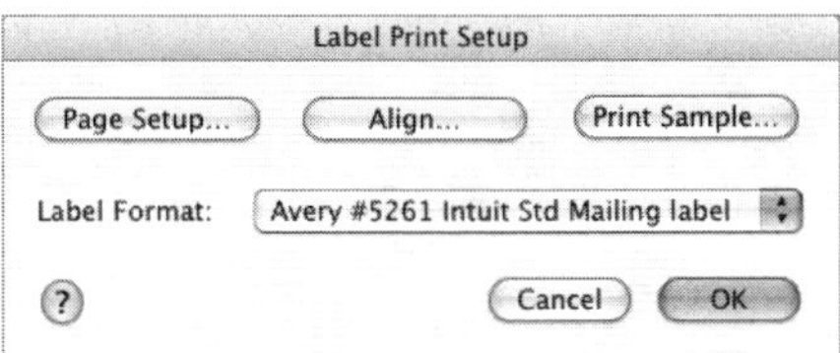

Figure 14 The Label Print Setup dialog.

✓ Avery #5261 Intuit Std Mailing label
Avery #5163 Mailing label
Avery #5260 Mailing label
Avery #5262 Mailing label
Avery #5261 Intuit Std Name & Phone
Avery #5163 Name and Phone
Avery #5260 Name and Phone
Avery #5262 Name and Phone
2 1/4" x 4" Rolodex cards
3" x 5" Rolodex cards

Figure 15 The Label Format pop-up menu specifies label size and format.

To set up for printing labels

1. Choose File > Print Setup > Mailing Label (**Figure 1**). The Label Print Setup dialog appears (**Figure 14**).
2. Choose an option from the Label Format pop-up menu (**Figure 15**): Formats correspond to standard Avery and Rolodex products and determine what will print on the label—mailing label or name and phone.
3. To set standard Mac OS page setup options, click the Page Setup button. Then use the Page Setup dialog that appears (**Figure 7**) to set printer, paper size, orientation, and scale options and click OK.
4. To adjust the horizontal and vertical offsets for printing on labels, click the Align button. Then use the Alignment dialog that appears (**Figure 8**) to enter offset amounts in 1/100ths of an inch and click OK.
5. To print test labels, click the Print Sample button. Then use the Print dialog that appears (**Figure 37**) to print a sample on your label stock.
6. Click OK to save your settings.

✔ Tips

- In step 4, if you click Print Sample, you can use the Print dialog to print sample labels with a grid for alignment. This can help you know what values to enter in the Offset boxes of the Alignment dialog (**Figure 8**).
- You must follow the steps in this section to specify, in advance, what labels you plan to print. Setting options in the Label Print Setup dialog (**Figure 14**) sets default options for printing all labels from that point forward.

To set up for printing 1099s

1. Choose File > Print Setup > 1099 (**Figure 1**). The 1099 Print Setup dialog appears (**Figure 16**).
2. To set standard Mac OS page setup options, click the Page Setup button. Then use the Page Setup dialog that appears (**Figure 7**) to set printer, paper size, orientation, and scale options and click OK.
3. To adjust the horizontal and vertical offsets for printing on the 1099, click the Align button. Then use the Alignment dialog that appears (**Figure 8**) to enter offset amounts in 1/100ths of an inch and click OK.
4. To print a test 1099, click the Print Sample button. Then use the Print dialog that appears (**Figure 37**) to print a sample on your 1099 forms.
5. Click OK to save your settings.

✔ Tip

- In step 3, if you click Print Sample in the Alignment dialog, you can use the Print dialog to print a sample 1099 with a grid for alignment. This can help you know what values to enter in the Offset boxes of the Alignment dialog (**Figure 8**).

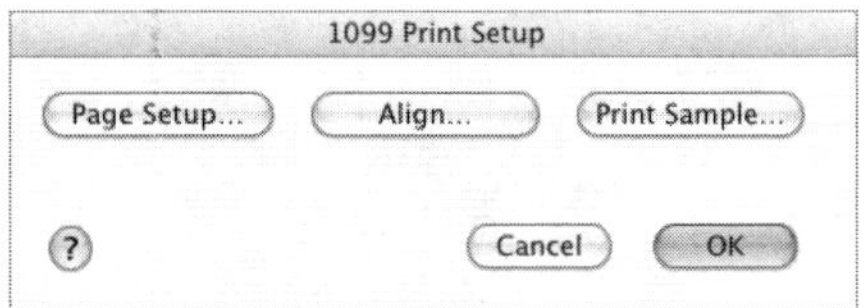

Figure 16 The 1099 Print Setup dialog.

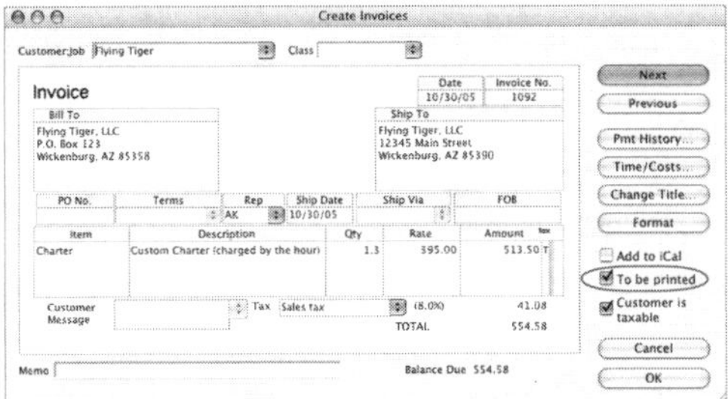

Figure 17 You indicate that a form needs to be printed by turning on the To be printed check box.

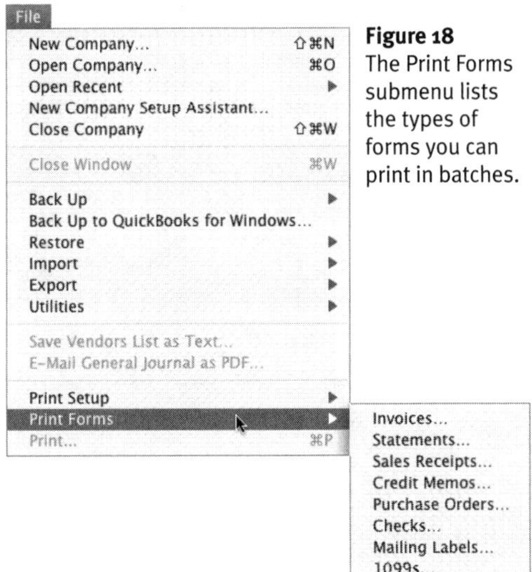

Figure 18 The Print Forms submenu lists the types of forms you can print in batches.

Printing Forms

You identify forms to be printed as you create them by turning on the To be printed check box on the right side of the form (**Figure 17**). This adds them to QuickBooks' internal list of forms to be printed.

When you're ready to print a specific type of form, you choose the corresponding command under the Print Forms submenu (**Figure 18**). You can then select the items you want to print (**Figure 19**) and click OK to start the print process..

In this part of the chapter, I explain how to get started printing all kinds of QuickBooks forms.

To print invoices, sales receipts, credit memos, or purchase orders

1. Choose a command from the Print Forms submenu under the File menu (**Figure 18**) to indicate the type of form you want to print.

   The Select *Form Type* to Print dialog appears (**Figures 19a**, **19b**, **19c**, and **19d**).

Continued on next page...

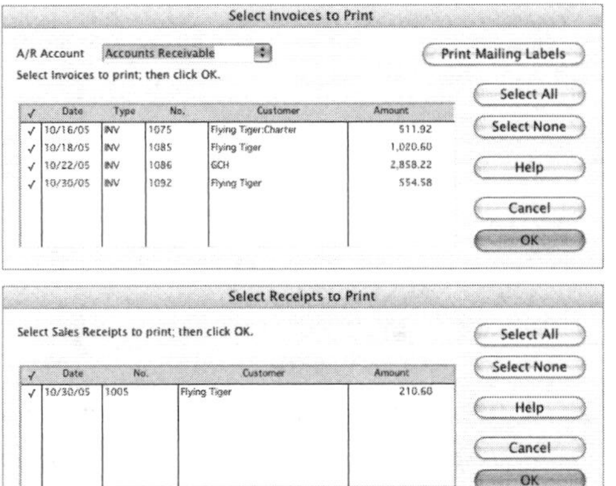

Figures 19a, 19b, 19c, & 19d Use a dialog to select the invoices (top-left), sales receipts (bottom-left), credit memos (top-right), or purchase orders (bottom-right) that you want to print.

Continued on next page...

2. To print invoices, in the Select Invoices to Print dialog (**Figure 19a**), choose an accounts receivable account from the A/R Account drop-down list, then click to place a check mark beside each invoice you want to print.

   Or

   To print sales receipts, in the Select Receipts to Print dialog (**Figure 19b**), click to place a check mark beside each sales receipt you want to print.

   Or

   To print credit memos, in the Select Credit Memos to Print dialog (**Figure 19c**), choose an accounts receivable account from the A/R Account drop-down list, then click to place a check mark beside each credit memo you want to print.

   Or

   To print purchase orders, in the Select Purchase Orders to Print dialog (**Figure 19d**), click to place a check mark beside each purchase order you want to print.

3. Click OK.

4. The Print dialog appears (**Figure 37**). Continue following instructions in the section titled "Using the Print Dialog" later in this chapter.

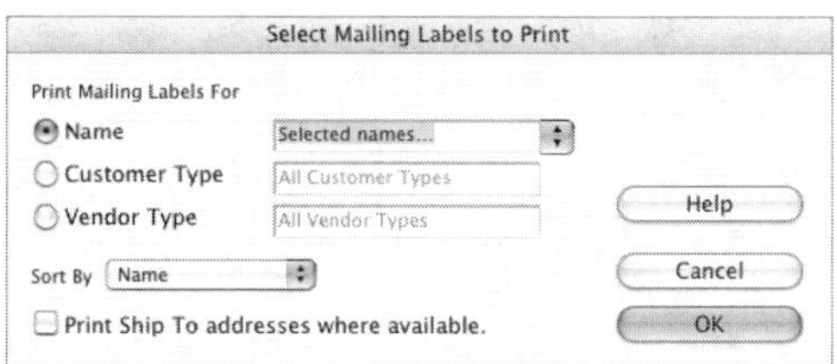

Figure 20 The Select Mailing Labels to Print dialog when printing mailing labels for invoices.

✔ Tip

- If you are printing invoices, you can print mailing labels for the invoices you are printing. Just click the Print Mailing Labels button in the Select Invoices to Print dialog (**Figure 19a**) before you click OK in step 3. Leave options in the Select Mailing Labels to Print dialog that appears (**Figure 20**) as set and click OK. Then click Print in the Print dialog. This feature prints using the label format you specify in the Label Print Setup dialog (**Figure 14**).

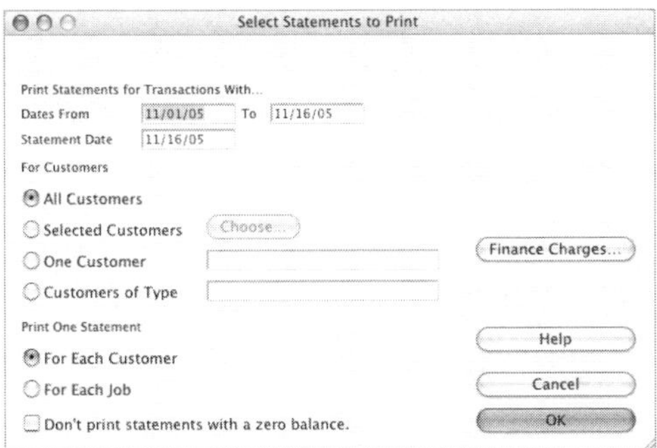

Figure 21 The Select Statements to Print dialog.

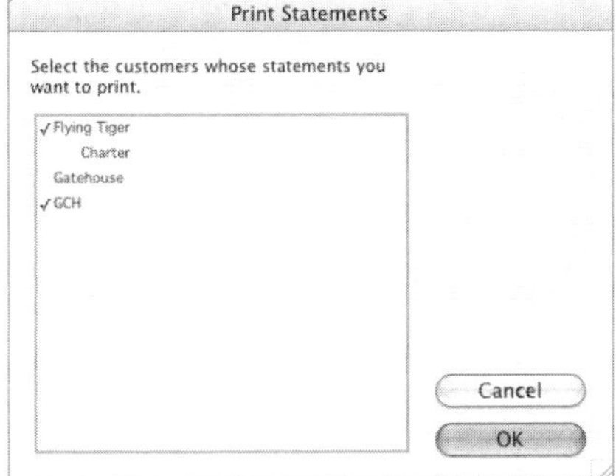

Figure 22 You can use this dialog to print statements for just some customers or jobs.

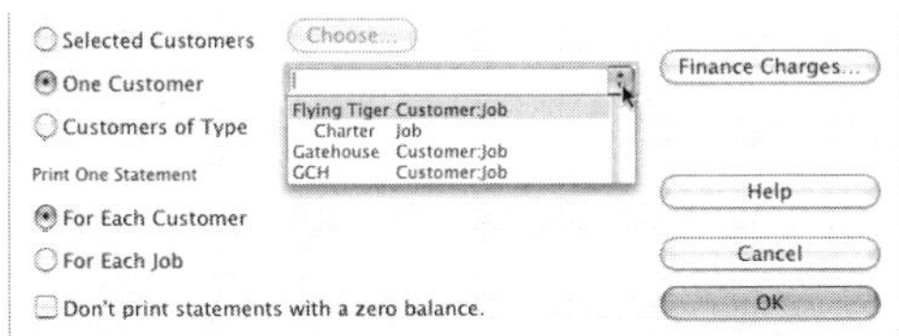

Figure 23 If you want to print a statement for just one customer, choose the customer from a drop-down list.

To print statements

1. Choose File > Print Forms > Statements (**Figure 18**). The Select Statements to Print dialog appears (**Figure 21**).

2. Enter date information at the top of the dialog:

   ▲ **Dates From** and **To** are the starting dates for the transactions to be included in the statement.

   ▲ **Statement Date** is the actual date of the statement.

3. Select a For Customers option:

   ▲ **All Customers** is all customers in your Customer List.

   ▲ **Selected Customers** enables you to click the Choose button and use the Print Statements dialog (**Figure 22**) to select the customers you want to print statements for. When you have finished checking off the customers you want to include, click OK.

   ▲ **One Customer** enables you to choose a customer from a drop-down list (**Figure 23**).

   ▲ **Customers of Type** enables you to choose a type of customer from a drop-down list. This option is only available if you have created and applied customer types.

4. Select a Print One Statement option:

   ▲ **For Each Customer** prints one statement per customer.

   ▲ **For Each Job** prints one statement per job. This means that customers with multiple jobs will get separate statements for each job.

Continued on next page...

Continued from previous page.

5. To omit statements with zero balances, turn on the Don't print statements with a zero balance check box.
6. Click OK.
7. The Print dialog appears (**Figure 37**). Continue following instructions in the section titled "Using the Print Dialog" later in this chapter.

✔ Tips

- Quicken does not store prepared statements. Instead, it creates customer statements on demand when you print.
- The One Customer (**Figure 23**) and Customer Type drop-down lists display the contents of lists you created in QuickBooks. I explain how to create lists in **Chapter 2**.
- To apply finance charges on statements, click the Finance Charges button. I tell you more about assessing finance charges in **Chapter 3**.

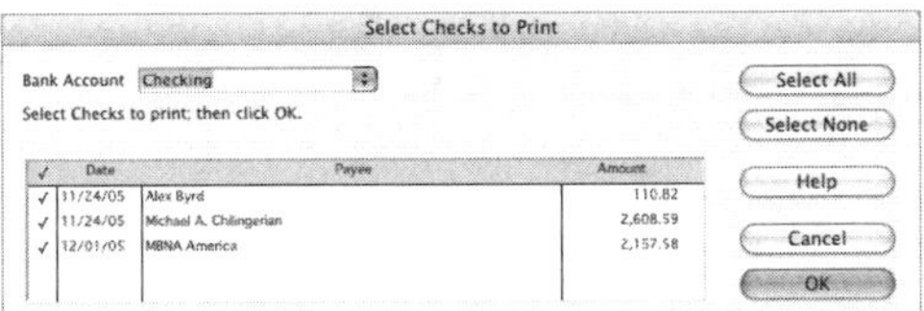

Figure 24 Use this dialog to select a bank account and the checks you want to print.

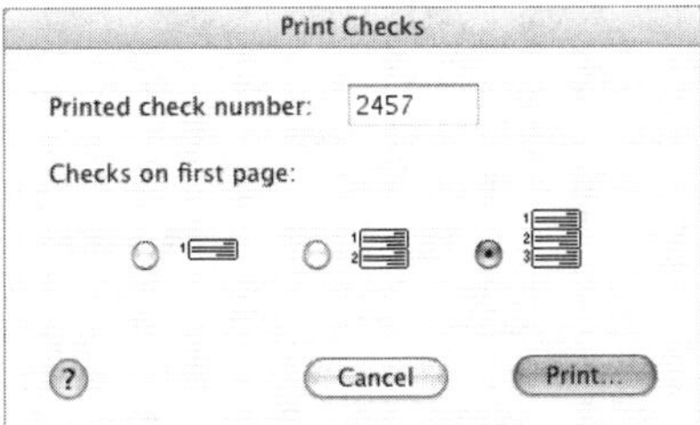

Figure 25 Enter the number of the first blank check and, if necessary, indicate how many checks are on the first sheet.

To print checks

1. Choose File > Print Forms > Checks (**Figure 18**). The Select Checks to Print dialog appears (**Figure 24**).
2. If necessary, choose the account you want to print checks for from the Bank Account drop-down list.
3. Click to place check marks beside each check you want to print.
4. Click OK.
5. In the Print Checks dialog (**Figure 25**), enter the number of the first blank check you will print.
6. If you are using Standard or Wallet checks, select one of the Checks on first page options.
7. Click Print.
8. The Print dialog appears (**Figure 37**). Continue following instructions in the section titled "Using the Print Dialog" later in this chapter.

✔ Tip

- Be sure to place check stock in the printer before completing step 8.

To print mailing labels

1. Follow the instructions in the section titled "To set up for printing labels" earlier in this chapter to choose the type of label you want to print.
2. Choose File > Print Forms > Mailing Labels (**Figure 18**) to display the Select Mailing Labels to Print dialog (**Figure 26**).
3. Select one of the three radio buttons to determine how names should be selected for printing and set appropriate options for your selection:
   - ▲ **Name** enables you to print all names—customers/jobs, vendors, employees, and other names—or selected names. Choose an option from the drop-down list (**Figure 27**). If you choose Selected names, you can use the Select Names dialog (**Figure 28**) to check off the names you want to print labels for.
   - ▲ **Customer Type** enables you to print customer names by customer type. Choose an option from the drop-down list. If you choose Selected Customer Types, you can use the Select Customer Types dialog to check off the types of customers you want to print labels for.
   - ▲ **Vendor Type** enables you to print vendor names by vendor type. Choose an option from the drop-down list. If you choose Selected Vendor Types, you can use the Select Vendor Types dialog to check off the types of vendors you want to print labels for.
4. Choose an option from the Sort By pop-up menu to specify the sort order for the labels: Name or Postal Code.

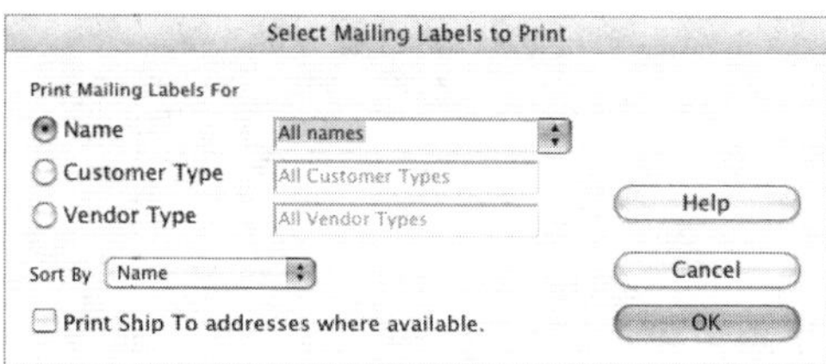

Figure 26 The Select Mailing Labels to Print dialog.

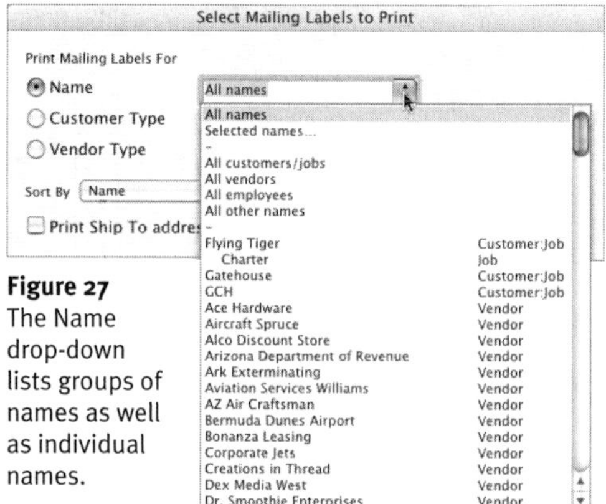

Figure 27 The Name drop-down lists groups of names as well as individual names.

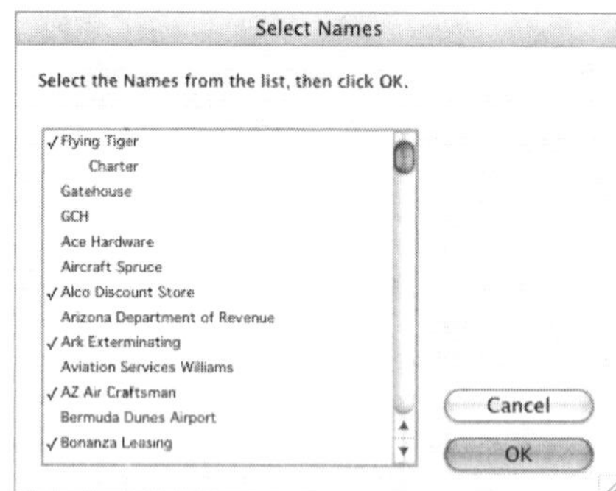

Figure 28 Use the Select Names dialog to select specific names for printing.

5. If you want a shipping address to print instead of a billing address, turn on the Print Ship To addresses where available check box.
6. Click OK.
7. The Print dialog appears (**Figure 37**). Continue following instructions in the section titled “Using the Print Dialog” later in this chapter.

✔ Tip

- The Name, Customer Type, and Vendor Type drop-down lists display the contents of lists you created in QuickBooks. I explain how to create lists in **Chapter 2**.

To print 1099s

1. Choose File > Print Forms > 1099s (**Figure 18**) to display the Printing 1099-MISC Forms dialog (**Figure 29**).
2. Choose a date range option from the pop-up menu or enter a starting and ending date in the two boxes.
3. Click OK.
4. In the Select 1099s to Print dialog (**Figure 30**), click to check off the vendors for which you want to print 1099 forms.
5. Click Print.
6. The Print dialog appears (**Figure 37**). Continue following instructions in the section titled "Using the Print Dialog" later in this chapter.

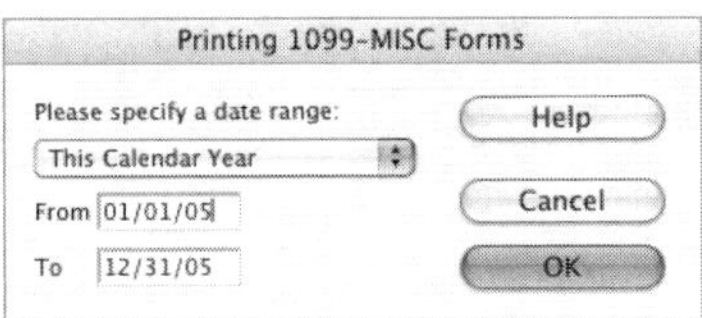

Figure 29 The Printing 1099-MISC Forms dialog.

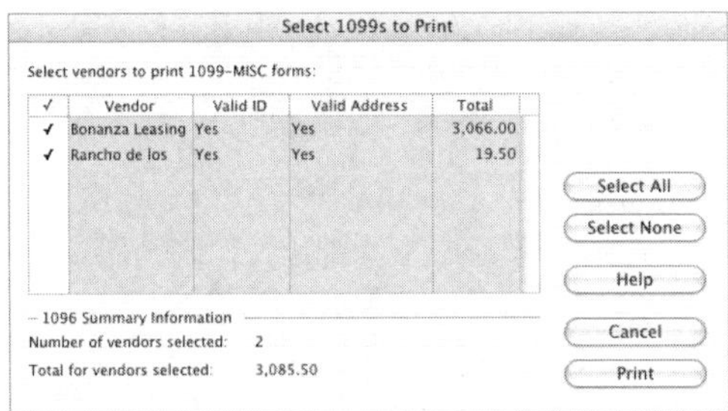

Figure 30 The Select 1099s to Print dialog.

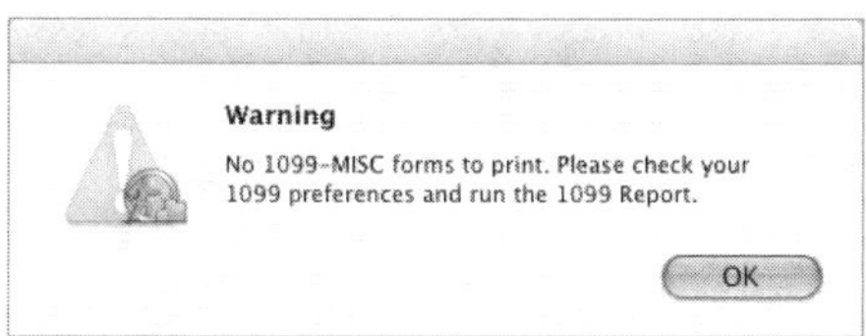

Figure 31 This warning appears if QuickBooks can't find any 1099 forms to print.

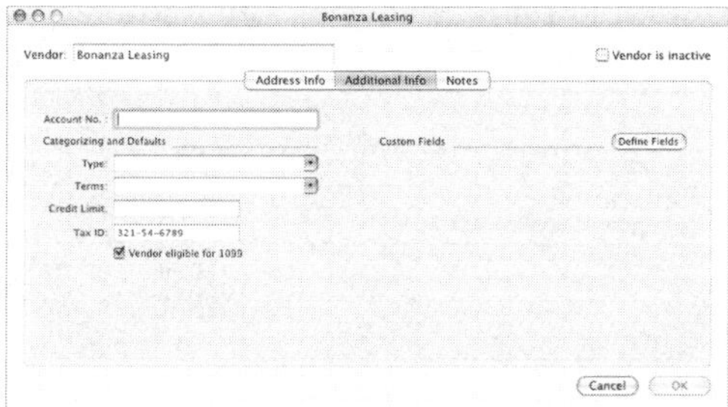

Figure 32 You must indicate that a vendor is eligible for 1099 forms in the vendor record.

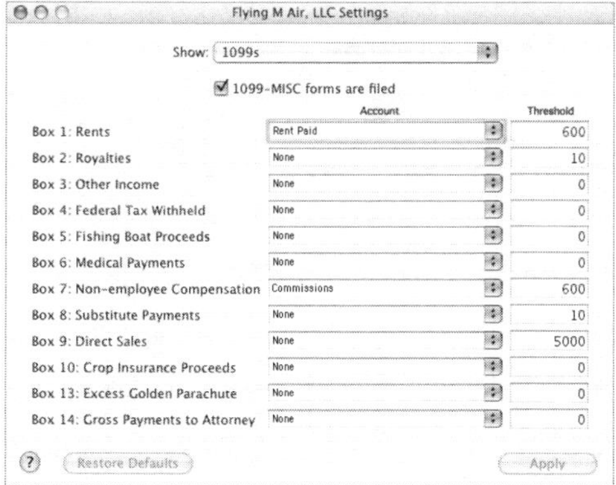

Figure 33 The 1099s section of the Settings window for a company.

✔ Tips

- If QuickBooks does not find any 1099 forms to print, it displays a dialog like the one in **Figure 31** after step 3. Click OK to dismiss it.
- If you plan to print 1099 forms for vendors, you must:
  - ▲ Turn on the Vendor eligible for 1099 check box in the Additional Info pane of the *Vendor Name* window (**Figure 32**).
  - ▲ Turn on the 1099-MISC forms are filed check box in the *Company Name* Settings window (**Figure 33**).
  - ▲ Properly match 1099 form boxes to accounts in the *Company Name* Settings window (**Figure 33**).
  - ▲ Use the accounts you matched in the *Company Name* Settings window (**Figure 33**) when recording payments to 1099 vendors.

I tell you more about setting up vendors in **Chapter 2** and about company settings in **Chapter 11**.

Printing Lists & Reports

In addition to printing forms and checks, QuickBooks can also print lists and reports.

As I explain in this part of the chapter, printing these things is as easy as displaying the list or report you want to print and choosing a menu command.

To print a list

1. Display the list you want to print (**Figure 34**).
2. Choose File > Print *List Name* List (**Figure 35**) or press [⌘ ⌘][P].
3. The Print dialog appears. Continue following instructions in the section titled "Using the Print Dialog" on the next page.

✔ Tip

- I tell you all about lists in **Chapter 2**.

To print a report

1. Display the report you want to print.
2. Choose File > Print Report (**Figure 36**) or press [⌘ ⌘][P].
3. The Print dialog appears. Continue following instructions in the section titled "Using the Print Dialog" on the next page.

✔ Tip

- I explain how to create and customize reports in **Chapter 9**.

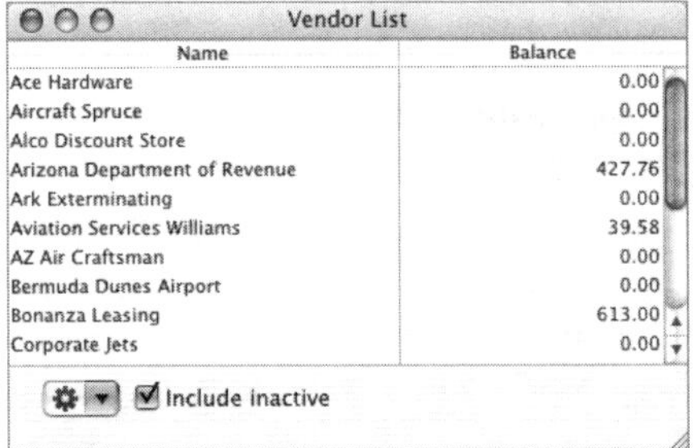

Figure 34 An example of a list window—in this case, the Vendor list.

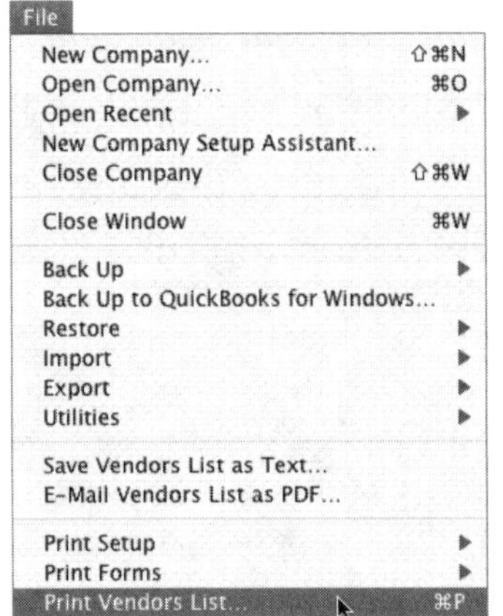

Figure 35 The File menu's Print command will display the name of the list that is in the active window.

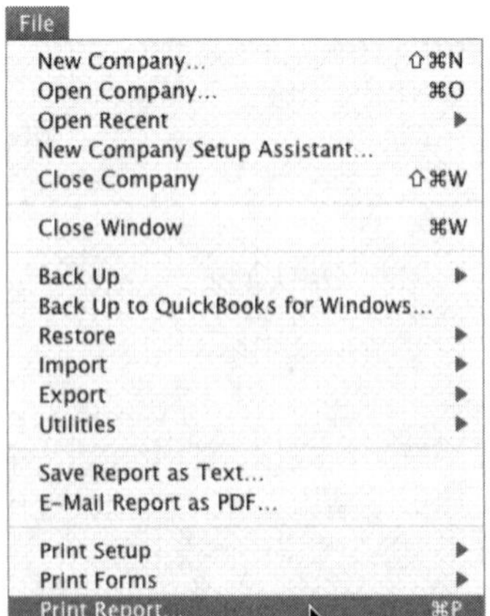

Figure 36 When a report window is active, the Print command becomes the Print Report command.

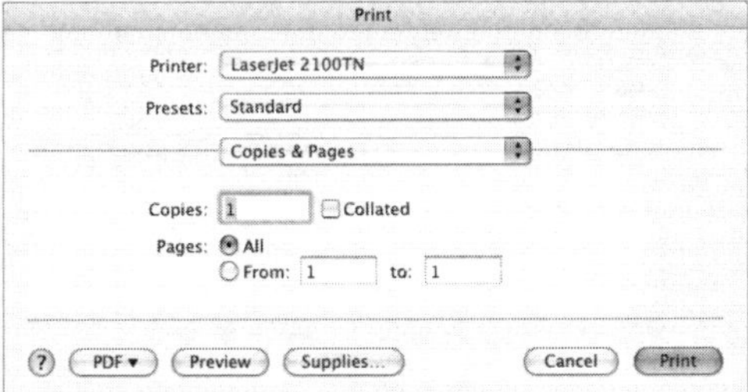

Figure 37 The Print dialog in Mac OS X 10.4.

Using the Print Dialog

Before you can print, you must face the Print dialog (**Figure 37**). This standard Mac OS dialog enables you to choose a printer, specify the number of copies you want to print, and indicate a page range for the document you are printing.

In this part of the chapter, I explain the basics of using the Print dialog to print forms, lists, and reports from within QuickBooks.

✔ Tip

- If you're brand new to Mac OS X and need help with the Print dialog and other Mac OS X interface features, check out one of my *Mac OS X Visual QuickStart Guides*. I think you'll find it helpful!

To set options in the Print dialog & print

1. Insert appropriate forms, check stock, or paper in your printer's print tray or feeder.
2. Follow instructions elsewhere in this chapter to print a form, check, list, or report. Eventually, the Print dialog appears (**Figure 37**).
3. Choose a printer from the Printer pop-up menu. This list will include all printers your computer has access to, including shared printers.
4. In the Copies box, enter the number of copies of each page you want to print. If you enter a value greater than 1, you can turn on the Collated check box to collate copies as they are printed.
5. To print fewer than all pages, select the From radio button in the Pages area and enter values in the From and to boxes to specify a page range.

Continued on next page...

Continued from previous page.

6. Set other options as desired.
7. Click Print. The document is spooled to the printer for printing.

✔ Tips

- You can obtain QuickBooks-compatible forms and check stock from the Intuit-Market Web site, `www.intuitmarket.com`.
- The PDF pop-up menu in the Print dialog (**Figure 38**) offers other options to output the file. Here are three of the most useful:
  - ▲ **Save As PDF** displays the Save dialog (**Figure 39**), which you can use to save the document as a PDF file. It can then be printed, e-mailed, or stored on disk for future reference.
  - ▲ **Fax PDF** displays a special Print dialog (**Figure 40**) that you can use to fax the document. This option is only available in Mac OS X 10.3 or later.
  - ▲ **Mail PDF** opens your default mail application and creates a new message with the document attached as a PDF. All you have to do is address the message and send it.
- Clicking the Preview button displays a preview of the document in Apple's Preview application, so you can see the way it will print when printed. You can then print from the Preview application, if desired.
- If you have printed forms or checks, a dialog like the one in **Figure 41a** or **41b** appears. If there was a problem during printing, enter the number of the first item that did not print correctly and click OK. That item and any items after it are marked to be printed again.

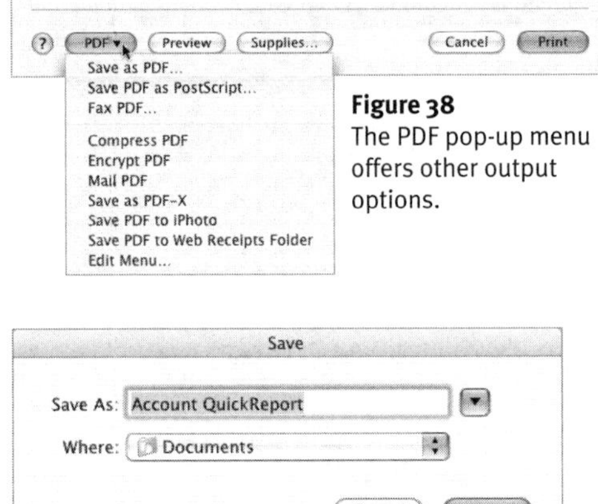

Figure 38 The PDF pop-up menu offers other output options.

Figure 39 Use the Save dialog to save the document as a PDF file.

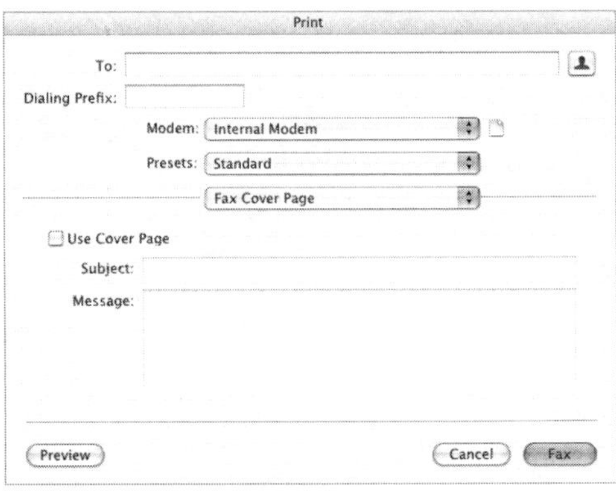

Figure 40 Mac OS X's built-in fax capabilities enable you to fax a document without printing it.

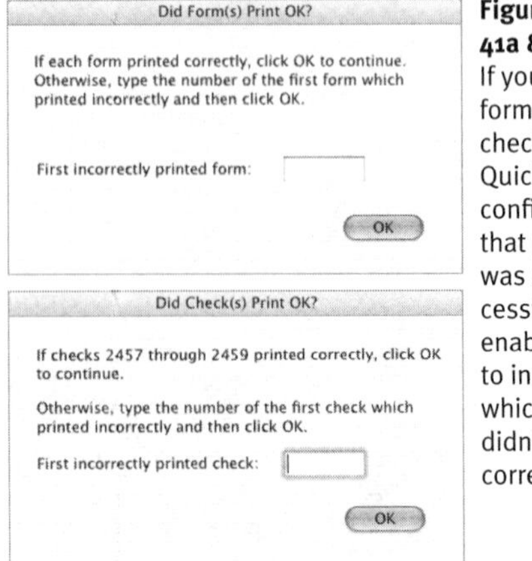

Figures 41a & 41b If you print forms or checks, QuickBooks confirms that printing was successful and enables you to indicate which items didn't print correctly.

Customizing QuickBooks

Customizing QuickBooks

The QuickBooks application is highly customizable. This makes it possible to set up QuickBooks in a way that makes you more productive.

QuickBooks offers three types of customization options:

- **QuickBooks Preferences** control general application operations, such as views, reminders, and menus. These options work throughout QuickBooks, no matter what company data file is open.
- **Company Settings** are options specific to your company, such as its address, tax ID, invoice format, finance charges, and passwords. These settings vary from one company data file to another.
- **Company Toolbar** enables you to customize the toolbar so it includes the buttons you want. These settings vary from one company data file to another.

This chapter explains how you can use all of these customization options to fine-tune QuickBooks to best meet your needs.

✔ Tip

- Many options are set based on your selections during the QuickBooks configuration process I cover in **Chapter 1**. As a result, your settings may not match the ones shown throughout this chapter.

QuickBooks Preferences

Like most applications, QuickBooks has a preferences window that enables you to set application-specific preferences. This part of the chapter looks at each of the QuickBooks preferences options.

To open & set QuickBooks preferences

1. Choose QuickBooks > Preferences (**Figure 1**) or press ⌘ ,. The QuickBooks Preferences window appears (**Figure 2**).
2. Choose the category of preferences you want to set from the Show pop-up menu (**Figure 3**).
3. Make changes to options as desired.
4. Click Apply.
5. Repeat steps 2 through 4 for each category of preferences you want to set.
6. Click the QuickBooks Preferences window's close button to dismiss it.

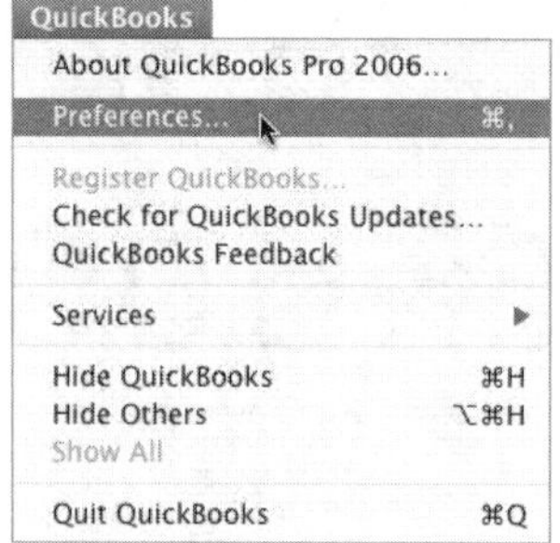

Figure 1 You open the QuickBooks Preferences window by choosing Preferences from the QuickBooks menu.

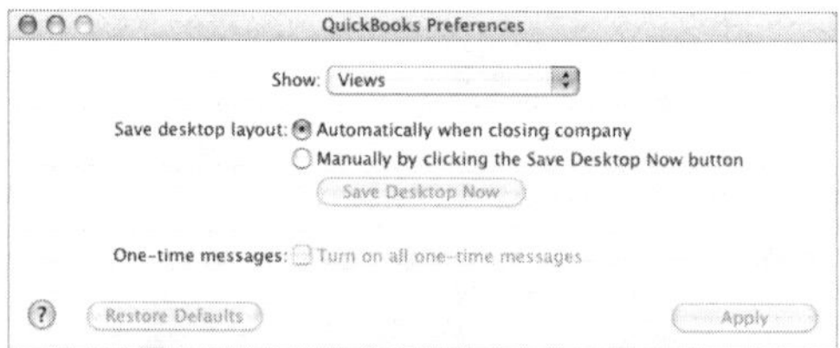

Figure 2 The Views options in the QuickBooks Preferences window.

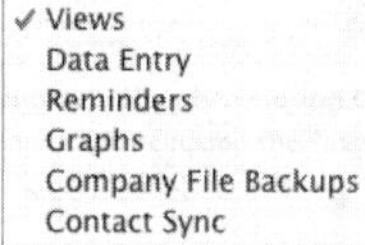

Figure 3 Choose the category of preferences you want to set from the Show pop-up menu.

Opening & Setting QuickBooks Prefs

Views preferences

Views preferences (**Figure 2**) control the appearance of QuickBooks when you open a data file, as well as the appearance of one-time messages.

- **Save desktop layout** enables you to specify what windows QuickBooks opens when you open a company file:
  - **Automatically when closing company** remembers which windows are open when you close a company file and automatically reopens the same windows when you open the company file again.
  - **Manually by clicking the Save Desktop Now button** enables you to memorize open windows so the same ones open the next time you open the data file. If you select this option, open and arrange windows the way you want to memorize them, then click the Save Desktop Now button.
- **One-time messages** turns on all one-time warning messages. This option is only available if you have disabled at least one one-time message.

Data Entry preferences

Data Entry preferences (**Figure 4**) modify the way data entry looks and works.

- **Data Entry** options control how data entry works:
  - **Pressing Return moves between fields** enables you to advance from one field to the next by pressing Return.
  - **Automatically place decimal point** assumes two decimal places for every value you enter. For example, with this option enabled, typing *1234* would enter *12.34* in the field.
  - **'QuickFill' transactions** enables the QuickFill feature, which automatically fills in transaction details based on the last transaction for that name.
  - **Warn when editing a transaction** displays a dialog like the one in **Figure 5** when you change a transaction and click Next or Previous instead of OK.
  - **Warn when deleting a transaction or unused list item** displays a dialog like the one in **Figure 6** when you delete a transaction or unused list item.
  - **Play a sound when recording a transaction** plays an entry sound when a transaction is recorded.
- **Employee List** enables you to specify whether employee names should be sorted by first name or last name in the Employee List window.
- **Time Format** enables you to choose between decimal hours or hours and minutes format for displaying time.

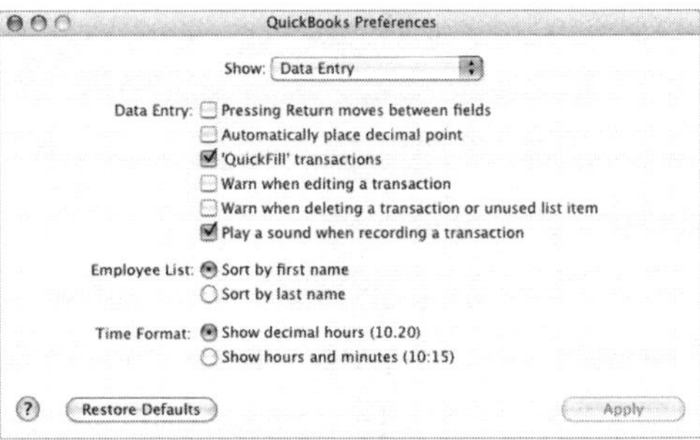

Figure 4 Data Entry preferences.

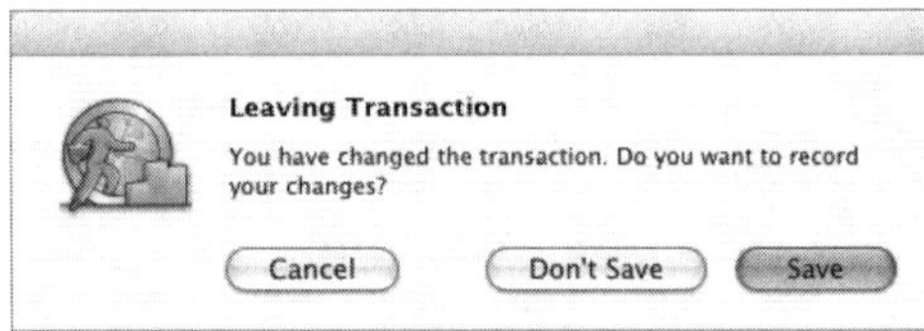

Figure 5 QuickBooks can display this dialog when you modify an existing transaction.

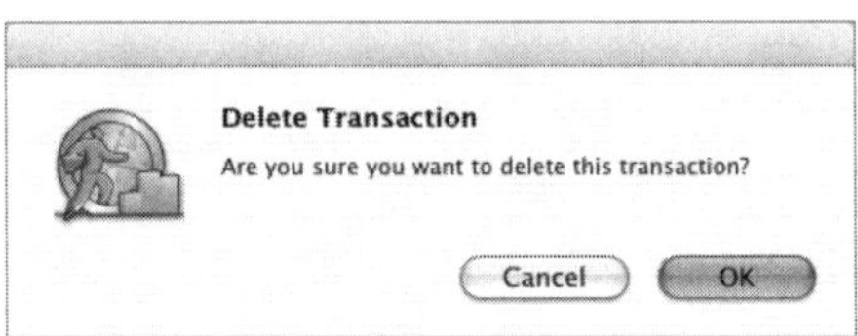

Figure 6 QuickBooks can display this confirmation dialog when you delete a transaction.

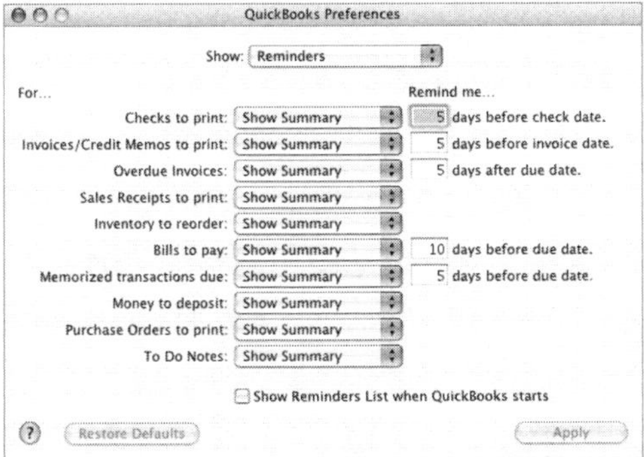

Figure 7 Reminders preferences.

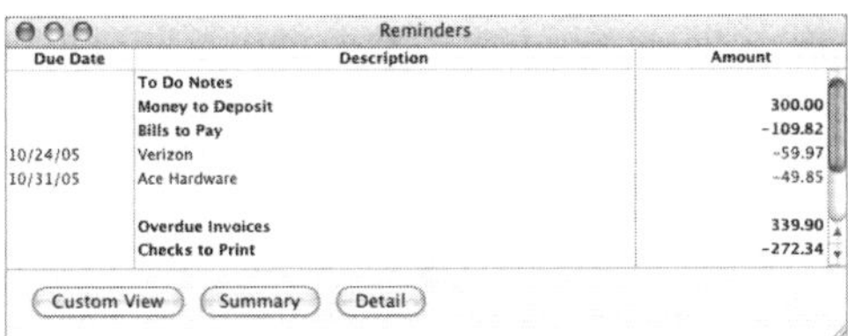

Figure 8 The Reminders list window, showing summaries and one detail list.

✓ Show Summary
Show List
Don't Remind Me

Figure 9 Use this pop-up menu to specify what should appear.

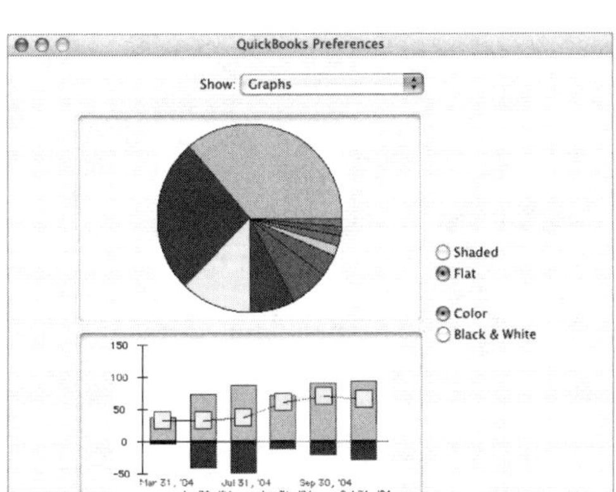

Figure 10 Graphs preferences.

Reminders preferences

Reminders preferences (**Figure 7**) control the way the Reminders window (**Figure 8**) looks and works.

- **For** options enable you to set the reminder display for each category of reminders. Choose an option from the pop-up menu (**Figure 9**). **Figure 8** shows an example with the Bills to pay option set to Show List and all others set to Show Summary.
- **Remind me** options enable you to set the number of days before or after an item to begin reminding you. Enter values in text boxes for applicable items.
- **Show Reminders List when QuickBooks starts** automatically displays the Reminders list window (**Figure 8**) when you start QuickBooks or open a company data file.

✓ Tip

- A reminder category only appears in the Reminders window (**Figure 8**) if reminders exist for that category.

Graphs preferences

Graphs preferences (**Figure 10**) enable you to set options for the appearance of QuickBooks graphs.

- **Shaded** or **Flat** determines whether charts appear 3D or 2D.
- **Color** or **Black & White** determines whether charts appear in color with different colors for each chart component or in black and white with different patterns for each chart component.

✓ Tip

- When you change one of the Graphs preferences options, the sample graphs show the effect of your change.

Company File Backups preferences

Company File Backups preferences (**Figure 11**) control whether QuickBooks automatically backs up your company file and/or reminds you to create a backup.

- **Automatically back up company files when closing** automatically creates a backup of your company file when you close it. If you enable this option, you can set the following options:
  - **Back up once every *N* times each company file is closed** specifies how often the file should be automatically backed up. The lower the number, the more often the file is backed up.
  - **Keep *N* backup files for each company** specifies how many versions of a backup file should be kept. The higher the number, the more backup history files are kept.
  - **Save backup files in** enables you to specify where backups are saved. Click the Change Folder button to display the Automatic Backup Folder dialog (**Figure 12**), select a disk location, and click Open.
- **Automatically back up company files to .Mac when closing** automatically backs up your company file to a .Mac account when you close the file. To use this feature, you must have a .Mac account and your .Mac login information must be entered in the Account screen of the .Mac preferences pane (**Figure 13**).

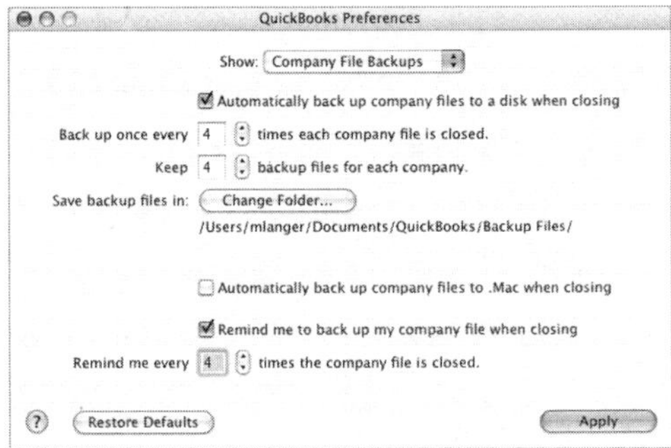

Figure 11 Company File Backups preferences.

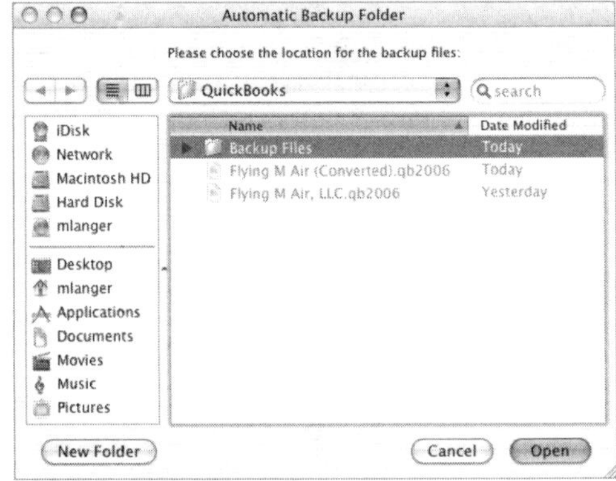

Figure 12 Use this dialog to select a location for automatic backups.

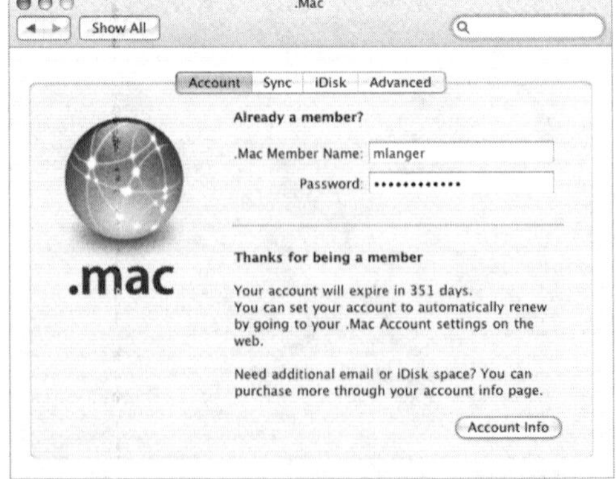

Figure 13 The Account screen of the .Mac preferences pane is where you can enter your .Mac account login information.

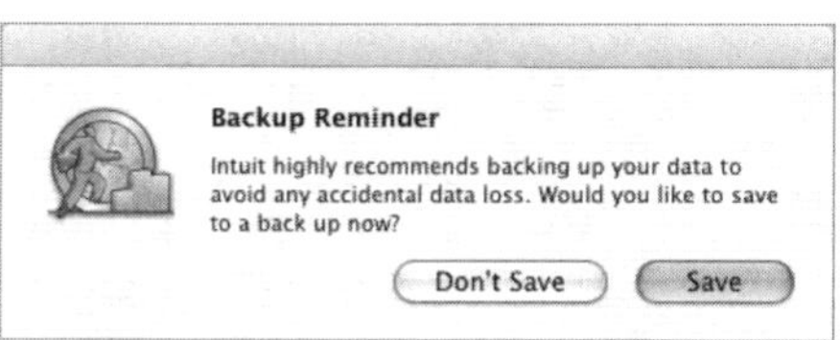

Figure 14 This Backup Reminder can appear when you close a company file or quit QuickBooks.

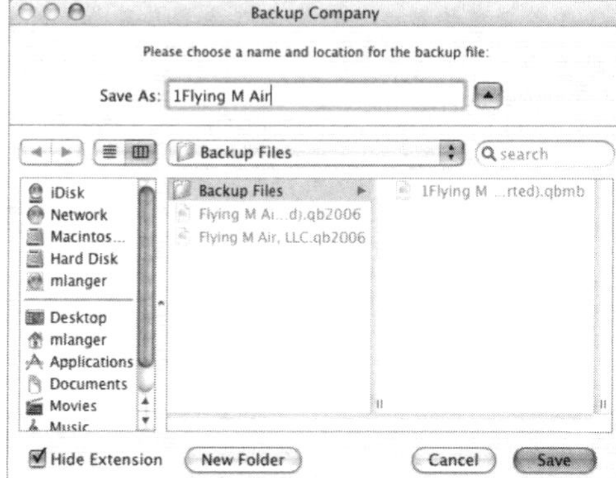

Figure 15 Use this dialog to manually create a backup copy of your company file.

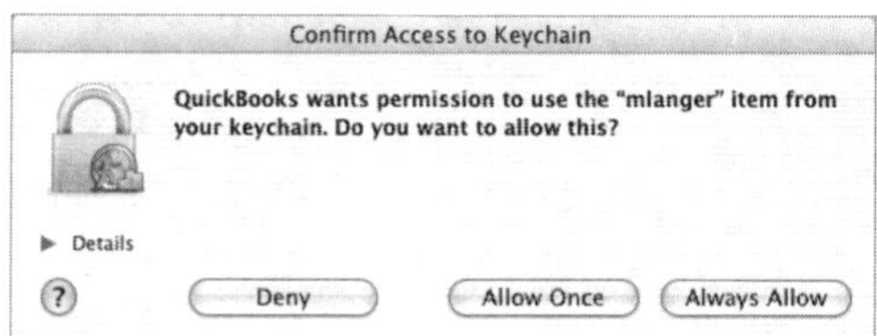

Figure 16 The first time you save to .Mac, a dialog like this may appear.

Figure 17 You'll be prompted to enter a password to further protect your company file when you back up to your .Mac account.

- **Remind me to back up my company file when closing** displays the Backup Reminder dialog (**Figure 14**) when you close a company data file. Clicking Save in this dialog displays a Backup Company dialog (**Figure 15**), which you can use to save a copy of the company file, preferably on another disk. If you enable this option, you can set one additional option:
  - **Remind me every *N* times the company file is closed** specifies how often you should be reminded. The lower the value, the more often QuickBooks bugs you.

✔ Tips

- To open the .Mac preferences pane (**Figure 13**), choose Apple > System Preferences and click the .Mac icon in the System Preferences window that appears.
- The first time QuickBooks backs up your company file to your .Mac account, your computer may display a dialog like the one in **Figure 16**. Click Always Allow to instruct your Mac to perform the backup without displaying this dialog again.
- The first time QuickBooks backs up your company file to your .Mac account, QuickBooks displays a dialog like the one in **Figure 17**. This dialog enables you to add additional security to your company file on your .Mac account. Enter the same password in each box. If you don't want to see this dialog again, turn on the Add Password to Keychain check box. Then click OK.
- To restore your company file from a backup, choose one of the options on the Restore submenu under the File menu and follow the instructions that appear.

Contact Sync preferences

Contact Sync preferences (**Figure 18**) enables you to synchronize your QuickBooks contacts with your Mac OS X Address Book contacts. Once enabled, synchronization occurs in the background without any further effort on your part.

- **Synchronize these contacts** enables you to toggle a check box for each type of QuickBooks contact: Customers, Employees, Other Names, and Vendors. Turn on the check box for each type of contact you want to synchronize with Address Book.

✔ Tips

- You must have Mac OS X 10.4 or later installed to use this feature.
- When you click Apply to initiate the first synchronization, the Sync Alert dialog may appear (**Figure 19**). Click Allow.
- When QuickBooks synchronizes with Address Book, it creates a new Address Book group for each category of QuickBooks contact that it syncs (**Figure 20**).

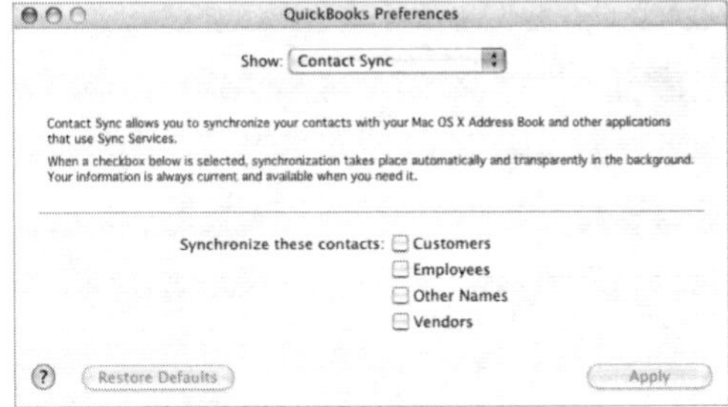

Figure 18 The Contact Sync preferences dialog, which is new in QuickBooks Pro 2006.

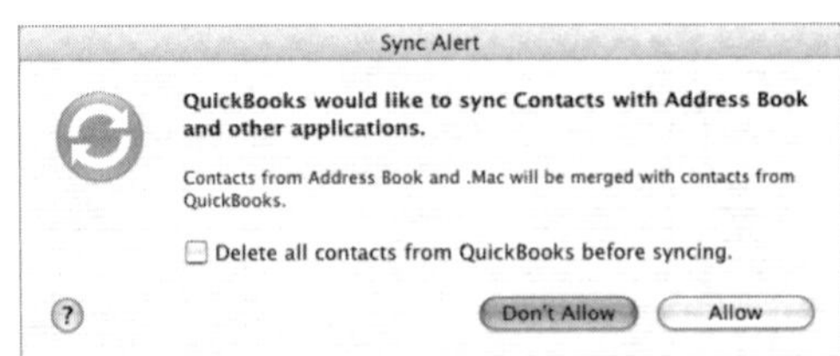

Figure 19 A dialog like this appears the first time QuickBooks attempts to sync with Address Book.

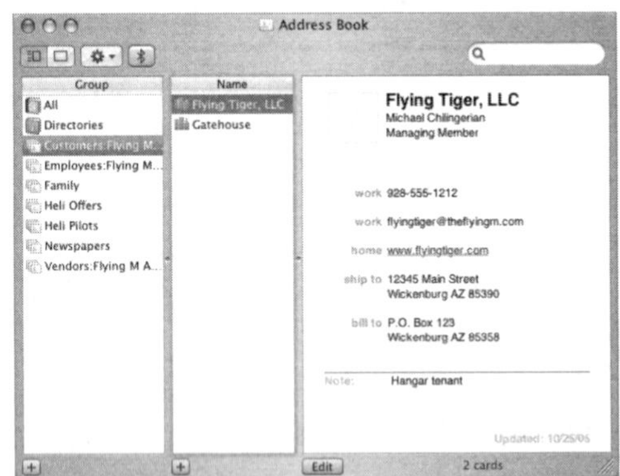

Figure 20 QuickBooks creates a new Address Book group for each category of QuickBooks contact.

Figure 21 QuickBooks' Company menu.

Figure 22 Company Information settings in the Company Settings window.

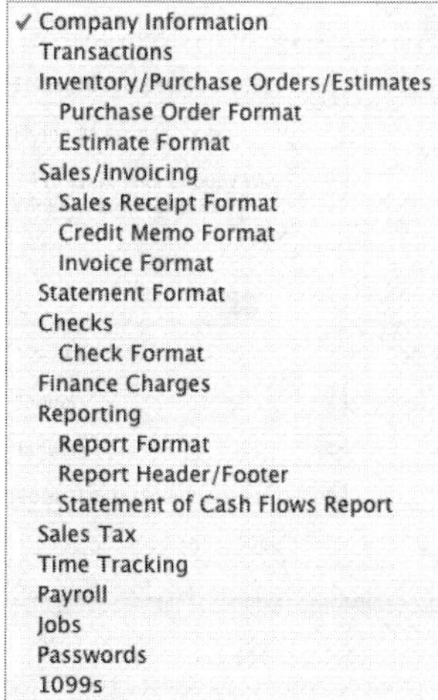

Figure 23 Use the Show pop-up menu to choose a category of settings.

Company Settings

QuickBooks' Company Settings window enables you to change 23 categories of information specific to your company data file. This information can be as basic as your company name and address or as obscure as the terms you use for pending and awarded jobs.

In this part of the chapter, I explain how to set options in the Company Settings window, and provide details about what each option is for.

✔ Tip

- I cover Finance Charges settings in **Chapter 3**.

To open & set Company Settings

1. Choose Company > Company Settings (**Figure 21**). The Company Settings window appears (**Figure 22**).
2. Choose the category of settings you want to set from the Show pop-up menu (**Figure 23**).
3. Make changes to options as desired.
4. Click Apply.
5. Repeat steps 2 through 4 for each category of settings you want to set.
6. Click the Company Settings window's close button to dismiss it.

✔ Tip

- As shown in **Figure 22**, the title of the Company Settings window is really the name of your company followed by the word *Settings*. For the sake of simplicity, I refer to it as the Company Settings window throughout this chapter.

Company Information settings

Company Information (**Figure 22**) includes your company's name and address, fiscal year, and tax information.

- **Company Name** is the name of your company, for internal use.
- **Legal Name** is your company's legal name for tax and other government purposes.
- **Address** is your company's complete address.
- **Country** is your country. The pop-up menu offers three options U.S., Canada, and Other.
- **Federal ID** is your company's Federal ID number for tax purposes.
- **First Month in Fiscal Year** is the name of the first month in your company's fiscal year. The pop-up menu includes all month names.
- **1st Month in Income Tax Year** is the name of the first month in your company's tax year. This option only appears if you choose U.S. from the Country pop-up menu.
- **Income Tax Form Used** is the form your company uses to file its income tax returns. Choose an option from the pop-up menu (**Figure 24**). This option only appears if you choose U.S. from the Country pop-up menu.

✔ Tip

- Your income tax return choice, when initially configuring QuickBooks for your company, determines, in part, the default accounts set up for your company.

Form 1120 (Corporation)
Form 1120S (S Corporation)
Form 1065 (Partnership)
Form 990 (Exempt Organization)
Form 990-PF (Ret of Priv Foundn)
Form 990-T (Bus Tx Ret)
✔ Form 1040 (Sole Proprietor)
<Other/None>

Figure 24 The Income Tax Form Used pop-up menu.

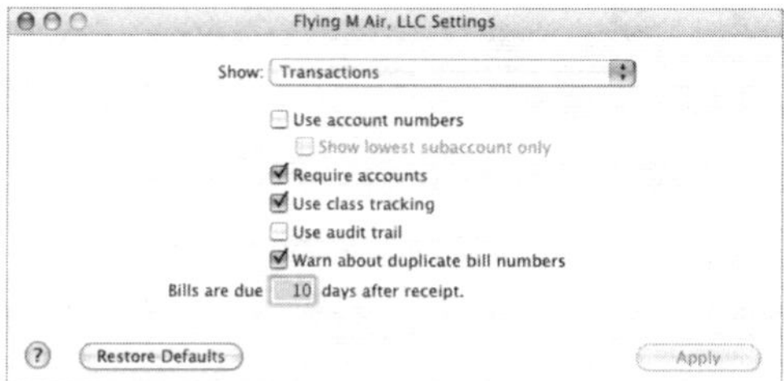

Figure 25 Transactions settings.

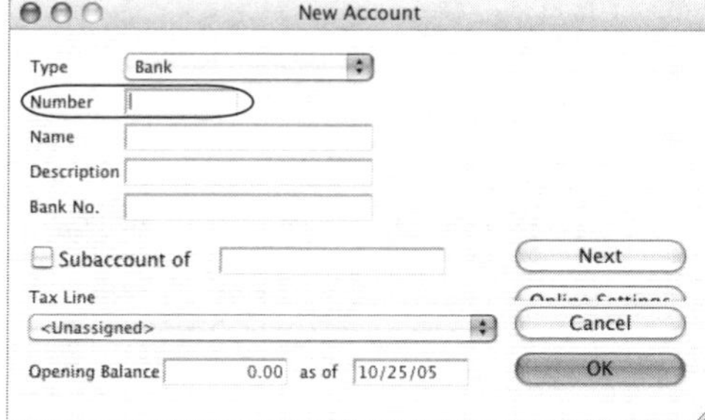

Figure 26 With the Use account numbers option turned on, you can enter an account number for an account when creating it.

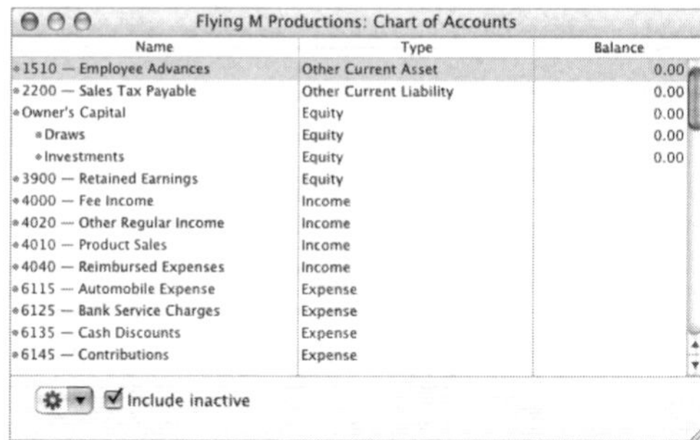

Figure 27 Account numbers appear as part of the account name in the Chart of Accounts.

Transactions settings

Transactions settings (**Figure 25**) are options for entering data in QuickBooks.

- **Use account numbers** enables you to assign account numbers to each account when you create (**Figure 26**) or edit it. Account numbers appear in the Chart of Accounts list window (**Figure 27**) and can be used to enter account information in transactions. If enabled, you can also enable another option:
  - **Show lowest subaccount only** shows the name of the lowest level of sub-account used in a transaction rather than the parent accounts and sub-accounts.
- **Require accounts** requires you to enter an account in every transaction.
- **Use class tracking** enables the class feature. This option must be turned on to create, maintain, and use the Class List.
- **Use audit trail** logs every transaction change to the audit trail report. With this option turned off, only the most recent change is logged.
- **Warn about duplicate bill numbers** displays a warning dialog when you enter a bill with the same number as an existing bill.
- **Bills are due *N* days after receipt** is the number of days QuickBooks uses to calculate the due date of your bills. You can always override the due date QuickBooks calculates when you enter the bill.

Inventory/Purchase Orders/ Estimates settings

Inventory/Purchase Orders/Estimates settings (**Figure 28**) control the way certain inventory and estimates features work.

- **Inventory and purchase orders are used** enables the inventory tracking and purchase order features. With this option turned on, you can set two related options:
  - **Warn if not enough stock to sell** displays a warning dialog (**Figure 29**) if you try to sell more units of an item than what is available.
  - **Warn about duplicate purchase order numbers** displays a warning dialog if you create a purchase order with the same number as an existing one.
- **Customer and/or job estimates are prepared** enables the estimate feature. With this option turned on, you can set another related option:
  - **Warn about duplicate estimate numbers** displays a warning dialog if you create an estimate with the same number as an existing estimate.

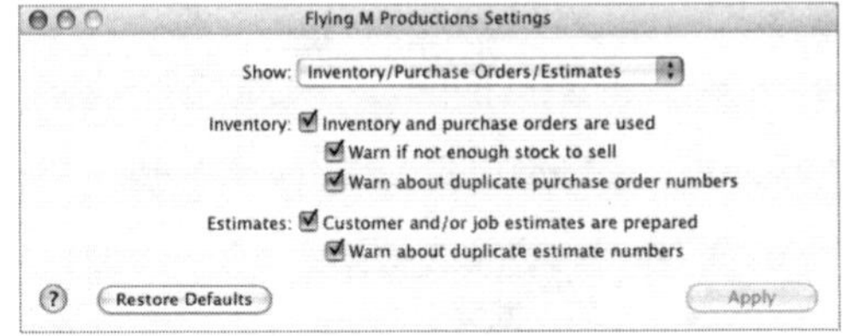

Figure 28 Inventory/Purchase Orders/Estimates settings.

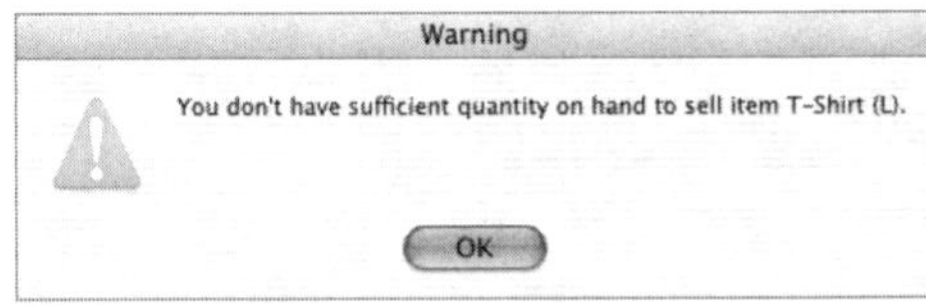

Figure 29 QuickBooks can warn you when you try to sell more items than you have.

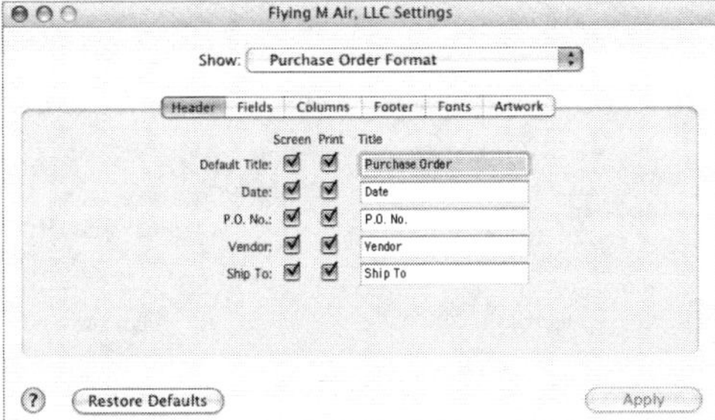

Figure 30 Header options of Purchase Order Format settings.

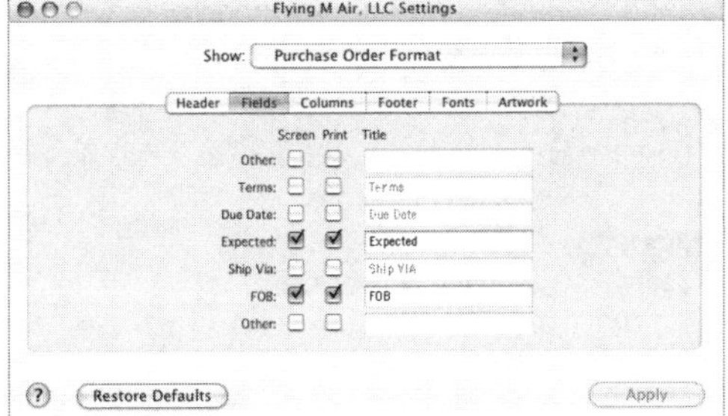

Figure 31 Fields options of Purchase Order Format settings.

Figure 32 Columns options of Purchase Order Format settings.

Purchase Order Format & Estimate Format settings

These two categories, which are almost identical, enable you to set formatting options for purchase orders and estimates. Each category includes six separate sections full of settings that determine how these documents will appear.

Here are the options in the Purchase Order Format category's settings; Estimate Format settings work the same way.

- **Header (Figure 30)** determines which header items appear onscreen and in print. Toggle check boxes and customize Title text as desired.
- **Fields (Figure 31)** determines which fields appear onscreen and in print. Toggle check boxes and customize Title text as desired.
- **Columns (Figure 32)** determines which columns of information appear onscreen and in print. Toggle check boxes to show or hide columns. To set the order in which columns appear, number the columns in the Order boxes. To set the print width of a column, enter percentages in the Print Width boxes. You can customize the text in the Title boxes, too.

Continued on next page...

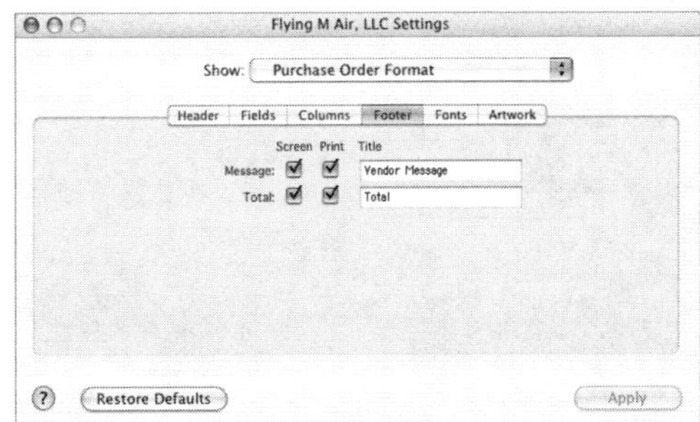

Figure 33 Footer options of Purchase Order Format settings.

Continued from previous page.

- **Footer (Figure 33)** determines which footer items appear onscreen and in print. Toggle check boxes and customize Title text as desired.
- **Fonts (Figure 34)** enables you to set the font, font size, font style, and font color for the form and the address fields. Choose an option from the Set font for pop-up menu **(Figure 35)**, then click the Show Fonts button to display the Font palette **(Figure 36)** and set options. Repeat this step for each part of the form for which you want to set font options. The sample areas show the effect of your changes.
- **Artwork (Figure 37)** has three separate options:
  - ▲ **Company Logo** enables you to drag or paste in a logo for use on the form. Open your logo in another application **(Figure 38)**, select it, and use the Copy command to copy it to the clipboard. Then switch back to Quick-

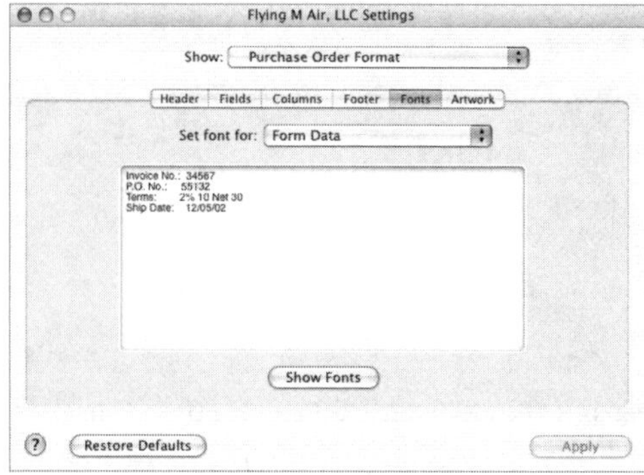

Figure 34 Fonts options of Purchase Order Format settings.

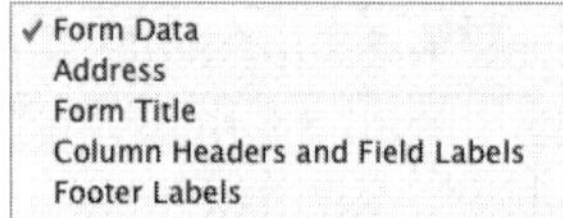

Figure 35 Use this pop-up menu to specify the form part you want to set Font options for.

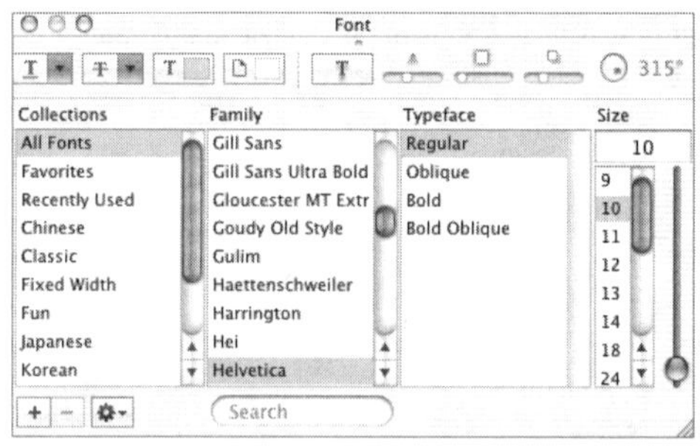

Figure 36 You can use a standard Mac OS font palette window to set font options.

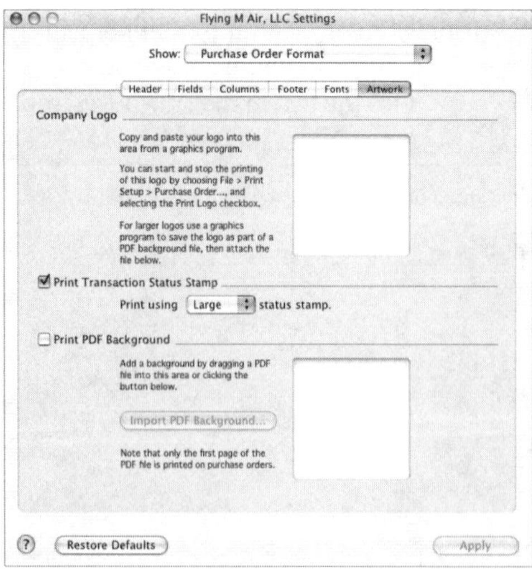

Figure 37 The Artwork options of Purchase Order Format settings.

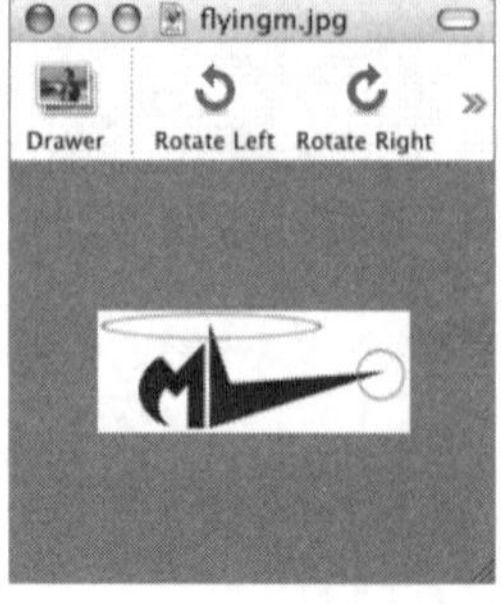

Figure 38 A company logo opened in Preview.

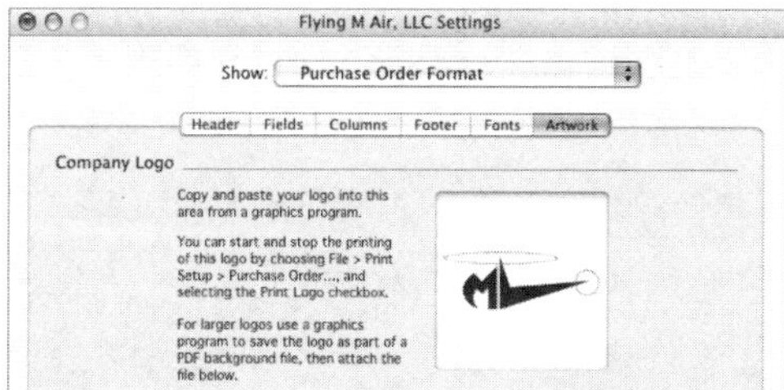

Figure 39 A company logo pasted into QuickBooks.

Figure 40 Use this dialog to import a PDF file.

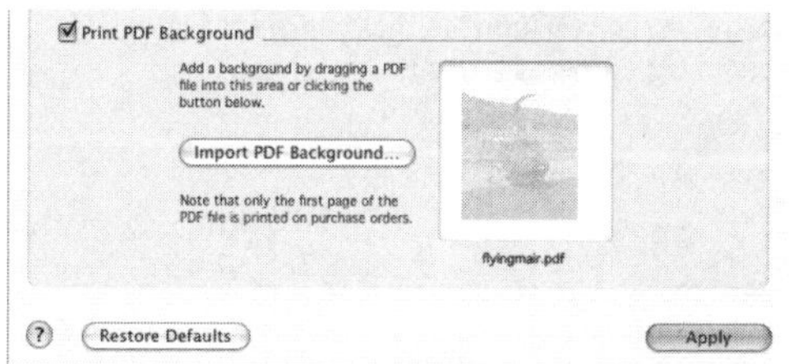

Figure 41 A PDF file imported into QuickBooks.

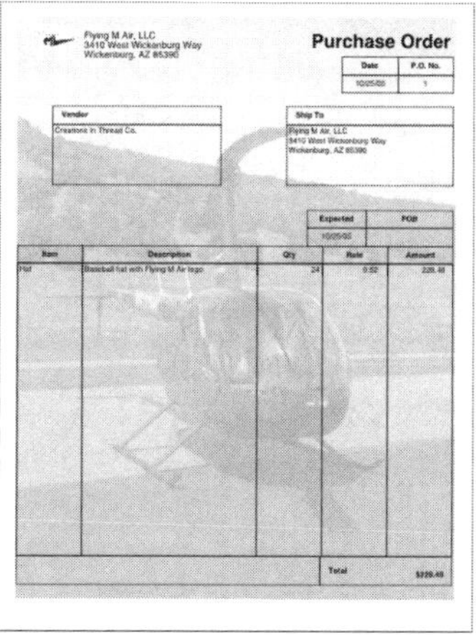

Figure 42 Here's an example of a Purchase Order with both a logo and a PDF background.

Books, open the Artwork settings pane (**Figure 37**), select the image well next to Company Logo, and paste it in (**Figure 39**).

- **Print Transaction Status Stamp** tells QuickBooks to include the transaction status on the purchase order. If you enable this option, you can choose an option from the Print Using pop-up menu: Small or Large. Note that this option does not appear for Estimate formats.
- **Print PDF Background** enables you to add a background image for the form. If you enable this option, click the Import PDF Background button and use the Background dialog that appears (**Figure 40**) to locate, select, and open a PDF file. The image appears in the image well (**Figure 41**).

✔ Tips

- To use your company logo in QuickBooks, it must be less than 1/2 inch square. To use a larger logo, save it as a PDF and import it as a PDF background.
- By default, logo printing is disabled. You can enable logo printing for a form by setting options in the Print Setup dialog for the form. I tell you about the Print Setup dialog in **Chapter 10**.
- You can include both a logo and a PDF background if you like. **Figure 42** shows an example.
- For best results, the PDF background image should be light colored or low contrast. Otherwise, it could make the document printed over it difficult to read.

Sales/Invoicing settings

Sales/Invoicing settings (**Figure 43**) are options for creating sales forms.

- **Usual FOB** is the default FOB setting for invoice and cash receipt forms.
- **Usual Shipping Method** is the default shipping method setting for invoice and cash receipt forms. The options on this pop-up menu match the options in the Ship Via List.
- **Default Markup Percentage** is the percentage used to automatically calculate a sales price based on an item's cost. This value is used when you create inventory parts, non-inventory parts, service items, and other charge items.
- **Track reimbursed expenses as income** accounts for an expense and a customer's reimbursement of the expense in separate expense and income accounts. With this option turned on, QuickBooks enables you to set the account for reimbursed expenses when you create (**Figure 44**) or edit an expense account.
- **Automatically apply payments** automatically applies a customer's payment to outstanding invoices. If the amount paid is less than the total amount due, QuickBooks applies payment to the oldest invoices first.
- **Warn about duplicate invoice numbers** displays a warning dialog when you create an invoice with the same number as an existing invoice.

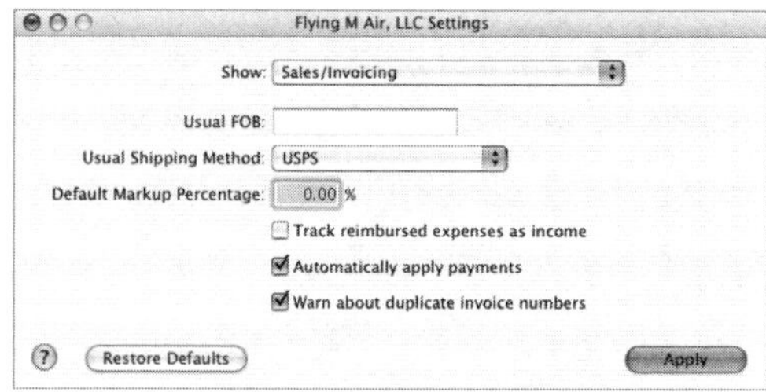

Figure 43 Sales/Invoicing settings.

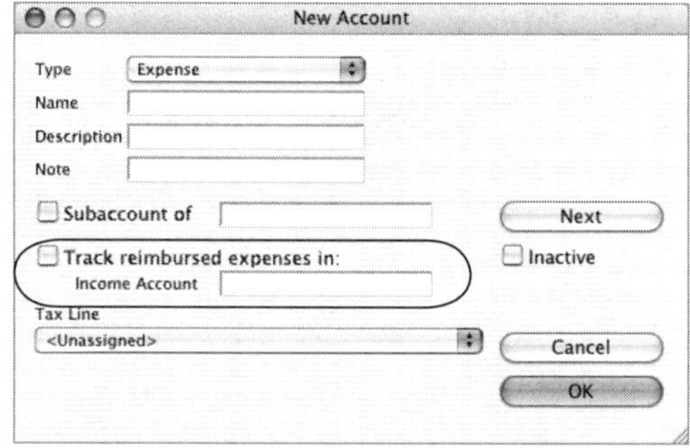

Figure 44 QuickBooks adds this check box and drop-down list to the New Account (and Edit Account) dialogs when you indicate that you want to track reimbursed expenses as income.

Sales/Invoicing Settings

✓ Product
Professional
Service
Custom

Figure 45 Use a pop-up menu to choose from among predefined formats.

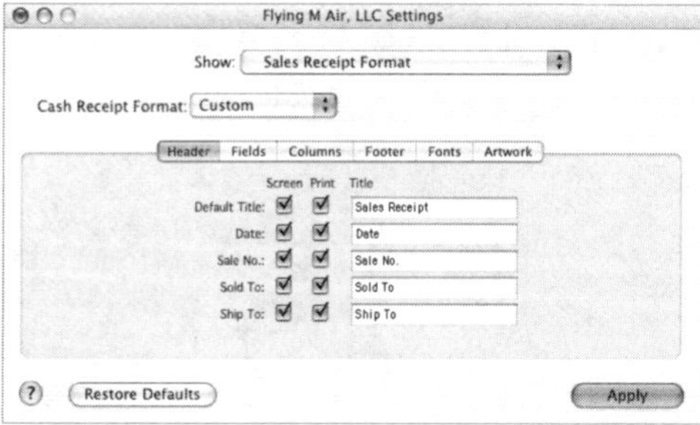

Figure 46 An example of the custom Header options for sales receipt formats.

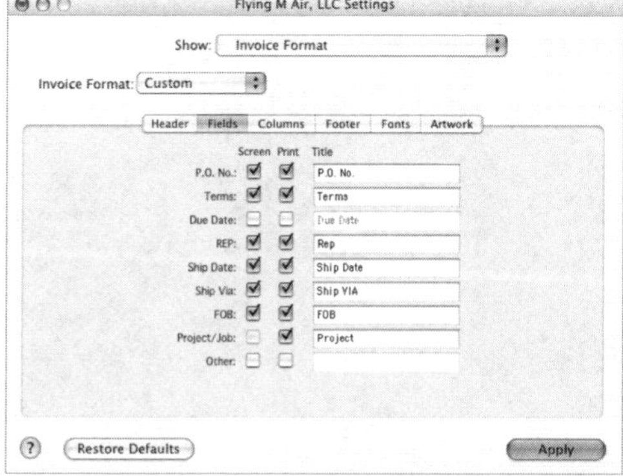

Figure 47 An example of the custom Fields options for invoice formats.

Sales Receipt Format, Credit Memo Format, Invoice Format, & Statement Format settings

These four categories of settings, which are almost identical, enable you to set formatting options for sales receipts, credit memos, invoices, and statements. Each category includes a pop-up menu you can use to choose from among predefined formats (**Figure 45**). If you choose the Custom option, you can use six separate sections full of settings to customize the appearance of these documents (**Figures 46 and 47**).

The customization options in these settings windows are almost identical to the ones for Purchase Order Format, which I illustrate and discuss earlier in this chapter. Consult that section to learn more about setting these options.

✔ Tip

- I illustrate the various predefined invoice and sales receipt formats in **Chapter 3**.

Checks settings

Checks settings (**Figure 48**) are options for working with checks.

- **Print account names on voucher** prints the names of accounts on the voucher part of a check form.
- **Change check date when check is printed** changes a check's transaction date to its print date.
- **Start with payee field on check** positions the insertion point in the Payee field of a check when you open it rather than selecting the Bank Account field.
- **Warn about duplicate check numbers** displays a warning when you enter a check that has the same number as an existing check.

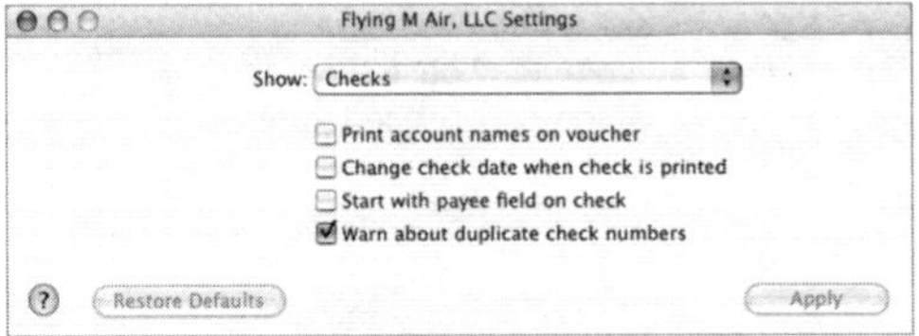

Figure 48 Checks settings.

Check Format settings

Check Format settings (**Figures 49 and 50**) enable you to set the fonts and paste in a custom logo for checks you print with QuickBooks.

The Font and Artwork customization options in this settings window are almost identical to the ones for Purchase Order Format, which I illustrate and discuss earlier in this chapter. Consult that section to learn more about setting these options.

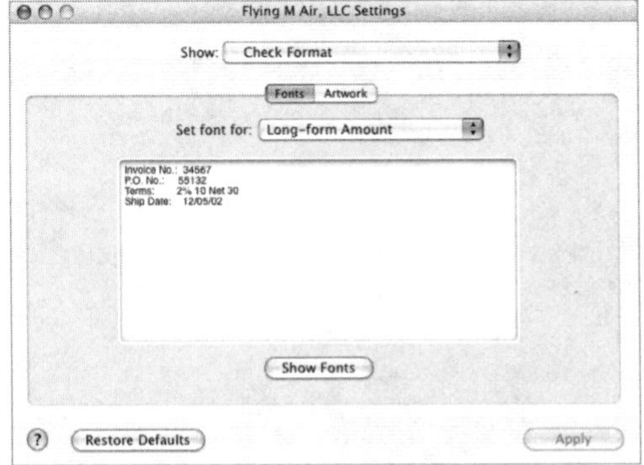

Figure 49 Font options in Check Format settings.

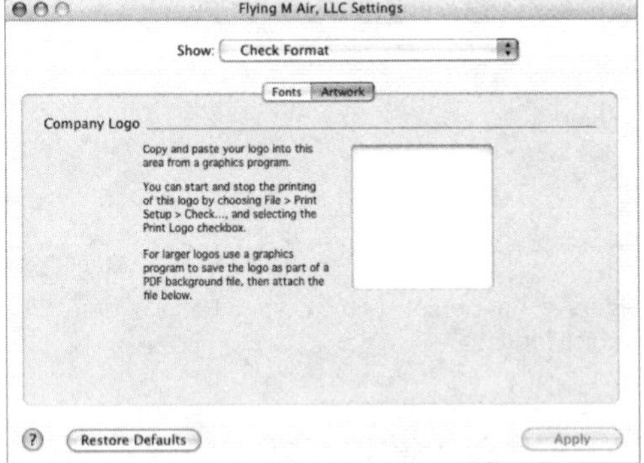

Figure 50 Artwork options in Check Format settings.

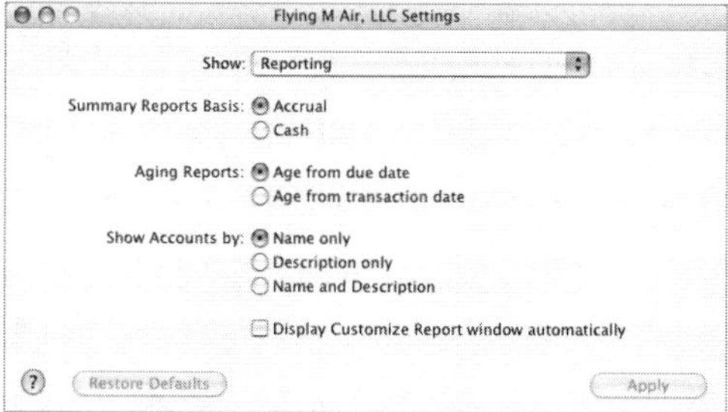

Figure 51 Reporting settings.

Reporting settings

Reporting settings (**Figure 51**) enable you to set basic reporting options.

- **Summary Reports Basis** lets you select between Accrual and Cash basis reporting for summary reports.
- **Aging Reports** lets you specify whether the age should be calculated from the due date or the transaction date.
- **Show Accounts by** enables you to specify whether account names, account descriptions, or account names and descriptions should appear on reports.
- **Display Customize Report window automatically** displays the Customize Report window every time you create a report, no matter how you create it.

Report Format settings

Report Format settings (**Figure 52**) enable you to set certain default formatting options for all reports you create.

- **General Number Options** set the way numbers appear:
  - **Divide all numbers by 1,000** reports numbers in thousands. In other words, it removes the last three digits of the number.
  - **Display Zero Amounts** displays zero amounts.
  - **Display Cents** includes both dollars and cents.
- **Negative Number Format** determines the appearance of negative numbers:
  - **Normally** displays negative numbers with a minus sign before them.
  - **In Parenthesis** displays negative numbers within parentheses.
  - **With a Trailing Minus** displays negative numbers with a minus sign after them.
  - **Show in Bright Red** displays negative numbers in red.
- **Font Style Settings for** enables you to set the font for various components of the report. Choose an option from the pop-up menu (**Figure 53**), then set options in the bottom half of the window. You can repeat this process for any combination of report components.

✔ Tip

- The options here are the same as those in the Format Report dialog, which I discuss in **Chapter 9**. They're just organized differently and they affect all reports.

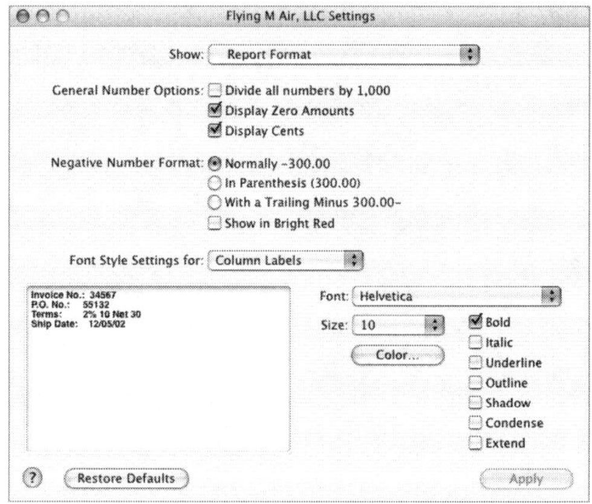

Figure 52 Report Format settings.

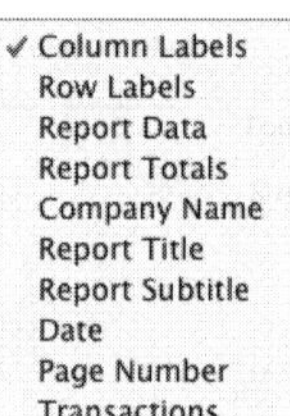

Figure 53 The Font Style Settings pop-up menu.

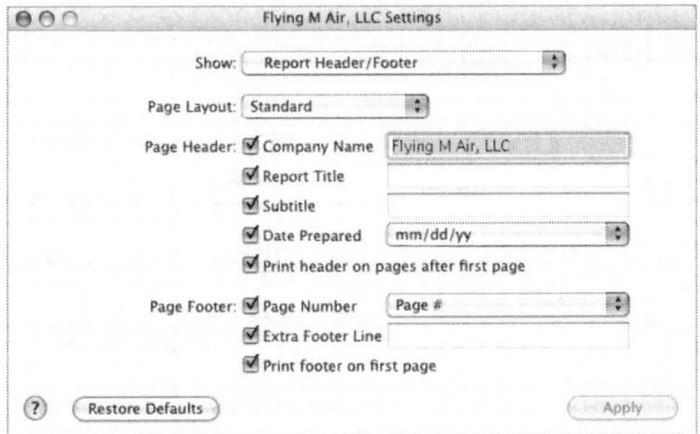

Figure 54 Report Header/Footer settings.

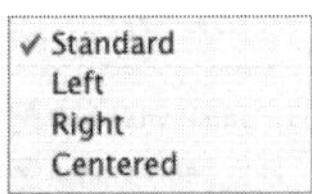

Figure 55 The Page Layout pop-up menu.

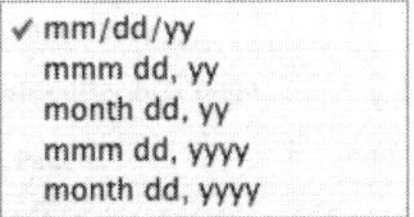

Figure 56 The Date Prepared pop-up menu.

Figure 57 The Page Number pop-up menu.

Report Header/Footer settings

The Report Header/Footer settings (**Figure 54**) enable you to set default formatting options for report headers and footers.

- **Page Layout** enables you to specify how the header and footer should be positioned on the page. Choose an option from the pop-up menu (**Figure 55**).
- **Page Header** controls what appears in the header:
  - **Company Name** is the name of your company, as it appears in the text box.
  - **Report Title** is the name of the report, as it appears in the text box.
  - **Subtitle** is the subtitle of the report, as it appears in the text box.
  - **Date Prepared** is the current date, formatted using one of the options in the pop-up menu (**Figure 56**).
  - **Print header on pages after first page** tells QuickBooks to print the header on all pages of the report—not just the first page.
- **Page Footer** controls what appears in the footer:
  - **Page Number** is the number of the current page, formatted using one of the options in the pop-up menu (**Figure 57**).
  - **Extra Footer Line** is additional text to include in the footer, as it appears in the text box.
  - **Print footer on first page** tells QuickBooks to print the footer on all pages of the report, including the first page.

✓ Tip

- The options here are the same as those in the Format Header/Footer dialog, which I discuss in **Chapter 9**.

Statement of Cash Flows Report

The Statement of Cash Flows Report settings **(Figure 58)** enables you to specify how accounts appear on the Statement of Cash Flows report. Use the check boxes and radio buttons to specify which accounts should be included in the report and where they should appear.

✔ Tip

- As noted in the Statement of Cash Flows Report window **(Figure 58)**, you probably won't need to customize this report. You can get further information about how this report applies to your business by consulting your accountant.

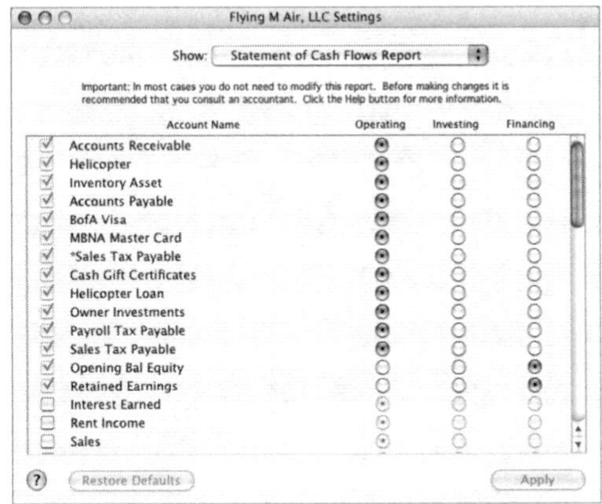

Figure 58 The Statement of Cash Flows Report settings.

Sales Tax settings

Sales Tax settings **(Figure 59)** control the way the sales tax feature works.

- **Customers are charged sales tax** turns on the sales tax feature. With this option turned off, you cannot set any of the other options in the window.
- **Sales Tax Payable** enables you to specify whether tax is payable monthly, quarterly, or annually.
- **Sales Tax Accrues** lets you specify whether sales tax is accrued as of the invoice date or the payment date for sales.
- **Most common sales tax** enables you to choose the most commonly applied sales tax from a pop-up menu. You can always override this choice when creating a sales form.
- **Mark taxable amounts with "T" when printing** prints the letter T beside each taxable item on a sales form.

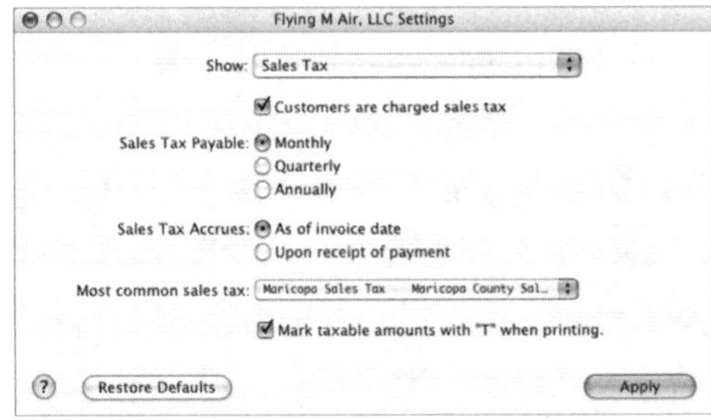

Figure 59 Sales Tax settings.

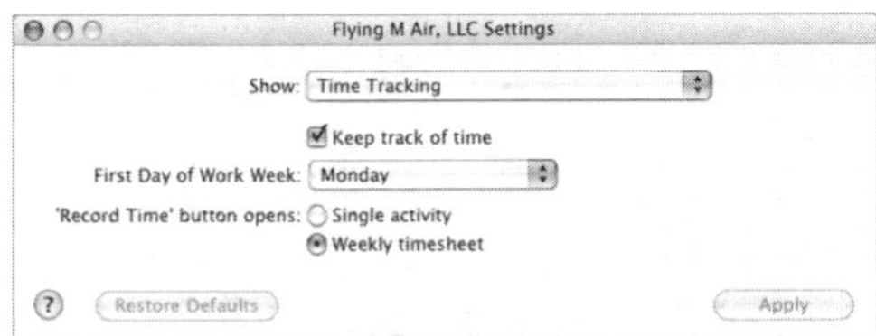

Figure 60 Time Tracking settings.

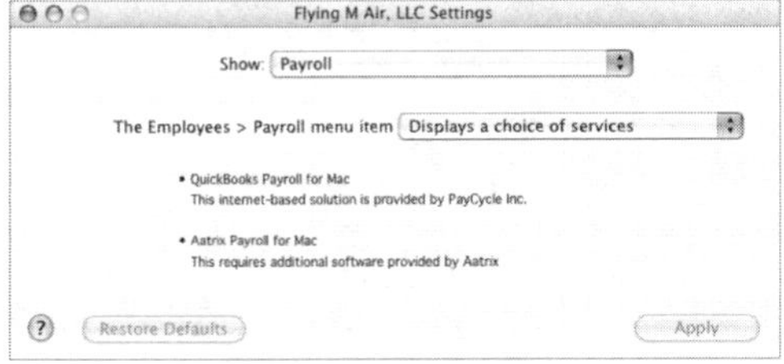

Figure 61 Payroll settings enable you to choose the service you want to use with QuickBooks to process payroll.

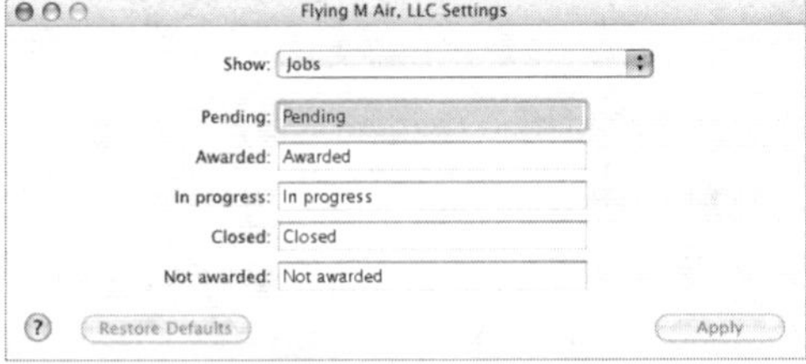

Figure 62 Jobs settings.

Time Tracking settings

Time Tracking settings (**Figure 60**) control how the time tracking feature works.

- **Keep track of time** turns on the time tracking feature. If this check box is turned off, you cannot set other settings in the window.
- **First Day of Work Week** is the first day of your company's work week. Choose a day from the pop-up menu.
- **'Record Time' button opens** enables you to specify whether clicking the Record Time button in a dialog opens a single activity form or a weekly timesheet.

Payroll settings

Payroll settings (**Figure 61**) enable you to indicate what the Payroll command on the Employees menu should do. Your options in the pop-up menu are:

- **Displays a choice of services** enables you to choose the payroll service you want to use.
- **Launches QuickBooks Payroll for Mac,** accesses an Internet-based solution provided by PayCycle Inc. This is the new payroll service that works with QuickBooks.
- **Launches Aatrix Top Pay** launches the Aatrix Top Pay software, which must be installed on your computer. This was the payroll service that worked with previous versions of QuickBooks.

Jobs settings

Jobs settings (**Figure 62**) let you set preferred terminology for job status options. Enter new text in the boxes you want to change. The text that appears in the boxes is what will appear as job status options.

Passwords settings

Passwords settings (**Figure 63**) enable you to password-protect your QuickBooks company data file and its transactions. Once passwords are set, QuickBooks displays a dialog each time a user attempts to perform a task that requires password entry (**Figures 64, 65, and 66**).

- **File Passwords** protect the data file from unauthorized access.
  - **Owner Password** allows unrestricted access to the entire file and all QuickBooks features.
  - **Data Entry Password** limits access to data entry features.
- **Transaction Password** prevents unauthorized users from modifying transactions on or before a specific date.
  - **Closing Date** is the cutoff date for protected transactions. Any transaction on or before this date cannot be modified without the password.
  - **Transaction Password** is the password to protect transactions.

✔ Tip

- To remove a password simply clear it from the appropriate box and click Apply.

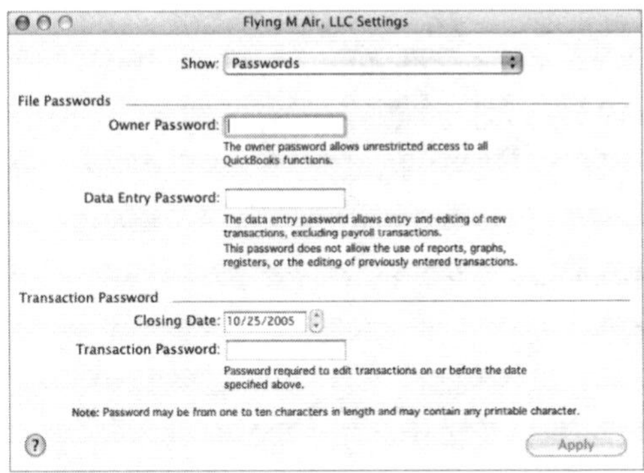

Figure 63 Passwords settings.

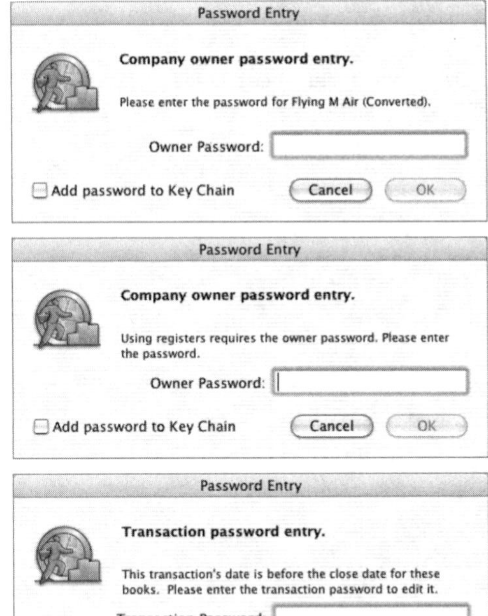

Figures 64, 65, & 66 Three examples of password prompt dialogs: to open a file (top), to use registers when logged in with a data entry password (middle), and to edit a transaction (bottom).

Figure 67 1099s settings.

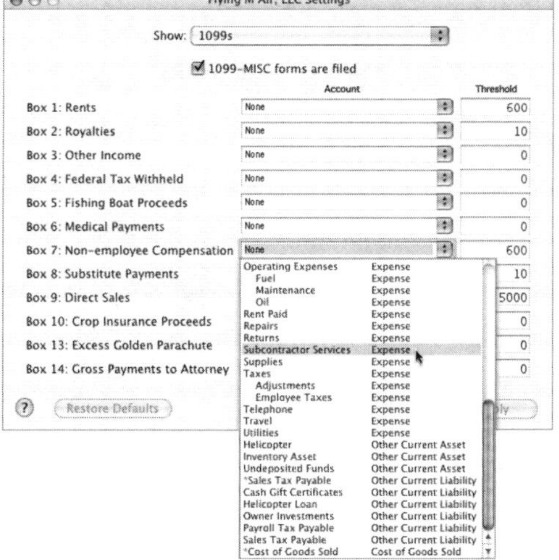

Figure 68 Choose an account from the drop-down list.

1099s settings

1099s settings (**Figure 67**) enable you to set up QuickBooks for tracking 1099-reportable payments to vendors.

Here's how it works. First, make sure the check box at the top of the window is turned on—this enables the 1099 reporting feature. Then use the drop-down list for each box number to choose the account in which related expenses are recorded. When you record expenses for a 1099 vendor, be sure to use one of the accounts you mapped to a box.

Here's an example. Suppose you use the Subcontractor Services account to record all payments to subcontractors that are reportable in Box 7 of 1099 forms. You would choose Subcontractor Services from the drop-down list beside Box 7: Non-employee Compensation (**Figure 68**). Then, when you record bills from or make payments to 1099 vendors, you'd use Subcontractor Services as the expense account for the transaction.

QuickBooks also enables you to change the threshold amounts for each box number. The default values are those set by the IRS at the time QuickBooks was published, but if these values change, you can change them here.

✔ Tips

- If you use more than one account for a box, you can choose Selected accounts from the drop-down list and use the dialog that appears to select the accounts to include.
- I tell you more about printing 1099 forms in **Chapter 10**.

Configuring the Toolbar

QuickBooks enables you to customize the toolbar so it shows the buttons you use most. This can help you be more productive by making it quicker and easier to access frequently used commands.

✔ Tip

- Toolbar customization is saved with the company file, not with QuickBooks itself. That means that every company file can have a different toolbar configuration.

To configure the toolbar

1. Choose Company > Configure Toolbar (**Figure 21**). The Configure Toolbar dialog slides out of the toolbar (**Figure 69**).

2. To change the appearance of the toolbar, choose an option from the Show pop-up menu at the bottom of the dialog (**Figure 70**):
   - ▲ **Icon & Text** displays the toolbar button's icon with the name of the button beneath it (**Figure 69**).
   - ▲ **Icon Only** displays just the button's icon (**Figure 71**).
   - ▲ **Text Only** displays just the button's name (**Figure 72**).

3. To display smaller versions of the buttons, turn on the Use Small Size check box. This makes it possible to display more buttons in the toolbar.

4. Modify the toolbar as follows:
   - ▲ To add a button to the toolbar, drag it from the middle of the dialog into place on the toolbar (**Figures 73 and 74**).

Figure 69 The Configure Toolbar dialog, with the toolbar outlined and ready for modification.

Figure 70 Use this pop-up menu to specify how the toolbar should appear.

Figures 71 & 72 The toolbar can also be displayed as just icons (top) or just text (bottom).

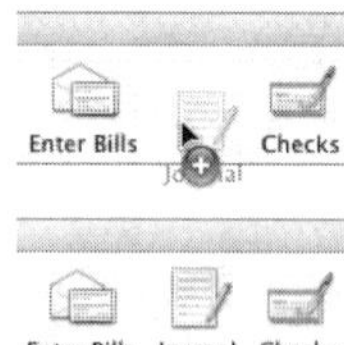

Figures 73 & 74 Drag an icon onto the toolbar. When you release the mouse button, it appears where you placed it.

- To remove a button from the toolbar, drag it off the toolbar.
- To move a toolbar button, drag it into a new position on the toolbar.
- To restore the toolbar to its default configuration, drag the default set of icons near the bottom of the dialog onto the toolbar.

5. When you're finished making changes, click Done. Your changes are saved and the Configure Toolbar dialog disappears.

✔ Tip

- To remove the toolbar, choose Company > Hide Company Toolbar (**Figure 21**).

Menus & Shortcut Keys

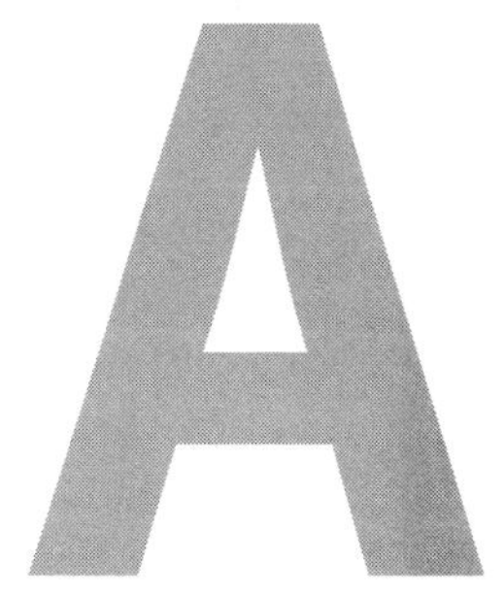

QuickBooks Menu

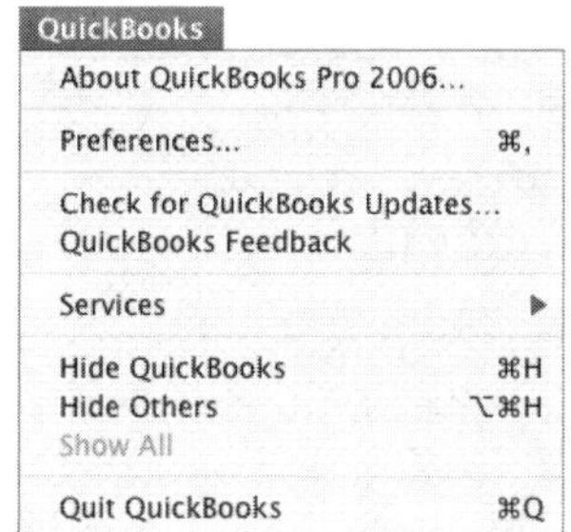

⌘ ,	Preferences
⌘ H	Hide QuickBooks
Option ⌘ H	Hide Others
⌘ Q	Quit QuickBooks

Menus & Shortcut Keys

This appendix illustrates all of QuickBooks' menus and submenus and provides a list of shortcut keys you can use to access menu commands.

To use a shortcut key, hold down the modifier key—which is usually ⌘—and press the keyboard key corresponding to the command. For example, to use the Create Invoices command's shortcut key, hold down ⌘ and press I.

✔ Tip

- Menus may vary depending on options set in preferences and the company settings file, as well as what window is open and active.

File Menu

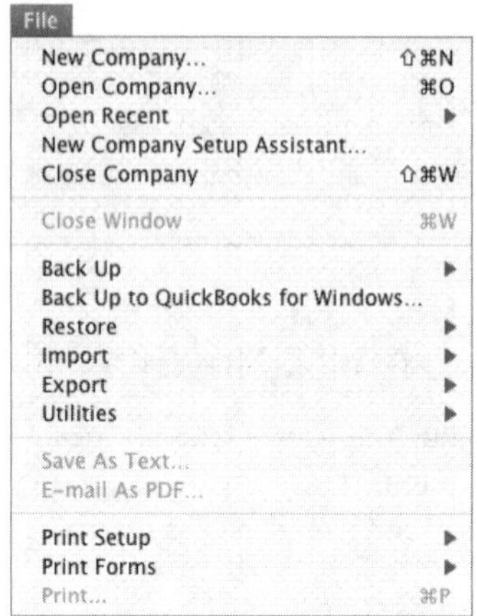

Shift ⌘ N	New Company
⌘ O	Open Company
Shift ⌘ W	Close Company
⌘ P	Print

Back Up submenu

To a Disk...
To .Mac...

Restore submenu

From a Disk...
From .Mac...

Import submenu

From IIF Files...
From Quicken Files...
From Web Connect...

Export submenu

Lists to IIF File...
Addresses To Text File...

Utilities submenu

Verify Data...
Rebuild Data
Condense Data...

Print Setup submenu

Invoice...
Statement...
Estimate...
Report/Graph/List...
Purchase Order...
Check...
Mailing Label...
1099

Print Forms submenu

Invoices...
Statements...
Sales Receipts...
Credit Memos...
Purchase Orders...
Checks...
Mailing Labels...
1099s...

Edit Menu

Edit	
Nothing to Undo	⌘Z
Redo	⇧⌘Z
Revert	
Cut	⌘X
Copy Accounts	⌘C
Paste	⌘V
Clear	
Select All	⌘A
Insert Line	⌘Y
Delete Line	⌘B
Edit Check	⌘E
New Check	⌘N
Delete Check	⌘D
Memorize Check...	⌘+
Make Inactive	
Re-sort List	
Notepad	
Transaction History...	⌘U
Void Check	
Copy Check	⌥⌘C
Go To Transfer	⌘G
Show List	⌘L
Use Register	⌘R
Mark As Pending	
Change Account Color...	
Find...	⌘F
Go To...	
Special Characters...	⌥⌘T

Shortcut	Command
⌘ Z	Undo
Shift ⌘ Z	Redo
⌘ X	Cut
⌘ C	Copy
⌘ V	Paste
⌘ A	Select All
⌘ Y	Insert Line
⌘ B	Delete Line
⌘ E	Edit *Item*
⌘ N	New *Item*
⌘ D	Delete *Item*
⌘ +	Memorize *Item*
⌘ U	Transaction History
Option ⌘ C	Copy *Item*
⌘ G	Go To Transfer
⌘ L	Show List
⌘ R	Use Register
⌘ F	Find
Option ⌘ T	Special Characters

Lists Menu

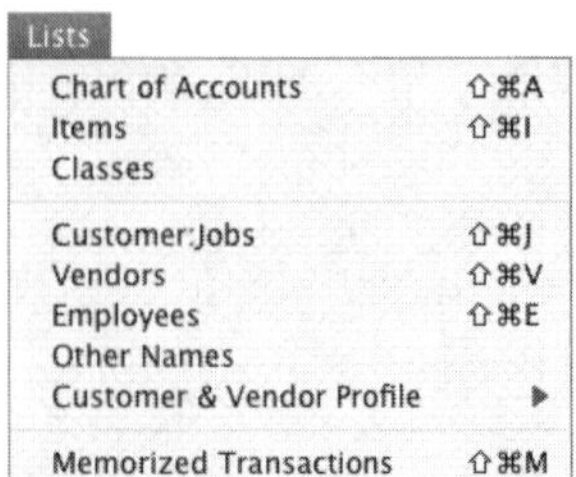

Shift ⌘ A	Chart of Accounts
Shift ⌘ I	Items
Shift ⌘ J	Customers:Jobs
Shift ⌘ V	Vendors
Shift ⌘ E	Employees
Shift ⌘ M	Memorized Transactions

Customer & Vendor Profile submenu

Customer Types
Vendor Types
Job Types
Terms
Customer Messages
Payment Methods
Ship Via

Company Menu

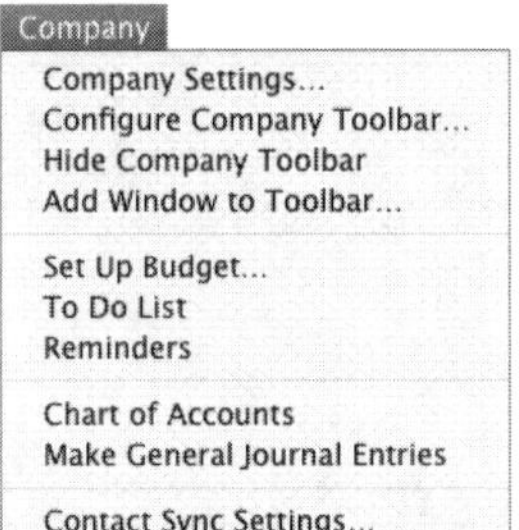

Customers Menu

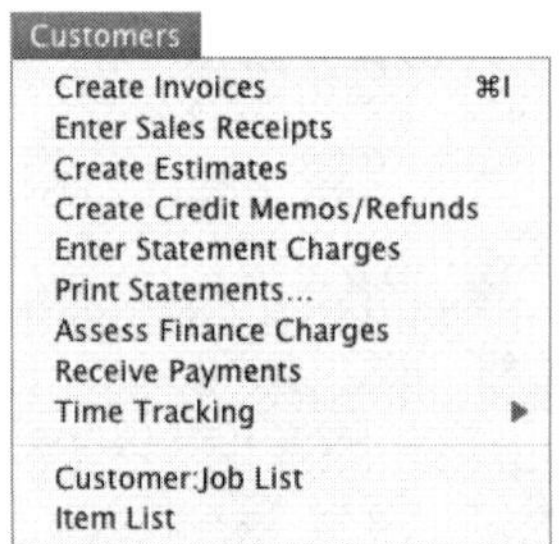

⌘ I	Create Invoices

Time Tracking submenu

Use Weekly Timesheet
Enter Single Activity

Vendors Menu

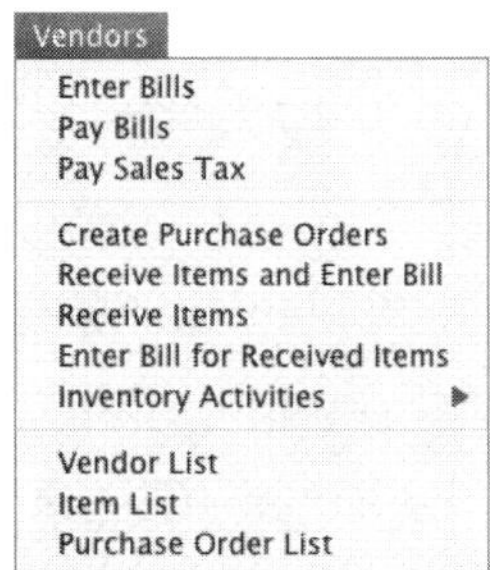

Inventory Activities submenu

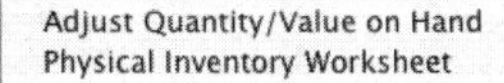

Banking Menu

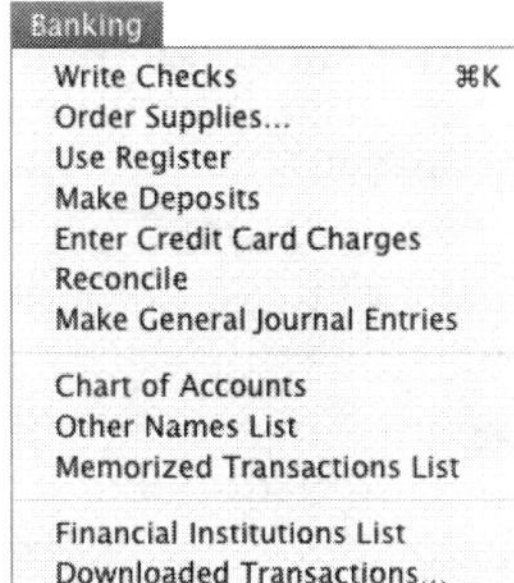

⌘ K	Write Checks

Employees Menu

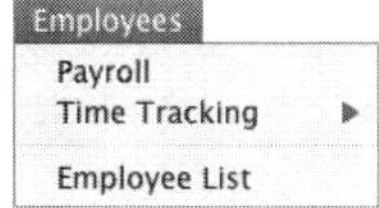

Time Tracking submenu

Use Weekly Timesheet
Enter Single Activity

Reports Menu

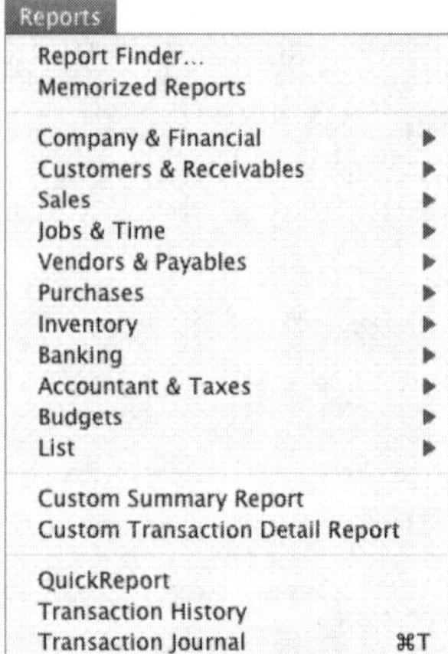

⌘T	Transaction Journal

Company & Financial submenu

Profit and Loss Standard
Profit and Loss Detail
Profit and Loss YTD Comparison
Profit and Loss Prev Year Comparison
Profit and Loss by Job
Profit and Loss by Class

Income by Customer Summary
Income by Customer Detail
Expenses by Vendor Summary
Expenses by Vendor Detail
Income and Expense Graph

Balance Sheet Standard
Balance Sheet Detail
Balance Sheet Summary
Balance Sheet Prev Year Comparison
Net Worth Graph

Statement of Cash Flows
Cash Flow Forecast

Customers & Receivables submenu

A/R Aging Summary
A/R Aging Detail

Customer Balance Summary
Customer Balance Detail

Open Invoices
Collections Report

Accounts Receivable Graph

Unbilled Costs by Job

Transaction List by Customer

Customer Phone List
Customer Contact List
Item Price List

Sales submenu

Sales by Customer Summary
Sales by Customer Detail

Sales by Item Summary
Sales by Item Detail

Sales by Rep Summary
Sales by Rep Detail

Sales Graph
Pending Sales

Jobs & Time submenu

Job Administration
Job Profitability Summary
Job Profitability Detail
Job Estimates vs. Actuals Summary
Job Estimates vs. Actuals Detail

Item Profitability
Item Estimates vs. Actuals
Profit and Loss by Job

Time by Job Summary
Time by Job Detail
Time by Name
Time by Item

Unbilled Costs by Job

Vendors & Payables submenu

A/P Aging Summary
A/P Aging Detail

Vendor Balance Summary
Vendor Balance Detail

Unpaid Bills Detail
Accounts Payable Graph
Transaction List by Vendor

1099 Summary
1099 Detail

Sales Tax Liability Report

Vendor Phone List
Vendor Contact List

Purchases submenu

Purchases by Vendor Summary
Purchases by Vendor Detail

Purchases by Item Summary
Purchases by Item Detail

Open Purchase Orders

Inventory submenu

Inventory Valuation Summary
Inventory Valuation Detail

Inventory Stock Status by Item
Inventory Stock Status by Vendor

Physical Inventory Worksheet
Inventory Price List

Banking submenu

Deposit Detail
Check Detail
Missing Checks

Accountant & Taxes submenu

Trial Balance
General Ledger
Journal
Audit Trail

Transaction List by Date

Transaction Detail by Date
Transaction Detail by Account

Account Listing

Income Tax Summary
Income Tax Detail

Budgets submenu

Profit and Loss Budget Overview
Profit and Loss Budget vs. Actual

Profit and Loss Budget by Job Overview
Profit and Loss Budget vs. Actual by Job

Budget vs. Actual Graph
Balance Sheet Budget Overview
Balance Sheet Budget vs. Actual

List submenu

Account Listing
Item Price List
Item Listing

Customer Phone List
Customer Contact List
Vendor Phone List
Vendor Contact List
Employee Contact List
Other Names Phone List
Other Names Contact List

Terms Listing
To Do Notes
Memorized Transaction Listing

Window Menu

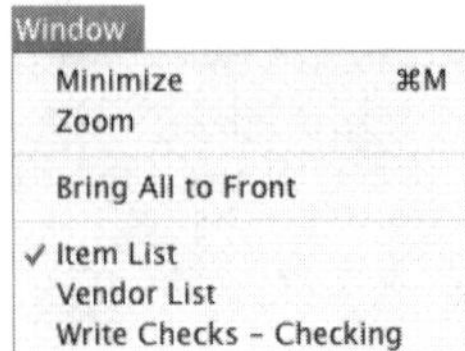

⌘M	Minimize

Help Menu

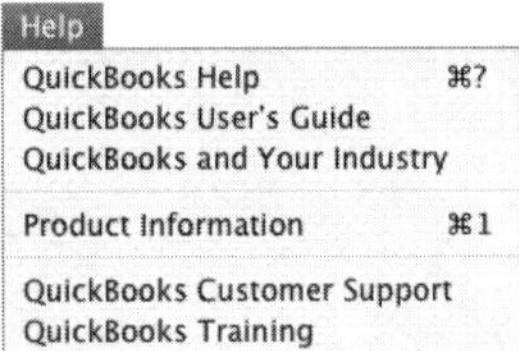

⌘?	QuickBooks Help
⌘1	Product Information

WINDOW & HELP MENUS

Index

1099 Print Setup dialog, 250
1099s
  printing
    forms, 258–259
    setup, 250
  settings, 287
1099s command (File menu), 250, 258

A

Aatrix Trop Pay, 201
Access Preferences screen, 208
Account Association dialog, 149
Account Not Found dialog, 43
Accountant & Taxes category
  Report Finder, 226
  Reports menu, 224
Accountant & Taxes menu commands, 297
accounting principles, xvi
accounts, xvii–xviii
  adding, 36–37
  deleting, 38
  modifying, 37
  options, 36–37
  reconciling, 179–182
  registers
    entering transactions, 162–164
    viewing, 156–157
  type supported, xvii, 34–35
Accounts completed screen, 25
Accounts Payable, xvii, 34
Accounts Payable graphs, 236
Accounts Receivable, xvii, 34, 91
  graphs, 236
  register window, 121
Action menu commands
  Add Job, 65
  Edit, 37
  Flat View, 32
  Hierarchical View, 32
  Make Active, 33
  Make Inactive, 33
  Mark as 'Done,' 79
  New, 36
  QuickReport, 157
  Show Only Open Purchase Orders, 185
  Show Sorted List, 32
Add a Contractor button, 211
Add Employee screen, 208, 210
Add Job command (Action menu), 65
Add One to Register button, 154
Adding an inventory item screen, 21
Adding lines of credit screen, 24
Adding Vendors with open balances screen, 23
Additional Info button
  New Customer dialog, 62
  New Employee dialog, 72
  New Vendor dialog, 68–69
Address Info button
  New Employee dialog, 71–72
  New Name dialog, 74–75
  New Vendor dialog, 67
Address Info pane, 66
Adjust Quantity/Value on Hand command (Vendors menu), 198
Adjust Quantity/Value on Hand window, 198
Align Checks dialog, 248
Align Windows button, 153
Approve Paychecks window, 215, 218
Assess Finance Charges command (Customers menu), 115
Assess Finance Charges dialog, 117
asset accounts, xvii, 34
Asset accounts screen, 25

B

Back Up menu commands, 292
Balance Sheet accounts, xviii, 34–35
bank accounts, xvii, 34
Bank accounts screen, 24
Banking category
  Report Finder, 225
  Reports menu, 223
Banking menu commands, 295, 297
  Downloaded Transactions, 149
  Enter Credit Card Charges, 123
  Financial Institutions, 146
  Make Deposits, 112
  Make General Journal Entries, 159
  Order Supplies, 248
  Reconcile, 180
  Reconcile Credit Card, 182
  Write Checks, 123
Basic Employee Information: Name and Address screen, 208
Bill To field (Create Invoices window), 93
billable items, entering, 98–100
Billable Time and Costs window, 100

bills
- entering, 190–195
- payments, 139–141

budget setup, 241–242
Budget *versus* Actual graphs, 236
Budgets category
- Report Finder, 226
- Reports menu, 224

Budgets menu commands, 297

C

cash
- deposits, 112
- sales, 92

Category option (Create Vacation and Sick Leave Policies screen), 206
Change button, 99
Change Graph Dates dialog, 238
Change Title button, 96
Change Type button, 75
Chart of Accounts, xvii, 29
- account types, 34–35
- adding accounts, 36–37
- deleting accounts, 38
- modifying accounts, 37
- options, 36–37

Chart of Accounts command (List menu), 156, 221
Chart of Accounts window, 31, 156
Check command (File menu), 247
Check Format settings, 280
Check No. field (Enter Sales Receipt window), 94
Check Print Setup dialog, 247
checks
- deposits, 112
- payments, 125–130
- printing
  - forms, 255
  - setup, 247–248

Checks command (File menu), 255
Checks settings, 280
Choose Billable Time and Costs dialog, 98, 175
Choose your QuickBooks start date screen, 16
Class List window, 58
Class lists, 29
- adding class, 59
- deleting class, 60
- modifying class, 60

Classifying transactions screen, 15
Combine Activities? radio buttons, 99
Combining personal and business expenses screen, 26
commands. *See also* individual menus
- Action menu
  - Add Job, 65
  - Edit, 37
  - Flat View, 32
  - Hierarchical View, 32
  - Make Active, 33
  - Make Inactive, 33
  - Mark as 'Done,' 79
  - New, 36
  - QuickReport, 157
  - Show Only Open Purchase Orders, 185
  - Show Sorted List, 32
- Banking menu
  - Downloaded Transactions, 149
  - Enter Credit Card Charges, 123
  - Financial Institutions, 146
  - Make Deposits, 112
  - Make General Journal Entries, 159
  - Order Supplies, 248
  - Reconcile, 180
  - Reconcile Credit Card, 182
  - Write Checks, 123
- Company menu
  - Company Settings, 115
  - Configure Toolbar, 288
  - To Do List, 30

commands, Company menu *(continued)*
  - Make General Journal Entries, 159
  - Reminders, 30
  - Set Up Budget, 241
- Customers menu
  - Assess Finance Charges, 115
  - Create Credit Memos/ Refunds, 118
  - Create Estimates, 101
  - Create Invoices, 93
  - Enter Sales Receipts, 93
  - Enter Statement Charges, 121
  - Receive Payments, 107, 109
- Edit menu. *See* individual commands
- Employees menu
  - Payroll, 203
  - Time Tracking, 176
- File menu
  - Import, 6
  - New Company, 8
  - Open Company, 6
  - Print Forms, 251
  - Print List, 31
  - Print Report, 260
  - Print Setup, 244
- List menu
  - Chart of Accounts, 156, 221
  - Customer & Vendor Profile, 29
- Reports menu
  - Memorized Reports, 240
  - Report Finder, 227
- Vendors menu
  - Create Purchase Orders, 186
  - Enter Bill for Received Items, 195
  - Enter Bills, 123
  - Inventory Activities, 196, 197
  - Pay Bills, 123
  - Pay Sales Tax, 124
  - Purchase Order List, 30, 185
  - Receive Items, 193
  - Receive Items and Enter Bill, 191

companies
New Company Setup Assistant, 8
Documents section, 26–27
General section, 9–16
Income & Expenses section, 17–18
Income Details section, 19–21
Opening Balances section, 22–25
open existing files, 4–7
Company & Financial category
Report Finder, 225
Reports menu, 223
Company & Financial menu commands, 296
Company File Backups preferences (QuickBooks Preferences window), 268–269
Company Info completed screen, 13
Company menu commands, 294
Company Settings, 115
Configure Toolbar, 288
To Do List, 30
Make General Journal Entries, 159
Reminders, 30
Set Up Budget, 241
Company Settings command (Company menu), 115
Company Settings window
Check Format settings, 280
Checks settings, 280
Company Information settings, 272
Credit Memo Format settings, 279
Estimate Format settings, 275–277
Inventory/Purchase Orders/Estimates settings, 274
Invoice Format settings, 279
Jobs settings, 285
opening, 271
Passwords settings, 286
Payroll settings, 285
Purchase Order Format settings, 275–277
Report Format settings, 282
Report Header/Footer settings, 283
Reporting settings, 281
1099s settings, 287
Sales/Invoicing settings, 278
Sales Receipt Format settings, 279
Sales Tax settings, 284
Statement Format settings, 279
Statement of Cash Flows Report settings, 284
Time Tracking settings, 285
Transactions settings, 273
Complete Employee Setup screen, 209–210
Configure Toolbar command (Company menu), 288
Configure Toolbar dialog, 288
Contact Sync preferences (QuickBooks Preferences window), 270
Convert from Quicken dialog, 6
Converting File dialog, 5
Copy to QuickBooks for Mac screen, 217
Copy window, 2
Cost of Goods Sold accounts, xvii, 35
Create a new QuickBooks file dialog, 6–7
Create Credit Memos/Refunds command (Customers menu), 118
Create Credit Memos/Refunds window, 118
Create Estimates command (Customers menu), 101
Create Estimates window, 101
Create Invoice button, 104
Create Invoices command (Customers menu), 93
Create Invoices window, 89, 93
Create Item Receipts dialog, 193
Create Item Receipts window, 190, 193
Create Pay Schedule screen, 205
Create Paychecks window, 215–218
Create Purchase Orders command (Vendors menu), 186
Create Purchase Orders window, 185
Create Vacation and Sick Leave Policies screen, 206
Credit Card accounts, xvii, 34
Credit card accounts screen, 23
credit cards
deposits, 113
entering charges, 135–138
Credit Memo Format settings, 279
credit memos
customer account adjustments, 118–120
printing forms, 251–252
Credit radio button, 134
credits
double-entry accounting system, xix
payments, 134
custom fields, Items lists, 56
Custom Fields button, 56
Custom Fields dialog, 56
Customer: Job List window, 61
Customer: Job Not Found dialog, 92
Customer: Jobs lists, 29
adding customer, 61–64
deleting customer, 66
jobs added to customer, 65
modifying customer, 66
Customer & Vendor Profile command (Lists menu), 29
Customer & Vendor Profile menu commands, 294
Customer Has Unapplied Payments dialog, 117
Customer Message List window, 86

Customer Messages lists, 30, 86
  adding customer message, 87
  deleting customer message, 88
  modifying customer message, 88
Customer Service Agreement, PayCycle, 211
Customer Service Agreement screen, 211
Customer Type window, 80
Customer Types lists, 29
  adding type, 80–81
  deleting, 82–83
  modifying type, 81
customers
  account adjustment
    credit memos, 118–120
    refunds, 118–120
    statement charges, 121
  adding, 61–64
  deleting, 66
  editing, 66
  jobs
    adding to, 65
    modifying, 66
  messages, 86
    adding, 87
    deleting, 88
    modifying, 88
  type
    adding, 80–81
    deleting, 82–83
    modifying, 81
Customers & Receivables category
  Report Finder, 225
  Reports menu, 223
Customers & Receivables menu commands, 296
Customers menu commands, 294
  Assess Finance Charges, 115
  Create Credit Memos/Refunds, 118
  Create Estimates, 101
  Create Invoices, 93
Customers menu commands *(continued)*
  Enter Sales Receipts, 93
  Enter Statement Charges, 121
  Receive Payments, 107, 109
customization, 263
  Company Settings window
    Check Format settings, 280
    Checks settings, 280
    Company Information settings, 272
    Credit Memo Format settings, 279
    Estimate Format settings, 275–277
    Inventory/Purchase Orders/Estimates settings, 274
    Invoice Format settings, 279
    Jobs settings, 285
    opening, 271
    Passwords settings, 286
    Payroll settings, 285
    Purchase Order Format settings, 275–277
    Report Format settings, 282
    Report Header/Footer settings, 283
    Reporting settings, 281
    1099s settings, 287
    Sales/Invoicing settings, 278
    Sales Receipt Format settings, 279
    Sales Tax settings, 284
    Statement Format settings, 279
    Statement of Cash Flows Report settings, 284
    Time Tracking settings, 285
    Transactions settings, 273
  graphs, 238
  QuickBooks Preferences window
    Company File Backups preferences, 268–269
    Contact Sync preferences, 270
customization *(continued)*
    Data Entry preferences, 266
    Graphs preferences, 267
    opening, 264
    Reminders preferences, 267
    Views preferences, 265
  reports, 228–230
    filters, 233
    formatting, 234
    header & footer formatting, 235
    options, 231–232
  toolbar configurations, 288–289
Customize Report dialog, 231–232
Customized Toolbar dialog, 5

D

Data Entry preferences (QuickBooks Preferences window), 266
Date Driven terms
  payments, 83
  setting options, 84
Date field (Create Invoices window), 93
Date Stamp button (New Customer dialog), 64
debits, double-entry accounting system, xix
defaults, list sort order, 32
Define Custom Fields for Items dialog, 56
Define Fields button, 56, 64
Define Fields dialog, 64
Delete Account command (Edit menu), 38
Delete Class command (Edit menu), 60
Delete Class dialog, 60
Delete Customer: Job command (Edit menu), 66
Delete Customer: Job dialog, 66
Delete Customer Message command (Edit menu), 88

Delete Customer Message dialog, 88
Delete Customer Type command (Edit menu), 83
Delete Customer Type dialog, 83
Delete Deposit command (Edit menu), 114
Delete Employee command (Edit menu), 73
Delete Employee dialog, 73
Delete Estimate command (Edit menu), 106
Delete Invoice command (Edit menu), 106
Delete Item command (Edit menu), 57
Delete Item dialog, 57
Delete Job Type command (Edit menu), 83
Delete Job Type dialog, 83
Delete Line command (Edit menu), 96
Delete Memorized Reports command (Edit menu), 240
Delete Memorized Transaction dialog, 173
Delete Other Name command (Edit menu), 76
Delete Other Name dialog, 76
Delete Payment command (Edit menu), 109
Delete Payment Method command (Edit menu), 88
Delete Payment Method dialog, 88
Delete Purchase Order command (Edit menu), 189
Delete Sales Receipt command (Edit menu), 106
Delete Shipping Method command (Edit menu), 88
Delete Shipping Method dialog, 88
Delete Terms command (Edit menu), 85
Delete Terms dialog, 85
Delete To Do Note command (Edit menu), 79
Delete To Do Note dialog, 79
Delete Transaction dialog, 106, 169, 189
Delete Vendor command (Edit menu), 70
Delete Vendor dialog, 70
Delete Vendor Type command (Edit menu), 83
Delete Vendor Type dialog, 83
deleting
  accounts, 38
  class, 60
  customer, 66, 88
  deposits, 114
  employees, 73
  estimates, 106
  invoices, 106
  items, 57
  memorized transactions, 173
  methods of payment, 88
  names, 76
  notes, 79
  payments, 109
  purchase orders, 189
  sales receipts, 106
  shipping methods, 88
  terms, 85
  transactions, 169
  types, 82
Deleting QuickBooks Account dialog, 38
Deposit radio buttons, 108
deposits, 111
  checks and cash, 112
  credit cards, 113
  deleting, 114
  modifying, 114
Description option
  Create Pay Schedule screen, 205
  Create Vacation and Sick Leave Policies screen, 206
dialogs. *See* individual dialogs
Direct deposit timing link, 207
Discount Info button, 108
Discount Information dialog, 108, 141
Discount items, 39, 49–50
Documents button, 26
Documents completed screen, 27
Documents screen, 26
Documents section (New Company Setup Assistant), 26–27
double-entry accounting system, xix
Downloaded Transactions command (Banking menu), 149
Downloaded Transactions window, 149
downloading transactions, 145, 148–151
  bank Web site login, 147
  financial institution support, 146
  reviewing, 152–154
  sign up, 147

E

Edit Account command (Edit menu), 37
Edit Account dialog, 37
Edit command (Action menu), 37
Edit Customer Message command (Edit menu), 88
Edit Customer Message dialog, 88
Edit Customer Type command (Edit menu), 81
Edit Customer Type dialog, 81
Edit Employee command (Edit menu), 73
Edit employee's Pay Info screen, 209
Edit employee's Tax Info form, 209
Edit Item command (Edit menu), 55
Edit Item dialog, 55
Edit Job Type dialog, 81

Edit menu commands, 293. *See also* individual commands
Edit Other Name command (Edit menu), 75
Edit Pay Policies screen, 205–206
Edit Payment Method command (Edit menu), 88
Edit Payment Method dialog, 88
Edit Shipping Method command (Edit menu), 88
Edit Shipping Method dialog, 88
Edit Terms command (Edit menu), 85
Edit Terms dialog, 85
Edit To Do dialog, 78
Edit To Do Note command (Edit menu), 78
Edit Vendor command (Edit menu), 70
Edit Vendor Type command (Edit menu), 81
Edit Vendor Type dialog, 81
editing. *See also* modifying
- accounts, 37
- class, 60
- customer, 66, 88
- deposits, 114
- employees, 73
- estimates, 106
- invoices, 106
- item, 55
- memorized transactions, 173
- names, 75
- notes, 78
- payment methods, 88
- payments, 109
- purchase orders, 189
- sales receipts, 106
- shipping methods, 88
- special transactions, 161
- terms, 85
- transactions, 169
- types, 81
- vendors, 70

Email Paystubs window, 217
Employee and Contractor Overview screen, 208
Employee List window, 71
employees
- adding, 71–72
- deleting, 73
- modifying, 73
- PayCycle, 208–211
- tracking time, 175
  - multiple activities, 177–178
  - single activity, 176

Employees earn option (Create Vacation and Sick Leave Policies screen), 206
Employees lists, 29
- adding employees, 71–72
- deleting employee, 73
- modifying employee, 73

Employees menu commands, 295
- Payroll, 203
- Time Tracking, 176

Enabling Inventory screen, 12
Enter Bill for Received Items command (Vendors menu), 195
Enter Bills command (Vendors menu), 123
Enter Bills window, 130–133, 190, 195
Enter Check Numbers screen, 216
Enter Credit Card Charges command (Banking menu), 123
Enter Credit Card Charges window, 135–138
Enter customers screen, 22
Enter Sales Receipts command (Customers menu), 93
Enter Sales Receipts window, 93
Enter Single Activity command (Employees menu), 176
Enter Single Activity window, 176
Enter Statement Charges command (Customers menu), 121
Entering historical transactions screen, 26
Equity accounts, xvii, 34–35
Estimate Format settings, 275–277
estimates
- creating, 101–103
- deleting, 106
- invoice creation, 104
- modifying, 106
- print setup, 244–246
- viewing, 105

Estimates screen, 14–15
Exit State Tax Information screen, 212
Expense accounts, xvii–xviii, 35
Expense accounts completed screen, 18
Expense Accounts screen, 17–18
expenses
- entering, 98–100
- payroll, 213

Expenses button, 98, 126
Export menu commands, 292

F

Federal Tax ID number, 11
Federal Taxes (941) accounts, 213
Federal Unemployment (940) accounts, 213
Feel free to change your answers screen, 10
fields, custom Items lists, 56
File menu commands, 292
- Import, 6
- New Company, 8
- Open Company, 6
- Print Forms, 251
- Print List, 31
- Print Report, 260
- Print Setup, 244

Filename for New Company dialog, 13, 16

files
- company, opening existing, 4–7
- converting from Quicken file, 6–7

Fill Down dialog, 242
filters, 165, 233
finance charges
- assessment, 117
- set up, 115–116

Financial Institutions command (Banking menu), 146
Financial Institutions window, 146
Find command (Edit menu), 165
Find dialog, 166
Find window, 165
Finder, open company file, 6
Finishing Up screen, 27
fiscal years, first month, 11
Fixed Asset accounts, xvii, 34
Flat View command (Action menu), 32
flat views, lists, 32
FOB field (Create Invoices window), 94
FOB (free on board), 94
footers, report formatting, 235
Format Header/Footer dialog, 235
Format Report dialog, 234
formatting custom reports, 234
forms, xix
- printing
  - checks, 255
  - credit memos, 251–252
  - invoices, 251–252
  - mailing labels, 256–257
  - purchase orders, 251–252
  - 1099s, 258–259
  - sales receipts, 251–252
  - statements, 253–254

free on board (FOB), 94
From Quicken File command (File menu), 6

G

General: Company Information screen, 10
General Journal Entry form, xix
General Journal Entry window, 159–160
General section completed screen, 16
General section (New Company Setup Assistant), 9–16
Graph command (File menu), 246
graphs
- payroll, 236–238
- print setup, 246

Graphs preferences (QuickBooks Preferences window), 267
Group items, 39, 47–48

H–I

Handling petty cash screen, 26
headers, report formatting, 235
Help menu commands, 298
Here are your expense accounts screen, 18
Here are your income accounts screen, 17
Hierarchical View command (Action menu), 32
hierarchical views, lists, 32
Hiring Info screen, 209
Hours are accrued option (Create Vacation and Sick Leave Policies screen), 206
Import command (File menu), 6
Import File button, 149
Import From Quicken Files command, 4
Import menu commands, 292
importing, downloading account transactions, 148–150
Income & Expenses button, 17
Income & Expenses graphs, 236
Income & Expenses section (New Company Setup Assistant), 17–18
Income accounts, xvii–xviii, 35
Income accounts completed screen, 17
Income Accounts screen, 17
Income Details: Introduction screen, 19
Income Details: Inventory screen, 21
Income Details: Items screen, 20
Income Details button, 19
Income Details section (New Company Setup Assistant), 19–21
Income Statement accounts, xviii, 35
Information dialog, 56
Information for your start date screen, 16
Information to have on hand screen, 22
Insert Line command (Edit menu), 96
installing QuickBooks, 2
Introduction completed screen, 19
Introduction to assets screen, 24
Introduction to equity accounts screen, 25
Intuit Market Web site, 248
Inventory Activities command (Vendors menu), 196, 197
Inventory Activities menu commands, 295
Inventory category
- Report Finder, 225
- Reports menu, 223

Inventory menu commands, 297
Inventory Part items, 39
- adding, 44–45

Inventory/Purchase Orders/Estimates settings, 274

INDEX

Inventory screen, 11
inventory tracking, 183–184
  adjusting balances, 196–199
  entering bills, 190–195
  purchase orders, 185–189
  receiving items, 190–195
Invoice Format settings, 279
Invoice No. field (Create Invoices window), 93
invoices, 92
  billable items, 98–100
  creating, 93–97, 104
  deleting, 106
  expenses, 98–100
  modifying, 106
  printing
    forms, 251–252
    setup, 244–246
  receiving payments, 107–108
  time, 98–100
  viewing, 105
Item List window, 39
Item Not Found dialog, 48
Items button, 98, 127
Items completed screen, 21
Items lists, 29
  custom fields, 56
  deleting item, 57
  discount item, 49–50
  group item, 47–48
  inventory part item, 44–45
  modifying item, 55
  non-inventory part item, 41–43
  other charge item, 41–43
  payment item, 51–52
  sales tax group item, 54–55
  sales tax item, 53
  service item, 41–43
  subtotal item, 46
  type items supported, 39–40

J

Job Info button (New Customer dialog), 63
Job Type List window, 80
Job Type lists, 29
  adding type, 80–81
  deleting, 82–83
  modifying type, 81
jobs
  customers
    adding to, 65
    modifying, 66
  deleting, 66
  editing, 66
  type
    adding, 80–81
    deleting, 82–83
    modifying, 81
Jobs & Time category
  Report Finder, 225
  Reports menu, 223
Jobs & Time menu commands, 296
Jobs settings, 285

K

keyboard shortcuts, 291
  Accountant & Taxes menu commands, 297
  Back Up menu commands, 292
  Banking menu commands, 295, 297
  Budgets menu commands, 297
  Company & Financial menu commands, 296
  Company menu commands, 294
  Customer & Vendor Profile menu commands, 294
  Customers & Receivables menu commands, 296
  Customers menu commands, 294
  Edit menu commands, 293
  Employees menu commands, 295
  Export menu commands, 292
  File menu commands, 292
  Help menu commands, 298
  Import menu commands, 292
keyboard shortcuts *(cont'd)*
  Inventory Activities menu commands, 295
  Inventory menu commands, 297
  Jobs & Time menu commands, 296
  List menu commands, 297
  Lists menu commands, 294
  Print Forms menu commands, 292
  Print Setup menu commands, 292
  Purchases menu commands, 297
  Reports menu commands, 296
  Restore menu commands, 292
  Sale menu commands, 296
  Time Tracking menu commands, 294–295
  Utilities menu commands, 292
  Vendors & Payables menu commands, 297
  Vendors menu commands, 295
  Window menu commands, 298

L

Label Print Setup dialog, 249
labels, printing
  forms, 256–257
  setup, 249
launching QuickBooks, 3
liabilities
  accounts, xvii, 34–35
  payroll, 213
List category
  Report Finder, 226
  Reports menu, 224
List command (File menu), 246
List menu commands, 294, 297
  Chart of Accounts, 156, 221
  Customer & Vendor Profile, 29

lists, xix
- activating, 33
- Chart of Accounts, xvii, 29
  - account types, 34–35
  - adding accounts, 36–37
  - deleting accounts, 38
  - modifying accounts, 37
  - options, 36–37
- Class, 29
  - adding class, 59
  - deleting class, 60
  - modifying class, 60
- closing, 31
- Customer: Jobs, 29
  - adding customer, 61–64
  - deleting customer, 66
  - jobs added to customer, 65
  - modifying customer, 66
- Customer Messages, 30, 86
  - adding customer message, 87
  - deleting customer message, 88
  - modifying customer message, 88
- Customer Types, 29
  - adding type, 80–81
  - deleting, 82–83
  - modifying type, 81
- To Do List, 30
  - adding note, 77–78
  - deleting note, 79
  - marking note as done, 79
  - modifying note, 78
- Employees, 29
  - adding employees, 71–72
  - deleting employee, 73
  - modifying employee, 73
- hiding, 33
- Items, 29
  - custom fields, 56
  - deleting item, 57
  - discount item, 49–50
  - group item, 47–48
  - inventory part item, 44–45
  - modifying item, 55
  - non-inventory part item, 41–43
  - other charge item, 41–43
  - payment item, 51–52

lists, Items *(continued)*
  - sales tax group item, 54–55
  - sales tax item, 53
  - service item, 41–43
  - subtotal item, 46
  - type items supported, 39–40
- Job Type, 29
  - adding type, 80–81
  - deleting, 82–83
  - modifying type, 81
- Other Names, 29
  - adding name, 74–75
  - deleting name, 76
  - modifying name, 75
- Payment Method, 30, 86
  - adding new payment method, 87
  - deleting payment method, 88
  - modifying payment method, 88
- printing, 31, 246, 260
- Reminders, 30, 89
- return to default sort order, 32
- Ship Via, 30, 86
  - adding new shipping method, 87
  - deleting shipping method, 88
  - modifying shipping method, 88
- sorting, 32
- Terms, 29
  - defining terms, 84–85
  - deleting terms, 85
  - modifying terms, 85
  - supported payment terms, 83
- types, 29–30
- Vendor Type, 29
  - adding type, 80–81
  - deleting, 82–83
  - modifying type, 81
- Vendors, 29
  - adding vendor, 67–69
  - deleting vendor, 70
  - modifying vendor, 70
- viewing, 31–32

Loans and Notes Payable screen, 24

Log In button, 147

Long Term Liability accounts, xvii, 34

M

mailing labels, printing
- forms, 256–257
- setup, 249

Mailing Labels command (File menu), 249, 256

Mailing Labels to Print dialog, 256

Make Active command (Action menu), 33

Make Deposits command (Banking menu), 112

Make Deposits window, 112

Make General Journal Entries command (Company menu), 159

Make Inactive command (Action menu), 33

Mark as 'Done' command (Action menu), 79

Mark Invoice As Final command (Edit menu), 97

Mark Invoice As Pending command (Edit menu), 97

Mark Sales Receipt As Pending command (Edit menu), 97

Marks Sales Receipt As Final command (Edit menu), 97

Maximum Available option (Create Vacation and Sick Leave Policies screen), 206

Memorize Report dialog, 239–240

Memorize Transaction command (Edit menu), 171

Memorize Transaction dialog, 171

Memorized Report List window, 240

Memorized Reports command (Reports menu), 240

Memorized Transaction List window, 172
Memorized Transactions lists, 29
memorizing
- reports, 219, 239–240
- transactions, 171–172
  - deleting, 173
  - Memorized Transaction List window, 172
  - modifying, 173
  - reminder and scheduling options, 174

menus, shortcut keys, 291
messages, customers, 86
- adding, 87
- deleting, 88
- modifying, 88

Microsoft Excel Visual QuickStart Guides, 230
Minimum expense accounts for QuickBooks Pro screen, 18
modifying. *See also* editing
- accounts, 37
- class, 60
- customer, 66, 88
- deposits, 114
- employees, 73
- estimates, 106
- invoices, 106
- item, 55
- memorized transactions, 173
- names, 75
- notes, 78
- payment methods, 88
- payments, 109
- purchase orders, 189
- sales receipts, 106
- shipping methods, 88
- special transactions, 161
- terms, 85
- transactions, 169
- types, 81
- vendors, 70

N

Name Not Found dialog, 128
names
- adding, 74–75
- deleting, 76
- modifying, 75

Navigating around the Assistant screen, 9
Net Worth graphs, 236
New Account command (Edit menu), 36
New Account dialog, 36
New Class command (Edit menu), 59
New Class dialog, 59
New command (Action menu), 36
New Company button, 3
New Company command (File menu), 8
New Company Setup Assistant, 1, 8
- Documents section, 26–27
- General section, 9–16
- Income & Expenses section, 17–18
- Income Details section, 19–21
- opening, 9
- Opening Balances section, 22–25

New Company Setup Assistant dialog, 8
New Customer: Job command (Edit menu), 61
New Customer dialog, 61–64
New Customer Message command (Edit menu), 87
New Customer Message dialog, 87
New Customer Type command (Edit menu), 80
New Customer Type dialog, 80
New Employee command (Edit menu), 71
New Employee dialog, 71–72
New Item command (Edit menu), 41
New Item dialog, 41
New Job dialog, 65
New Job Type command (Edit menu), 80
New Job Type dialog, 80
New Name dialog, 74–75
New Other Name command (Edit menu), 74
New Payment Method command (Edit menu), 87
New Payment Method dialog, 87
New Shipping Method command (Edit menu), 87
New Shipping Method dialog, 87
New Terms command (Edit menu), 84–85
New Terms dialog, 84–85
New To Do button, 78
New To Do button (New Customer dialog), 64
New To Do dialog, 77–78
New To Do Note command (Edit menu), 77
New Vendor command (Edit menu), 67
New Vendor dialog, 67–69
New Vendor Type command (Edit menu), 80
New Vendor Type dialog, 80
Non-inventory Part items, 39, 41–43
Non-inventory Parts screen, 20
notes
- deleting, 79
- marking as done, 79
- modifying, 78
- new to do notes, 77–78

Notes button
- New Customer dialog, 64
- New Employee dialog, 72
- New Vendor dialog, 69

INDEX

O

Open Company button, 5
Open Company command (File menu), 6
Open dialog, 5, 149
Open Purchase Orders dialog, 191
Opening Balances: Accounts screen, 23
Opening Balances: Customers screen, 22
Opening Balances: Introduction screen, 22
Opening Balances: Vendors screen, 23
Opening Balances button, 22
Opening Balances section (New Company Setup Assistant), 22–25
Options for Transferring Billable Time dialog, 99
Order Supplies command (Banking menu), 248
Ordering QuickBooks supplies screen, 27
Other Asset accounts, xvii, 34
Other Charges items, 39, 41–43
Other charges screen, 20
Other company information screen, 11
Other Current Asset accounts, xvii, 34
Other Current Liability accounts, xvii, 34
Other Expense accounts, xvii, 35
Other Income accounts, xvii, 35
Other Names List window, 74
Other Names lists, 29
  adding name, 74–75
  deleting name, 76
  modifying name, 75

P

Page Setup dialog, 246
Passwords settings, 286
Pay Bills command (Vendors menu), 123
Pay Bills window, tracking bills, 139
Pay Date option (Create Pay Schedule screen), 205
Pay Method field (Enter Sales Receipt window), 94
Pay Period option (Create Pay Schedule screen), 205
Pay Sales Tax command (Vendors menu), 124
Pay Sales Tax dialog, 142–143
Pay Schedule Confirmation screen, 205
Paycheck Records Web site, 208
paychecks, creating, 215–218
PayCycle
  adding employees, 208–211
  Customer Service Agreement, 211
  opening, 203–204
  pay schedule and policies, 205–207
  state tax setup, 212
  Web site, 202
Payment items, 40, 51–52
Payment Method List window, 86
Payment Method lists, 30, 86
  adding new payment method, 87
  deleting payment method, 88
  modifying payment method, 88
Payment Method Not Found dialog, 52
payments, 123–124
  bills, 139–141
  credit card charges, 135–138
  credits, 134
  deleting, 109
  entering bills, 130–133
payments *(continued)*
  methods
    adding new, 87
    deleting, 88
    modifying, 88
  receiving
    application to open invoice, 107–108
    modifying, 109
    viewing history, 110
  sales tax, 142–143
  terms
    defining, 84–85
    supported, 83
  writing checks, 125–130
Payments to Deposits window, 112
payroll, 201–202
  budget setup, 241–242
  creating paychecks, 215–218
  graphs, 236–238
  PayCycle
    adding employees, 208–211
    Customer Service Agreement, 211
    opening, 203–204
    pay schedule and policies, 205–207
    state tax setup, 212
    Web site, 202
  processing, 213–214
Payroll command (Employees menu), 203
Payroll settings, 285
Physical Inventory Worksheet command (Vendors menu), 197
Physical Inventory Worksheet report, 197
Pmt History button, 110
PO No. field (Create Invoices window), 93
policies, PayCycle, 205–207
predefined reports, 219
preferences
  access, 208
  data entry, 266
  graphs, 267

preferences *(continued)*
QuickBooks Preferences window
Company File Backups, 268–269
Contact Sync, 270
Data Entry, 266
Graphs, 267
opening, 264
Reminders, 267
Views, 265
reminders, 267
views, 265
Preferences - Accounting Software Integration screen, 214
Preferences completed screen, 15
Print Checks dialog, 255
Print Credit Memo button, 109
Print Credit Memo dialog, 109
Print dialog, 31, 261–262
Print Forms command (File menu), 251
Print Forms menu commands, 292
Print List command (File menu), 31
Print Report command (File menu), 260
Print Setup command (File menu), 244
Print Setup dialog, 244–246
Print Setup menu commands, 292
Printer Setup screen, 215
printing, 243
forms
checks, 255
credit memos, 251–252
invoices, 251–252
mailing labels, 256–257
purchase orders, 251–252
1099s, 258–259
sales receipts, 251–252
statements, 253–254
lists, 31, 260
Print dialog, 261–262
reports, 260
printing *(continued)*
setup
checks, 247–248
estimates, 244–246
graphs, 246
invoices, 244–246
labels, 249
lists, 246
purchase orders, 244–246
reports, 246
1099s, 250
statements, 244–246
Printing 1099-MISC Forms dialog, 258
Product sales with QuickBooks inventory screen, 12
Purchase Order Format settings, 275–277
Purchase Order list, 30, 185
Purchase Order List command (Vendors menu), 30, 185
Purchase Order List window, 185
purchase orders
creating, 186–188
deleting, 189
modifying, 189
printing
forms, 251–252
setup, 244–246
Purchase Order list, 185
viewing, 185
Purchases category
Report Finder, 225
Reports menu, 223
Purchases menu commands, 297

Q

QuickBooks
installation, 2
launching, 3
New Company Setup Assistant, 8
Documents section, 26–27
General section, 9–16
Income & Expenses section, 17–18
QuickBooks, New Company Setup *(continued)*
Income Details section, 19–21
Opening Balances section, 22–25
upgrading to latest version, 3
QuickBooks menu commands, 291
QuickBooks Payroll for Mac, 201, 203
QuickBooks Preferences window
Company File Backups preferences, 268–269
Contact Sync preferences, 270
Data Entry preferences, 266
opening, 264
Reminders preferences, 267
Views preferences, 265
QuickBooks Pro 2006 icon, 2
QuickBooks Web Connect files, 148
Quicken, xvi
converting to QuickBook file, 6–7
Web site, 4
Quicken Conversion Results window, 7
QuickReports, 219, 221–222
QuickReports command (Actions menu), 157
QuickZoom feature, 221–222

R

Receipt of payment screen, 19
receipts, sales
billable items, 98–100
deleting, 106
entering, 93–97
expenses, 98–100
modifying, 106
printing forms, 251–252
receiving payments, 107–110
viewing, 105

Receive Items and Enter Bill command (Vendors menu), 191
Receive Items command (Vendors menu), 193
Receive Payments command (Customers menu), 107, 109
Receive Payments window, 107
receiving items, tracking inventory, 190–195
Recent Files list, 3
Reconcile Adjustment dialog, 181
Reconcile command (Banking menu), 180
Reconcile Credit Card command (Banking menu), 182
Reconcile window, 180
Reconciliation Complete dialog, 181
reconciling accounts, 179–182
Refund button, 120
refunds
  customer account adjustment, 118–120
  customer account adjustments, 118–120
registering QuickBooks, 3
reminders, memorized transactions, 174
Reminders command (Company menu), 30
Reminders list screen, 15
Reminders lists, 30, 89, 139
Reminders preferences (QuickBooks Preferences window), 267
Reminders window, 89
Rep field (Enter Sales Receipt window), 94
Report command (File menu), 246
Report Filters dialog, 166, 233
Report Finder, 225–227, 237
Report Finder command (Reports menu), 227
Report Finder window, 227
Report Format settings, 282
Report Header/Footer settings, 283
Report Print Setup dialog, 246
Reporting settings, 281
reports, 219–220
  customizing, 228–230
    filters, 233
    formatting, 234
    header & footer formatting, 235
    options, 231–232
  memorizing, 239–240
  printing, 246, 260
  QuickReports, 221–222
  Report Finder, 225–227
  Reports menu, 223–224
Reports menu commands, 223–224, 296
  creating graphs, 237
  Memorized Reports, 240
  Report Finder, 227
Restore menu commands, 292

S

Sale menu commands, 296
Sale No. field (Enter Sales Receipt window), 93
sales, 91
  customer account adjustment
    credit memos, 118–120
    refunds, 118–120
    statement charges, 121
  deposits, 111
    checks and cash, 112
    credit cards, 113
    deleting, 114
    modifying, 114
  entering, 92
    billable items, 98–100
    creating invoice, 93–97
    expenses, 98–100
    sales receipts, 93–97
    time, 98–100
  estimates
    creating, 101–103
    invoices creation, 104
sales *(continued)*
  finance charges
    assessment, 117
    set up, 115–116
  graphs, 236
  receipts. *See* sales receipts
  taxes. *See* sales taxes
Sales category
  Report Finder, 225
  Reports menu, 223
Sales/Invoicing settings, 278
Sales Receipt Format settings, 279
sales receipts
  billable items, 98–100
  deleting, 106
  entering, 93–97
  expenses, 98–100
  modifying, 106
  printing forms, 251–252
  receiving payments
    application to open invoice, 107–108
    modifying, 109
    viewing history, 110
  viewing, 105
Sales Tax Group items, 40, 54–55
Sales Tax information screen, 14
Sales Tax screen, 14
Sales Tax settings, 284
sales taxes
  items, 40, 53
  payments, 142–143
Sample Files list, 3
Save to File dialog, 262
Schedule Memorized Transaction window, 173
schedules
  memorized transactions, 174
  PayCycle, 205–207
searching transactions, 165–167
Sections and topics screen, 10
Select Credit Memos to Print dialog, 252
Select dialog, 6

Select For to Print dialog, 251
Select Invoices to Print dialog, 252
Select Item Receipt dialog, 195
Select Mailing Labels to Print dialog, 252
Select Name Type dialog, 75
Select Purchase Orders to Print dialog, 252
Select Receipts to Print dialog, 252
Select 1099s to Print dialog, 258
Select Statements to Print dialog, 253
Select your type of business screen, 11
Service items, 39, 41–43
Service Items screen, 20
Set Date dialog, 177
Set Title dialog, 96
Set up all your accounts? screen, 18
Set Up Budget command (Company menu), 241
Set Up Budget dialog, 241
Set Up Budget window, 241
Setting up a new QuickBooks company screen, 9
Setup hints for your business screen, 12
Ship Date field (Create Invoices window), 94
Ship To field (Create Invoice window), 93
Ship Via field (Create Invoices window), 94
Ship Via List window, 86
Ship Via lists, 30, 86
  adding new shipping method, 87
  deleting shipping method, 88
  modifying shipping method, 88
shipping methods, 86
  adding new, 87
  deleting, 88
  modifying, 88
shortcut keys, 291
  Back Up menu commands, 292
  Banking menu commands, 295, 297
  Budgets menu commands, 297
  Company & Financial menu commands, 296
  Company menu commands, 294
  Customer & Vendor Profile menu commands, 294
  Customers & Receivables menu commands, 296
  Customers menu commands, 294
  Edit menu commands, 293
  Employees menu commands, 295
  Export menu commands, 292
  File menu commands, 292
  Help menu commands, 298
  Import menu commands, 292
  Inventory Activities menu commands, 295
  Inventory menu commands, 297
  Jobs & Time menu commands, 296
  List menu commands, 297
  Lists menu commands, 294
  Print Forms menu commands, 292
  Print Setup menu commands, 292
  Purchases menu commands, 297
  Reports menu commands, 296
  Restore menu commands, 292
  Sale menu commands, 296
  Time Tracking menu commands, 294–295
  Utilities menu commands, 292
  Vendors & Payables menu commands, 297
shortcut keys *(continued)*
  Vendors menu commands, 295
  Window menu commands, 298
Should I user QuickBooks for inventory? screen, 12
Show Only Open Purchase Orders command (Action menu), 185
Show Sorted List command (Action menu), 32
Single or multiple sales tax rates? screen, 14
Sold To field (Enter Sales Receipt window), 93
sorting, lists, 32
Standard terms
  payments, 83
  setting options, 84
State Income Tax accounts, 213
state taxes, PayCycle, 212
State Unemployment Tax accounts, 213
Statement Charges screen, 19
Statement Format settings, 279
Statement of Cash Flows Report settings, 284
statements
  charges, 121
  printing
    forms, 253–254
    setup, 244–246
Statements command (File menu), 253
subaccounts, 35
subclasses, 58
Subtotal items, 39, 46
subtypes, 80

T

Tax Accounts, 213
taxes
  first month of income, 11
  sales
    items, 40, 53
    payments, 142–143

terms
  defining, 84–85
  deleting, 85
  modifying, 85
Terms field (Create Invoices window), 94
Terms List window, 83–84
Terms lists, 29
  defining terms, 84–85
  deleting terms, 85
  modifying terms, 85
  supported payment terms, 83
time
  entering on invoices, 98–100
  tracking, 175
    multiple activities, 177–178
    single activity, 176
Time button, 98
Time/Costs button, 98
Time Tracking command (Employees menu), 176
Time Tracking menu commands, 294, 295
Time Tracking screen, 15
Time Tracking settings, 285
timesheets, tracking employee time, 177–178
title bars, identifying active window, 31
To Do List, 30
  adding note, 77–78
  deleting note, 79
  marking note as done, 79
  modifying note, 78
To Do List command (Company menu), 30
To Do List window, 77, 89
toolbar configuration, 288–289
tracking
  inventory, 183–184
    adjusting balances, 196–199
    entering bills, 190–195
    purchase orders, 185–190
    receiving items, 190–195
  time, 175
    multiple activities, 177–178
    single activity, 176
Transaction Cleared dialog, 182
Transaction History - Invoice dialog, 110
transactions, 29, 155
  classes
    adding, 59
    deleting, 60
    modifying, 60
  deleting, 169
  downloading, 145, 148–150
    bank Web site login, 147
    financial institution support, 146
    reviewing, 152–154
    sign up, 147
  memorizing, 171–172
    deleting, 173
    Memorized Transaction List window, 172
    modifying, 173
    reminder and scheduling options, 174
  modifying, 169
  opening, 168
  reconciling accounts, 179–182
  searching, 165–167
  special, 158
    account register window, 162–164
    General Journal Entry window, 159–160
    modifying, 161
  tracking time, 175
    multiple activities, 177–178
    single activity, 176
  viewing account registers, 156–157
  voiding, 106
Two ways to handle bills and payments screen, 15
types
  customer
    adding, 80–81
    deleting, 82–83
    modifying, 81
  jobs
    adding, 80–81
    deleting, 82–83
    modifying, 81
types *(continued)*
  vendors
    adding, 80–81
    deleting, 82–83
    modifying, 81
Types of Pay screen, 205

U–V

Undeposited Funds accounts, 111
Understanding your QuickBooks start date screen, 16
upgrading QuickBooks, 3
Use Weekly Timesheet command (Employees menu), 177
Using QuickBooks for contact management screen, 27
Using QuickBooks in Canada screen, 26
Utilities menu commands, 292
Vendor List window, 67
Vendor Not Found dialog, 43, 133
Vendor Type List window, 80
Vendor Type lists, 29
  adding type, 80–81
  deleting, 82–83
  modifying type, 81
vendors
  adding, 67–69
  deleting, 70
  modifying, 70
  type
    adding, 80–81
    deleting, 82–83
    modifying, 81
Vendors & Payables category
  Report Finder, 225
  Reports menu, 223
Vendors & Payables menu commands, 297
Vendors completed screen, 23
Vendors lists, 29
  adding vendor, 67–69
  deleting vendor, 70
  modifying vendor, 70

Vendors menu commands, 295
  Create Purchase Orders, 186
  Enter Bill for Received Items, 195
  Enter Bills, 123
  Inventory Activities, 196, 197
  Pay Bills, 123
  Pay Sales Tax, 124
  Purchase Order List, 30, 185
  Receive Items, 193
  Receive Items and Enter Bill, 191
View and Print Paychecks window, 216
views, lists, 32
Views preferences (QuickBooks Preferences window), 265
Void Deposit command (Edit menu), 114
Void Estimate command (Edit menu), 106
Void Invoice command (Edit menu), 106
Void Sales Receipt command (Edit menu), 106
voiding transactions, 106, 169

W

Wage Accounts, 213
Web sites
  Intuit Market, 248
  Paycheck Records, 208
  PayCycle, 202
  Quicken, 4
Weekly Timesheet window, 177
Welcome to QuickBooks window, 3
Welcome to the New Company Setup Assistant screen, 9
We're ready to create your company file now screen, 13
What are the preferences? screen, 13
Window menu commands, 298
Write Checks command (Banking menu), 123
Write Checks form, xix
Write Checks window, 120, 125–130
writing checks, payments, 125–130

X–Y–Z

Your company income tax form screen, 11
Your Equity accounts screen, 25
Your income and expense accounts screen, 13
Your invoice format screen, 14